Painting Landscapes

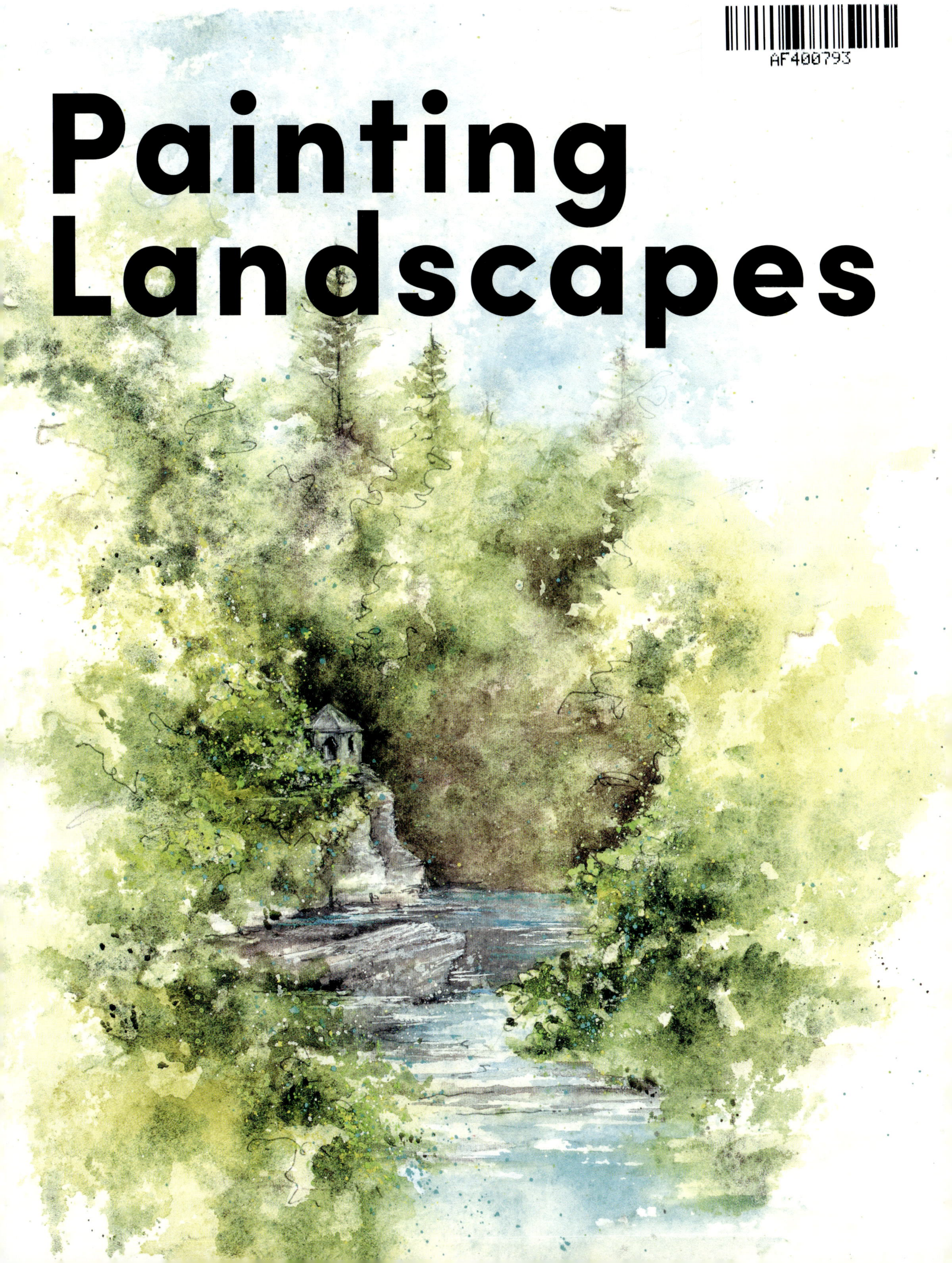

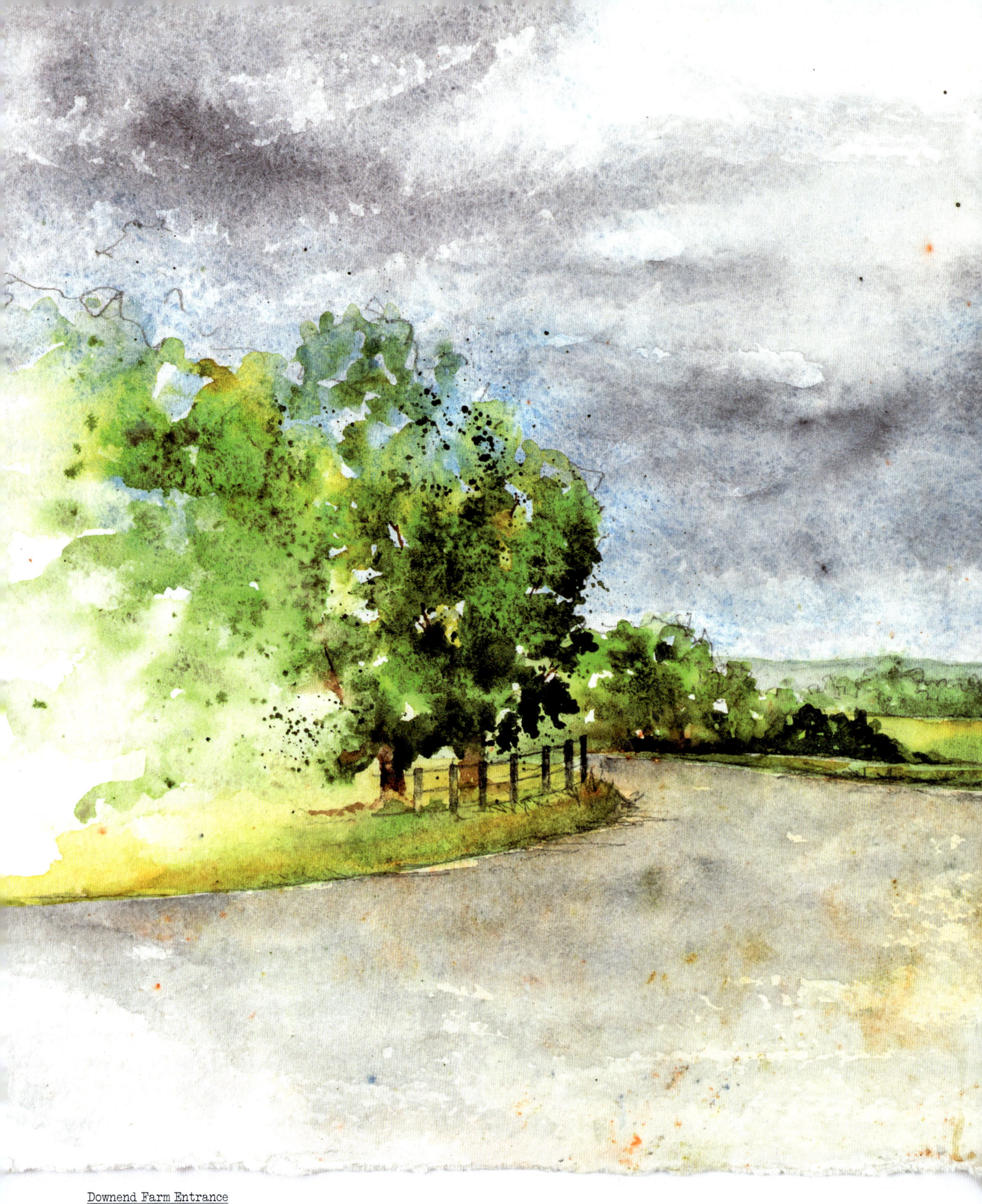

Downend Farm Entrance
530 × 250mm (20⅞ × 9¾in)
See also page 60.

Alison C. Board

Painting Landscapes

A creative approach
in watercolour and
mixed media

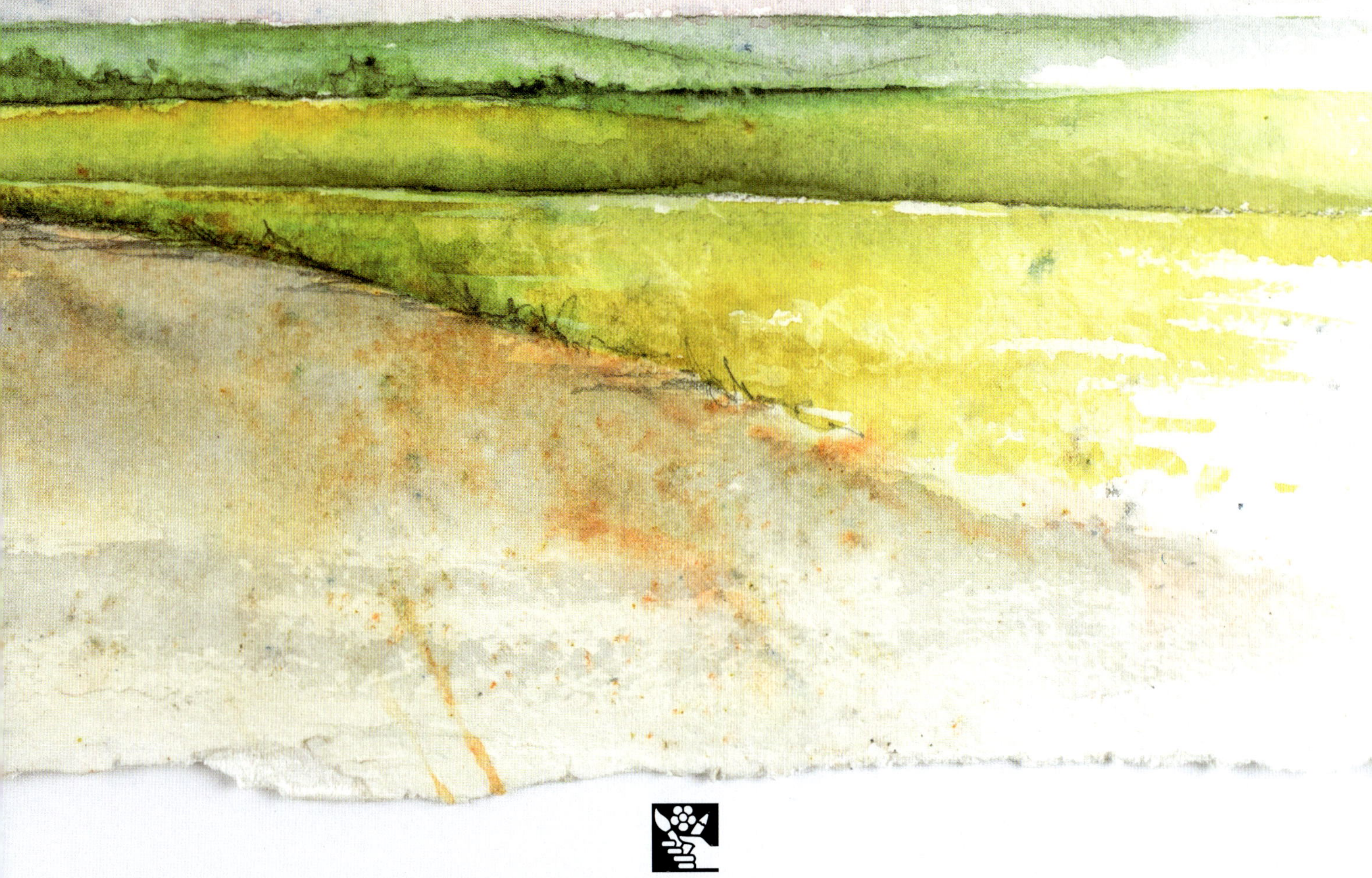

SEARCH PRESS

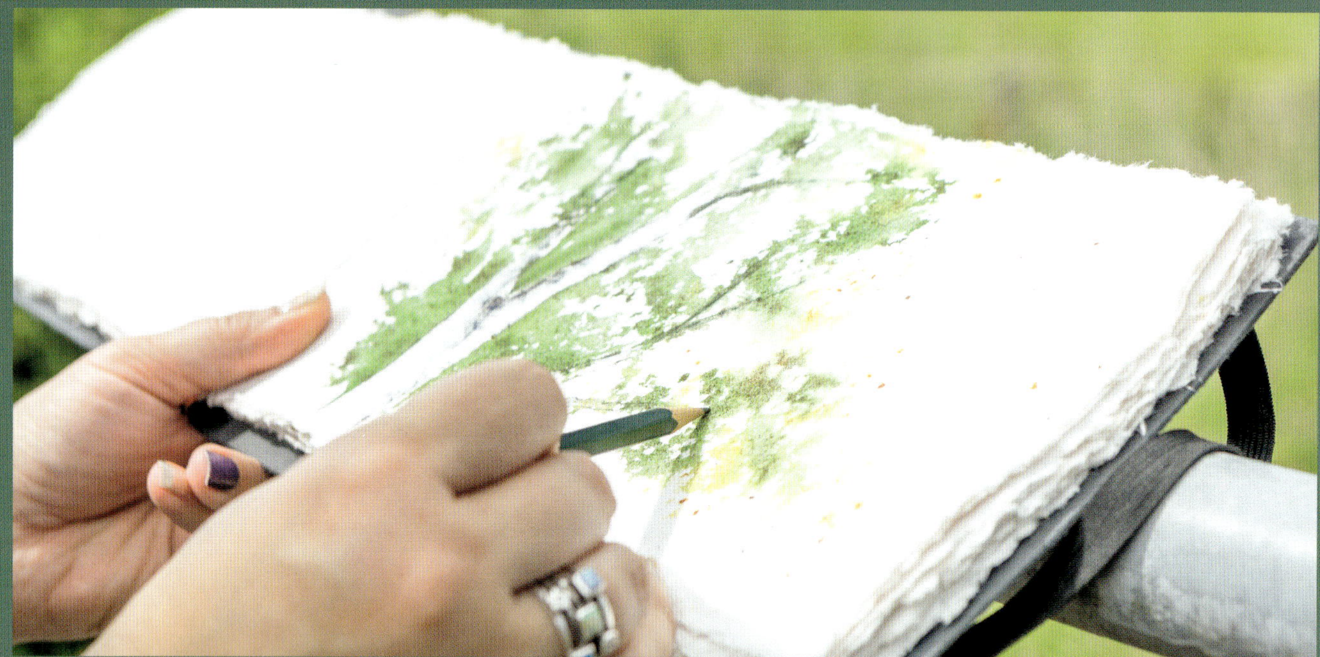

First published in 2026
Search Press Limited
Wellwood, North Farm Road,
Tunbridge Wells, Kent TN2 3DR

1 2 3 4 5 6 7 8 9 10

Text copyright © Alison C. Board, 2026

Photographs by Mark Davison (www.markdavison.com) for Search Press
Studios, except for pages 50, 62 (tr), 64 (tr), 68 (tr), 69 (tr), 70 (tr),
71 (tr), 73 (R), 75 (tr), 76 (tr), 77 (tr), 80 (tr), 82 (tr), 84 (tr), 86 (tr), 88 (tr),
89 (tr), 90 (tr), 92 (tr), 94 (tr), 96 (tr), 116 (t), 128, 134, 140, 146 and 152
© Alison C. Board; and pages 66 (tr), 72 (tr) and 78 (tr) © Richard Foot

Photographs and design © Search Press Ltd, 2026

ISBN: 978-1-80092-315-7
ebook ISBN: 978-1-80093-301-9

Bookmarked Hub
Bonus material for this book can be found on the Bookmarked
Hub. Search for this book by title or ISBN: the files can be
found under 'Book Extras'. Membership of the Bookmarked
online community is free: www.bookmarkedhub.com

Publishers' note
The Publishers and author can accept no responsibility
for any consequences arising from the information,
advice or instructions given in this publication.

For errata, please visit our website (www.searchpress.com)
or the Bookmarked Hub (www.bookmarkedhub.com).

You are invited to visit the author's website:
www.learningtopaint.co.uk

Follow Alison on social media: @aliboardartist

GPSR information can be found at www.searchpress.com
Printed in China, AP012026

DEDICATION

To Mum, Dad and Beez for everything they do for me,
always there, forever supportive and for Uncle Mike who
was the teacher I aspire to be.

ACKNOWLEDGEMENTS

I can't begin to thank the Search Press team enough, for
believing in my idea for this book and for, once again,
guiding me through every process as it began to grow
and fully form. I'd particularly like to thank Beth, my
editor extraordinaire, and Emma and Mark for their
creative expertise.

To my students past and present but particularly
The All A–Board Artists, who shape me as a teacher
and challenge me to new creative adventures with their
ideas and enthusiasm.

I'd particularly like to thank my family and friends who
have put up with me forgetting birthdays, not being
around and always asking me how it's going so that
I feel loved and supported every day… you know who
you are.

Contents

INTRODUCTION

Landscapes as a source of inspiration for painting were not my first love, but they have grown in importance for me over time. It's not that I didn't appreciate the magnificence of a wonderful view or marvel at the textures in a group of trees; I can't really tell you why other subjects made their way to my paper first. Perhaps it was because I felt that all the facets of a landscape were too overwhelming to interpret and I couldn't think of how I would make my way through the process. Or perhaps I simply felt humbled by the many amazing landscape painters that I have admired.

When I began to realize that I needed to focus on my response, and how I see and interpret the subject, I felt more at ease with choosing to paint landscapes. I became eager to get my individual stories down on paper.

Individuality in expression is very important to me and something that I constantly encourage in others. Throughout this book I will share my thought processes, all the while hoping to ignite ideas for how you might confidently approach a similar subject.

In practical terms, there are some elements that I have discovered over the years that help with the obvious hurdles to landscape painting and I'm excited to share them with you in this book. Even seemingly small things, like how to feel comfortable when you are out on location, can be the key to unlocking the creative parts of you that are itching to get out.

I hope that this book will encourage you, not only to find ways of expressing your creativity in your paintings, but also to dig a little deeper to unlock your unique and personal interpretations of what you see.

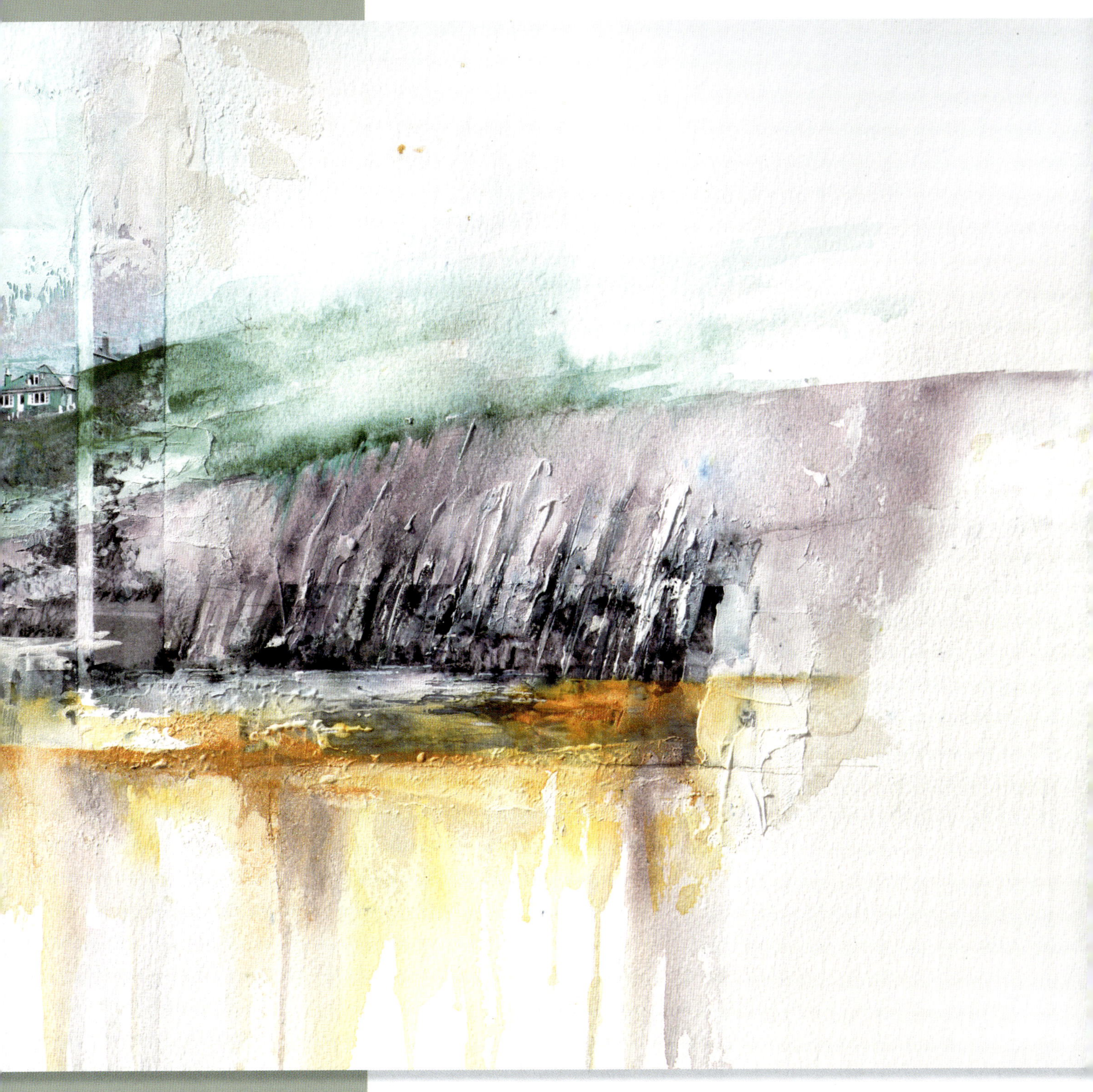

<u>Craig Yr Awel</u>
443 × 327mm (17½ × 13in)

Inspired by the landscape

It is sometimes challenging to put into words what inspires us. Often it is a feeling, a personal response that someone else might struggle to understand, but I do think that there are common themes that we can all relate to.

A landscape has the power to reconnect us with nature and our history on this planet. We are all aware of the benefits that being in nature affords us; our health, our wellbeing and the incredible feeling of being part of something much bigger than ourselves are all aspects of how we can react to a landscape, no matter the scale of what we are seeing.

We may also consider those who have gone before us and feel a personal connection to a location, or be thinking of the generations yet to come and how our actions ripple through time. No matter how we respond to a landscape, it can often be a very deep and meaningful experience.

In this chapter, I have considered various ways in which you might find yourself starting a landscape painting.

You may be very new to it as a subject or may be seeking ways to expand on skills you have already acquired.

I have also made a point of considering different situations, as many people may not be able to access locations easily – but this should not be a barrier to a successful painting experience.

One aspect to consider before starting any creative project is that it is not often a linear adventure – we don't start at 'A' and finish at 'Z'. I hope this chapter encourages you to embrace the many diverse ways of collecting together your inspiration, and perhaps returning to ideas or exploring aspects you may have set aside.

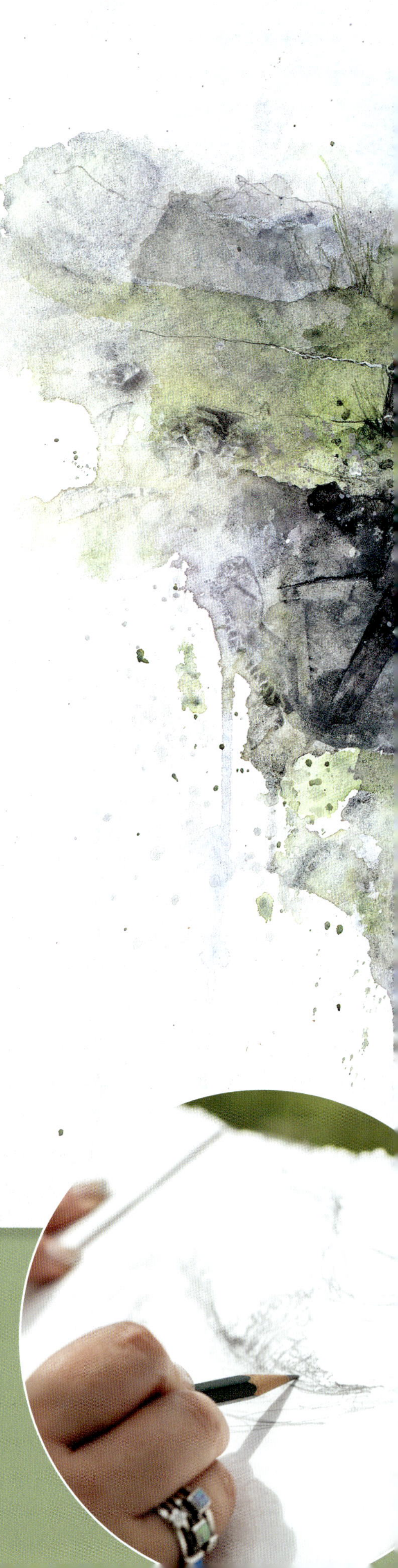

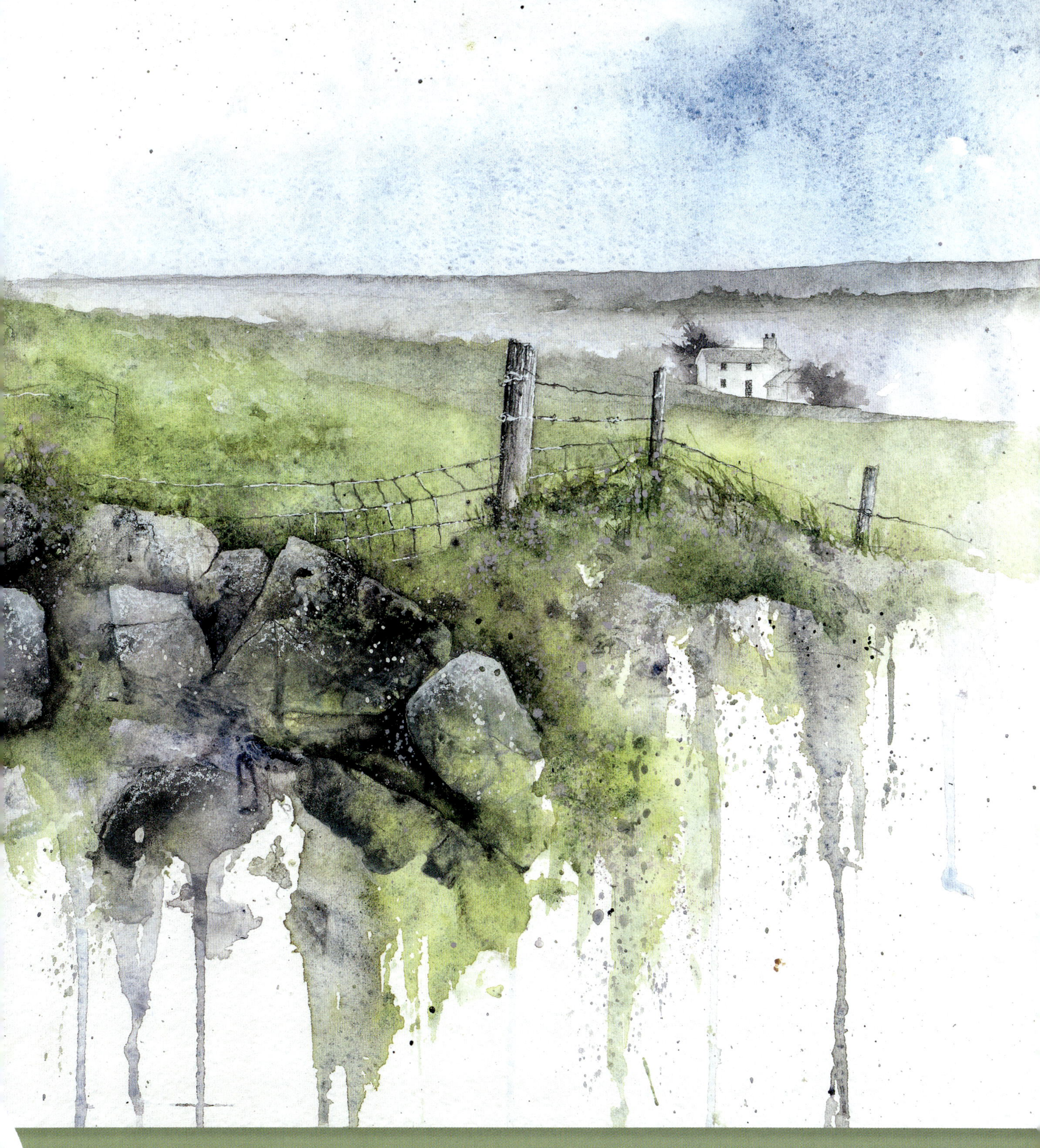

<u>Carn Llidi Descent</u>
385 × 285mm (15¼ × 11¼in)

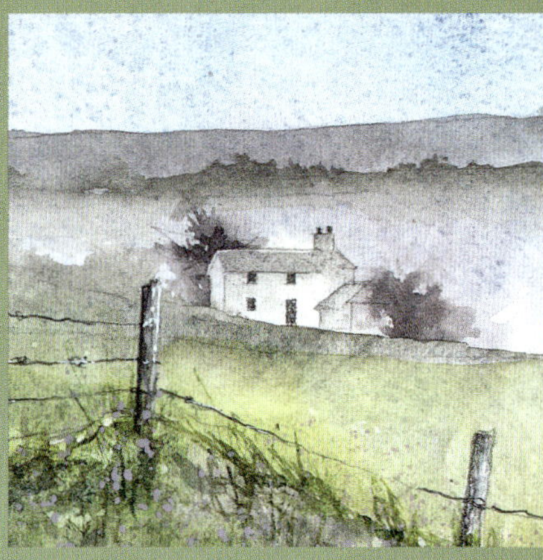

WHY ARE WE CAPTIVATED BY LANDSCAPES?

From early paintings establishing our place and balance in the natural world, through storytelling of mythological and historical themes in the Renaissance, to the more picturesque responses of the Romantics, art and writing reveal how humans are irrefutably linked to the landscapes they encounter.

Today, we have a wealth of interpretations to inspire us, more advanced materials and resources than ever before, and the ability to be able to freely decide what the landscape means to us as individuals.

For me, a landscape will always provide me first with a sense of being grounded, and then very often with wonder at what I see and encounter. It doesn't have to be a great swathe of countryside; I could find myself in a wood surrounded by birch trees or low down in the grass looking up at the clouds. No matter where I am, I have a sensation of calm and a desire to find a way of creatively responding to what I am experiencing.

I know that in the beginning, when I first started painting, I struggled to find that spark of inspiration if I hadn't visited a particular location, but I have since found that there are many ways to connect with the environment I am interpreting. It will not always be possible to visit those places that you find intriguing but there are definitely ways to discover your unique interpretation of them, and feel confident in your exploration.

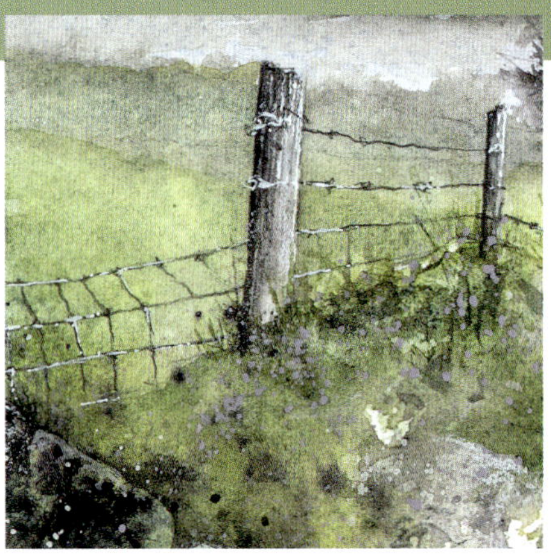

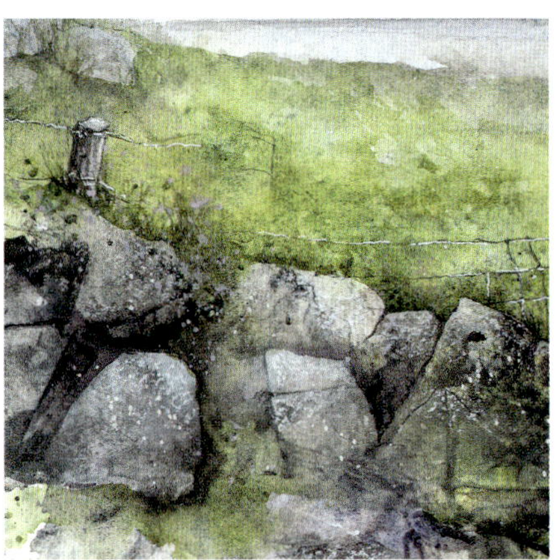

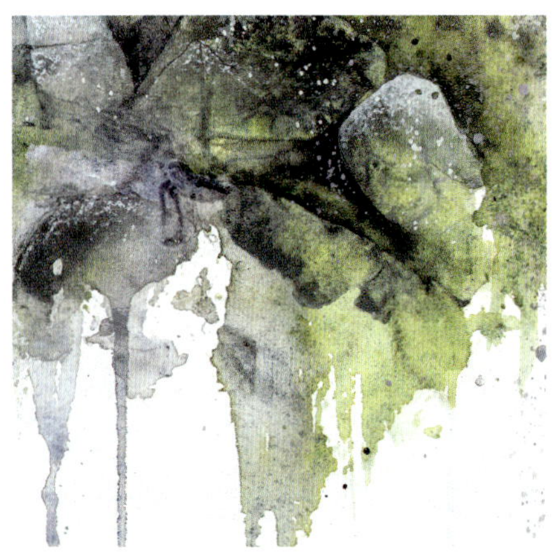

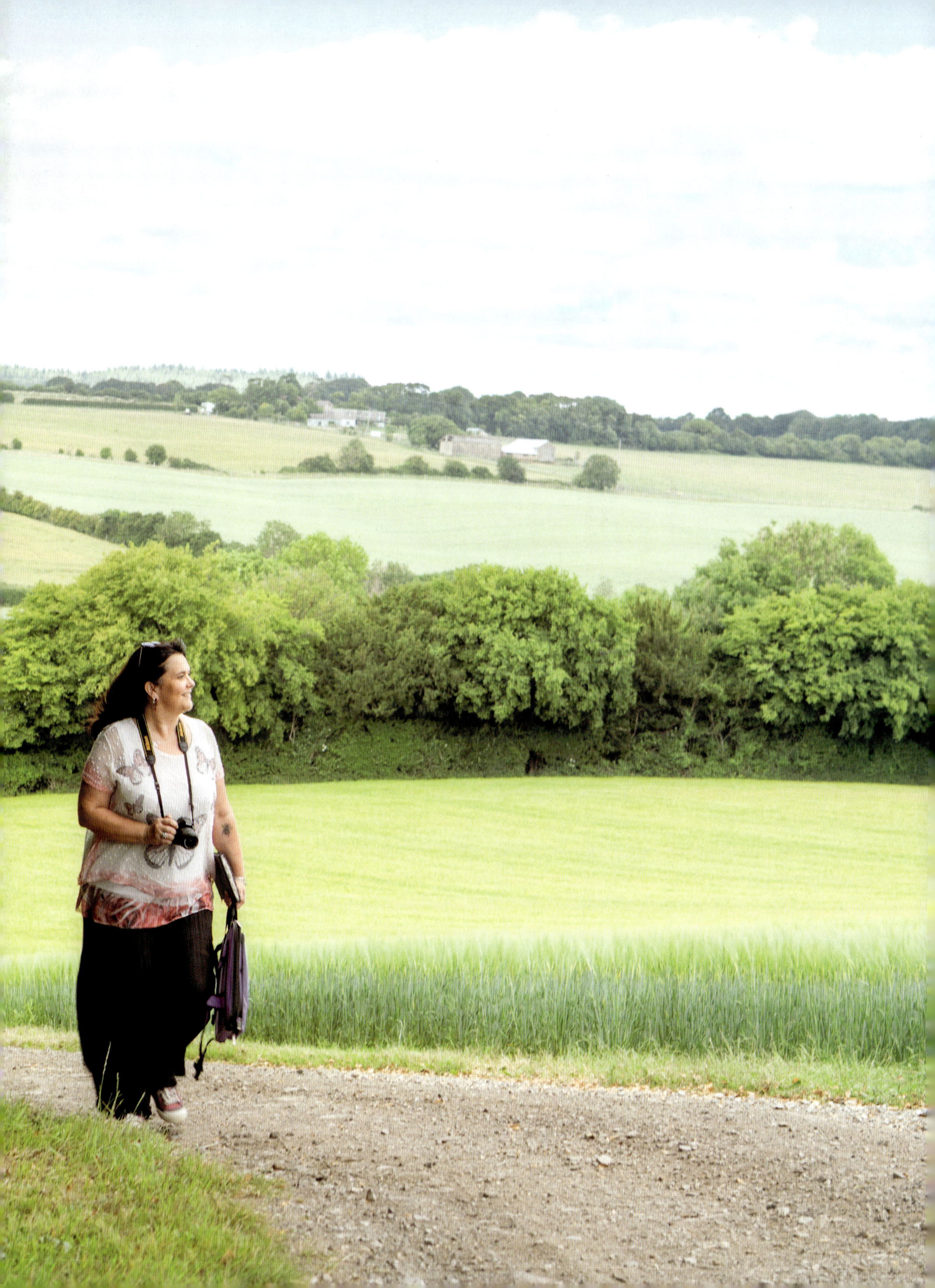

INSPIRATION, GATHERING AND EXPERIMENTING

In order to create a successful landscape painting, and for it to feel like a unique and personal interpretation, we usually require a certain amount of information before we feel confident. I call this process 'Inspiration, gathering and experimenting' and I often use a flow chart to help me get started. I find that having a loose structure of questions to ask myself helps me to reach conclusions and stop getting tied up with endless loops of repetition that don't lead me anywhere. I must point out that a loop isn't always a bad thing; it's better to paint something and be creative than not; but if your loop results in procrastination, then maybe you need a little nudge to find your way out.

On the page opposite, you will find a flow chart to help you get started when you feel lost, or to offer ideas if you are stuck. Over the next pages I dive a little deeper with my advice on how each of these elements might work for you. There are similar flow charts for other situations on pages 21 and 25.

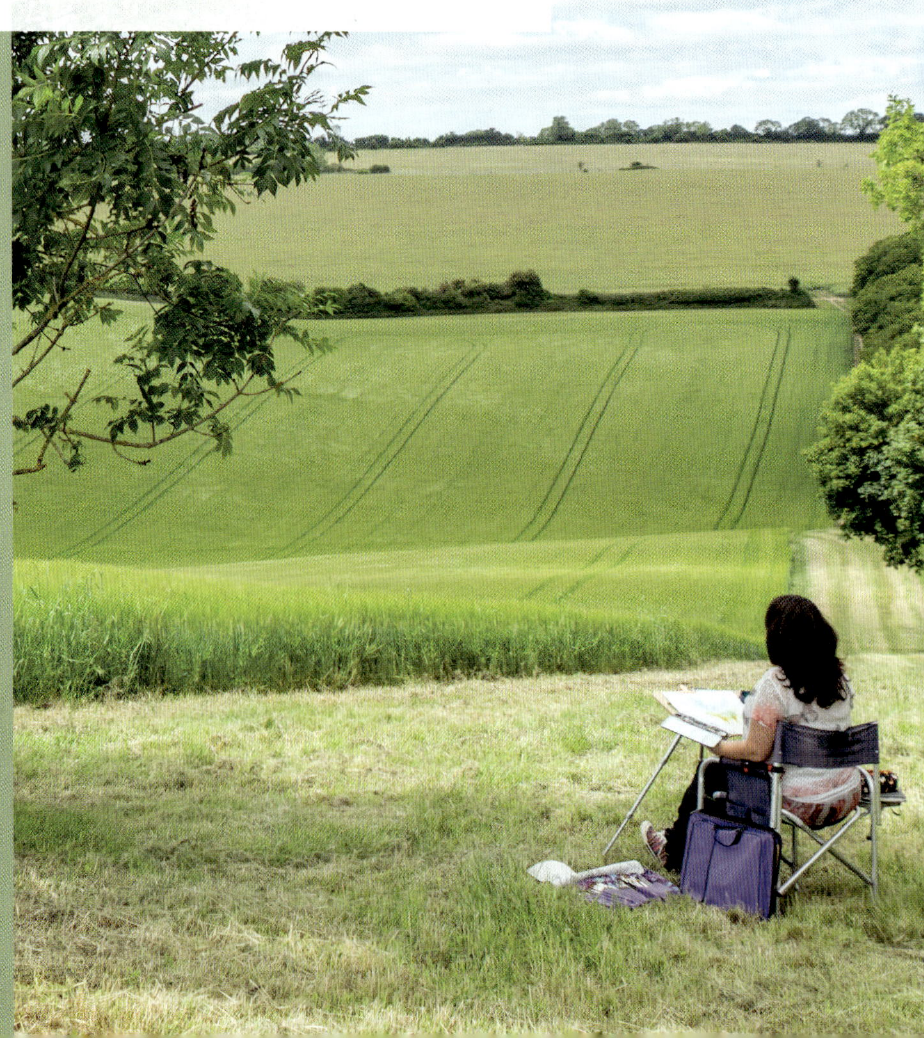

Inspiration, Gathering and Experimenting

Inspiration

Your chosen landscape, or a place
you're considering painting

Have you been there?

Are you going there?

Do you have a personal connection to it?

Can you get there?

Gathering

What do you already know? Do you want to do some research?
What can you find out about it?

Photos you have taken

Royalty-free photos from a reputable site

Talking to someone who has been there

Sketches you have created

Notes or annotations you have made on location

Personal connections

Memory sketches from a trip or recollection

History of the location: geographical, events and notable people

Dive right in and create with existing skills or intuition

Experimenting

How will your research turn into further practical outcomes?

Revisit previous ideas

Develop outcomes from the previous stage

Explore materials

Test techniques

Dive right in and create with existing skills or intuition

Your painting

SEEKING INSPIRATION

At the top of the flow chart on page 13 you will have seen that I suggest 'Inspiration' as a possible first step. It doesn't have to come first – sometimes you might be experimenting with your materials when inspiration strikes – but I still believe you have to seek it.

We are not machines; we are complex creatures who don't all think and perform in the same way and so require a variety of mechanisms for stimulation and creativity.

Consider the following:

- Do you have a personal connection to the location? This might be due to your passion for where you live or maybe where you grew up, or perhaps it's the site of a much-cherished holiday.

- Is there a historical or cultural significance to a location? You may visit the site of a famous battle or enjoy the peace of a chapel nestled in the hills.

- Perhaps there is an instinctive connection: there are often locations in which we experience quite a visceral response to what we see. We can't necessarily explain it, but it takes our breath away when we least anticipate it, and we want to find creative ways to share this response with others.

AN IMPORTANT NOTE

The process of seeking inspiration isn't magic, therefore don't be disheartened if inspiration is elusive. Not every landscape is going to consume you instantly – you may come to see its beauty gradually, in the same way that a piece of music might grow on you over time. I often have to find the key to unlock how I want to paint or sketch what I am seeing, and that is when the second section of the flow chart, 'Gathering', can help.

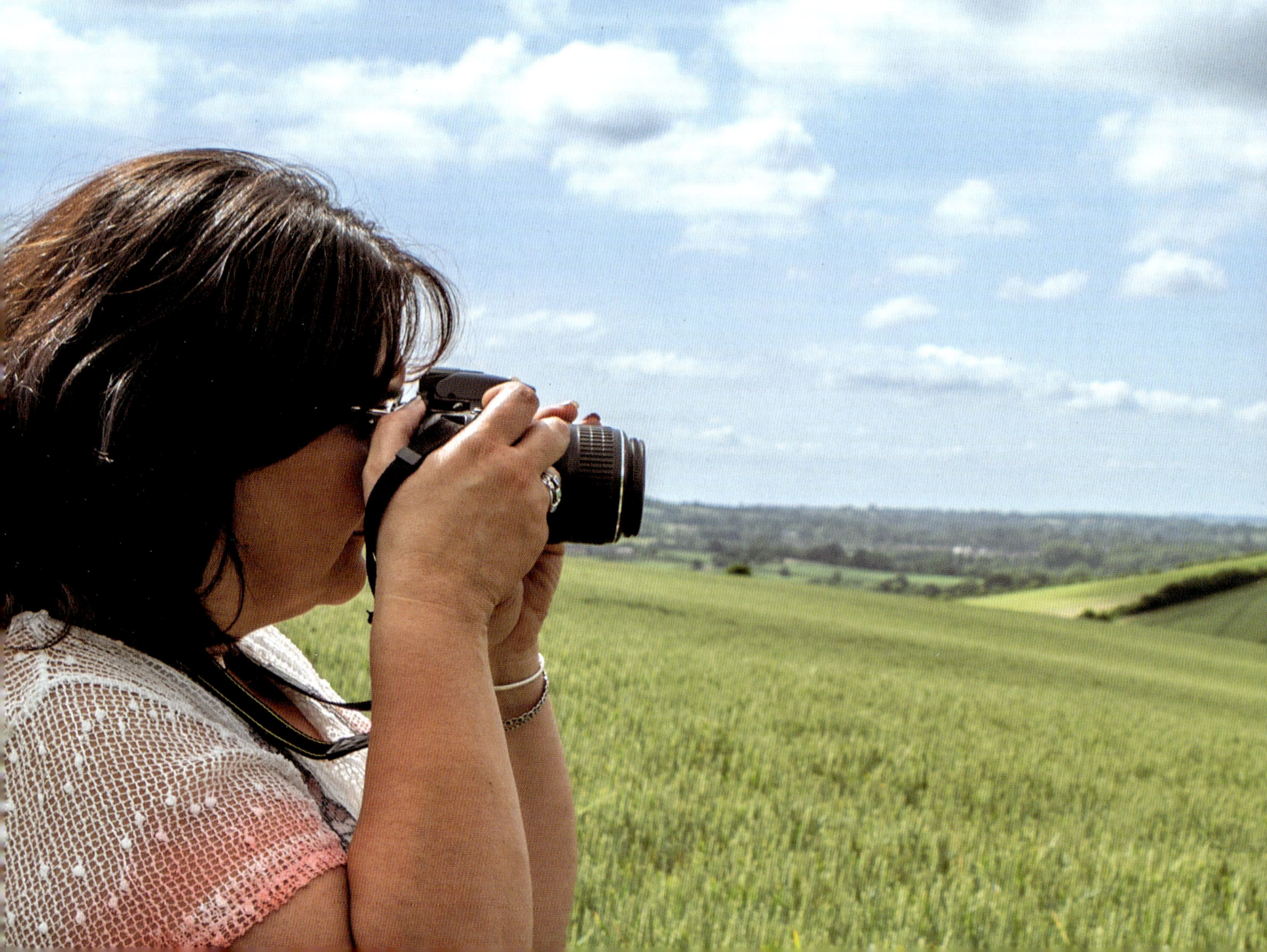

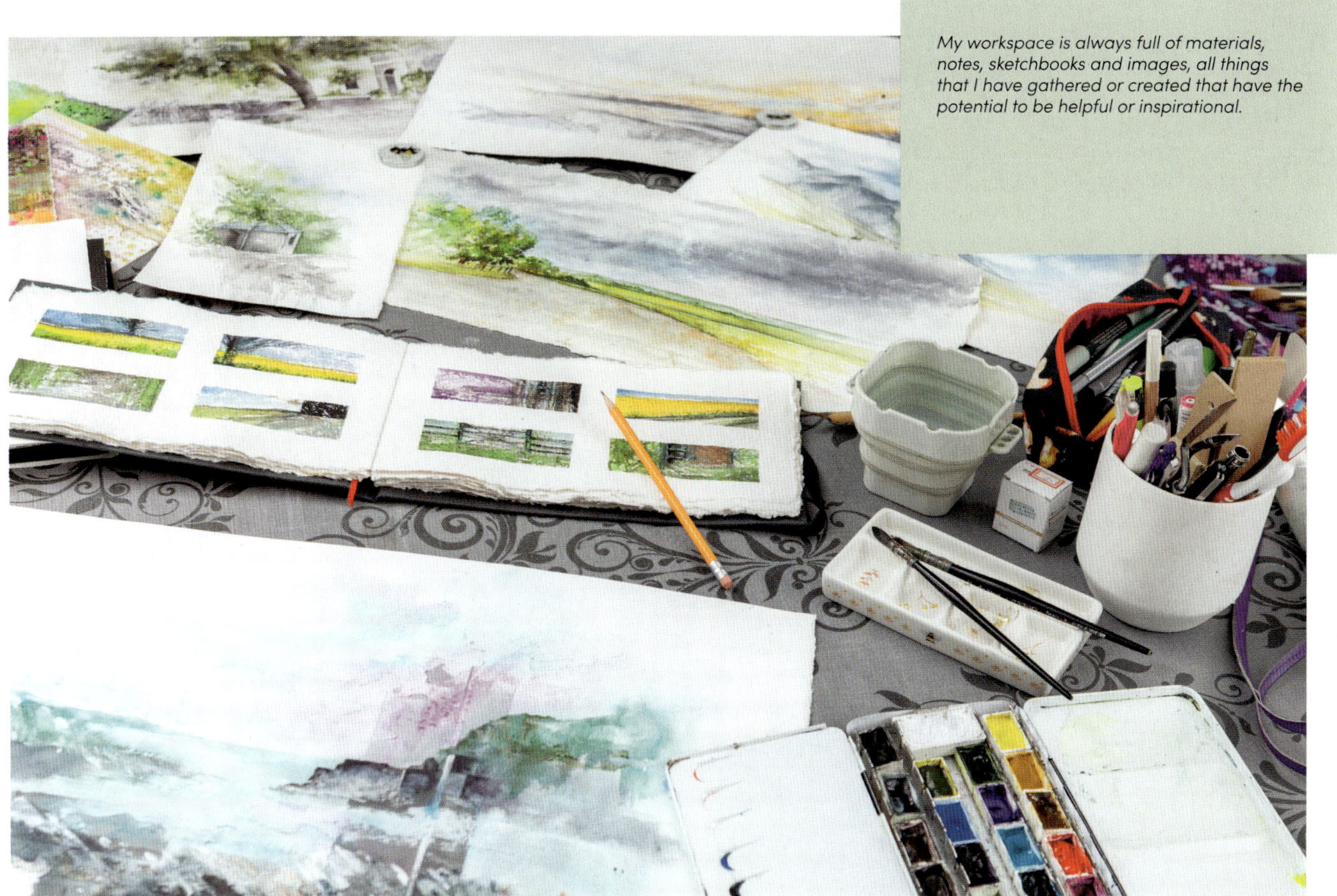

GATHERING INFORMATION

In formal art tuition, gathering information is more commonly known as research, but I always think that makes it sound too academic and like a chore. I therefore prefer to call it 'gathering' as I feel that allows it more scope to be a fun part of the process.

If we look again at our flow chart on page 13, you will see I have made several suggestions for how you might start to develop your ideas; some are instinctive, some practical, and some are more investigative.

The most traditionally artistic way of responding to a landscape is to go and experience it yourself so that it is right there before you. On pages 19–21, I give you some advice - born of my own experience - on how to get the most out of sketching on location.

Sometimes, you have to become a detective, and your information may have to come from external sources. I am aware that some of you reading this book may not be in a position to go out into the landscape and experience it for yourself. While there are many reasons why you might not have the opportunity to do so, let me reassure you that there are plenty of ways in which you can create wonderful landscape paintings and not have to be out in all weathers.

If painting on location or working from photographs doesn't excite you, then working with your existing skills or experimenting with materials might be more useful. I have included on pages 22–23 one of my favourite techniques, 'Memory sketches', as a way of moving from inspiration to a practical, physical outcome.

No matter which path you choose, you are going to need to capture your experiments in a way that helps you to investigate the results and document your ideas, so before we dive into practical solutions, I'd like to share how I go about preserving my findings.

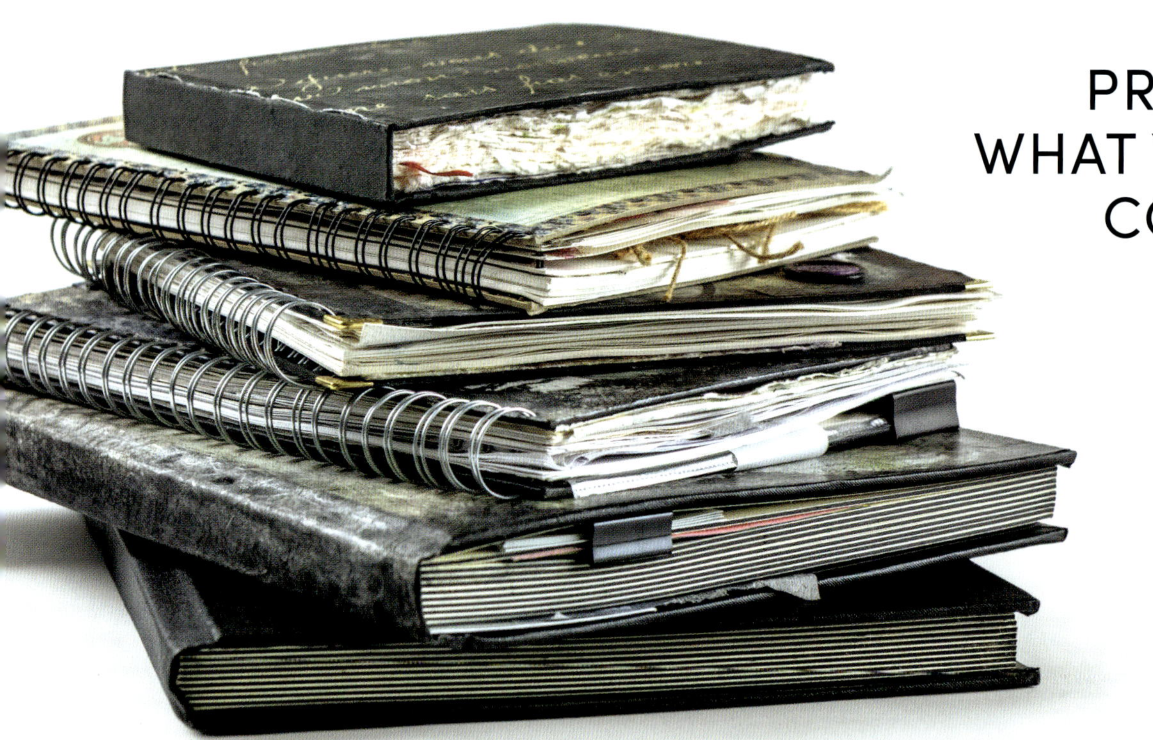

One of the most traditional ways to record your creative ideas is to use a sketchbook. You will probably buy more sketchbooks than you ever require… or maybe that's just me? I have often struggled to find the 'perfect' book to suit my needs, and I don't think there is one specific style or brand that I instinctively reach for. So I have come to the conclusion that my choice of sketchbook very much depends on my mood and what materials I feel like using on any given day.

KEEPING A SKETCHBOOK

Here are a few things I have discovered over the years:

- Whatever you do, don't start a new sketchbook on the first page – it's too much pressure. No one said a sketchbook has to be chronological; save that first page for something else or for a delicious technique experiment you have discovered. Maybe a photograph or a colour chart (like the one on page 44) would be better placed at the start?

- Take ownership of your sketchbook. I like to cover mine or paint them so that they feel personal to me. This is also a great exercise to stop a sketchbook staying too pristine and therefore too perfect to be used.

- You don't have to use a traditional sketchbook. I've seen plenty of stationery appropriated and turned into sketchbooks in interesting and creative ways – even vintage novels that have been covered in paint and worked back into.

- I like a big book, but you might find the size overwhelming, so choose something small and manageable, particularly if the idea of popping it in a pocket or small bag appeals; that way, your sketchbook can always be with you.

- Everything is valid. There is an inexhaustible list of things that you can include in your sketchbook – you are not confined to sketches alone. Some of my favourite inclusions are drawings, colour swatches, writing, collage, leaves/grasses collected on site, research on artists, ideas for future paintings, textures, tracings and memory sketches. Remember also that not everything has to be 'finished'.

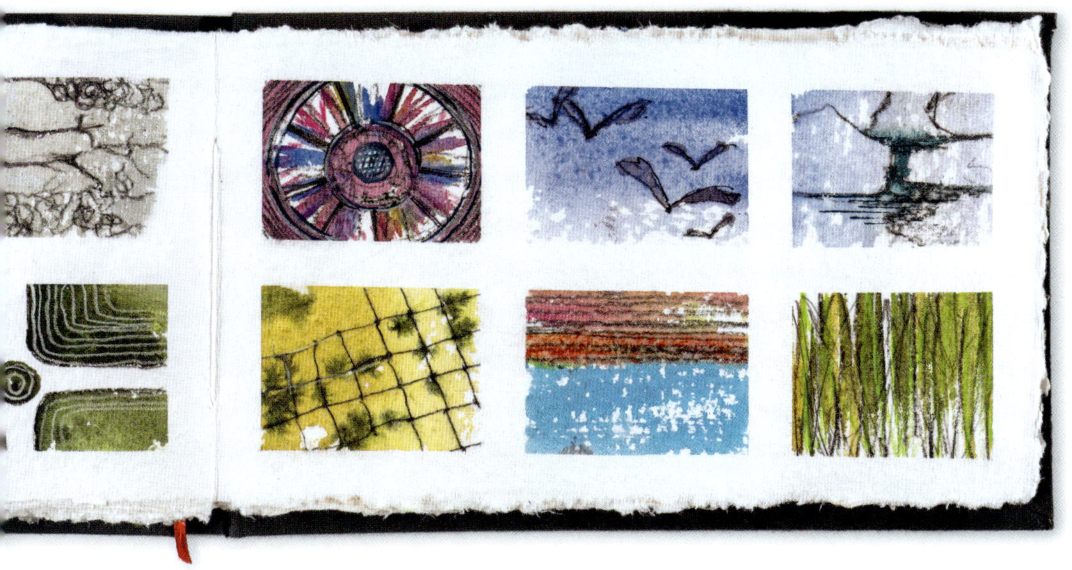

A REFLECTION OF YOU

We often struggle to put into words our responses to places we have seen or visited. Sketching them in a small and private way can be very rewarding and help us to feel like we have really experienced a location.

You may wish to describe this collection more as a visual diary than a sketchbook. I love to write in mine alongside any images that I may have gathered; these notes are just for me and are a delightful *aide-mémoire* for the next or future project.

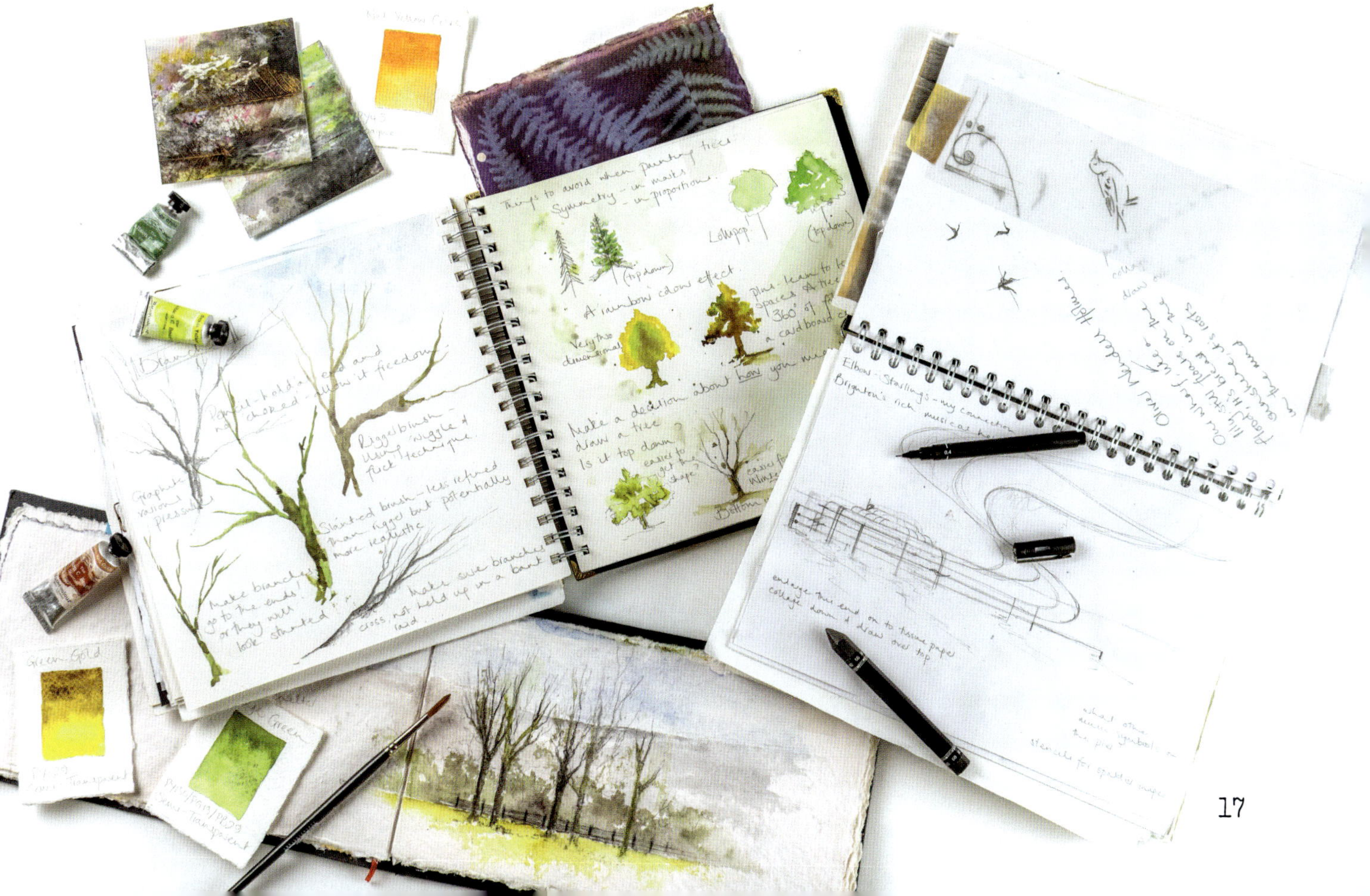

USING PHOTOGRAPHY

Another way of keeping a visual diary is to use photographs. You don't need to be a professional photographer or use fancy equipment to benefit from working from photographs; you don't even have to take the pictures yourself – you can use reliable royalty-free images if you have full permission to do so.

Here is my advice on using photographs when gathering information:

USING YOUR OWN PHOTOGRAPHS:

- You don't need an expensive, hi-tech camera; a phone or tablet is absolutely fine to use.
- Avoid taking photos in bright sunshine; try to capture interesting shadows and tones.
- Be careful of including people's personal or private property in your pictures – always ask permission first.
- A photo that you will paint from doesn't have to be a technically 'good' photo. You might choose to focus solely on a single tree or a selection of rocks that would work more successfully in a different project or composition.
- Take as many photographs as you can so you have all angles and details covered.

USING OTHER PEOPLE'S PHOTOS

- If you have friends or family who travel, ask to see their holiday photos – they will love reliving their adventures, and you will get a feel for what made a location special.
- Use reputable websites to source royalty-free images. If you're not sure where to find such sites, ask an art group, either online or in person, where its members source their images.

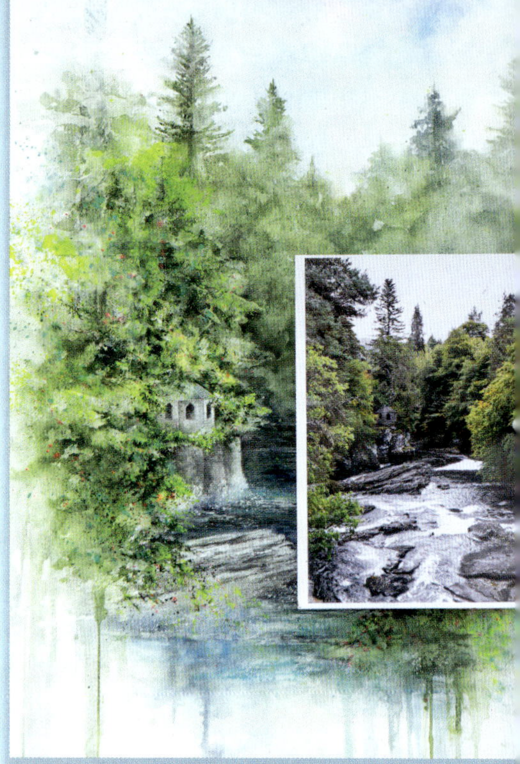

The Summer House (see pages 152–158)
I took this photograph as the view I wanted was from a bridge in the middle of a busy road and not conducive to stopping to paint.

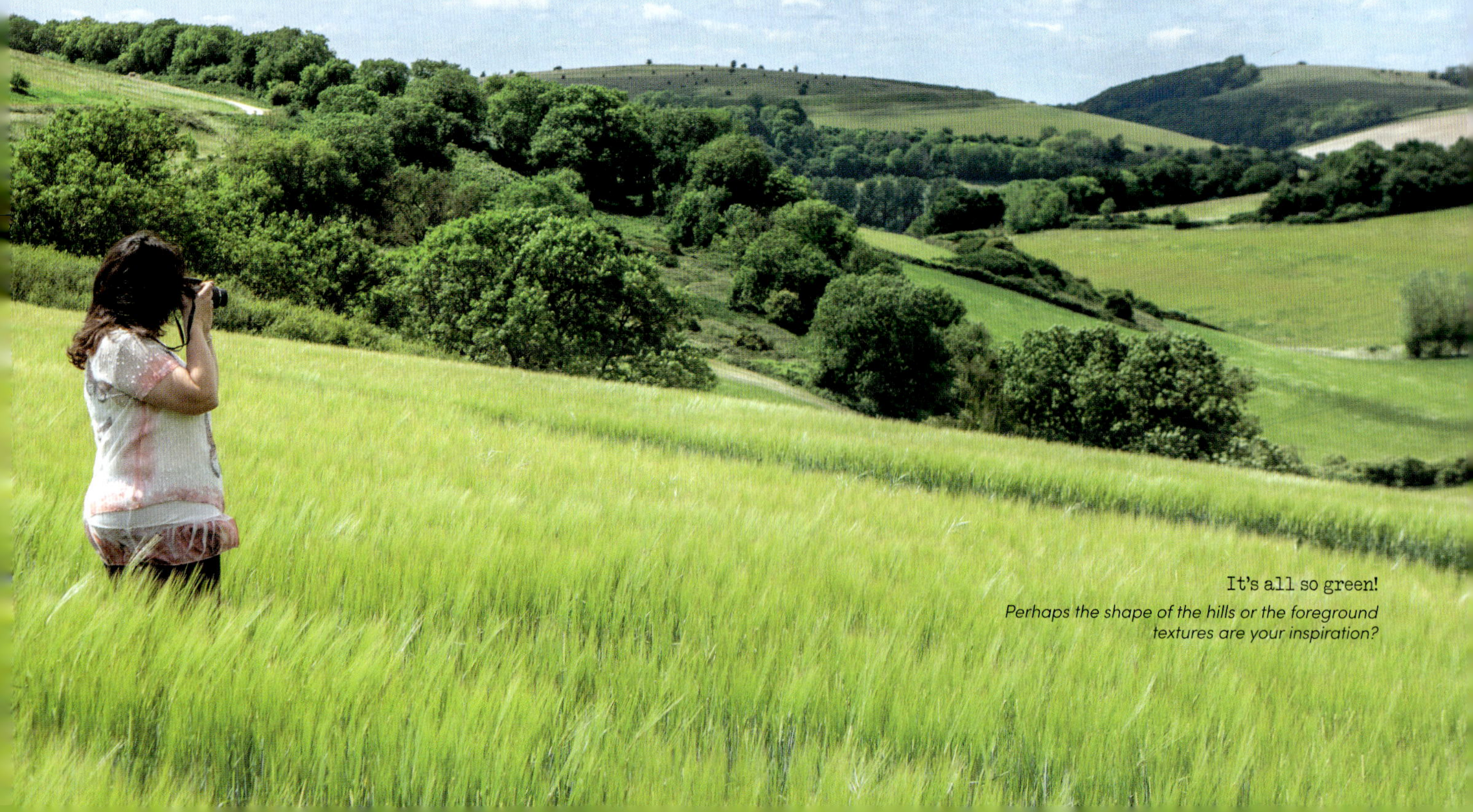

It's all so green!
Perhaps the shape of the hills or the foreground textures are your inspiration?

SKETCHING AND PAINTING OUTDOORS

As I suggested on pages 15–16, a traditional method for understanding a landscape is to sketch or paint while you are experiencing it. You may wish to capture a few details or spend the whole day creating a more comprehensive painting, which can be fun but also daunting if you haven't tried it before.

You will probably have questions before you embark such as: *What do I need to take? Will there be somewhere I can relax and sketch? Will other people want to see what I am doing?* And, of course, the thing that can hold us back: *what if my sketch or painting doesn't meet my expectations?*

Let's see if I can answer some of these questions straight away; you can find a flow chart to help you work through the more artistic considerations on page 21.

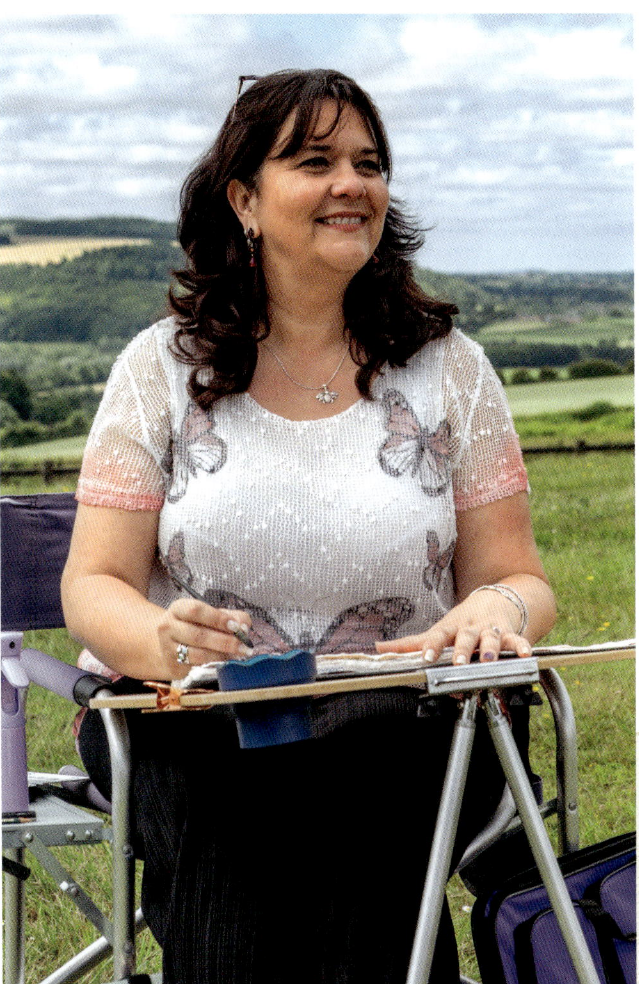

'WHAT SHOULD I PACK?'

There are usually two types of artists when it comes to painting outdoors: those who like to travel light and those who prefer the comfort of their materials. I definitely fall into the second category: I get so frustrated if I don't have all my 'stuff' with me and I like to be comfortable so I can concentrate. The photo on page 33 shows some of the items I consider essential.

'WILL THERE BE SOMEWHERE I CAN RELAX AND SKETCH?'

Choose your location wisely. Challenge yourself with your choice of subject, but not to the point where it stops you from feeling as though you have achieved something. If working outdoors is new to you, focus on something small and manageable – a few trees or a simple building rather than a 360-degree view of every species of native plant. Find a suitable place to work from and if need be, take your own chair, as I do, so you can be comfortable.

'GO ALONE OR GO WITH OTHER PEOPLE?'

This is something only you can answer. There is definitely safety in numbers sometimes, and it can be particularly helpful if you are going with someone with more experience, who is going to encourage you. Or maybe you prefer solitude in order to get 'in the zone' and concentrate. It may be a case of different needs at different times.

'HOW DO I DEAL WITH SPECTATORS?'

Most of the time, people passing will be truly interested in what you are doing, and usually well-meaning. You don't need to tell them that you think it's not very good/ you are only a beginner/it's your interpretation (delete as applicable); let them see what you are up to and make a new friend. If they are anything less than encouraging, that's all about them and no reflection on your creativity. As the saying goes, 'if you can't say anything nice then say nothing at all'.

Creativity is infectious: if you feel comfortable, share your thoughts with any passing observers, as they may, in turn, offer a valuable observation of their own.

PRACTICAL TECHNIQUES FOR BEING CREATIVE OUTDOORS

No matter if your creative excursion is planned or spontaneous, and whether you are alone or with friends, to be suddenly confronted with a landscape can be quite daunting.

Here is a visual reference for some of the things you might want to think about when you get to your chosen spot. This isn't by any means a definitive guide and I invite you to add your own suggestions to suit your situation as you become more confident with painting on location.

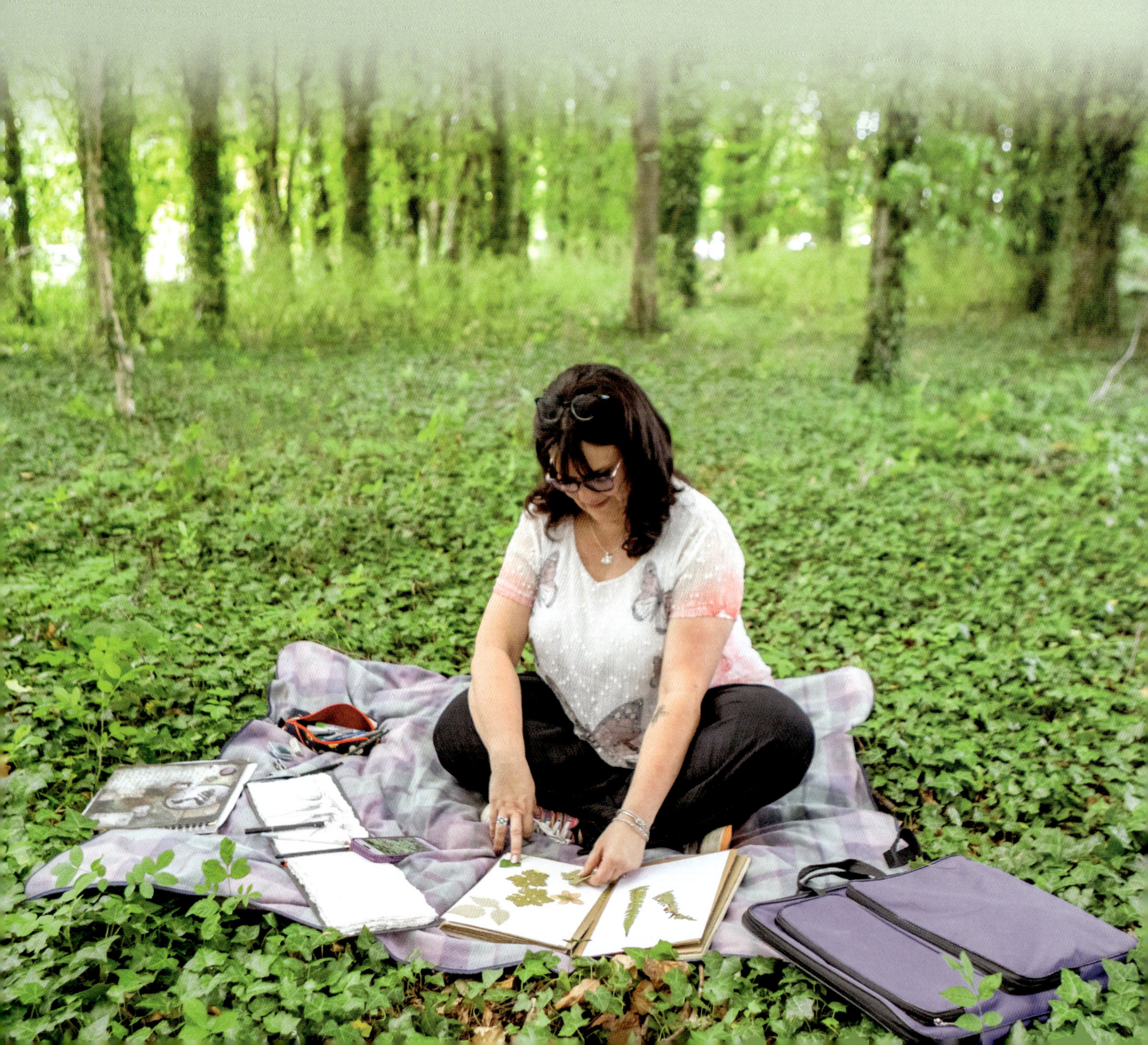

Working Outdoors

1. Arrive at location

a. Wander around; look carefully at what interests you.

b. Hone your observation skills. How about looking above, below or at the corner of your subject?

c. Take photographs – lots of them.

d. Sit and 'be' – make notes of the sounds, smells and colours to help you recall the scene later.

e. How long are you planning on staying? Is it worth setting yourself a minimum or maximum amount of time, or are you just going to see what happens?

2. Get comfy!

Even for five minutes. Don't let discomfort or distractions hinder you.

Take a big, deep breath and close your eyes before making any marks on the paper.

3. Consider these starting ideas

a. Start small – sketch something achievable.

b. Draw the 'whole' quickly and without accuracy to become accustomed to the scene.

c. Use colour, not line – just splash some colour on the paper, and make shapes instead of focusing on detail.

d. Use line and no colour – concentrate on contour and texture by making interesting marks on the paper.

4. Take notes

Write notes during your time on location – anything that might help you to recall the place, or perhaps an observation on your sketch. Keep it positive to help you progress with your ideas.

5. Gather information

Collect anything and everything: a leaf, a grass, a rubbing, a print – make some unconventional observations.

MEMORY SKETCHES

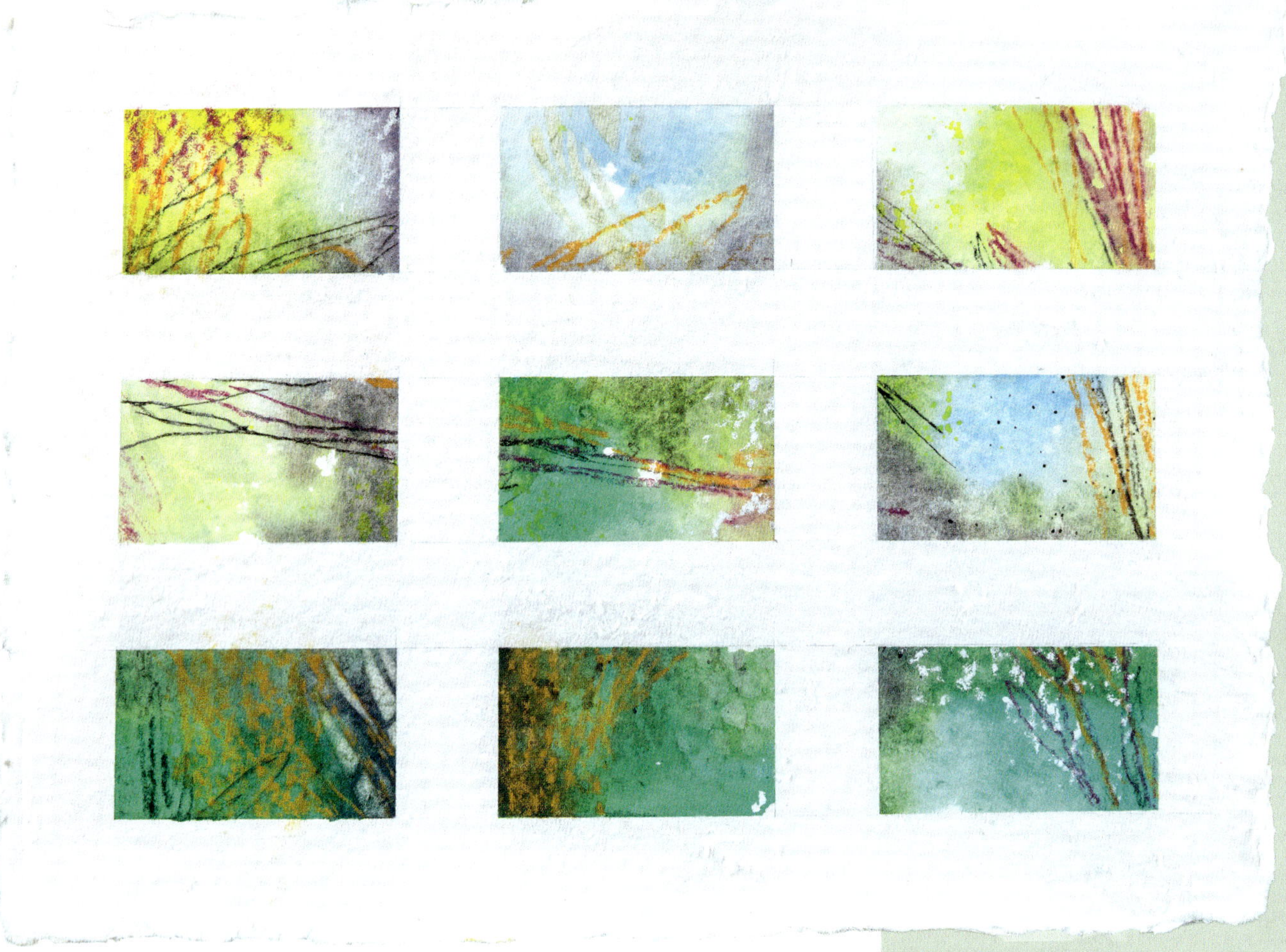

A memory sketch is a way of interpreting your landscape without it needing to be representational. It is a device I use often to start off my artistic process, a way of staying free from becoming too overwhelmed by the painting ahead or to clear a creative block when I'm stuck and don't know what is important to me. I create memory sketches when I have come back from a walk or a trip out, as the images I have in my head are often the most resonant elements of the trip.

Equally, when I paint a scene that I do not know, I listen to people describe the location, to discern what is important to them. As such, memory sketches can also be called 'imagination sketches'; they are a wonderful way to experiment, make mistakes and take the pressure off a more traditional approach to creating a scene.

Memory sketches are one of my favourite warm-up exercises, and I encourage you to have a go at them as they are fun to explore and are a creative way of moving from your figurative (realistic) observations to something more experimental and unique.

HOW TO CREATE A MEMORY SKETCH

1 Research, visit or recall a place that you wish to paint.

2 Choose a painting surface to work on (see page 32) and decide on the size of your surface. This is always dependent on my mood, how much time I have to invest in the exercise and what materials I currently have available to me.

3 Divide the surface up into smaller sections using tape or drawn lines: I prefer low-tack tape as I love peeling it back at the end to reveal the colours and textures of each individual study. The number of individual cells is entirely up to you.

4 Select materials that are inspiring you today – go with your instinct, or deliberately challenge yourself to try some new experiments.

5 Draw, paint, spatter, scrape, blow, stick, scratch – whatever you feel like doing that sums up the colours/ textures/atmosphere/geography/season/weather of the location you have in mind. Some experiments will work, some will not; you are simply making small discoveries along the way.

6 Extra layers can be achieved by adding bold marks using unusual materials such as stencils or printing blocks.

7 If you have masked off your cells with tape, carefully remove the tape and review each cell, either as a combination or individually. Consider how each memory sketch came about. Did you find a new way of expressing something? Did a new material work for you? Did you isolate an aspect that you hadn't considered before?

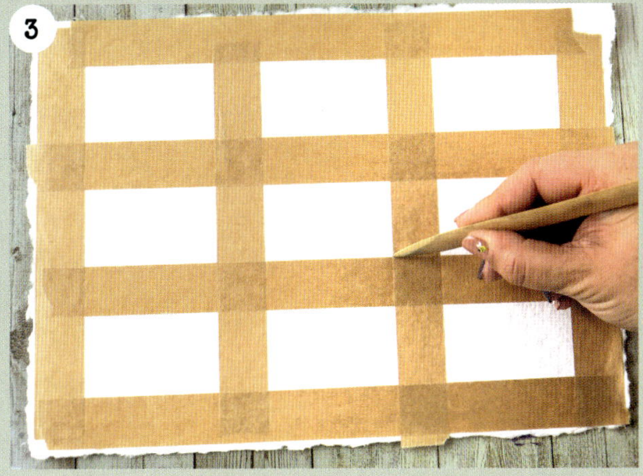

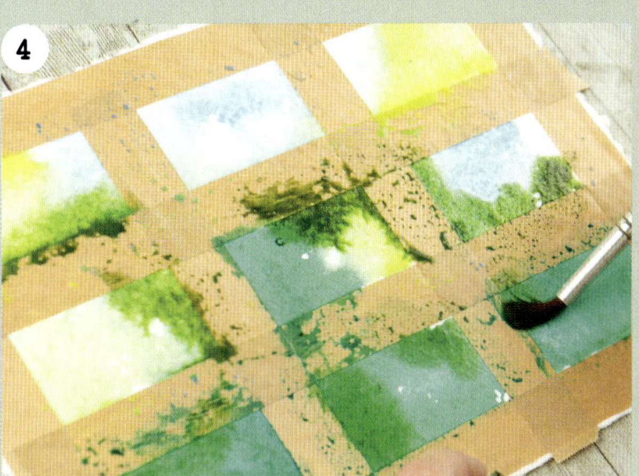

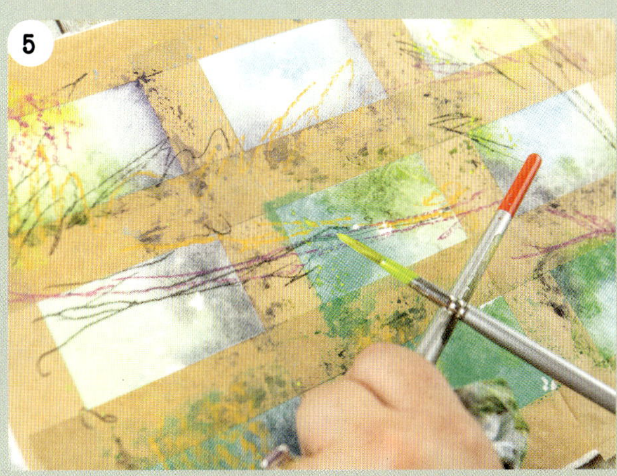

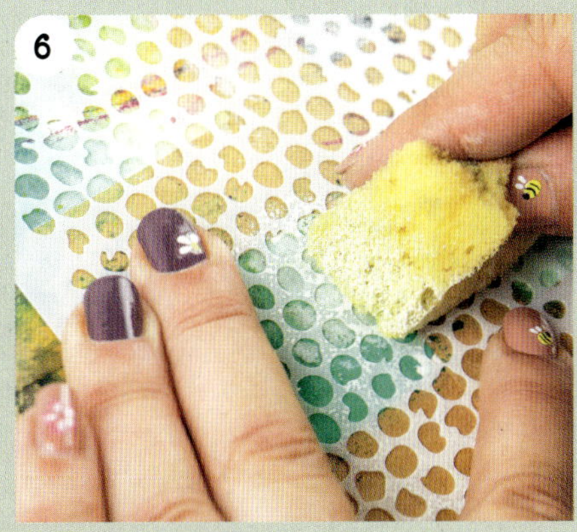

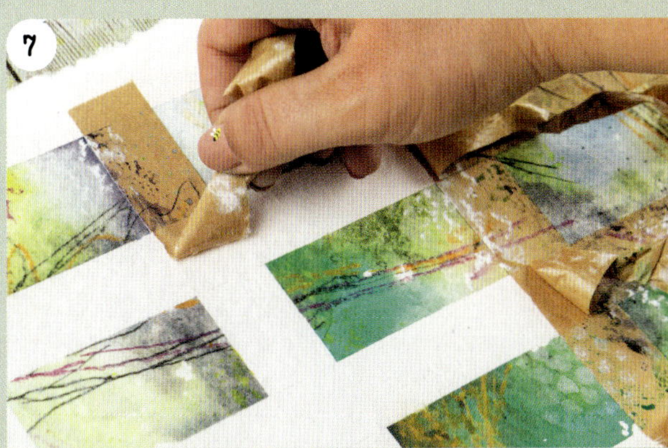

YOUR UNIQUE APPROACH

When we start to get more confident with how we gather information for our chosen landscape and ways in which explore creative outcomes, our attention turns to what we can do to express our individuality.

The flow chart opposite, on page 25, shares a few of my suggestions for where you might start to find your own way to be creative, taking the ideas from the previous pages a little further. This is not an exhaustive list as I am sure you will begin to think of your own ideas, and they can be applied to painting on location and painting in a studio setting to suit your situation. We will explore some of these ideas further in chapter 5, 'Creative thinking' (see page 98).

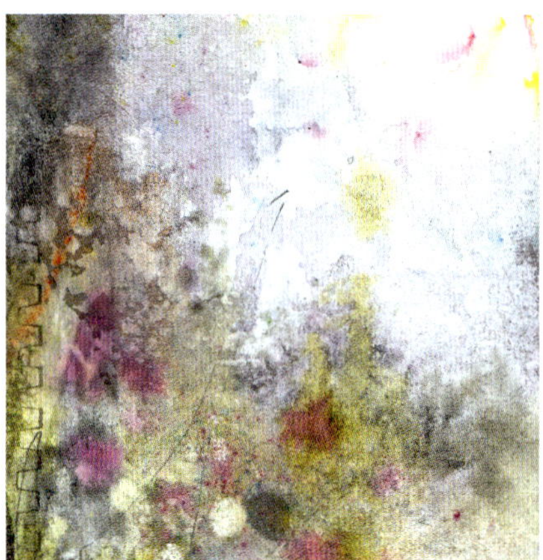 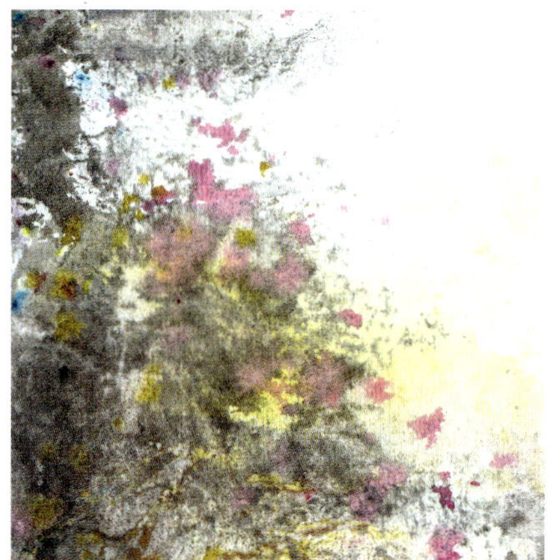 

A NOTE ABOUT BREAKING THE RULES

Before we dive into how you may wish to explore your own interpretations of landscapes, I'd like to share how important it is to me that, no matter what advice is given, you need to find your own path through a project – be it traditional or unconventional.

Creative people have broken rules as long as there has been creativity. I like to think of the more formal regulations of art as 'guidelines' rather than rules, insofar as you can choose to follow them – they may be useful tools to help you assess what is or isn't working, but ultimately you make the choices about what you include or exclude.

There are really two schools of thought about formal rules: do you learn them all when you are a beginner and risk being overwhelmed by what you should or shouldn't do, or do you fill the gaps in your knowledge when you have an issue? Based upon my experience, I fall firmly into the latter category. I am primarily self-taught, and as frustrating as it is when I don't know how to fix a creative problem, it doesn't stifle my urge to be creative, make mistakes and enjoy the process.

I have shared the painting project *Storm Bert* on pages 26 and 27 to demonstrate that understanding how I was feeling about what I was seeing was more important than employing any formal or traditional ways of expressing the landscape.

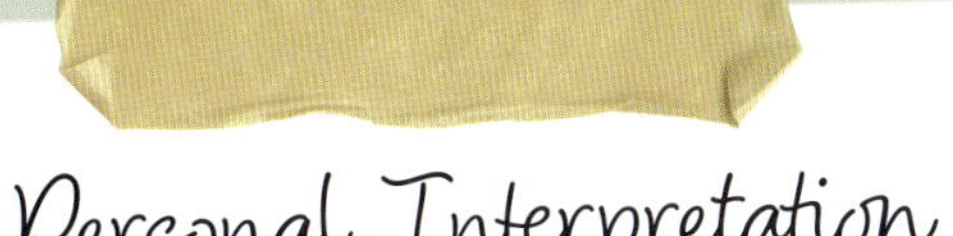

Personal Interpretation

1. Your landscape

a. Do you want to replicate it faithfully?

b. Do you want to explore something different?

c. Do you want to break the rules and take creative risks?

d. Is this one painting or a series of views?

2. Storytelling

What is it about the place that speaks to me?

a. What is its history and how can I show this?

b. What is the intended emotional reaction to the location? Can it be shown through mood and/or atmosphere?

c. What is the importance of the location, to me or to others?

3. Choosing the focus of your interpretation

a. Could you use colour creatively? You could perhaps use jarring colours, a monotone selection, a limited palette or your favourite hues.

b. Can you emphasize textures? You may want to think about the tools you use – and whether they are traditional or experimental – the mediums that you choose or the marks that you make to show what is important to you.

c. How about playing with the composition? Maybe you like the geometry of the landscape, or the perspective? Can you explore these with small 'thumbnail' sketches or by changing your viewpoint?

d. What if you used your imagination? Being in a landscape and closing your eyes can help you to concentrate on more than what you see. Or perhaps you wish to remove certain elements that you don't think will work in the final painting.

e. Instead of working from a photograph or on location, are you able to imagine a view or recall what you have seen?

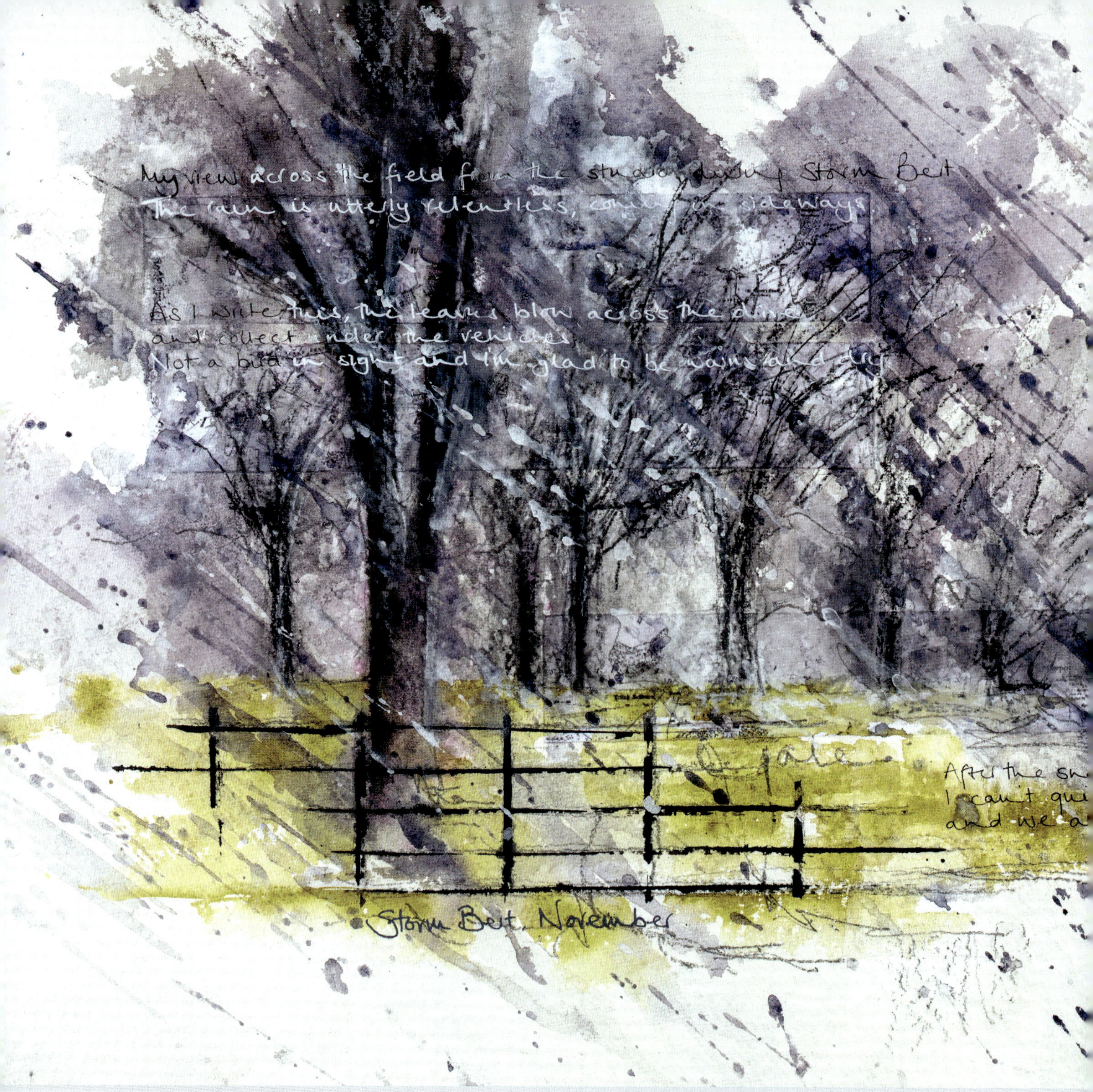

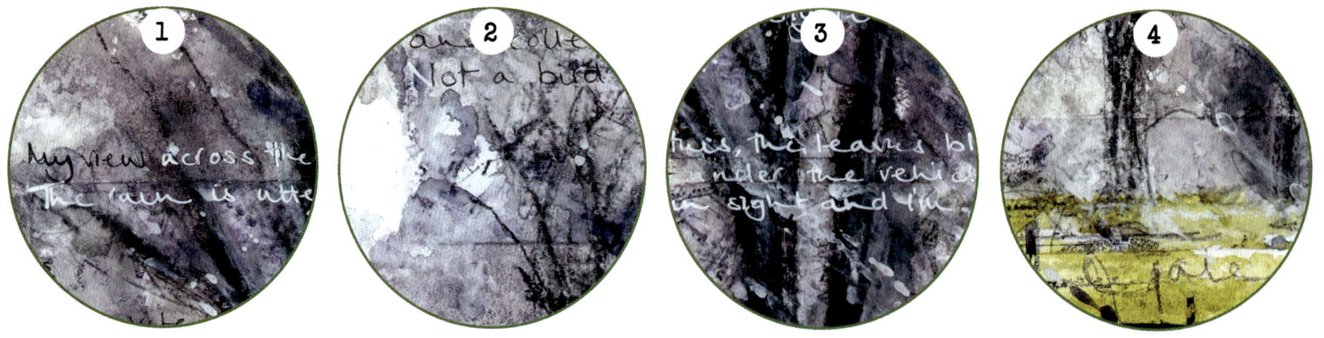

My view across the field from the studio during Storm Bert.
The rain is utterly relentless, coming in sideways

As I write this, the leaves blow across the drive
and collect under the vehicles
Not a bud in sight and I'm glad to be warm and dry

After the sn
I can't qui
and we a

Storm Bert, November

INTERPRETING *STORM BERT*

This painting shows how I have interpreted my response to the landscape in the ways described previously in this chapter.

1 History of location

This is a view I see every day from my studio, being dramatically altered by the weather.

2 Exploring something different

I adhered pieces of map left over from another project to paper I wasn't familiar with (see page 106).

3 Storytelling

I recorded my observations both literally and with descriptive language (see page 110).

4 Colour palette to reflect the weather

I combined dusky colours with brighter shades, and left the white of the paper to show contrast.

5 Textures and marks to reflect the intensity of the weather

Throwing the paint across the surface to mirror the rain hitting the window.

6 Different art media used (watercolour, ink, crayon, text)

Using whatever I could find at my desk, I experimented with different materials to make a variety of marks.

CONCLUSION

There is no right or wrong way to approach landscapes as a subject, and equally no set way for you to explore how you record them. What matters is that your subject inspires you, and drives you to interpret what you see in meaningful ways. It could be that the scene is well known, or that you have discovered a corner of the planet to which you feel a profound connection – or maybe because when you saw the scene, you thought about that tube of colour that you haven't yet had the opportunity to use.

Materials and techniques can all be discovered and learned about, some of which I will cover in the next chapter but finding that spark of inspiration is usually the first step that makes us want to explore a subject further.

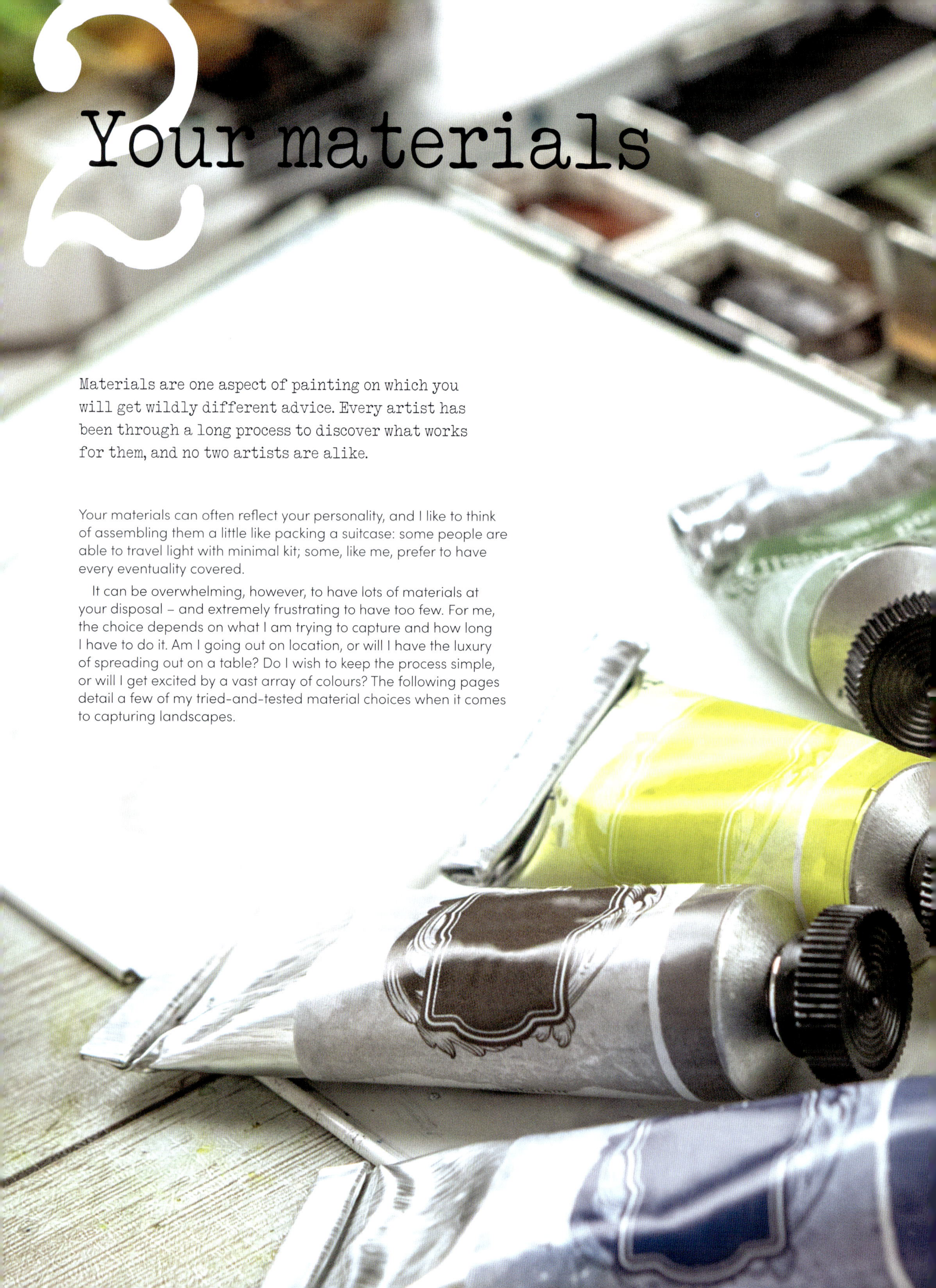

2 Your materials

Materials are one aspect of painting on which you will get wildly different advice. Every artist has been through a long process to discover what works for them, and no two artists are alike.

Your materials can often reflect your personality, and I like to think of assembling them a little like packing a suitcase: some people are able to travel light with minimal kit; some, like me, prefer to have every eventuality covered.

It can be overwhelming, however, to have lots of materials at your disposal – and extremely frustrating to have too few. For me, the choice depends on what I am trying to capture and how long I have to do it. Am I going out on location, or will I have the luxury of spreading out on a table? Do I wish to keep the process simple, or will I get excited by a vast array of colours? The following pages detail a few of my tried-and-tested material choices when it comes to capturing landscapes.

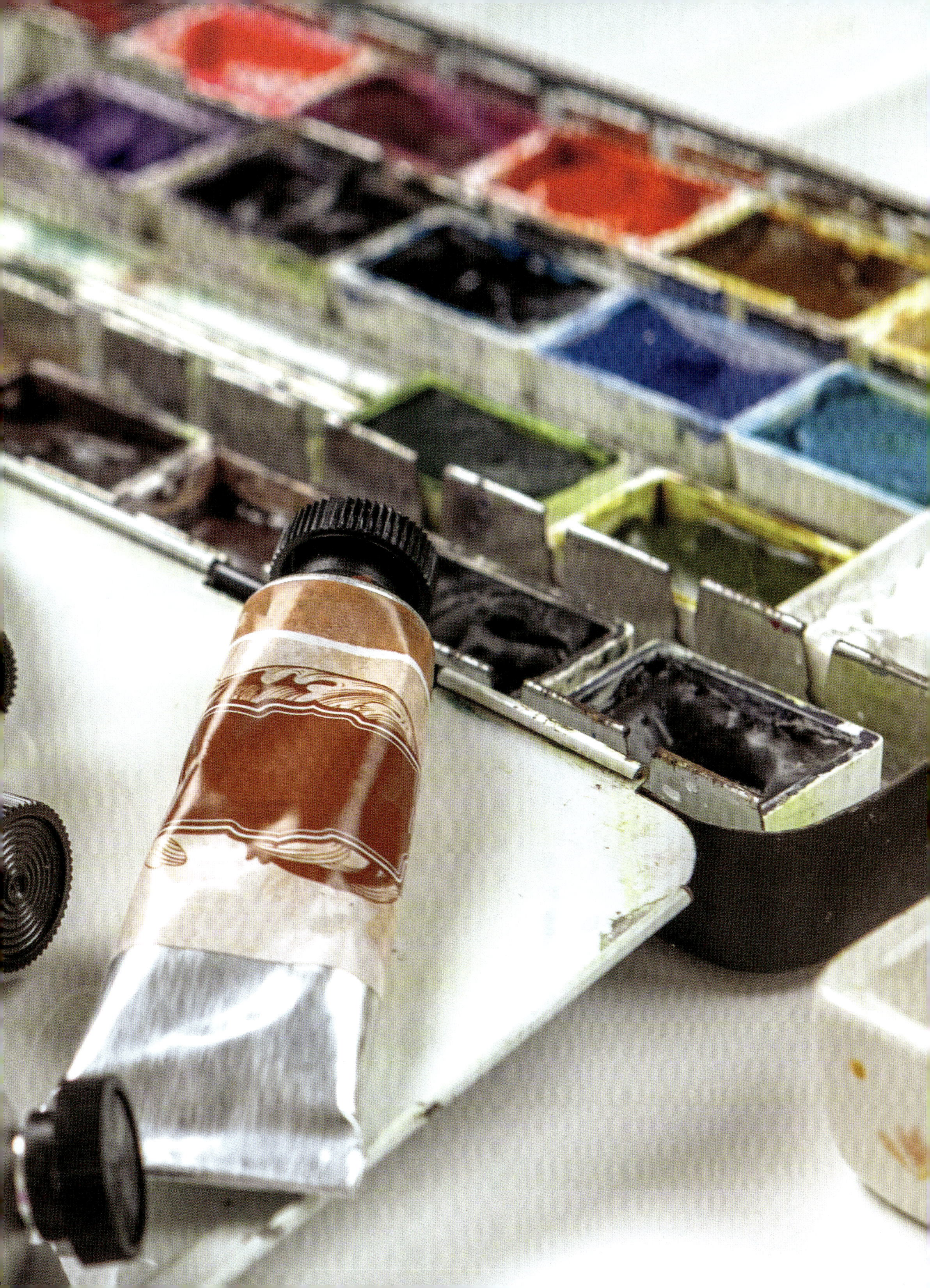

PAINTING MATERIALS

The array of art materials available is astonishing - how are you supposed to know what might be right for <u>you</u>? It took me a long time to work out where I felt most comfortable, and the experiments that I had along the way were fascinating, as I tried out lots of things to see if they fit.

I am a mixed-media artist, which means that I don't stick to only one medium in my work – I like to make individual marks with individual tools rather than use just the one tool and make my choice fit with what I'm doing. I do narrow it down a little, however, as I tend to use water-soluble media, so all the things I use work in harmony with each other.

Another influence on my choice of materials is their impact on the planet. You wouldn't necessarily associate art materials with ecological concern, but as this is equipment I use every day, I need to be just as aware of what I am using as with everything else I consume.

MEDIUMS/MEDIA

'Medium' is a term often used to describe paint or ink but is sometimes extended to include dry materials, such as pastel, pencil or charcoal. My particular choice regarding the ingredients of my materials is reflected in the paints I choose to use as a few pigments are created from animal by-products – for example, ivory black pigment is usually obtained from charred animal bones; and if you are vegan, you may also wish to avoid honey as a pigment binder in watercolour.

If you like to use acrylic paint, you may wish to think about how you dispose of the water you use. While artists account for only a tiny percentage of the distribution of microplastics, I feel that an individual can often be the catalyst for a ripple of change.

SURFACE/SUPPORT

This is what you paint on – be it paper, board, canvas or a specialist surface designed exclusively for your choice of medium, such as Pastelmat®, which is designed for use with chalk pastels.

Again, it may not be immediately apparent that paper has the potential to make an environmental impact, but artists' papers can sometimes be manufactured using large quantities of water, or animal-derived products such as gelatine to prepare them for painting. Any ethical company or distributor will make information available for you to research; and there is a vast amount of reputable information on the internet to inform your values and impact your purchasing habits. (See page 32 for information about the paper I like to use.)

BRUSHES AND ACCESSORIES

I haven't used animal-hair brushes for a while now; I actually prefer a synthetic hair as I am so horrible to my brushes that it became expensive to replace them all the time. There are now some excellent animal-hair substitutions on the market, with synthetic filaments to replicate the water- and colour-holding properties of more traditional fibres.

Accessories can range from a humble water pot to a fancy easel. If you have the opportunity to treat yourself, it is satisfying – but not essential – to have tools that are specially made for the job. Many items can be found around the house, such as kitchen paper, an old white plate for mixing (instead of a palette) or a cotton bud (swab) for blending chalks.

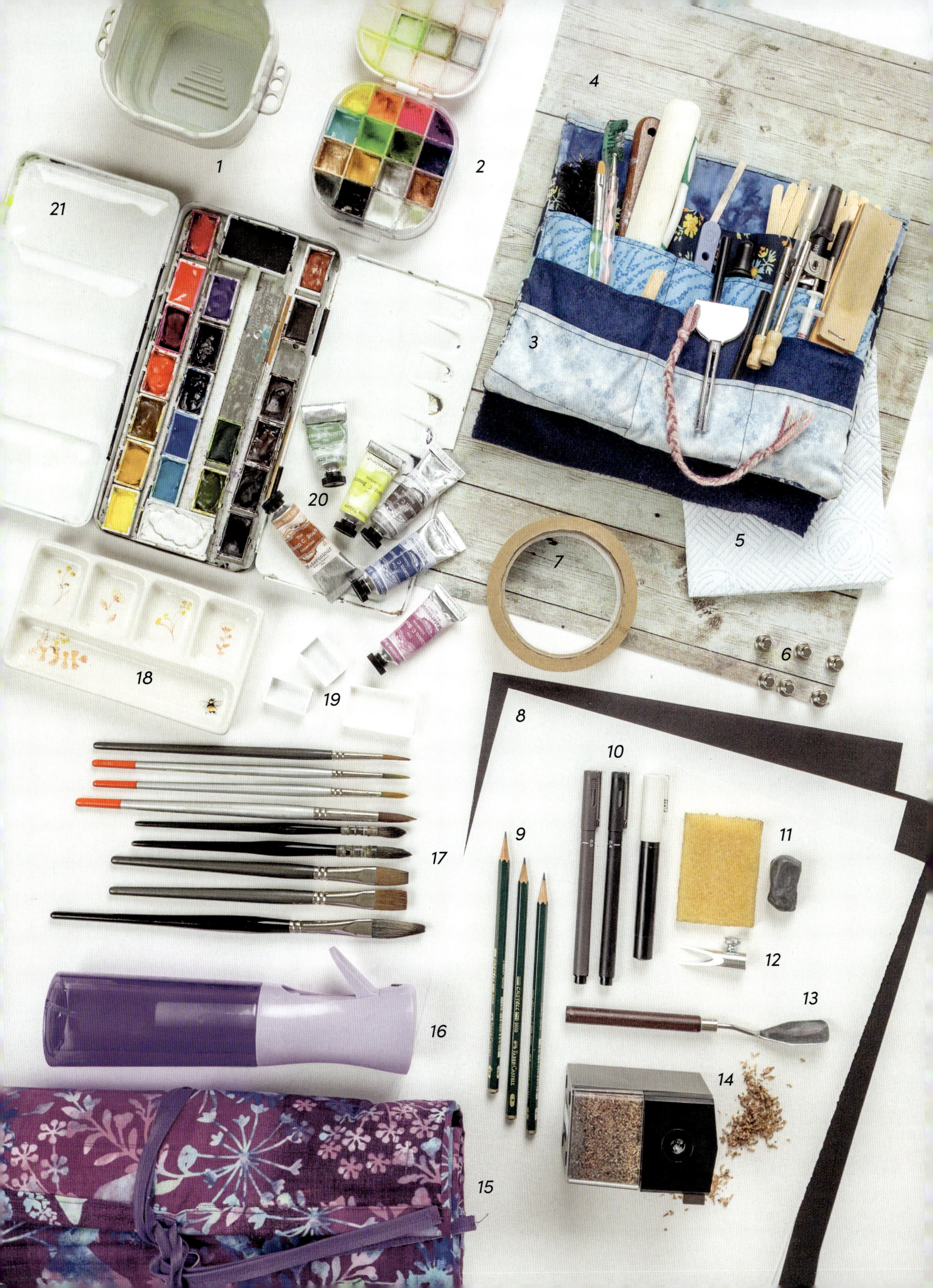

UNDERSTANDING YOUR PAPER

MAKING THE RIGHT CHOICES FOR YOU

Of all the materials to consider, paper is one of the most important to me as it needs to respond to the paints and techniques in a way that works for what I am trying to express. Luckily, you can experiment with many different types and textures, which have the potential to make a world of difference to your work.

My personal preference is for watercolour paper and, although I do dip into alternative surfaces to keep my work fresh and experimental, I return every time to a paper that will take all the media I like to use. I don't use one specific brand or type of paper; my choice depends on what I'm working towards or the combinations of media I plan on using in the piece.

- I prefer **cotton or natural-fibre paper** that is internally sized (that is, treated with the element that stops it acting like blotting paper) so that I get longer to float my colour on the surface before it dries. A few favourite brands of mine are Fabriano Artistico, Millford, much of Hahnemühle's range, and handmade papers from India (Artway INDIGO).

- I like a paper that is a **strong white** as opposed to a more traditional, creamier white. This way, it shows off the colours I am using and is easier to photograph or reproduce without the background of the paper looking yellow.

- I tend to use a **'Not' or a Rough surface**. Not is a general term for Cold-Pressed papers as the surface is neither smooth nor rough – it's somewhere in the middle. It's worth noting that a Not/Rough surface isn't a general standard; it's particular to the range that the paper is in – not all Rough papers are the same.

- I also like **papers that do something different** while retaining their properties – that is, a paper that has a regular texture that will show up the brickwork in a building, a black watercolour paper that adds a bit of drama, or a pastel paper that I can paint on before applying dry media.

My advice is to purchase some trial packs of paper and see what works for you, or identify an artist whose work you admire and find out what surfaces they prefer.

Fabriano Artistico, 300gsm (140lb) Not

Millford, 300gsm (140lb) Not

Artway INDIGO, 250gsm (no imperial equivalent)

Pastelmat®, 360gsm (170lb)

Tilseds Black Watercolour, 320gsm (140lb)

Hahnemühle Cornwall, 450gsm (210lb)

Hahnemühle Andalucia, 500gsm (230lb)

Hahnemühle Agave, 290gsm (135lb)

Hahnemühle Sugar Cane, 290gsm (135lb)

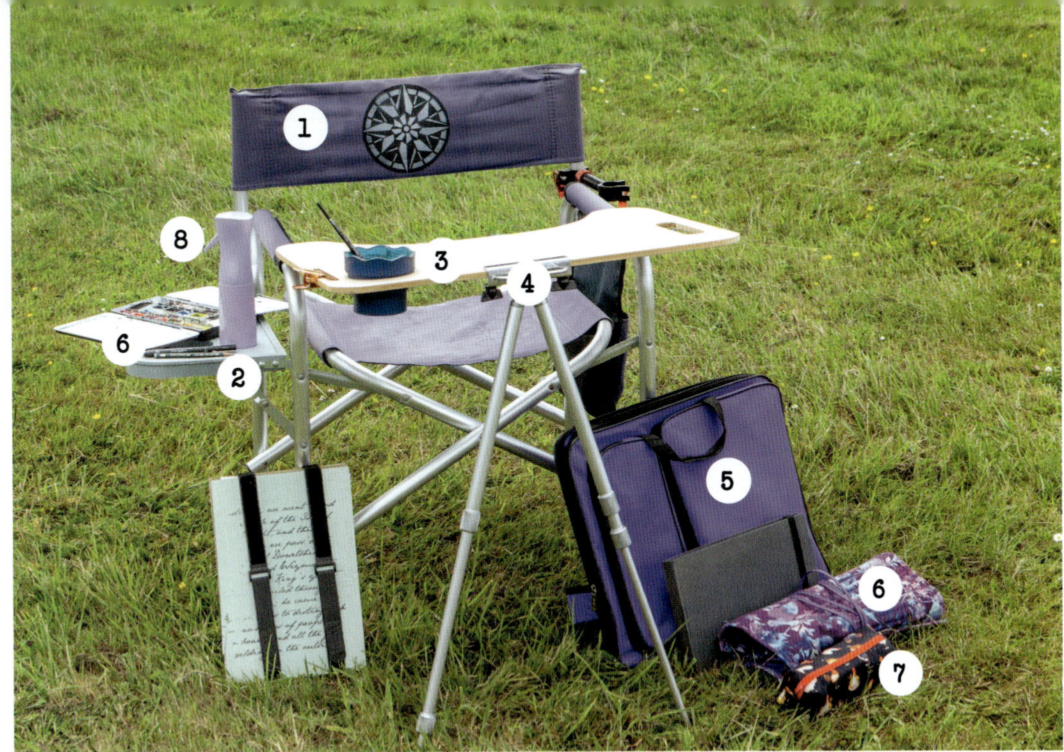

My location painting essentials

YOUR LOCATION PAINTING KIT

I'm not a minimalist when it comes to the materials I take out with me. I like to be comfortable, so I won't be distracted and I like to make decisions about what to use as the landscape presents itself before me. Of course, I can't take all my materials out with me, but I always try to take a little of everything and in smaller containers or quantities, so that I don't have to compromise the marks I'm making because I've decided I want to travel light.

Here I explain why I've chosen all the things that form my location painting kit:

1 **A comfy chair:** mine is lightweight but still comfortable as I'm not one to be perched on something precarious, getting a bad back. My chair even has an attachment to hold an umbrella, either for shade or to hold back a light rain shower.

2 My chair has **a side table** so that I don't have to balance materials on my drawing board (**3**) or lap.

3 **A drawing board:** mine is large, and I designed it myself so that it curves around my lap, has a hole to take a water pot, and a carry handle for ease of transportation. There are lots on the market or find someone with some carpentry skills to make you something bespoke.

4 **An easel:** I find conventional easels too upright or cumbersome, and too time-consuming to assemble. Mine is comprised of just two legs that attach to my drawing board.

5 **A folder of a decent size and capacity,** which can carry pads, a sketchbook or sheets of paper, so that I can decide on location what I feel like using.

6 I won't compromise on the paints or brushes I take out, so my **regular tin of colours** and my **brush roll** go everywhere with me.

7 My **pencil case** holds an abridged version of any mixed-media materials I am currently experimenting with, including sketching pens, charcoal pencils and graphite stick.

8 Then there are the **more unusual items** like mark-making tools (toothbrush, sponge, Lego), spray bottle (a large one so it also holds the water for my main pot) and my flower press that also keeps tissue paper for collecting rubbings or fragile found objects.

9 And I never forget my **camera or smartphone** (not shown)!

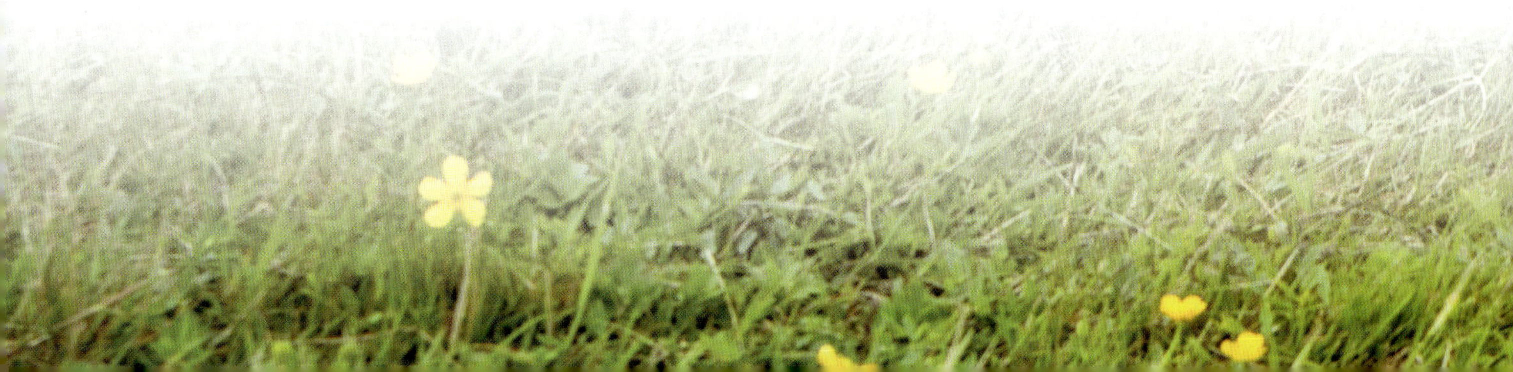

BE INSPIRED BY YOUR MATERIALS

I believe that it's just as possible to be inspired by your materials as it is by what you are painting. If you are compelled to tell a story visually or share through images what is important to you, your materials need to reflect that narrative in the best way that they can. My opinion is that if I sit down to paint and I feel it's a chore to mix a specific colour, or disheartened that I'm fighting my paper, I won't be my best creative self.

My materials and tools are an extremely important part of my work; I want my tools to help me, to inspire me and to do the best job they can at showing off the decisions I have made about my work. Yes, you can use a stick of charcoal and a piece of wallpaper to make art, and if that's what inspires you then that's what you should equip yourself with, but equally you may find huge amounts of joy in buying paint, brushes and paper that excite you when they arrive.

There are three areas of my work that have the most significance or importance to me and they are **colour**, **surface** and **texture**. They are the elements I look for when I search for inspiration and the materials that bring me the most joy; therefore when I'm at the stage of gathering or experimenting, my materials can give me a huge boost and help me express myself. I've expanded on these here so that you can understand why they help me and perhaps it might be a starting point for you too.

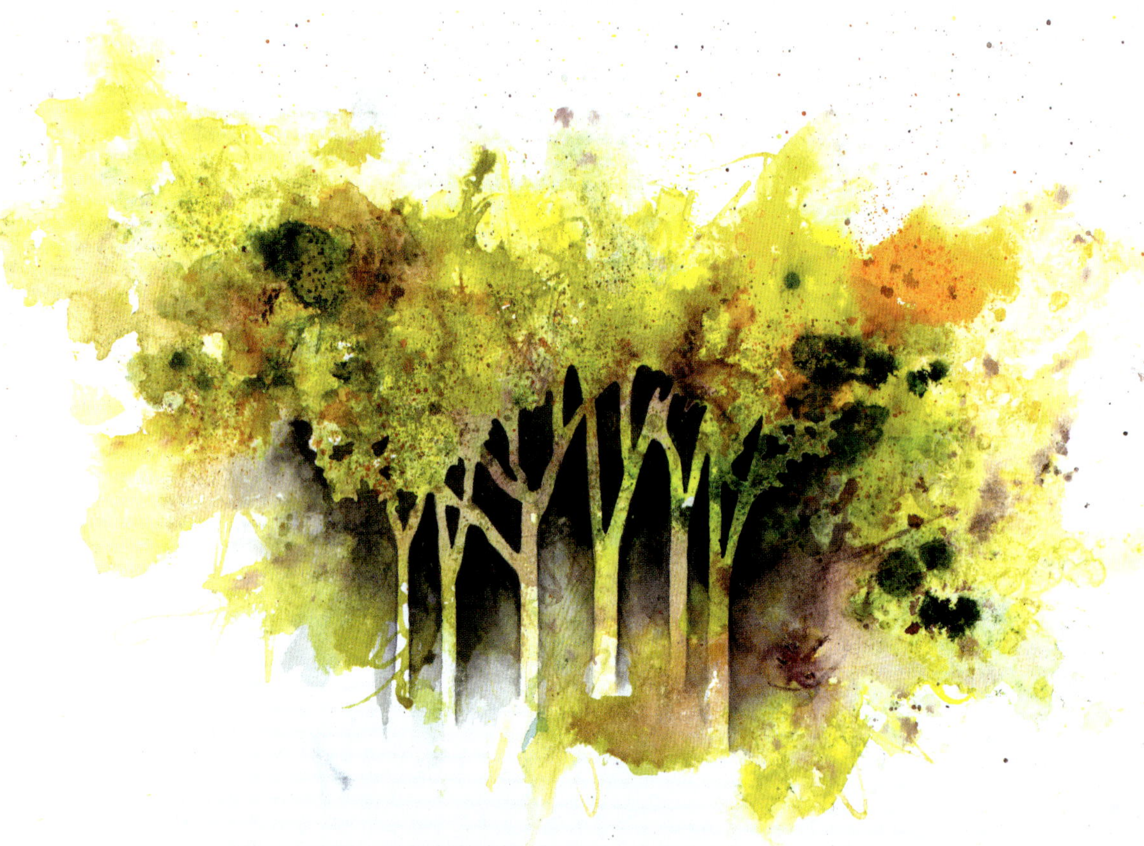

Negative trees

400 × 300mm
(15¾ × 11¾in)

This experiment was all of my paint and textures applied without any idea of where it was going, including a delicious fluorescent yellow acrylic ink that I had just purchased. I then painted the dark areas over the top in order for the marks and colours to look like bright foliage against the rich spaces between the trunks.

COLOUR

Yes, it is probably wise to learn how to mix colour properly from the point of view of acquiring traditional skills. BUT! If you see a new colour and it becomes your favourite shade, or you think to yourself, 'oooh, that looks interesting!', then experiment with it. Why wouldn't you want to use a metallic gold or a rich black – or even a fluorescent yellow?

SURFACE

Are you bored of painting on the same paper or board every time? Is there a more exciting surface out there that might work better with the combinations of materials that you have? What if you use something unusual like wood or fabric instead of traditional paper? What if you interfere with your paper by adding collage or a resist before you start painting?

We can very easily get stuck in using the same materials every time we sit down to paint, and often need to encourage ourselves to use something a little different.

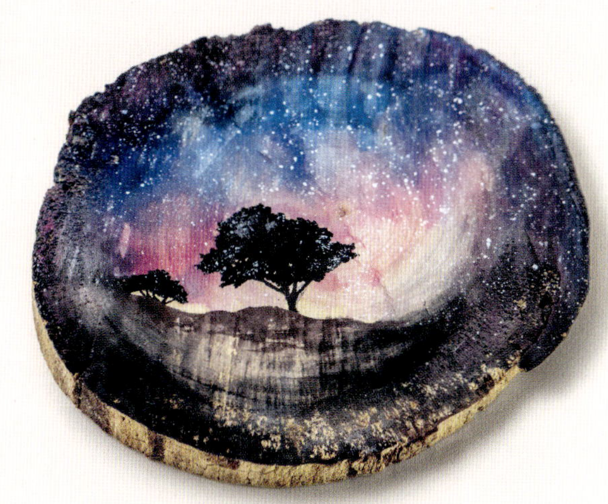

Ancient Trees

200 × 185mm (7⅞ × 7¼in)

At the time of seeing a news report of a very famous tree being felled, one came down in high winds at the bottom of my garden. Everywhere I looked I was either reading about trees falling or seeing one out of my studio window.
It felt apt to use the tree itself as an alternative surface, even though I did have to wait quite a long time for it to be dry enough to paint on.

TEXTURE

Are you trying to replicate the specific texture of an object, and can that object be involved in the texture-making process? Are there implements in your kitchen, garage or shed that might give you an interesting pattern? If you prefer to take a more traditional approach, are there mediums that you could mix in with your paint to create thickness or richness? See page 102 for more texture-making ideas.

Mark making (which is discussed further on pages 52–55) is an element of painting that can transform your work, particularly if the item used to make the mark is unusual, or it creates an interesting pattern.

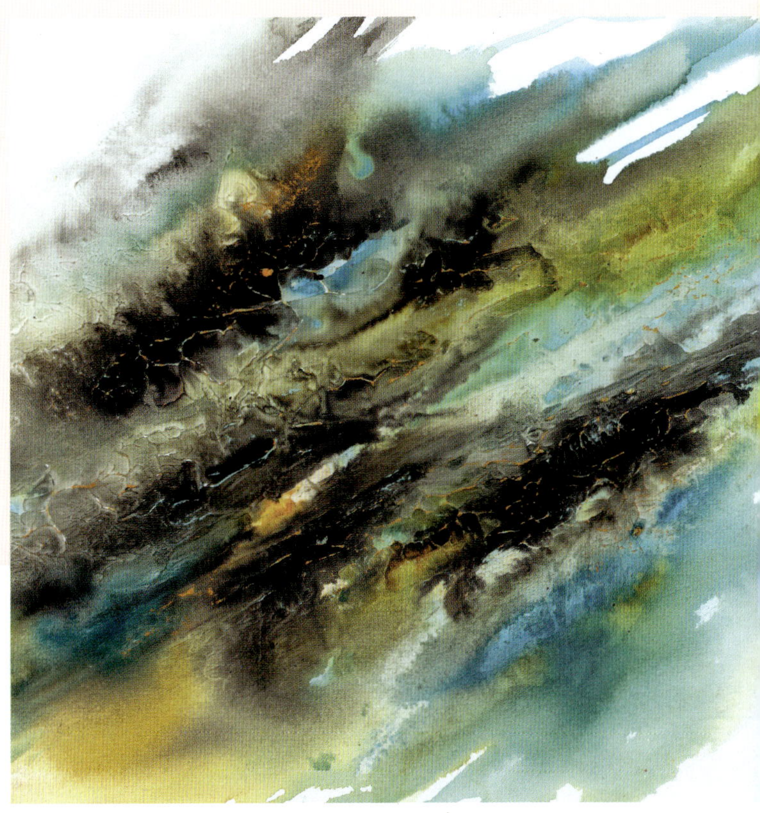

Bark in modelling paste

240 × 300mm (9½ × 11¾in)

At the same time that the piece of wood used for 'Ancient Trees' was drying out, the bark that surrounded it started to contract and fall away, leaving me with pieces that were begging to be used as texture tools. After smearing thick modelling paste on to paper, I pressed into them with pushed pieces of bark (outer side down), removed them, allowed the paste to dry fully and then dripped acrylic ink into the textures.

RELATING YOUR MATERIALS TO YOUR LANDSCAPE

No matter how much you practise techniques or how advanced your painting theory, one question remains: how do you use your materials in your interpretation of the landscape?

Let's think back to the flow chart on page 13 ('Inspiration, gathering and experimenting'), which might help us to link your materials and your interpretation of the scene together:

- If your intention is to faithfully capture the landscape before you, what colours do you see and are they present in your palette?

- If you are working from a photograph, a memory or someone else's experiences of the scene, how are the colours shown/described and what can you do to interpret them?

- Do you have a favourite colour among your materials that you feel might produce an interesting and alternative way of describing something?

- If you are working from sketches you have made on location and want to expand these into more thoroughly investigated paintings, would a different surface make them work better/be more interesting?

- Do you have a story to tell, as I did with my 'Ancient Trees' on page 35? If so, can you think of another way of presenting it or is there a surface such as a map (see pages 106–107) that might help you to share the connection?

- If you decide to paint on a surface that you haven't experienced before, do you need to do some tests, or explore how others have done something similar? What materials do you have that might work on it?

- Did you collect something from your scene that would help you to describe the texture of your subject? Or maybe there is a utensil in your kitchen that makes an exciting mark on the paper?

As you can see, we don't have to forage too far for potential solutions to more exciting and creative ways of expressing ourselves. If you are a more experienced painter and have found yourself a little stuck for new ways to express yourself, asking your materials for help has certainly always been a solution for me.

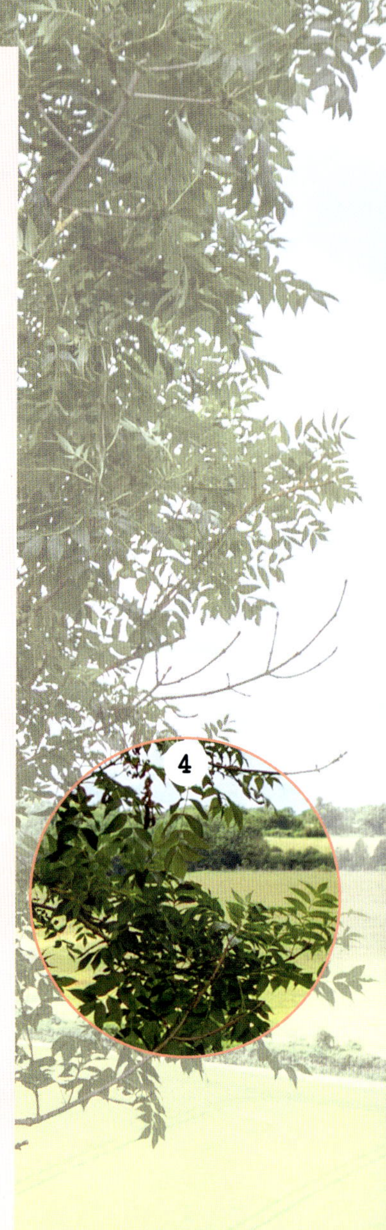

HOW MIGHT I TACKLE
THIS LANDSCAPE?

1 How many different greens do I need for this scene, both for the larger expanses of colour and within the busier areas, or do I feel like pushing the boundaries and including something more unusual?

2 If I want to show subtle changes in colour, do I think watercolour is best or should I use a medium that has greater blending potential such as pastel? If I use watercolour, would a 'double' sky be most appropriate here? (See page 132.)

3 How can I describe these textures? The tractor trails in this field offer an opportunity for mark making. Can they best be described with a brush or a stick dragged through paint?

4 If I gathered some fallen leaves from this tree, would they make an interesting texture when printed with paint on the paper?

5 Would using tissue paper and a crayon for a rubbing help me to understand the texture of this trunk? Perhaps I could use collage to include the rubbing in my painting (see pages 108–109).

CONCLUSION

So far, we have talked about ways that you might get started with the potential that your materials have to help you express yourself. Painting and drawing do, of course, have a set of traditional ways of making these elements come together, in the same way that music has scales, notes and octaves to give us structure. I call these 'painting fundamentals' and I outline those that I think will be helpful in the next chapter.

Painting fundamentals

No matter your skill level, it is important to regularly set aside
time not only to discover what your materials can do for you but also
to underpin your knowledge with theory so that each time you meet
a new challenge, you have the confidence to navigate through it.

This doesn't mean that these fundamental principles have to
be rigidly adhered to – artists have been breaking the rules
for centuries (see page 24) – but they sometimes provide us
with a way of assessing what hasn't quite worked in a piece.
It is also worth repeating that painting – and in fact creativity
– is not a straight, linear path. It has facets, curveballs,
accidents, serendipity and emotion tied up in it, all of which
means that you will constantly be trying to assess what is
happening in the quest for a finished painting.

This chapter sets out some of the more widely known
fundamentals, but you may also find chapter 6, 'Problem
solving', helpful if you are feeling stuck (see page 112).

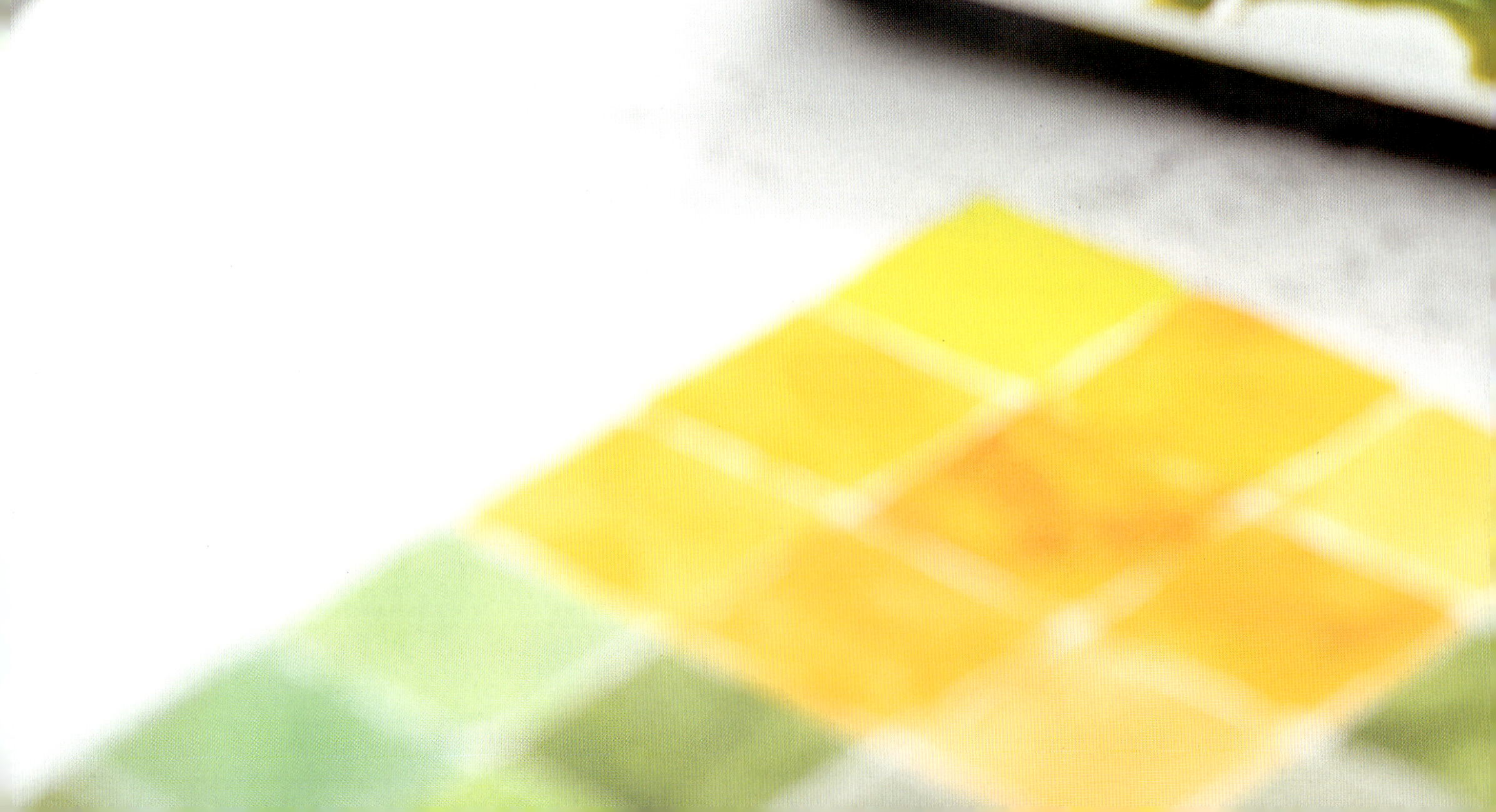

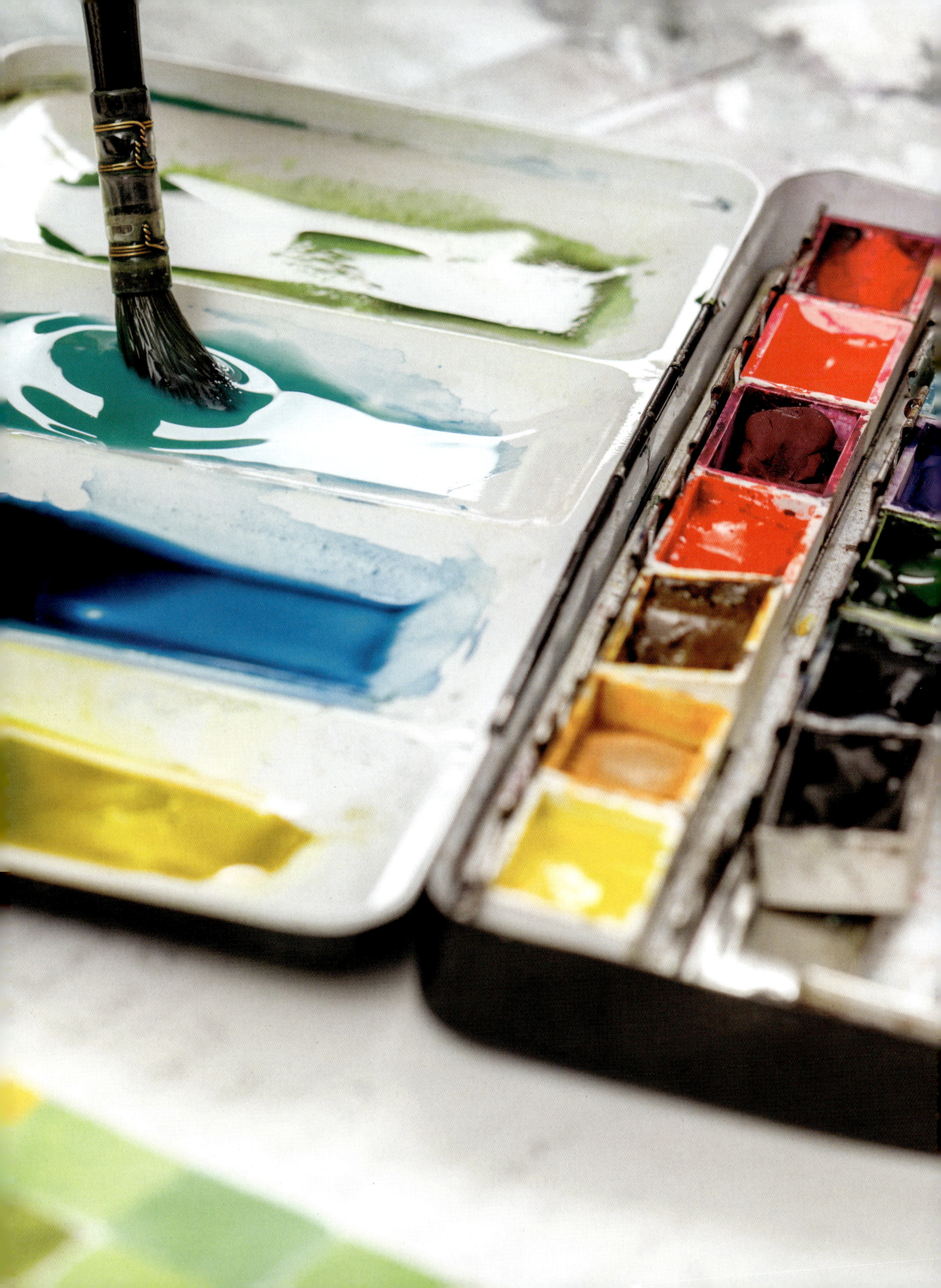

COLOUR THEORY

Whenever I teach fundamentals, I tend to start with colour theory as it is one of the first places you can learn to break all the rules and still come out with vibrant and atmospheric colour mixes!

General colour theory tells us that there are three primary colours: red, yellow and blue, which – when mixed one with another – make secondary combinations of green, orange and violet. The supposition is that you can mix everything you could possibly need from a very small number of colours.

This theory doesn't quite work for me, as it doesn't consider the clarity of each of those colours, the biases that they might contain (for example, there are greenish yellows, orangish yellows and sometimes even brownish yellows) and the fact that painting is a 'subtractive' process, in that the more you mix, the further you get away from light.

I tend to suggest that it may be more useful to have two reds, two yellows and two blues, giving greater opportunity for success when mixing, but as you will soon see I expand on this selection quite quickly for both convenience and speed – more on this on page 42.

Any artist will give you their opinion on where you should start with this process: deciding whose advice is applicable to you can be a minefield. May I suggest that you choose an artist whose work you admire, and investigate which colours and brands they use to create their paintings? The chances are that if their work appeals to you, their colour choices will too.

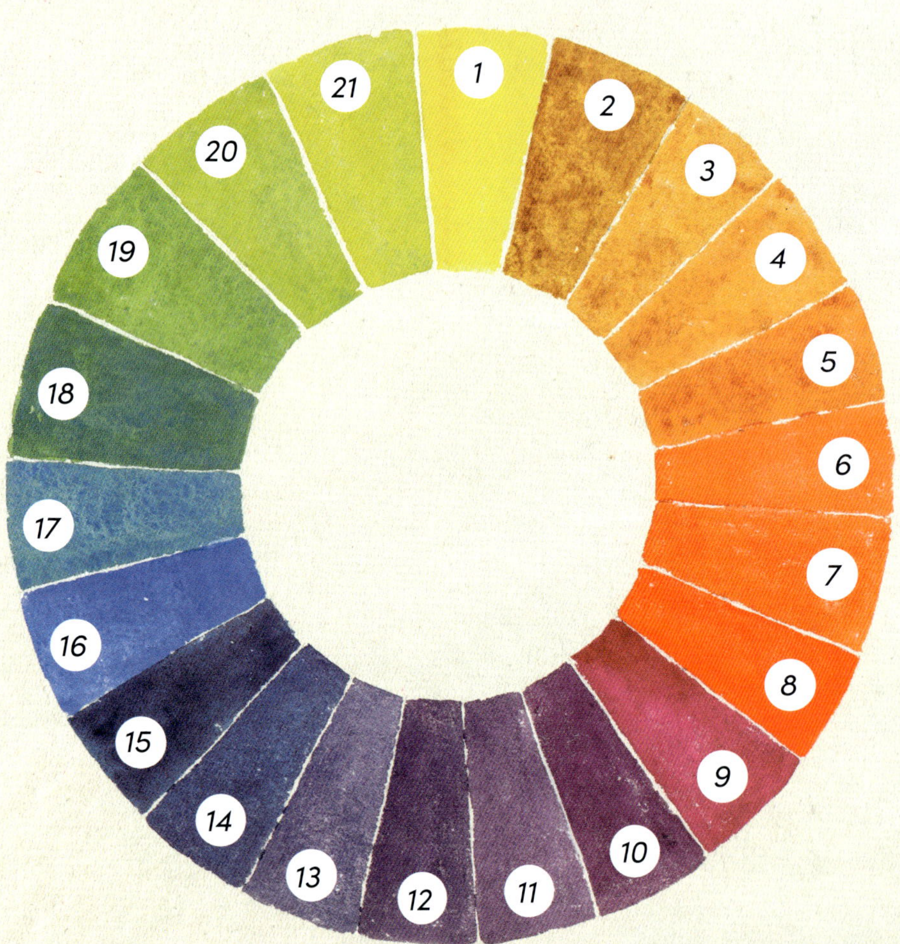

The traditional colour wheel

All of these paints are from my own range: The Alison C. Board Collection.

1 Hansa Yellow
2 Bee's Gold
3 Bee's Gold with a small amount of Scarlet Lake
4 Bee's Gold with slightly more Scarlet Lake
5 Orange made up of equal parts Bee's Gold and Scarlet Lake
6 Scarlet Lake with slightly more Bee's Gold than no. 7
7 Scarlet Lake with a small amount of Bee's Gold
8 Scarlet Lake
9 Quinacridone Magenta
10 Quinacridone Magenta with a small amount of Prussian Blue
11 Quinacridone Magenta with slightly more Prussian Blue
12 Violet made up of equal parts of Quinacridone Magenta and Prussian Blue
13 Prussian Blue with slightly more Quinacridone Magenta than no. 14
14 Prussian Blue with a small amount of Quinacridone Magenta
15 Prussian Blue
16 Cobalt Blue
17 Cobalt Blue with a small amount of Hansa Yellow
18 Cobalt Blue with slightly more Hansa Yellow
19 Green (made up of equal parts Cobalt Blue and Hansa Yellow)
20 Hansa Yellow with slightly more Cobalt Blue
21 Hansa Yellow with a smaller amount of Cobalt Blue than no. 20

MY COLOUR CHOICES

My choice of colours reflects several aspects of painting that are important to me; as such they may well be very different from the colours you choose. My colour choices have evolved from the way my work has developed over the years, helping to communicate my response to how I see a subject and the way I wish to express it on paper.

I work mainly in watercolour, with lots of other media added in for different effects, which means I want my watercolours to be vibrant; have clear, translucent qualities; to create texture. I want them to flow on the surface without much interference – and I want them to be free of animal-based ingredients. That's a big ask for a small tube of paint!

I also prefer to squeeze colour from the tube into an empty pan and allow it to set so that it's all ready for me as soon as I start to paint.

On the right is a selection of my own brand of colours, with their inherent qualities listed below, all of which allow me to tackle landscapes effectively.

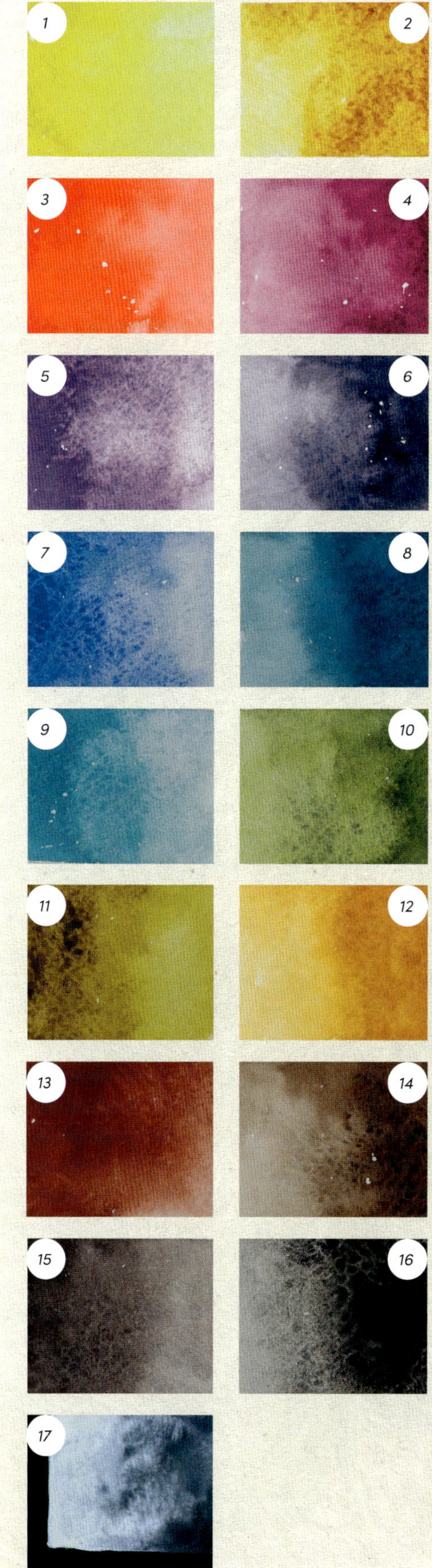

1 Hansa Yellow
A semi-opaque, vibrant yellow that makes bright greens.

2 Bee's Gold
A transparent yellow, versatile for oranges, greens and browns.

3 Scarlet Lake
A vivid, transparent red that makes excellent oranges. Has a luminous quality when used alone.

4 Quinacridone Magenta
A semi-transparent crimson, more stable than its traditional counterparts.

5 Ultramarine Violet
A semi-transparent, granulating colour that makes soft shadows and excellent bluebells.

6 Dusky Violet
A convenient colour that is semi-transparent, granulates and gives excellent tones and shadows.

7 Cobalt Blue
A semi-transparent, granulating colour that is an all-rounder for natural blues, greens and violets.

8 Prussian Blue
A traditional colour that is semi-transparent, giving depth to mixes, particularly greens and greys.

9 Cobalt Turquoise
A semi-transparent, granulating colour that has a greenish tone; perfect for water.

10 Foliage Green
A convenient colour that is semi-transparent, granulates and provides very natural greens for landscapes.

11 Green Gold
A green with a very yellow bias that gives vibrant mixes for fresh greens.

12 Natural Yellow Ochre
An opaque yet clean version of the natural straw colours found in many locations.

13 English Red Oxide
A semi-opaque brown that has a red bias, suitable for warm brown requirements.

14 Burnt Umber
A slightly granulating, opaque, traditional colour that has wide-ranging applications in landscapes.

15 Hematite Genuine
A very unusual granulating colour that is semi-transparent and useful in mixes, particularly greys.

16 Black Iron Oxide
A black that provides transparent and granulating greys and mixes for interesting textures.

17 Titanium White (shown on black watercolour paper)
A very opaque gouache colour, used instead of white watercolours to block out or create highlights.

LANDSCAPE COLOUR THEORY

Following on from thinking generally about colour theory, I want to share a few ideas about how to choose colours that might be more applicable to your personal interpretation of the landscape. It moves us on from the more traditional wheel on page 40 and shows how my individual colour choices work for me.

- In the landscapes I like to paint, the most prevalent colour is green and it can get very dull – and time consuming- to mix the green I need. A gorgeous array of greens can now be purchased ready-made for you – many of them are fabulous pigments that have been sourced with the artist in mind. You can trust that the manufacturers know what they are doing in the preparation of your paint.

- You don't have to follow the traditional rules of colour theory. It is, after all, your painting to interpret as you wish, so if you want to paint bright pink skies with orange trees then you must do so. As we've already discussed, inspiration and creativity can be very hard to come by, so when you are in the mood, paint in whatever way you wish.

- Very generally speaking, warm colours advance and cool colours recede – but this is all relative. Your distant hills could be painted orange if your foreground is the sharpest of flame reds; equally your foreground could be a soft blue if your far-away trees are a frosty grey. See also page 68: aerial perspective.

- Experimentation is key. Find colours you love; if the thought of including an exciting turquoise is the catalyst for starting a painting, don't let traditional rules hold you back. Those rules can be helpful if you are having an issue with your colour choices, but they are not hard and fast. For example, a turquoise can produce many interesting greens instead of a traditional blue. You will see from my palette on pages 41 and 44 it is a staple in my selection

My landscape colour wheel

This takes the same form as the colour wheel on page 40, and substitutes the traditional colours with those you might find in a landscape. This shows the way that these colours have the potential to relate to each other but on page 44 you will discover an alternative way of exploring colour mixes.

1 *Cobalt Blue*
2 *75% Cobalt Blue with 25% Natural Yellow Ochre*
3 *75% Natural Yellow Ochre with 25% Cobalt Blue*
4 *Natural Yellow Ochre*
5 *75% Natural Yellow Ochre with 25% Foliage Green*
6 *75% Foliage Green with 25% Natural Yellow Ochre*
7 *Foliage Green*
8 *75% Foliage Green with 25% Hematite Genuine*
9 *75% Hematite Genuine with 25% Foliage Green*
10 *Hematite Genuine*
11 *75% Hematite Genuine with 25% Dusky Violet*
12 *75% Dusky Violet with 25% Hematite Genuine*
13 *Dusky Violet*
14 *75% Dusky Violet with 25% Cobalt Blue*
15 *75% Cobalt Blue with 25% Dusky Violet*

Opposite, <u>A Walk through the Woods</u>
280 × 380mm (11 × 15in)
A painting that uses traditional colours in places but then more unusual choices for textural effect. The bright reds and blues spattered on the surface punctuate the more muted shades used in the background.

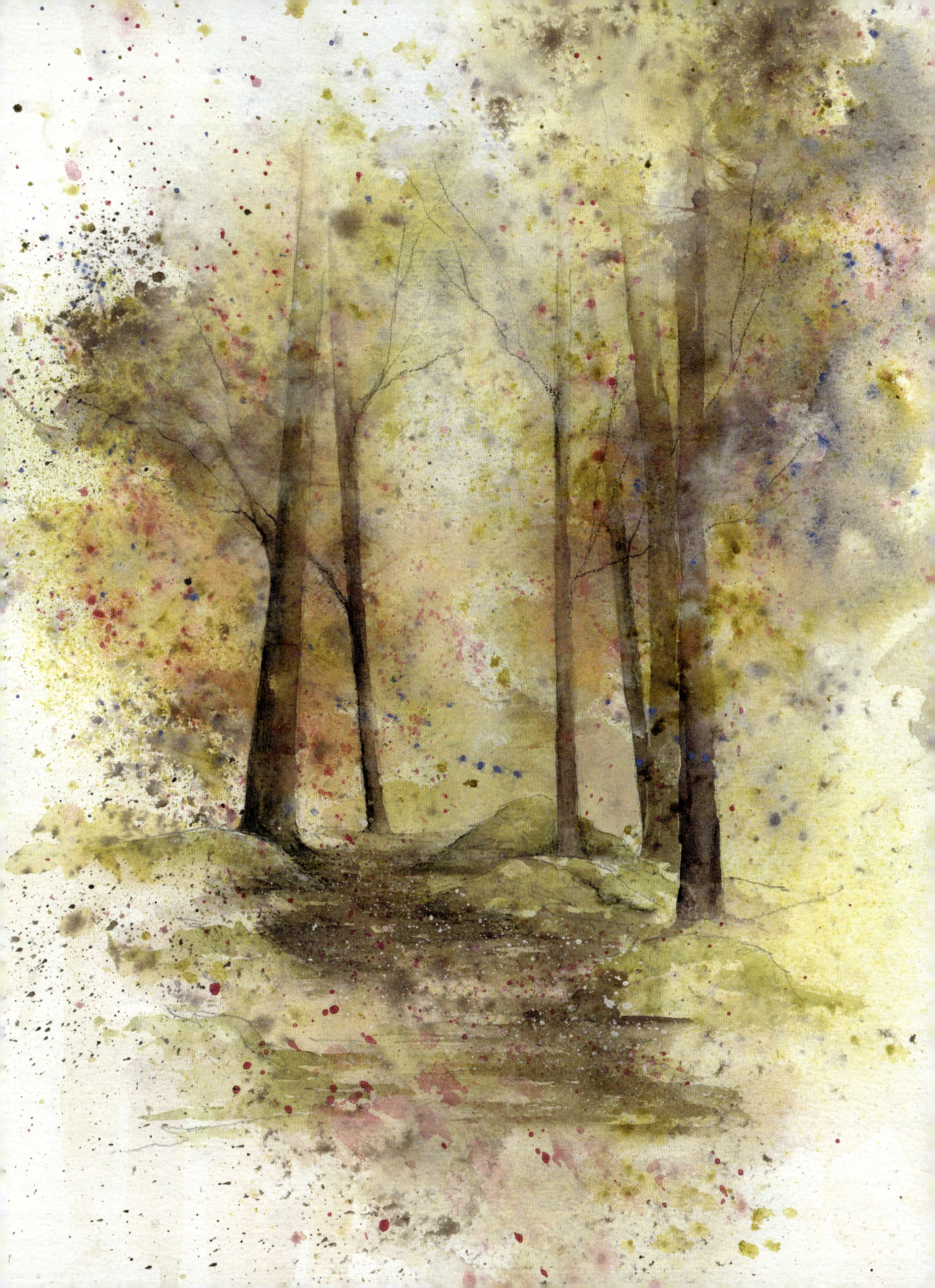

MIXING GREENS

As I mentioned on page 42, I enjoy having ready-made greens in my colour palette – they are convenient, and they do interesting things on the paper – but the skill of being able to mix colours and discover new shades is useful, and helps us to understand colour better. A chart like the one below can take time to produce but is great to have as reference, particularly if you enjoy faithfully replicating the greens you observe in the landscape. Create it on your favourite paper, or better still, on a different paper to see how the surface affects the colour. Keep it safe to consult for future projects.

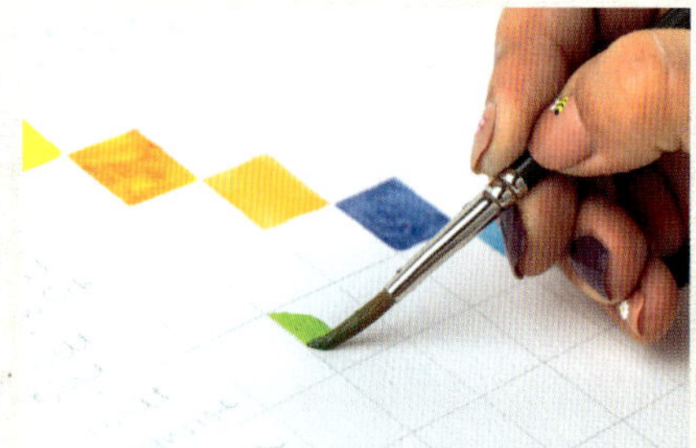

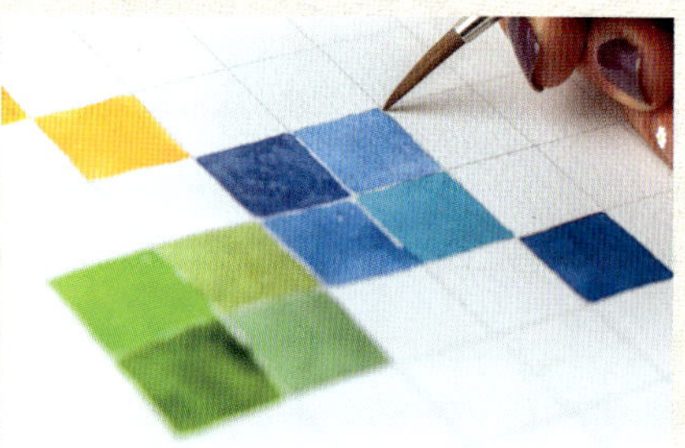

1 Draw a grid that corresponds to the number of colours you wish to include in the chart. I've chosen nine colours for this demonstration, so I have 81 squares in total in a grid of 9 × 9 squares. List your colours both along the top and down the side of the grid, including as much information as you see fit (you may want to include brand names to keep a record). Fill the like-for-like squares (on the diagonal if using the same colour order along both edges) with colour straight from the tube first; here I have thinned them a little with water to make them flow.

2 Then, inside each square where two different colours meet, mix the corresponding colours together in roughly equal proportions. 50:50 doesn't always work in terms of **quantity** as some colours will be more powerful than others, so you may want to consider 50:50 **intensity** instead.

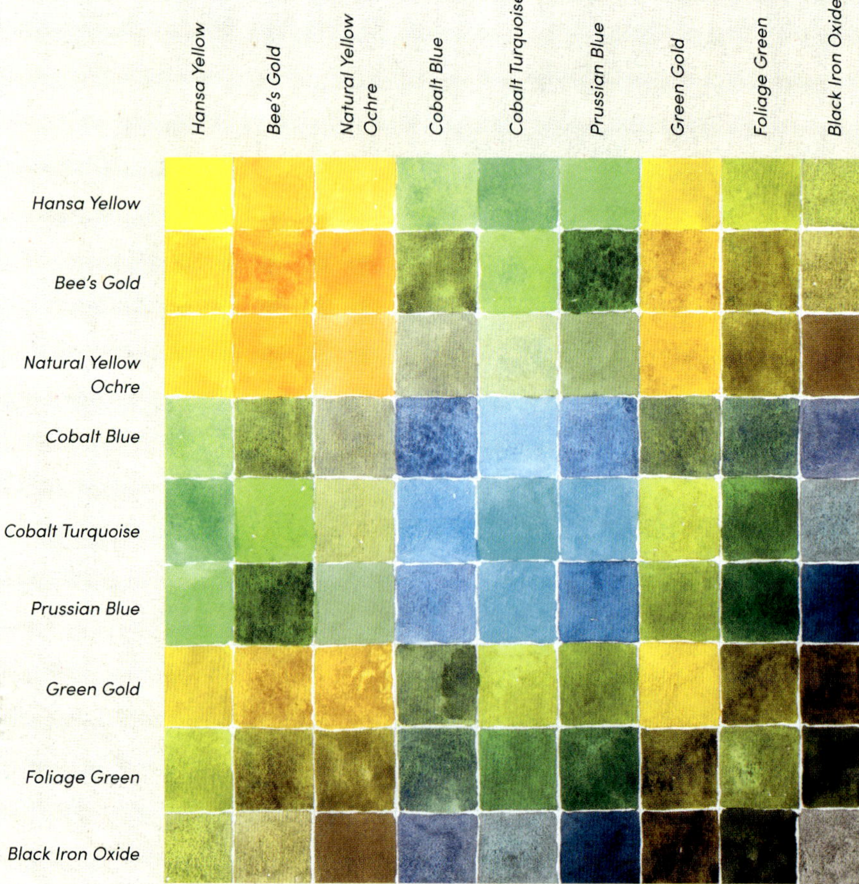

The grid repeats, so you can either leave one half of it blank or, as I have done here, test yourself to see if you can mix the same colour twice.

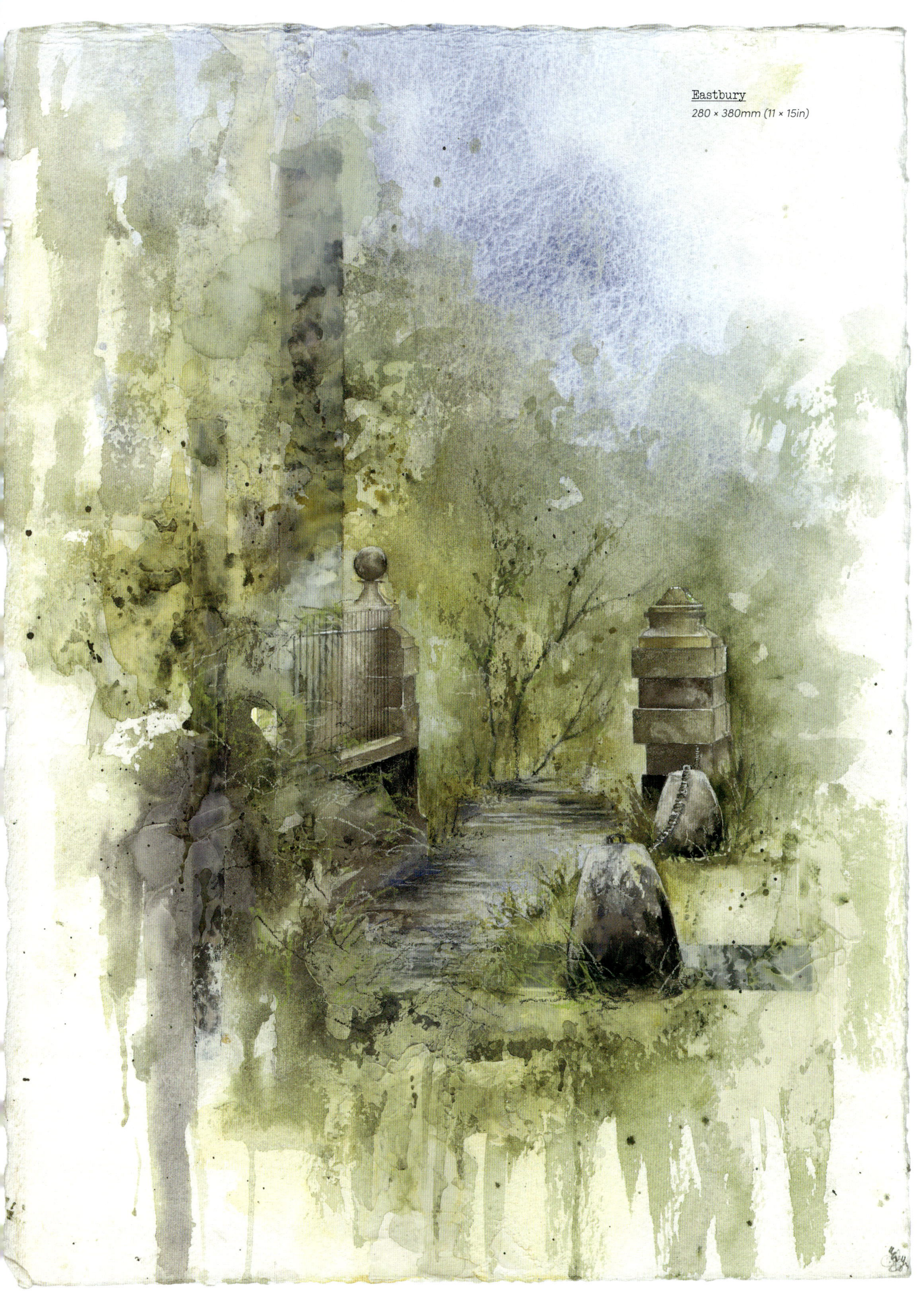

Eastbury
280 × 380mm (11 × 15in)

TRADITIONAL COMPOSITION

Composition – the way in which we put elements together in a painting – is another building block of art and something that seems easy, but with which many painters struggle.

There are several traditional ways of considering and structuring composition, such as the 'Rule of Thirds' and 'The Golden Section', both of which use mathematics to guide us towards pleasing configurations in our creations, helping us to place objects or elements in specific areas on the surface.

The **Rule of Thirds** divides the page both vertically and horizontally, placing points of interest on the intersections of these lines.

The **Golden Section** is a guideline that uses the mathematical ratio of 1:1.618, sometimes also referred to as the Fibonacci Sequence, to arrange elements that naturally guide the viewer's eye towards a focal point or grouping of objects.

To me, a mathematical approach overlooks one important element of composition and that is what is pleasing to the individual. We design our living spaces in particular ways that suit us, even if it isn't a conscious decision. For example, I like odd numbers, and I prefer asymmetry to symmetry – but this might not be the same for you. The Rule of Thirds suggests that we divide our proposed painting into nine equal parts and then place the main subject along one of the lines or at an intersection – but I personally find that too forced a suggestion.

All this presupposes that there is no room to break the rules, and as I am sure you are starting to appreciate, I like to find the cracks in the theory for an alternative route towards my goals.

The Rule of Thirds, applied.

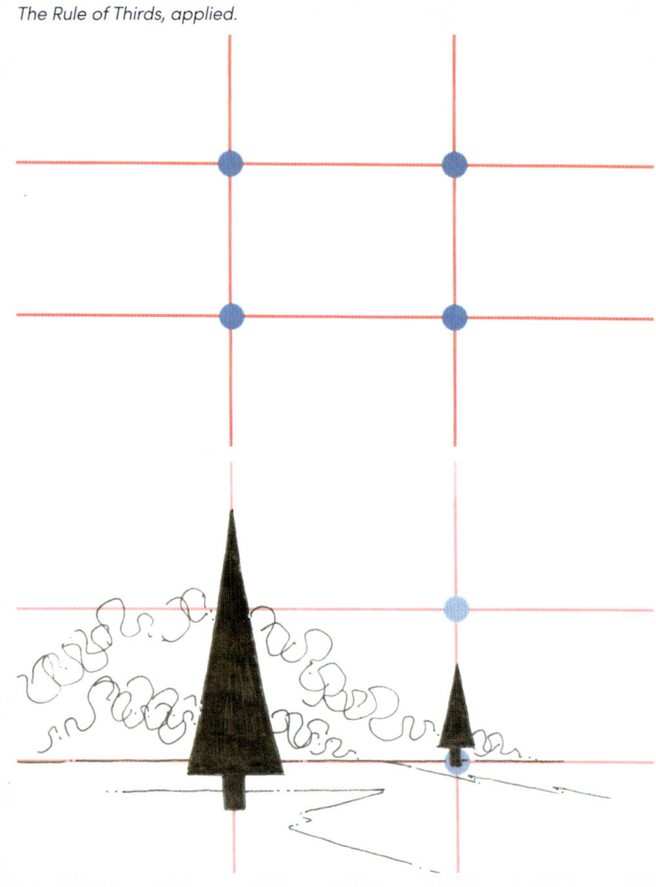

The Golden Section, applied.

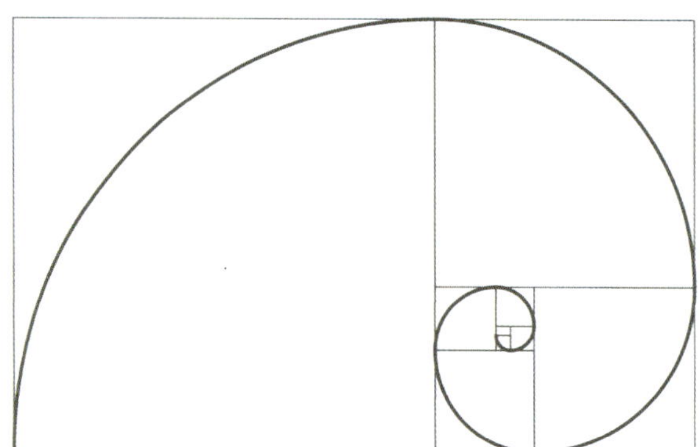

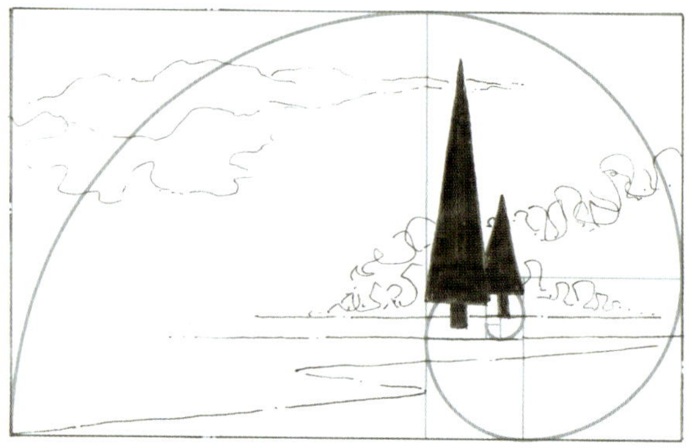

COMPOSITION USING THE ALPHABET

If the mathematical element of composition doesn't work for you, there may be another way of considering composition.

Try using letters of the alphabet to see which ways of presenting the elements of your painting work best for you. Here, I've featured an English-language (Latin) alphabet but you can apply these principles to the individual letters of your own alphabet, depending upon the structure of those characters.

As I favour asymmetry, I gravitate towards letters such as J and L, rather than T and W, but we all have an aesthetic that we prefer, and our paintings will reflect our preferences.

Try some of the examples on the right to see which you lean towards. The way I have presented them here is not exhaustive but it should give you a few compositional ideas to help you get started.

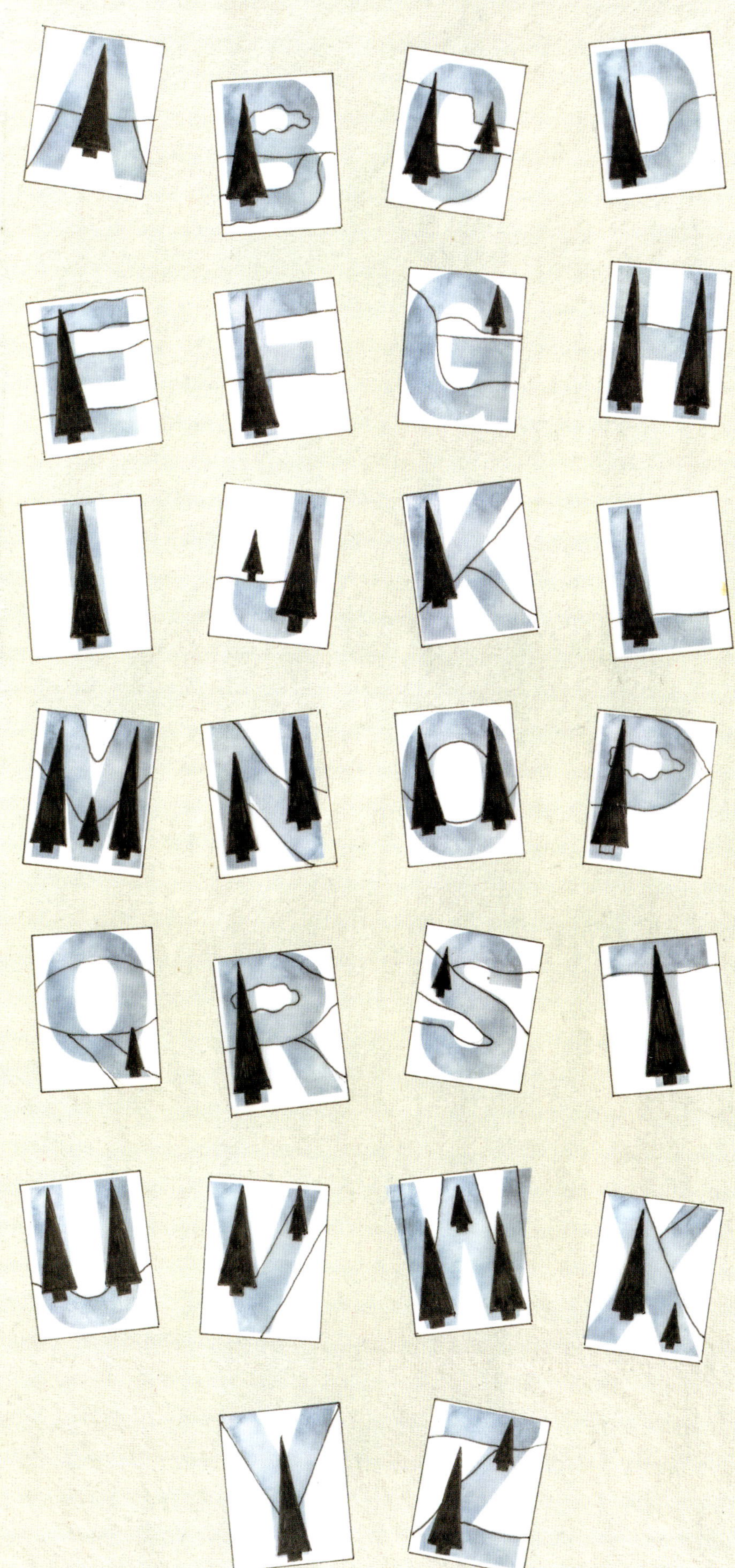

A QUICK WORD ABOUT DARKS

So far in this chapter, I've talked about some of the formal building blocks of painting and how you might relate them to landscapes. At this point, I want to add something that could be considered part of the earlier discussion on colour, but relates to tone and mark making too, and that is how you use darks in your work.

You may be cautious about adding darks to a painting that you are pleased with, as they seem very final, and can often make you hold your breath as you apply them. They are a necessary part of the process, though – the darker the darks, the lighter your lights will look, and that's what gives your subjects form.

While watercolour features heavily in my work, I deviate from traditional methods of leaving lights behind, preferring instead to over-apply my darks, so that I can bring back my highlights with the addition of a pale colour in another medium such as gouache or soft pastel. What I do enjoy about watercolour, though, are many of the delicious darks that can be made with the paints, as they have a luminosity to them that I find lacking in other media.

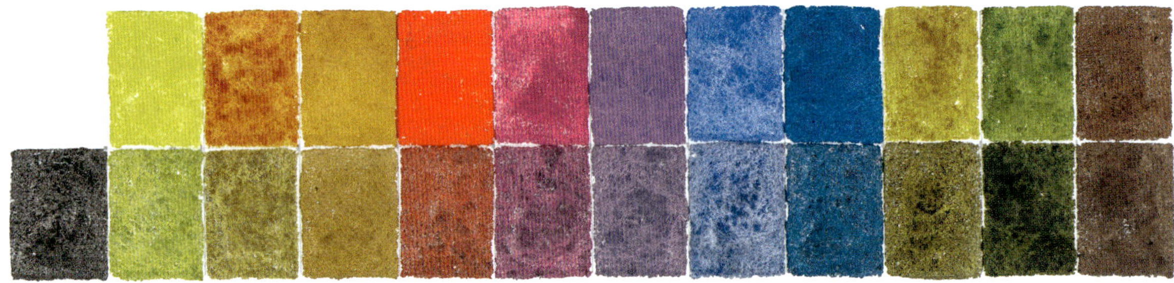

This colour chart of darks, above, was created by the addition of black. Adding black to watercolour is sometimes seen as a 'bad' way to create darks and because traditional painters do have a point, but like many aspects of art, it depends on which black you choose as not all black paints are the same. The top row is comprised of colours straight from the tube (with a little water to make them flow), and the bottom row is that same colour, with a touch of Black iron oxide combined. The colours change from being bright, to having a depth without compromising their luminosity.

Complementary pairs are colours that are opposite each other on the colour wheel and, when combined, they make interesting darks or shadow colours.

This chart, right, has been constructed using complementary pairs. Refer to the colour wheel on page 40, and you will see that I have numbered the colours 1–21; some are 'primary' (red, yellow and blue) and some are 'secondary' (orange, green and violet).

16: Cobalt Blue
5: Orange made up of equal parts Bee's Gold
*   and Scarlet Lake*
1: Hansa Yellow
12: Violet made up of equal parts of
*   Quinacridone Magenta and Prussian Blue*
9: Quinacridone Magenta
19: Green made up of equal parts Cobalt Blue
*   and Hansa Yellow.*

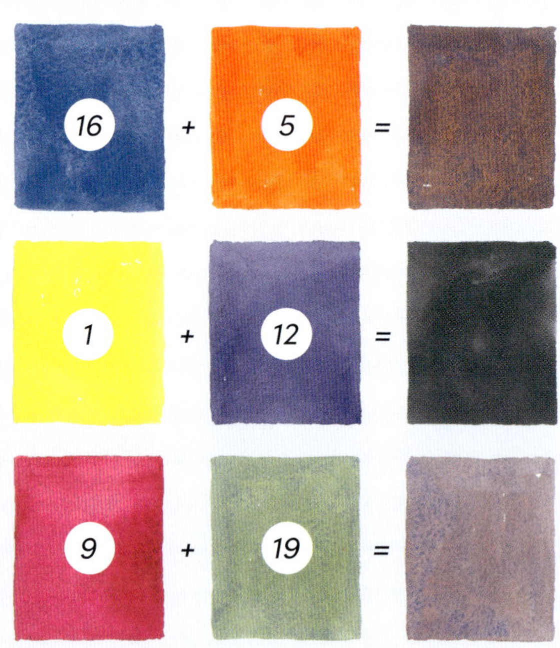

THE IMPORTANCE OF TONE

When we talk about tone, we need to understand exactly what we mean. I use it to describe how dark or light a colour is; tone can also describe a range of techniques including mixing (adding grey to a colour).

Tone is sometimes called 'value' instead, and very much depends on the medium you are using. Watercolour requires more – or less – water to help you achieve a range of tones. Other media, like acrylic, might need white for pale tones and black for darker ones. You will need to do a certain amount of tailoring to your paint to meet your tonal needs.

Whatever medium you are using, tone can be used in landscape painting to suggest distance (see page 68), so understanding it and gaining proficiency in it is extremely useful. Painting a simple landscape featuring just shapes and tones can depict atmosphere in a short time and is a great exercise in watercolour, as it also teaches you how much water is required to make the paint flow and how much you need on your brush for the space you are filling (see pages 50–51).

If we want our landscapes to have mood and character then understanding tone can be one of the first steps to achieving this.

Below, a comparison of how tones are achieved in three different media, either by adding water or white for paler results.

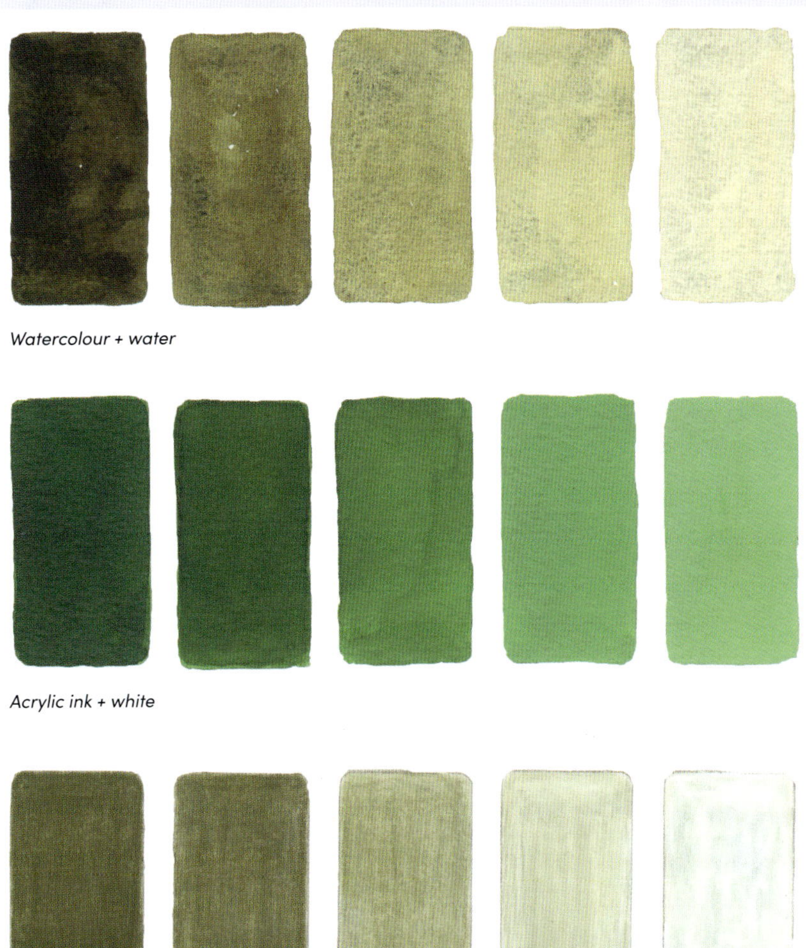

Watercolour + water

Acrylic ink + white

Pastel + white

HOW TONE CAN DEPICT ATMOSPHERE

To show how a simple landscape can be filled with atmosphere if the tonal values are balanced, let's consider this view of Loch Loyne in the Highlands of Scotland.

EXPLODED SECTIONS

1 We must remember that the sky is both far away and overhead, and while that is a challenge, it can be very useful to frame what is going on below. As this photograph is all about the hills, and using them to show how far away the water stretches, the sky is less important in this instance (though that doesn't mean it has to be boring).

2 This hill shows us that while it is a distinct shape, it has soft edges, which can be used to depict something misty and far away. Notice how pale the far hill is in comparison to the sloping hillside in front of it.

3 There is a very strong patch of dark trees in the foreground that will help us to bring this element towards us. At the same time, because it is not right at the front, the dark tone here will help draw viewers deeper into the picture.

4 Too much going on in this area could 'fight' with the dark area of trees; it might steal our focus and be too heavy at the bottom.

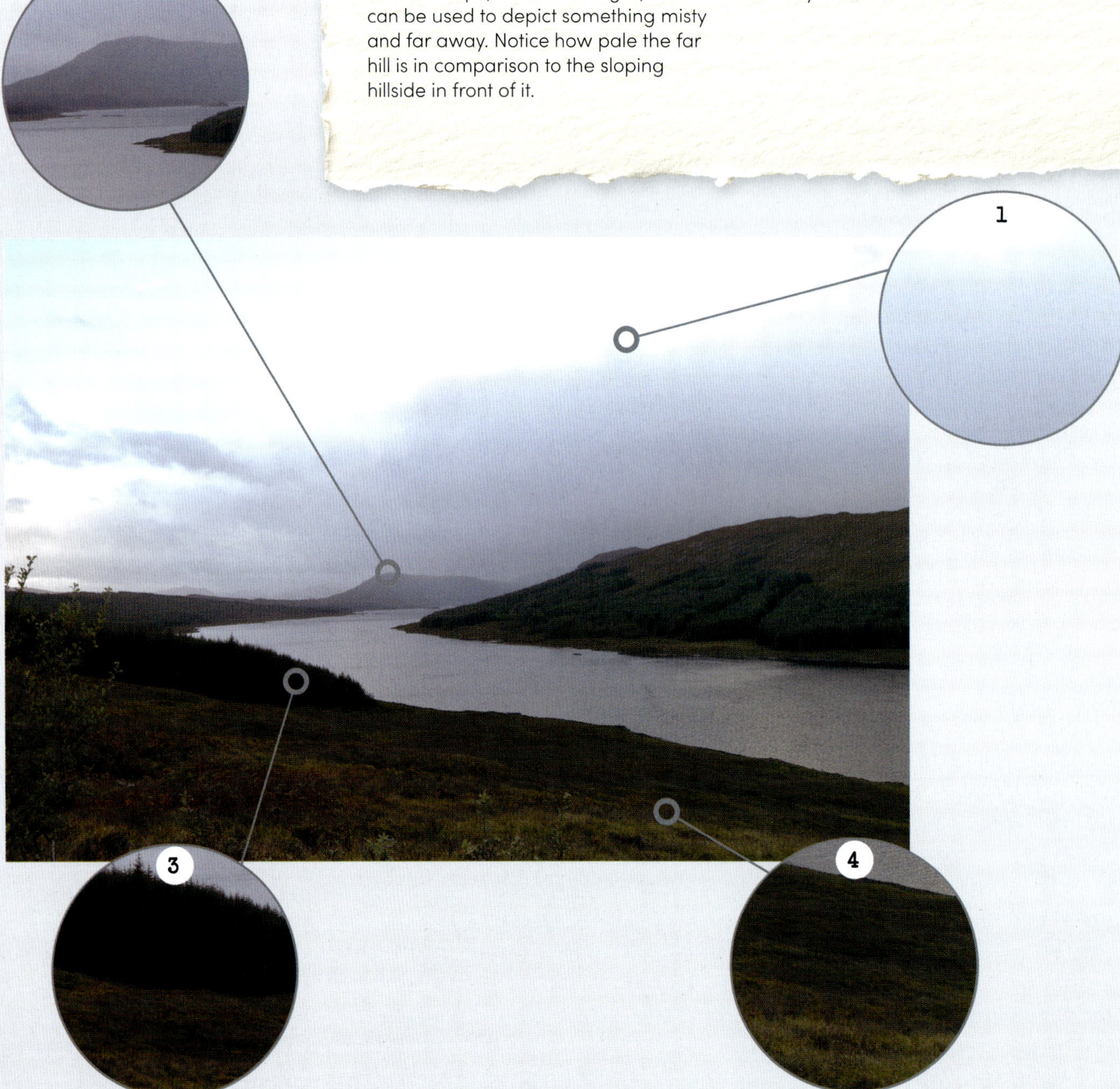

Now that we have isolated the parts that are going to give us the best information, we need to translate them into tones and textures to create an original version of this view.

EXPLODED SECTIONS

1 In order to best demonstrate how tone can be useful to us, I've chosen to create this scene in monochrome, using Dusky Violet watercolour as it has properties that give it a large tonal range. It can be used neat and dark, but, with the addition of water, can be made into softer versions. The chart on the left shows how I have made sure that I have the correct amounts of water mixed in before I start.

2 I've left the sky area soft so that it doesn't steal our attention. As I am using watercolour, this means I have applied it to a damp surface to create shapes that hint at clouds but without hard edges.

3 That misty hill is a slightly stronger tone than the sky so that it shows the shape but without dominating. Watercolour is a perfect medium for describing that disappearing edge, tucking it behind the stronger toned hill in front of it.

4 and **5** As we saw when looking at the photograph, the deep tone and texture of the trees make us lift our gaze, away from the ground closest to us and onwards into the distance. I have also added touches of darker tone to the shores where land meets water, drawing us along the loch to the hills beyond.

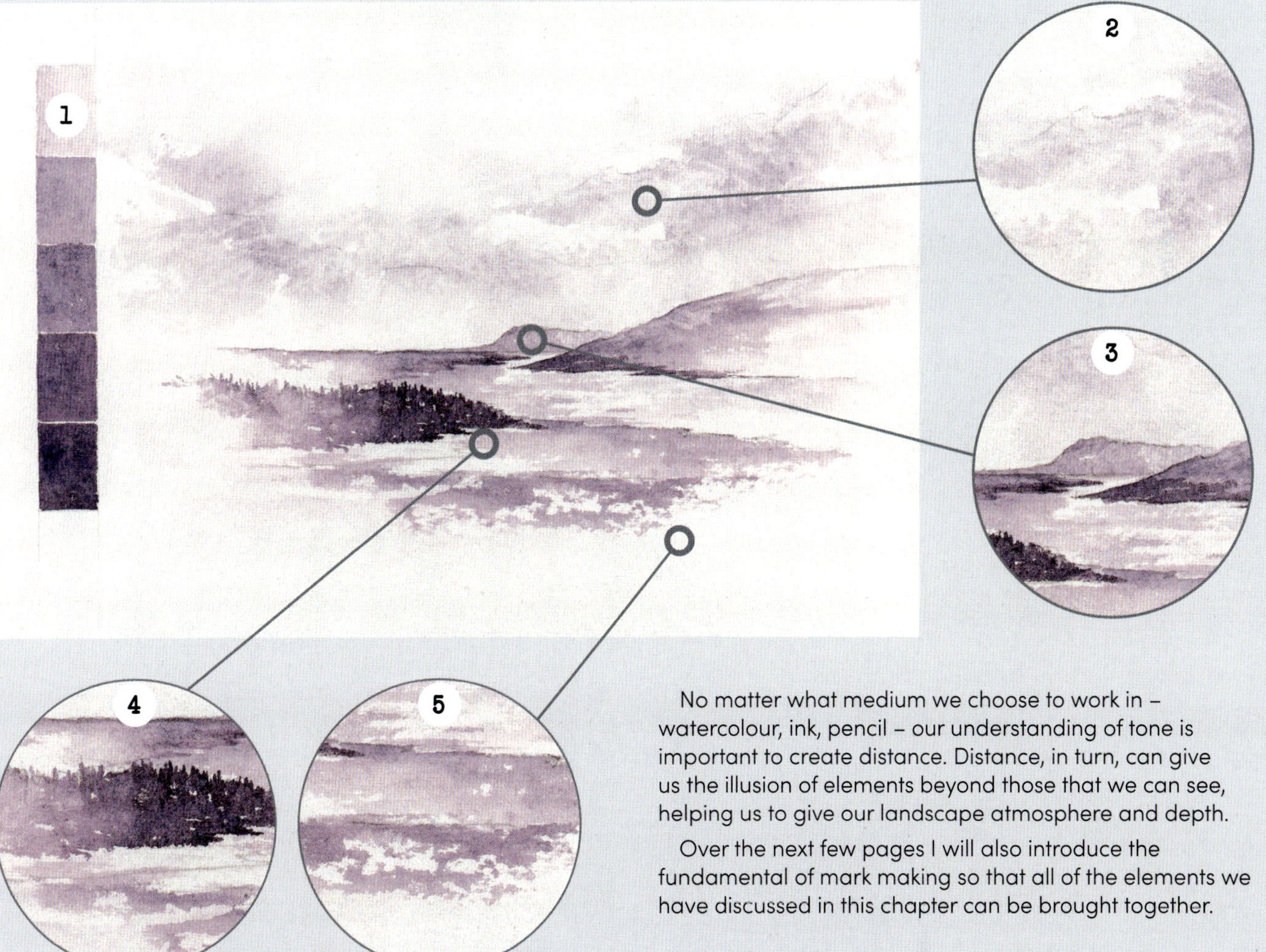

No matter what medium we choose to work in – watercolour, ink, pencil – our understanding of tone is important to create distance. Distance, in turn, can give us the illusion of elements beyond those that we can see, helping us to give our landscape atmosphere and depth.

Over the next few pages I will also introduce the fundamental of mark making so that all of the elements we have discussed in this chapter can be brought together.

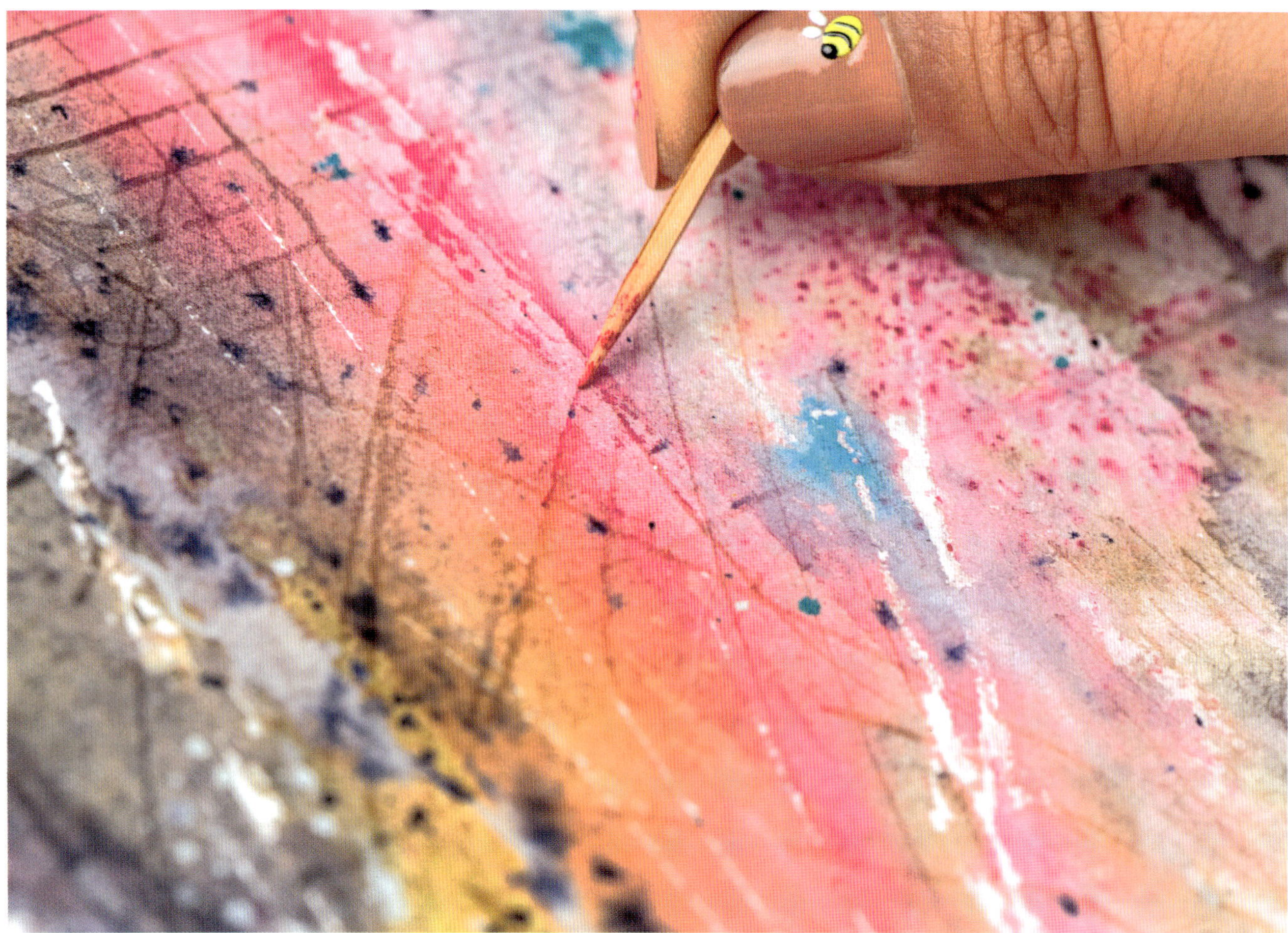

MARK MAKING

Mark making, literally making marks on your surface, helps you to form a visual vocabulary that develops and becomes increasingly important as your skills progress.

Mark making can provide your painting with so many things – it can describe your subject, express your response and create a mood for the piece. The marks don't even have to be realistic or representational – they can be abstract and unusual, neat and controlled, or loose and gestural.

WHY IS MARK MAKING IMPORTANT?

When you start learning to draw and paint, there are so many things to think about that mark making may fall down the list of priorities of elements you are tackling, but it might just become the component that makes your paintings unique to you, like a form of creative handwriting. It makes you able to communicate your thinking visually.

Mark making can seem overwhelming if you are a beginner. It took me a long time to understand its importance, and I'm still learning, myself: I keep finding new techniques or new tools to experiment with. My advice is to try and relax a little, enjoy doodling rather than forcing the technique and allow your brain to wander off while your hand is making interesting marks

A sketchbook page showing how one pen can be used to create a variety of marks and textures.

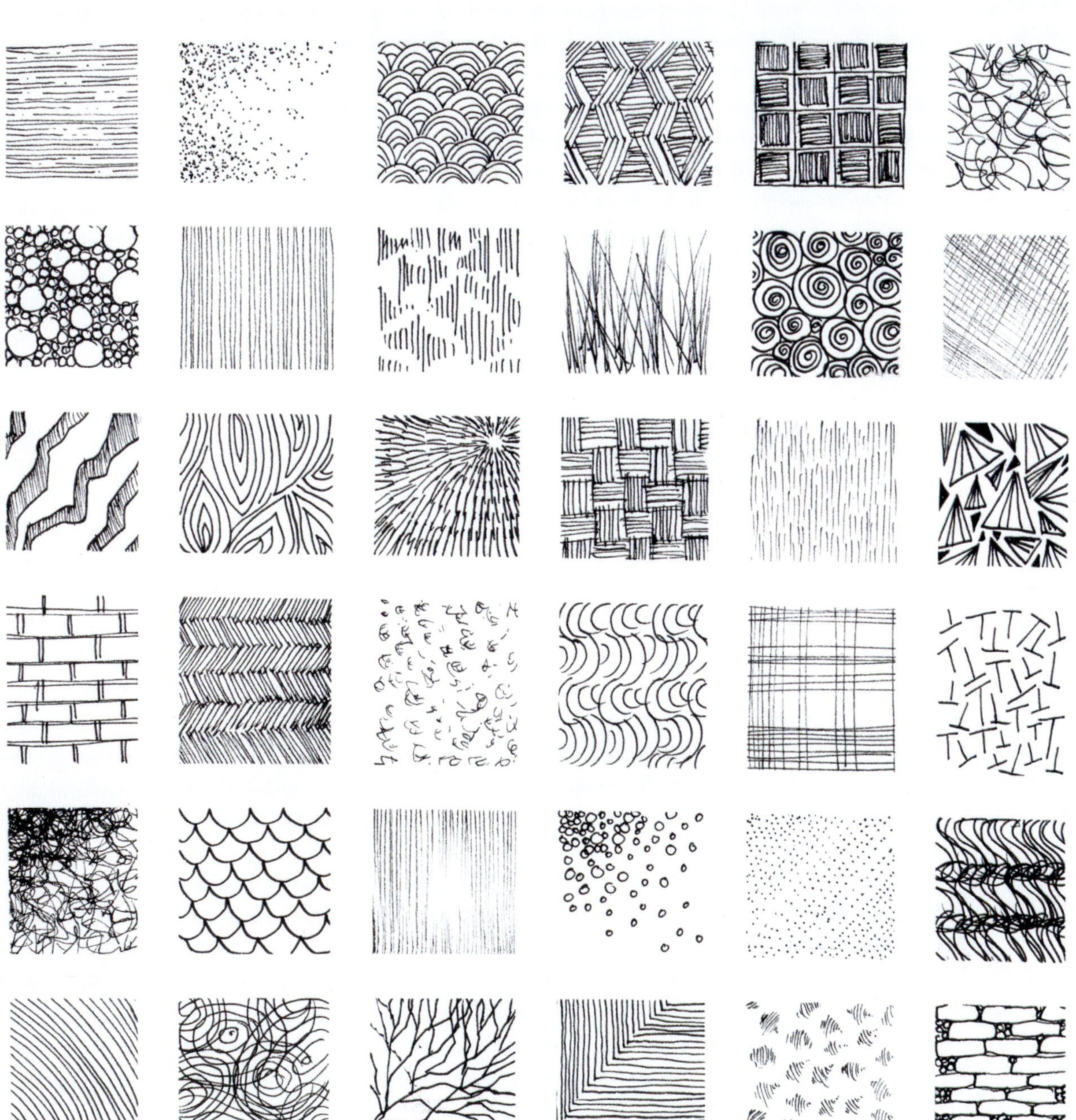

To help you develop your mark-making vocabulary, here are a few of my personal favourite tools and techniques that I use to express different elements in a painting:

TOOLS

1 Sticks/paintbrush handles

You can make grasses, branches and fine lines look more natural if you lessen control over your tools; or use something unusual like a bamboo skewer.

2 Lego and bubble wrap

The regularity of marks made from these items, when used as stamps, can suggest foreground flowers, the texture of a building or a man-made element in your composition.

3 Craft stencils

Use stencils to suggest both positive and negative patterns in large areas that require extra detail. These are usually applied towards the end of a painting.

TECHNIQUES

4 Circles

Add halos to objects to break up repetitious areas of colour using bottle caps dipped in paint.

5 Spatter

Use to suggest texture or movement, or to break up marks that have become too ordered and unnatural (see page 89).

6 Resists

Wax, oil pastel and masking fluid can all be used to repel paint or to preserve white or pale coloured areas; apply the resist to the paper before adding any paint.

In chapter 5, 'Creative thinking', I show how I use some of these tools and techniques to do more than simply paint a landscape, and you can find more information about other materials that I work with. (See page 98.)

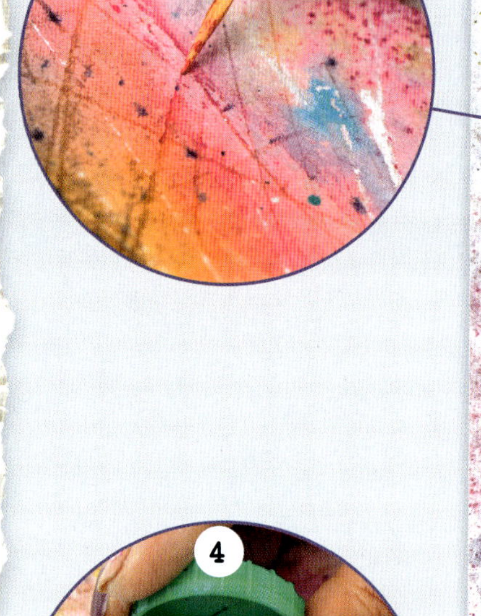

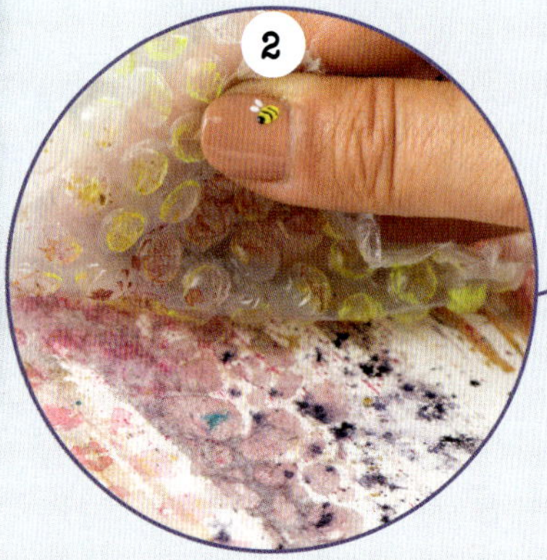

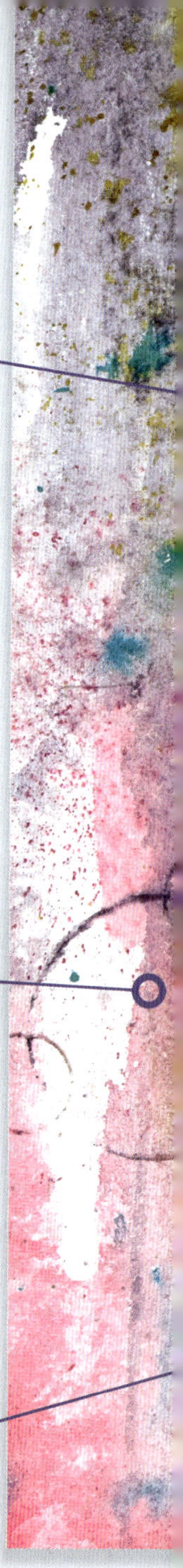

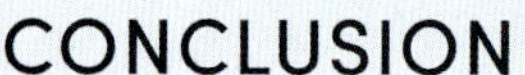

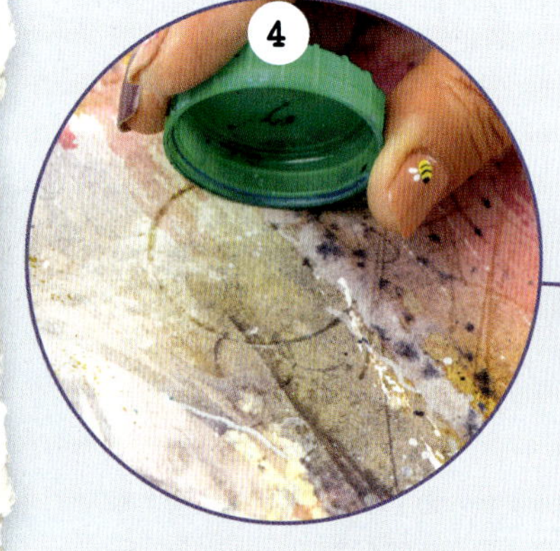

CONCLUSION

Thinking about the materials you choose and linking them to a few fundamentals of painting can really help you to find out what works for you, and give you the confidence to express yourself.

If you are more experienced, experimenting with mark making and particular colour combinations is often the way to unlock your unique style and help you to understand what makes the landscape special to you.

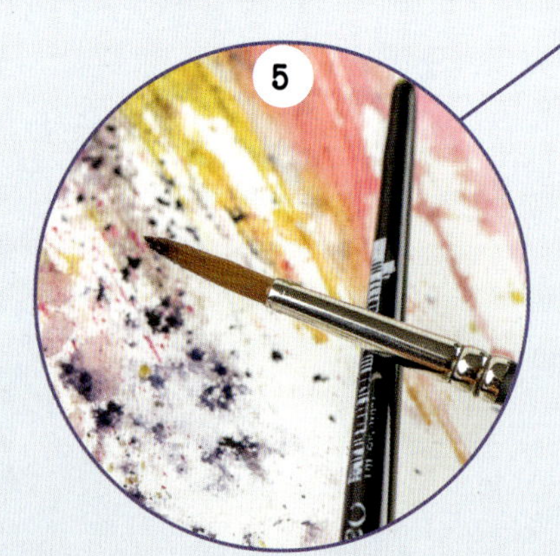

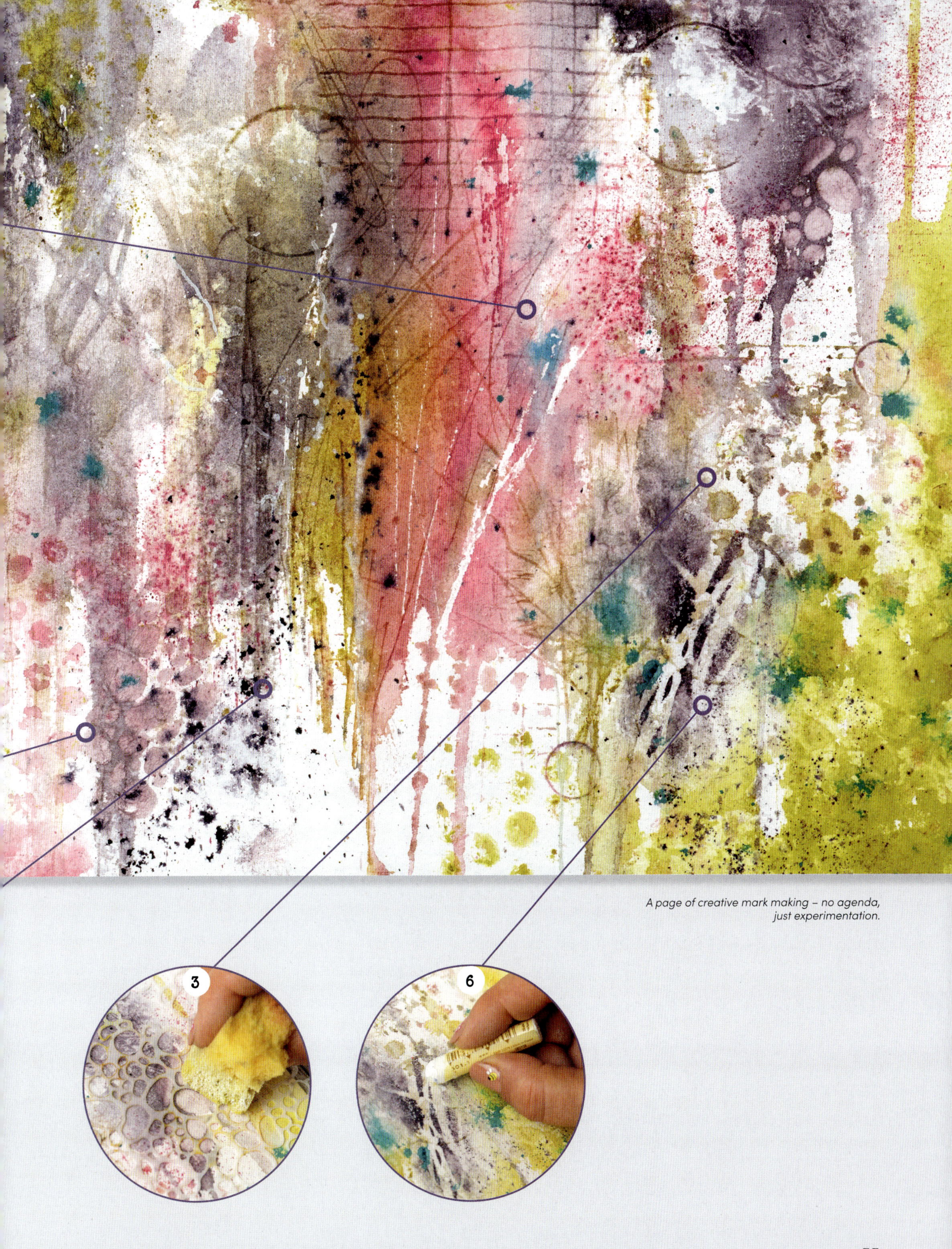

A page of creative mark making – no agenda, just experimentation.

CREATING 'THE BLUE LAGOON'

This painting pulls together some of the fundamentals we have been considering in this chapter and demonstrates how I have made this view unique to me through my choice of colours, marks, and so on.

It isn't always possible, nor desirable, to include every single fundamental, but if a painting isn't doing what you would like it to, then considering the suggestions I have made below and in the rest of this chapter may be a good place to start.

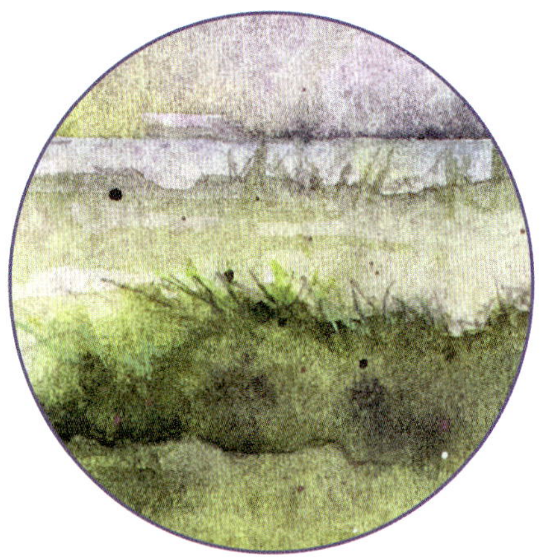

Colour theory (see pages 40–43)

Here, I have included one of my favourite colour combinations – green and violet – in a single landscape. I'm pushing the boundaries of colour temperature here on purpose, making the distant elements as important as those in the foreground, to lead your eye past the rock and beyond.

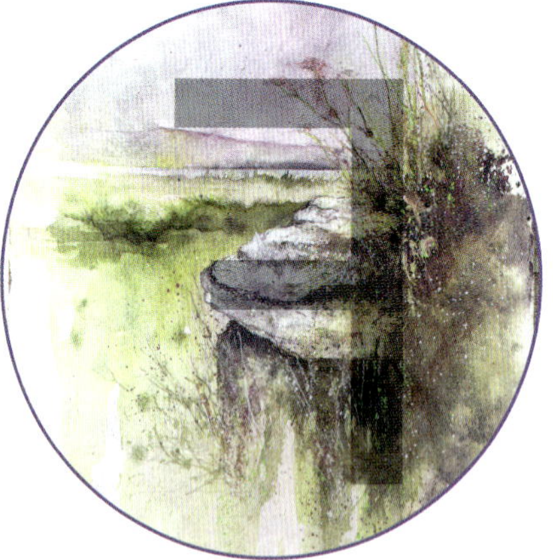

Composition (see pages 46–47)

The composition of this painting is based on a back-to-front letter F so its asymmetry is even more pleasing to my eye.

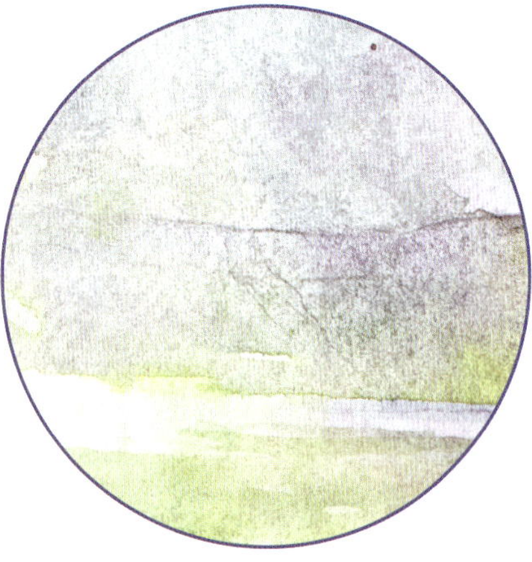

Tone – atmosphere (see pages 50–51)

I've used watercolour to create soft shapes and to make the area where land meets sky 'disappear'.

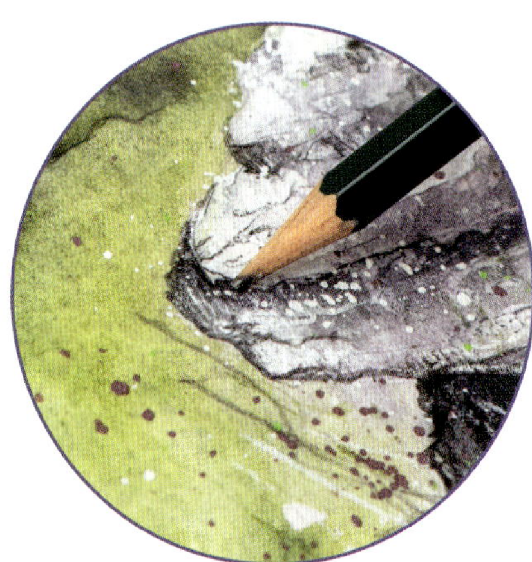

4. Tone – darks (see page 48)

I made sure I had a good selection of darks to bring out the paler areas of all the components, both in the distance and close-up.

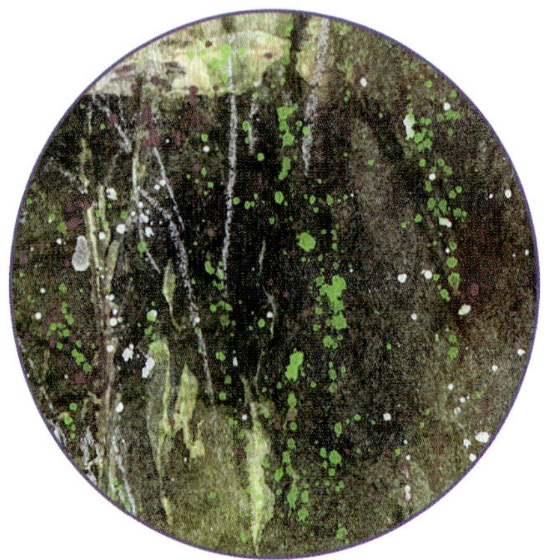

5. Mark making – spatter (see pages 54–55)

Spatter is probably my favourite final flourish to add to a painting. I don't know why – although perhaps it is the action that I enjoy as much as the result.

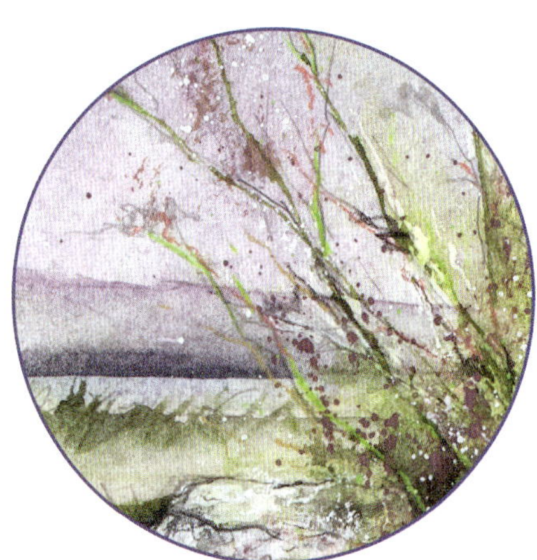

6. Mark making – lines (see pages 54–55)

I used many different tools here to create the random grasses, including sticks, the point of a paintbrush handle and pencils.

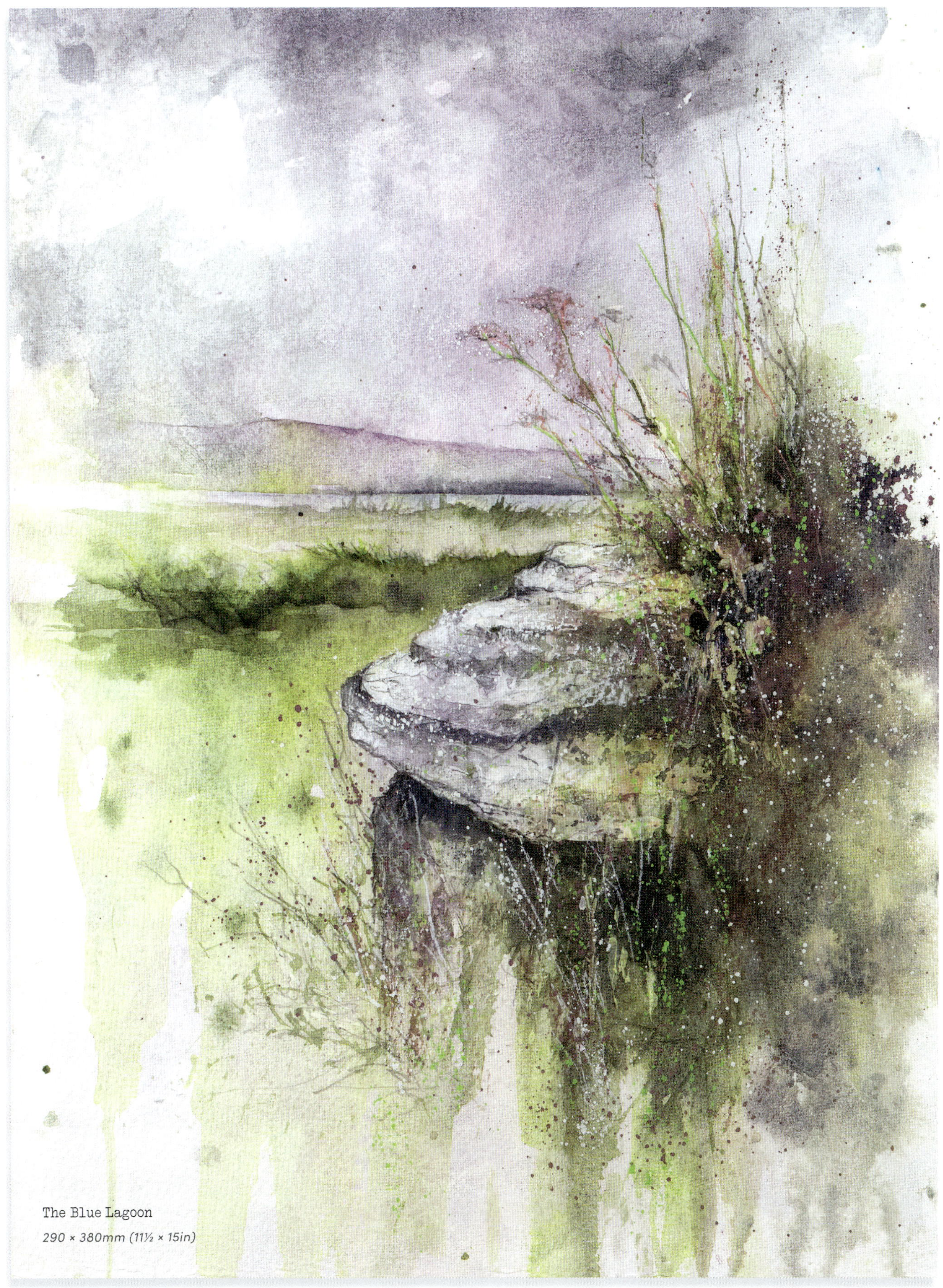

The Blue Lagoon
290 × 380mm (11½ × 15in)

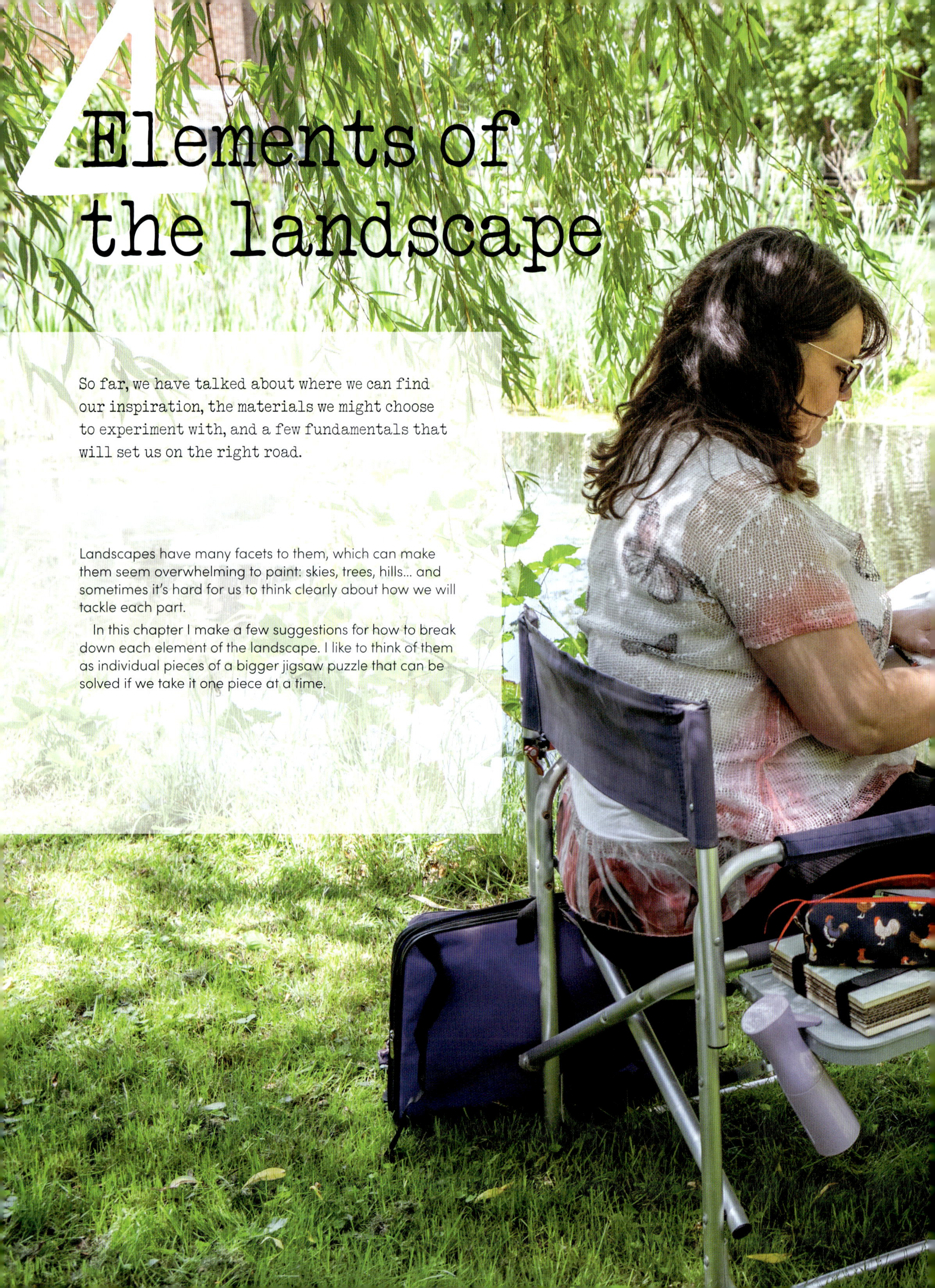

4 Elements of the landscape

So far, we have talked about where we can find our inspiration, the materials we might choose to experiment with, and a few fundamentals that will set us on the right road.

Landscapes have many facets to them, which can make them seem overwhelming to paint: skies, trees, hills... and sometimes it's hard for us to think clearly about how we will tackle each part.

In this chapter I make a few suggestions for how to break down each element of the landscape. I like to think of them as individual pieces of a bigger jigsaw puzzle that can be solved if we take it one piece at a time.

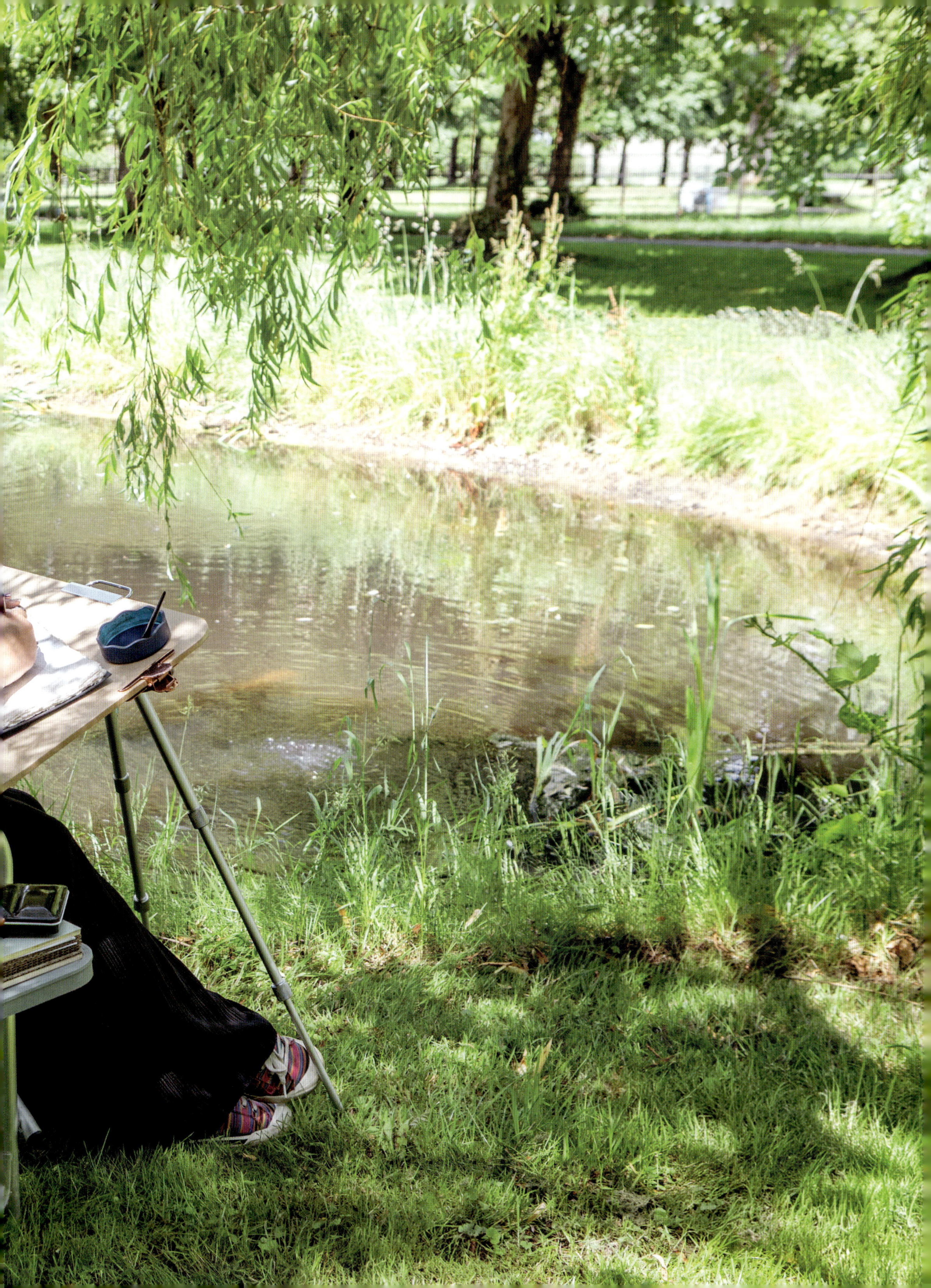

THE JIGSAW-PUZZLE APPROACH

Earlier in this book, I admitted that landscapes did not immediately inspire me – they were simply full of too many elements to consider, when I didn't believe I had the skills to get them all down on paper.

I realized I was thinking about this all the wrong way: I needed to tackle the various elements individually first, and acquire a repertoire of skills that I could draw on when the time came to combine them in one whole project.

Now, I am not saying that you should place landscape elements in isolation from each other when you come to tackle a painting: this will make it look too much like theatre scenery and be too disparate. However, studying their nuances separately will help you to discover techniques and give you confidence so that when dealing with them all together, you feel more able to take them on and enjoy what connects them.

Throughout this chapter you will see examples of photographs I have taken, sketchbook explorations and completed paintings alongside experiments that I feel are relevant to what we are considering. The pages are designed to give you ideas to ponder, starting points for inspiration and more techniques you may wish to explore.

Downend Farm Entrance

530 × 250mm (20⅞ × 9¾in)

You can see that this view had the potential to be overwhelming but by simplifying some of the elements and deciding that the focus was on the foreground rather than the hills beyond, I was able to piece the painting together. (The full painting can be seen on pages 2–3.)

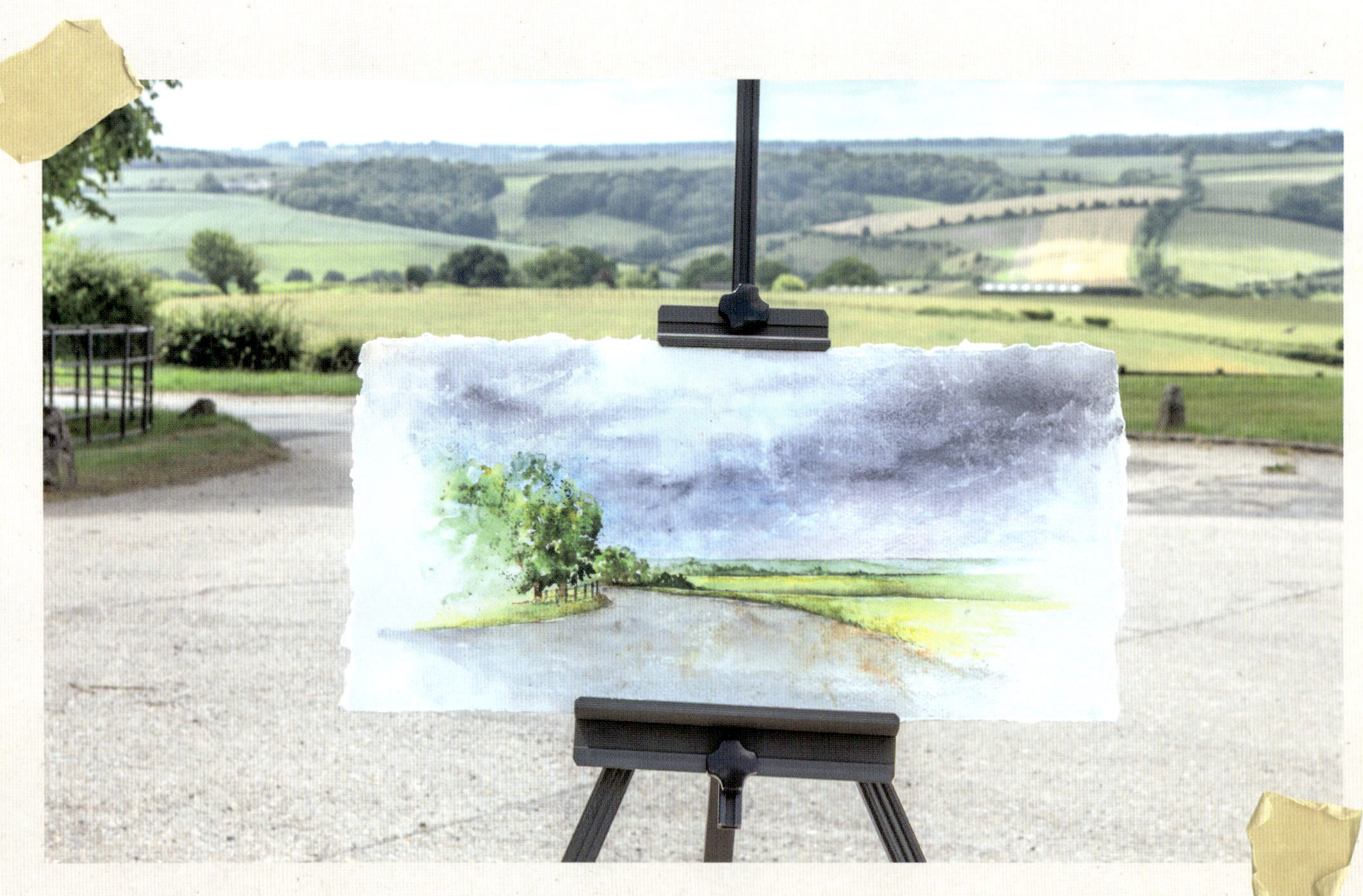

Basic sky

Where better to begin our look at individual landscape elements than with a sky? Skies offer the opportunity to explore techniques, mood, weather and atmosphere so you can make them as simple or as complex as you wish.

Skies take a little time to become confident with when you first start your landscape painting adventures. Don't be afraid to experiment and you will soon discover that you are observing the sky wherever you go.

1 If you like to use watercolour to capture the movement and elements of a sky, try laying down single or multiple colours onto damp paper.

2 Allow the colour to sit on the surface of the paper for a few seconds. This will help the pigment to settle and give you more opportunity to manipulate it – don't leave it for too long though; just long enough to take a big, deep breath is probably enough!

3 Scrunch up a sheet of kitchen paper and gently roll it into the colour to lift out cloud shapes. I call this technique 'rag rolling'.

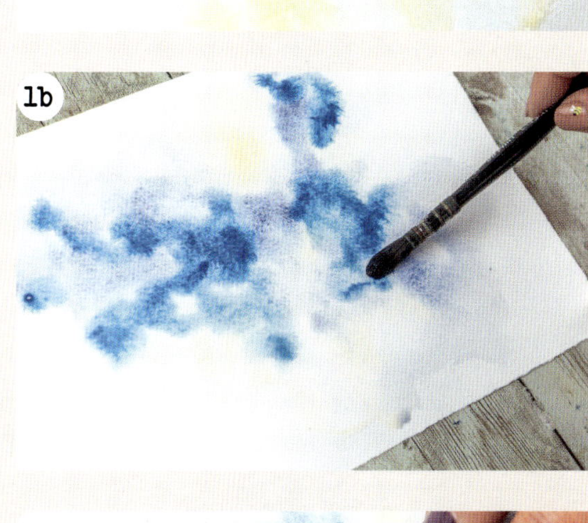

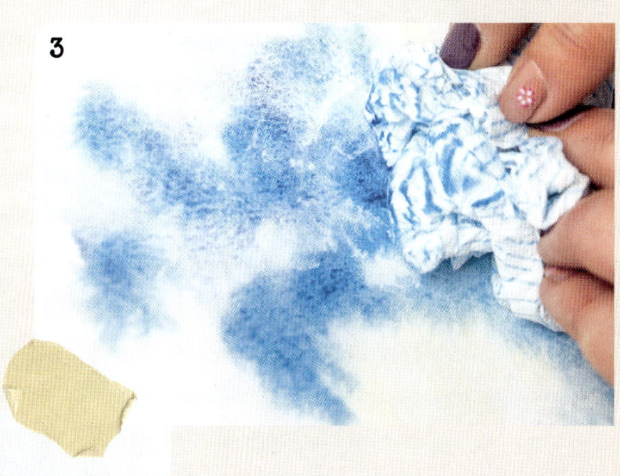

Sketchbook cloud study: a simple sky with rag-rolled clouds.

Experiment with colours to show varying seasons or times of the day.

Cloudy sky

There are so many cloud shapes to observe and experiment with. Artists have spent lifetimes watching the way that the sky alters throughout the day.

Clouds can be wispy and almost imperceptible, or heavily textured; you may wish to document specific types or keep them more general. The addition of clouds can set the mood and provide us with a wonderful textural element.

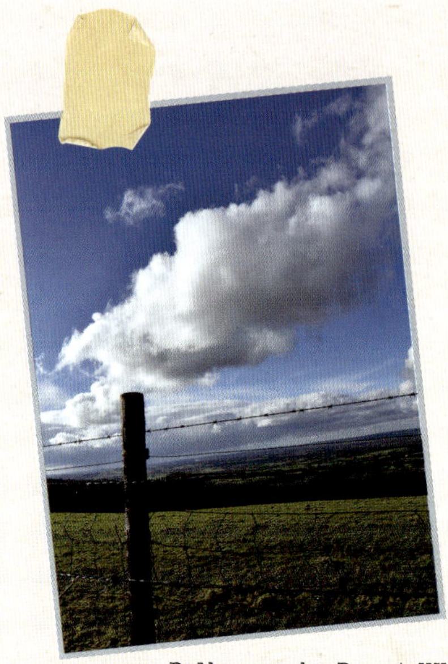

Bulbarrow sky, Dorset, UK
When photographing skies, get some elevation so you can see across a distance.

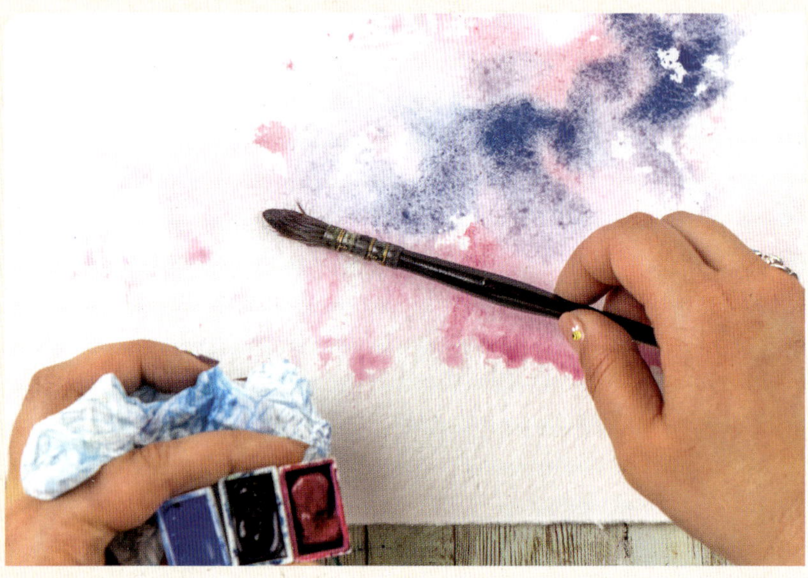

1 Combine layers of colour for interesting mixes. Mix on the paper rather than in your palette, allowing your paint to find its own way across the surface.

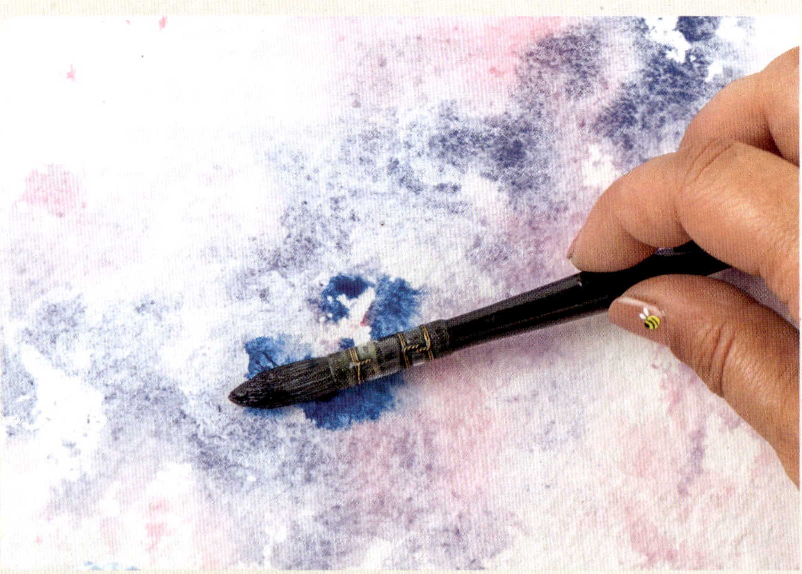

2 Hold your brush at different angles to create a variety of marks; for example, put your hand over the top of the handle to allow all the bristles to touch the paper.

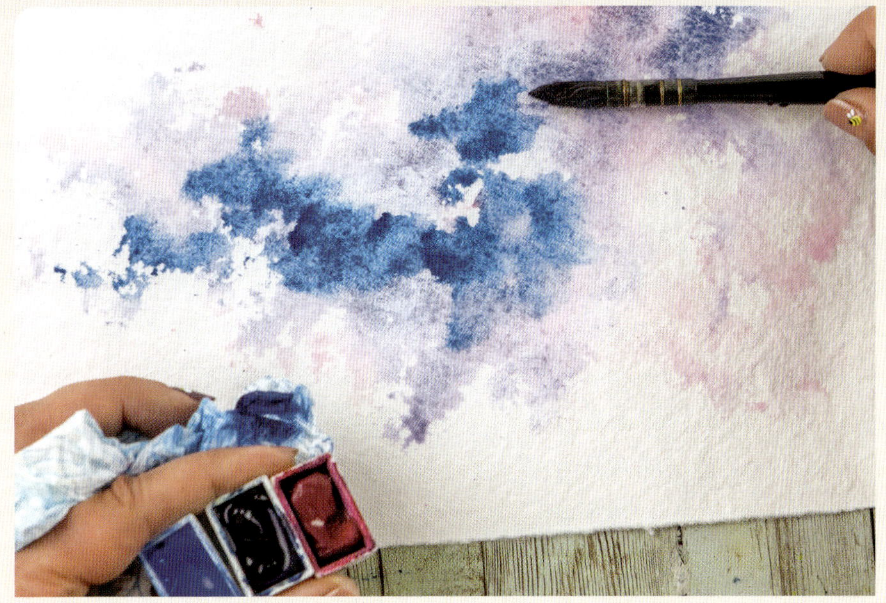

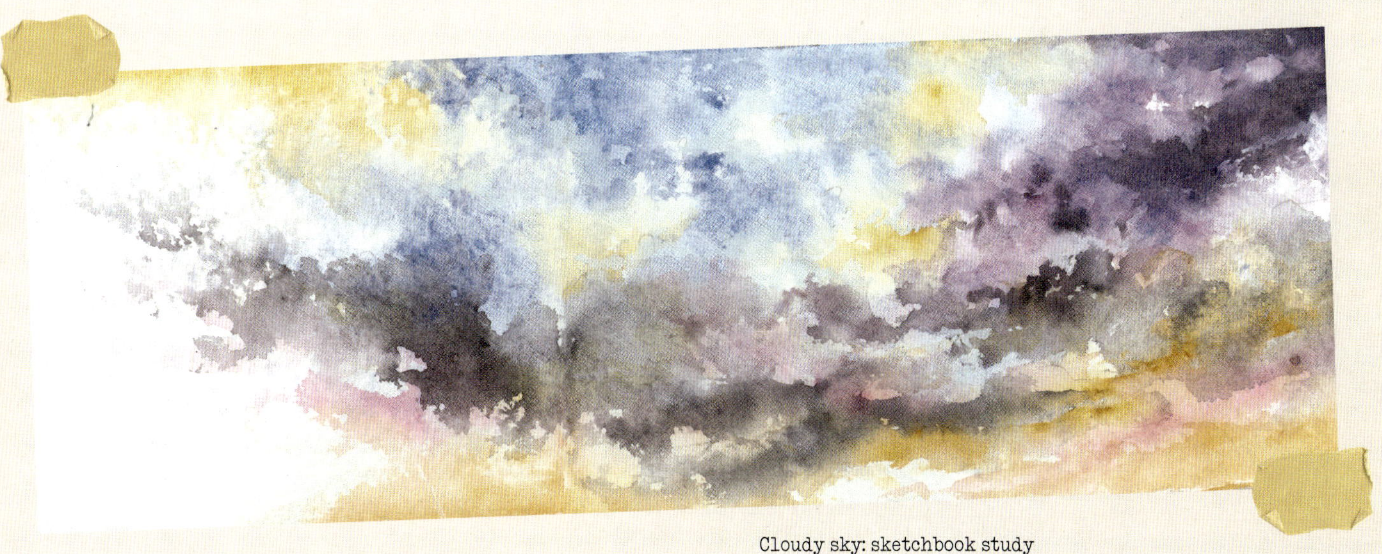

Cloudy sky: sketchbook study
An experiment with layers of texture and strong colour.

Sunrise, sunset

It's hard to not be seduced by the opportunity to depict that extra drama at the start and end of the day. It's also fun to experiment with a different medium to diversify how you commit your interpretation to paper.

Here I have started with a coloured surface, notably one that will allow me to layer up lots of chalk pastel so that I can smudge and blend. It's wonderful to use chalk pastel as it has the never-ending property of being able to be edited and changed. Pastels can be a great medium to learn with.

Dorset sunset
Understanding how clouds can be lit from behind.

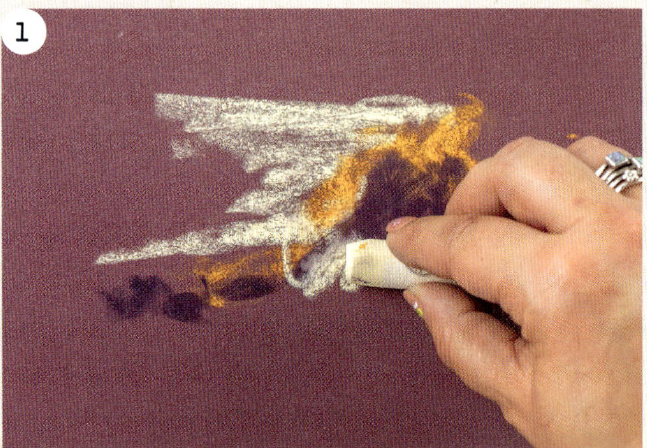

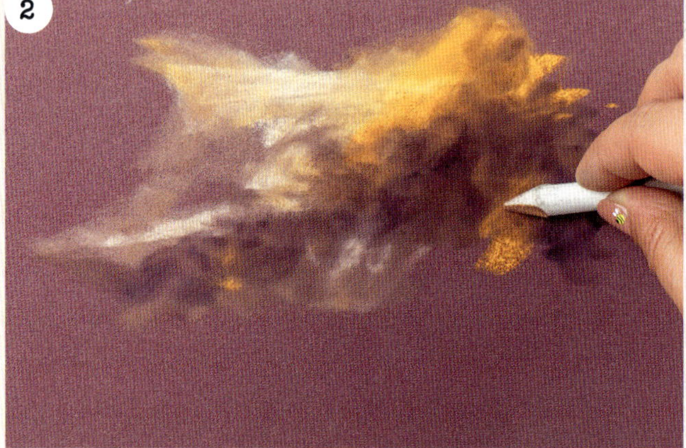

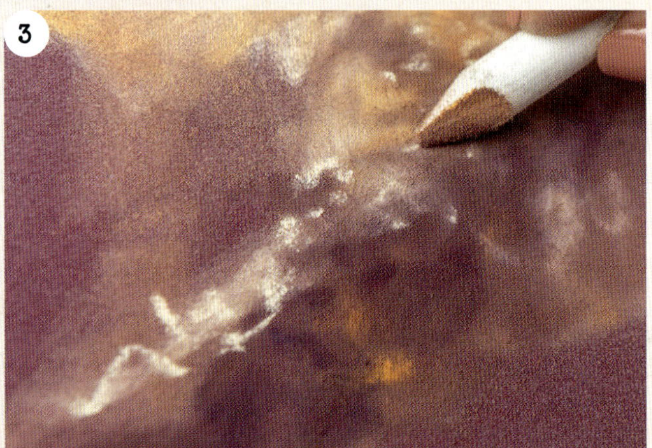

1 Try using dramatic, contrasting colours for your sky and then adding lights for variation in tone – for example, here I have used violet and orange.

2 Blending will help you to attain soft and hard edges – see pages 92 and 139.

3 Don't be afraid to add small, scribbled details to the edges of clouds to show where they have broken away.

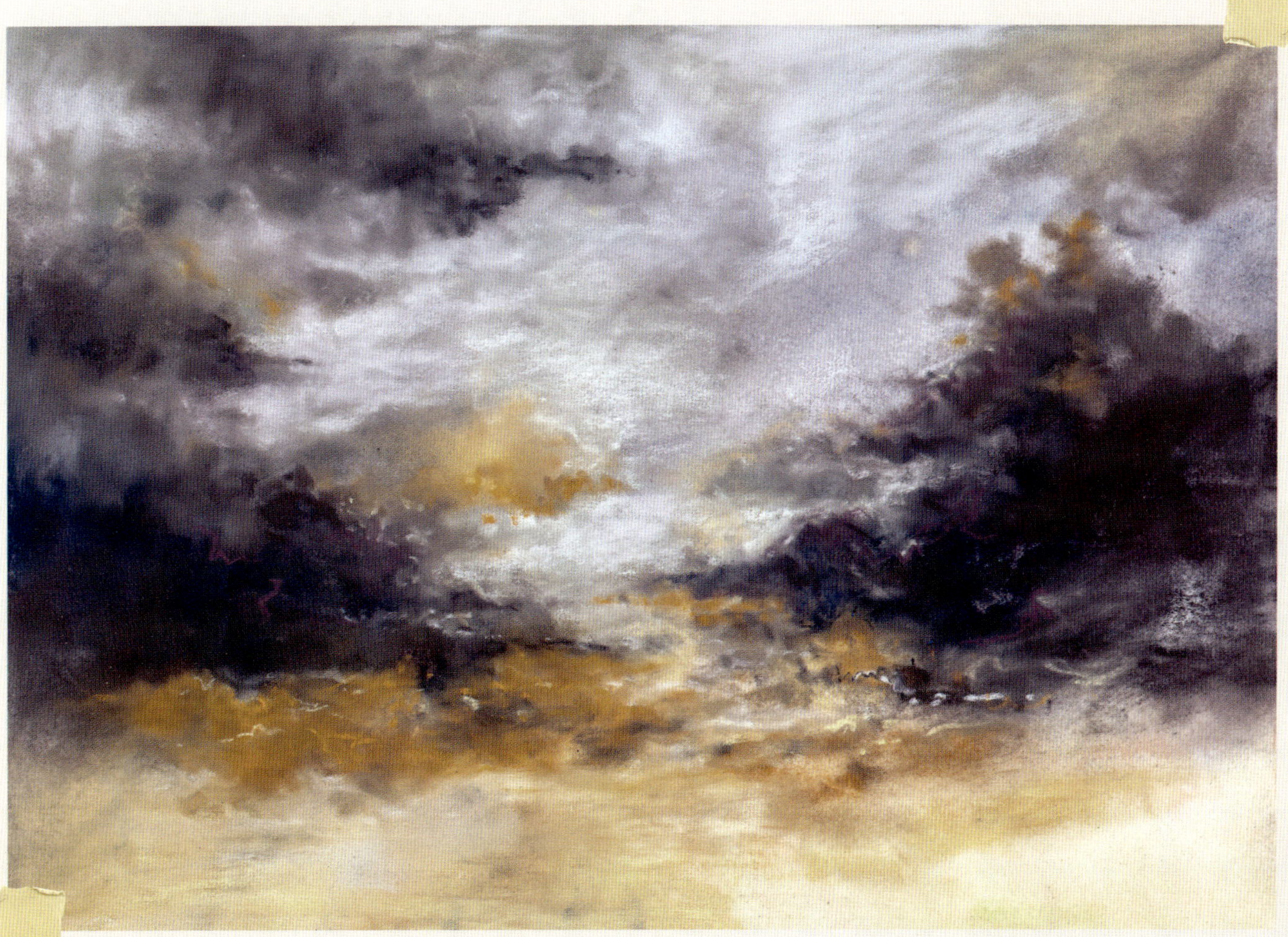

Pastel sunset: sketchbook experiment

In this experiment you can see that I've played with colour, using violet and orange to give drama and by using a dark tone to show off the lighter areas. The texture has been created with variations in the marks, whether I need them to show large areas or small details.

Hills and mountains

A hill or mountain can be a wonderful backdrop to establish distance in a scene, but it can equally be a main feature. As well as experimenting with different ways in which to paint hills and mountains, you may like to consider how to use them to describe the geography and weather conditions of your landscape.

Don't be afraid to combine media – sometimes unlikely combinations create textures that describe your subject perfectly.

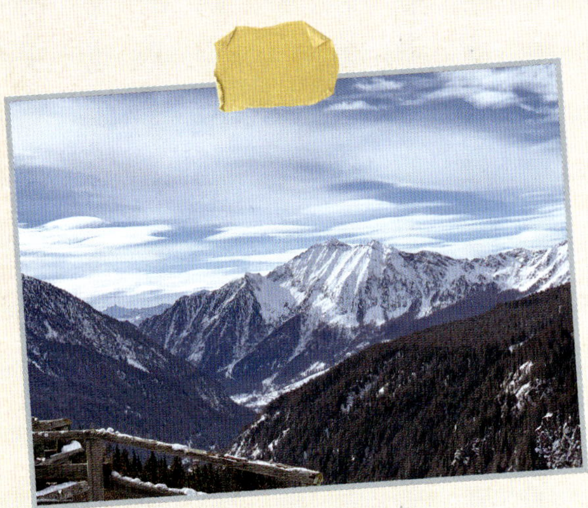

Gressoney, Italy

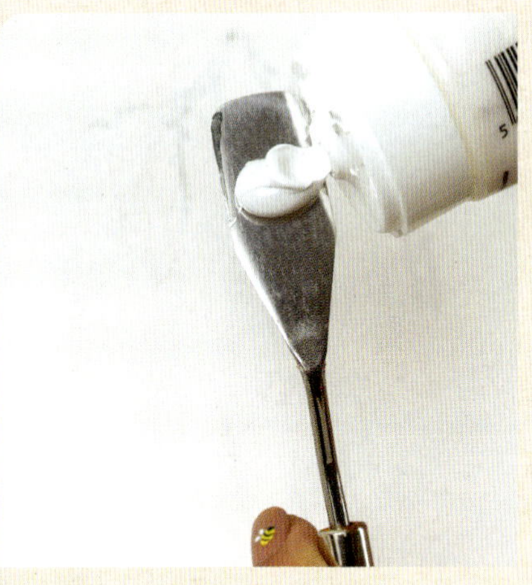

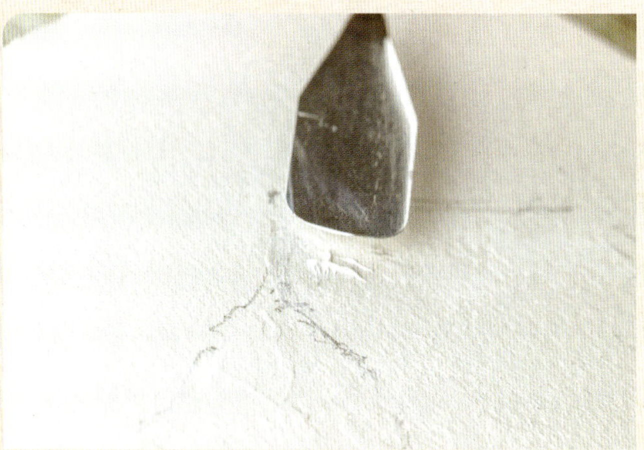

1 Use white acrylic paint, laid down on watercolour paper, to create 'broken' textures. Acrylic repels watercolour and so will give the illusion of snow or rock.

2 Try to apply it with a 'skimming' action that results in hits and misses on the surface.

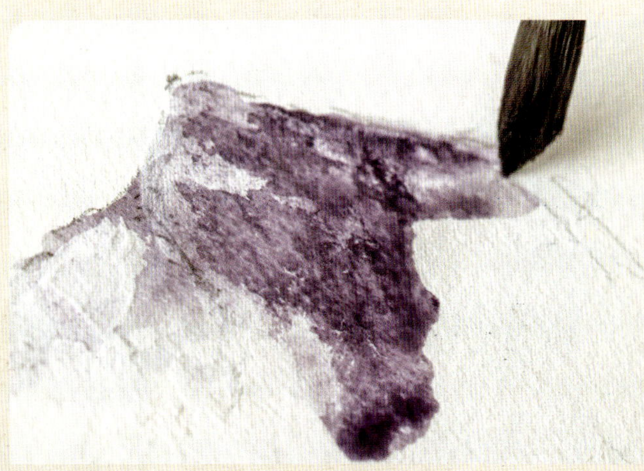

3 When watercolour is applied, it will be repelled by the acrylic and fall into the spaces between, thus describing the rocks poking up between areas of snow.

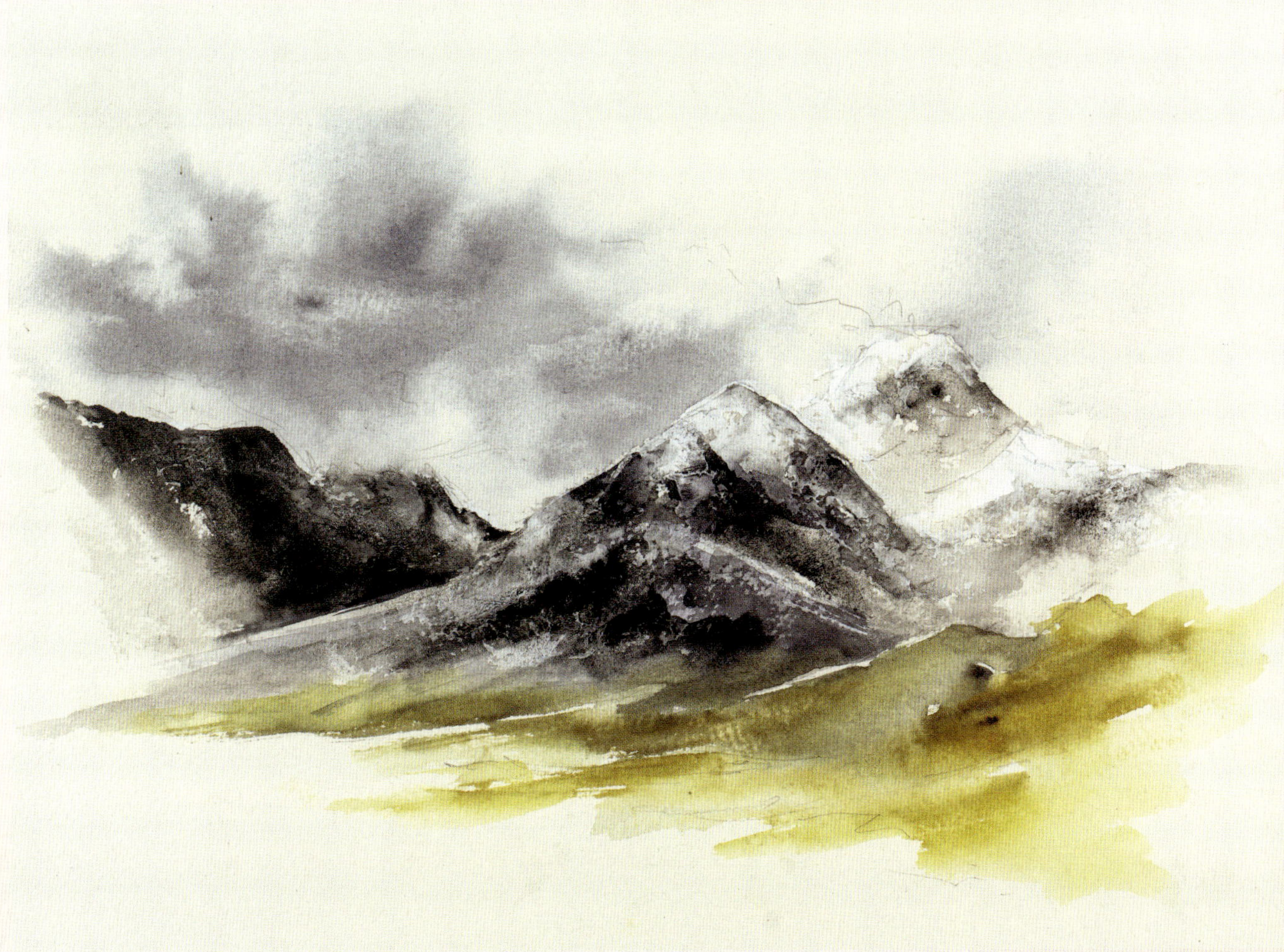

Mountains: study

I used exactly the technique described opposite for this study, watering down my paint to achieve a variety of tones alongside the texture.

Hills and mountains: aerial perspective

Mountains and hills can suggest distance, both through their relative size and through aerial perspective. Aerial perspective is distance described by tone (see pages 49–51) as opposed to size, and is achieved by making distant objects paler and often colder in colour, reflecting the atmosphere around them.

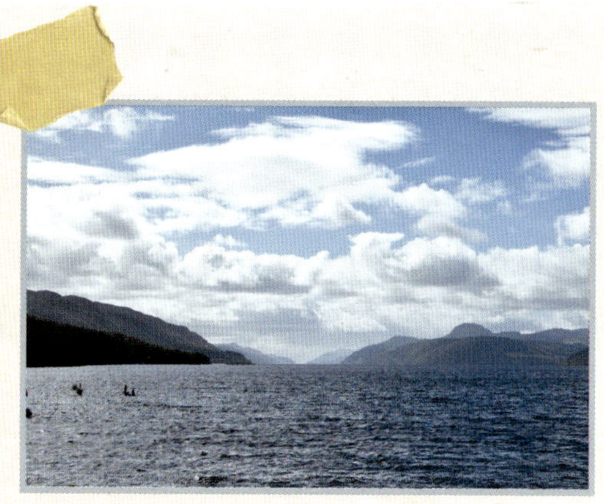

Dores Beach, Inverness, Scotland, UK

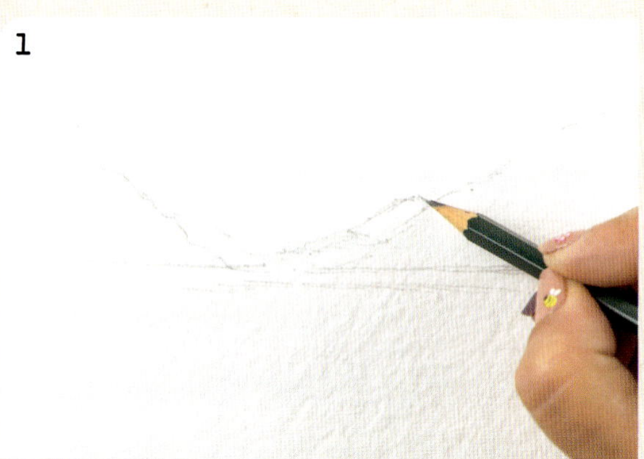

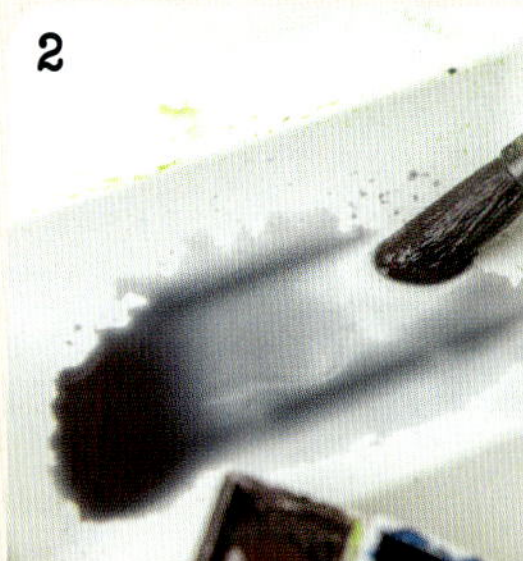

1 Think of the mountains in layers; you don't want them to look too 'cut out' but you do need to consider them – and draw them – one section at a time.

2 Even if you have chosen to paint in a warm colour, get to know how much water will make pale and strong versions of it to suggest recession.

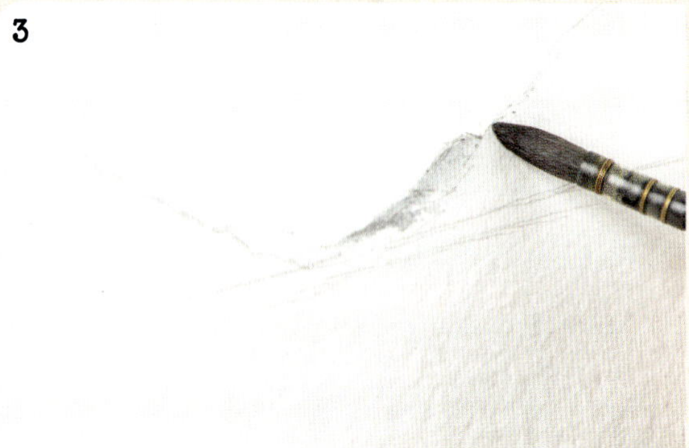

3 Allow each layer to dry fully, or they may merge too much and look flat rather than suggest proximity or distance.

Dores Beach

Experiment with your colour palette to achieve aerial perspective – using just one colour can create a sense of distance if your tones are well balanced (see pages 50–51). Here you can see that I have concentrated on the edges of the mountains where they meet the water, leaving a thin line of white to accentuate the strong tones above.

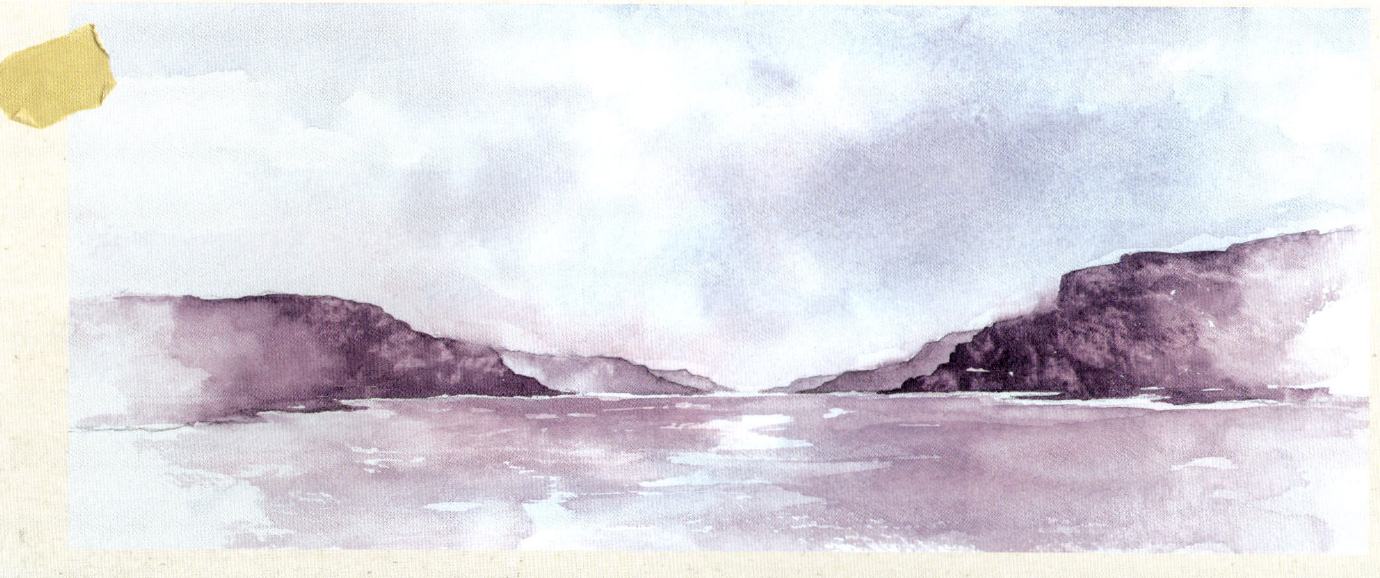

Hills and mountains as geography

Featuring hills and mountains can be an excellent way of establishing the geography of your location. The sharpness or softness of the formations – along with the colour palette you choose to describe where you are painting – all help the viewer to understand where you are situated.

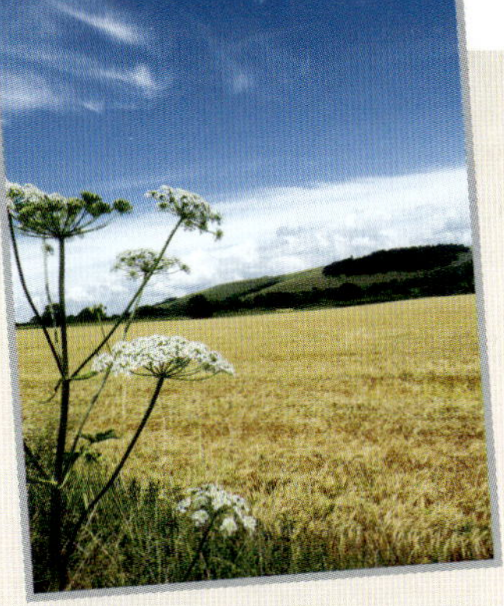

Towards Hambledon, Dorset, UK

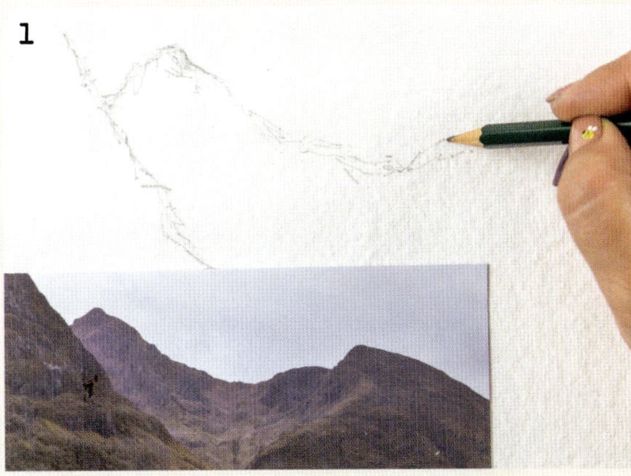

1 Look at the shape that the hills or mountains form, as their height, and therefore scale, will be determined by this.

2 Choose your colours or tones to suit the surrounding landscape.

3 Use the texture of your surface, or your brush strokes, to show whether your hill is a point of focus, or in the background – greater texture and contrast will draw the eye.

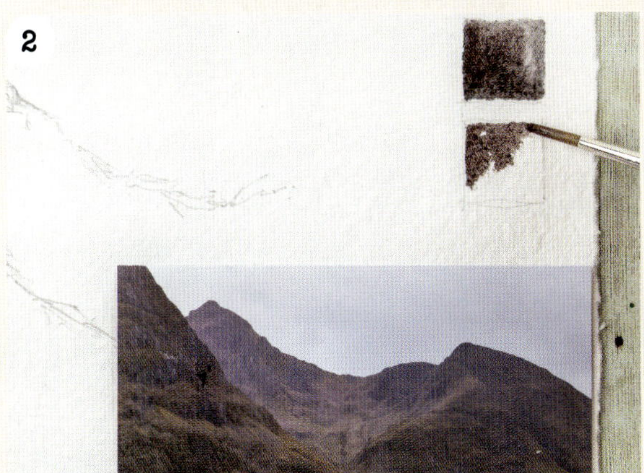

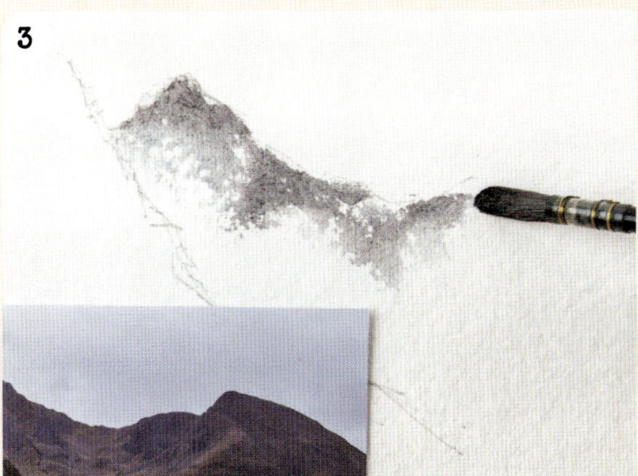

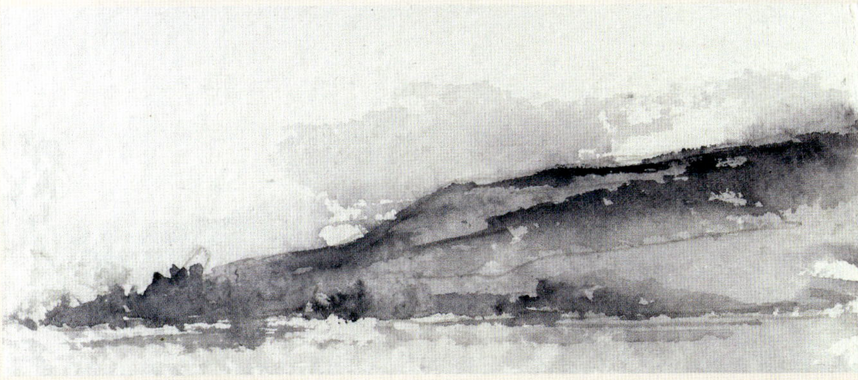

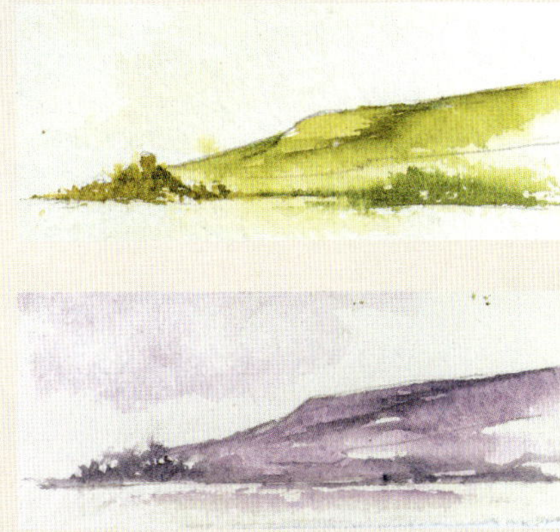

Hills: sketchbook study

I played with the colours that I could potentially use for this simple hill study: this prompted me to consider the impact of my choices on other parts of the painting and whether or not they suited the geography of the surroundings.

Where hills and sky combine

Despite your best efforts, it can be tricky to avoid hills and mountains looking like cardboard cut-outs; so it might be worth considering blurring the contours where they meet the sky, both to show any weather aspects and to give atmosphere and realism to your painting.

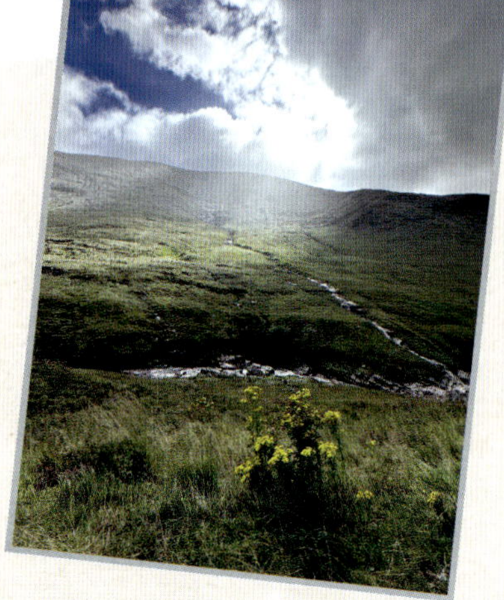

Glen Etive, Scottish Highlands, UK

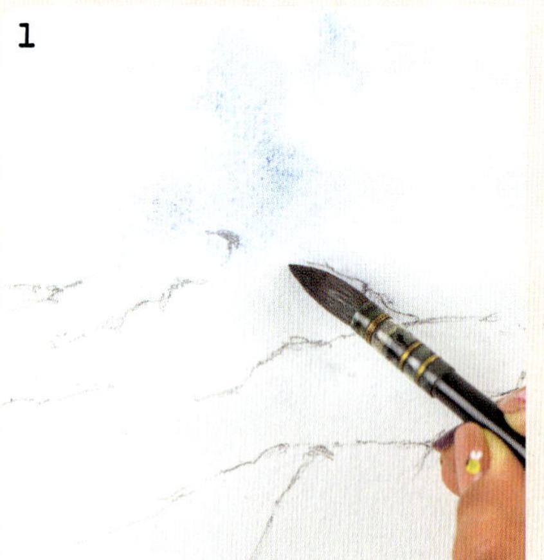

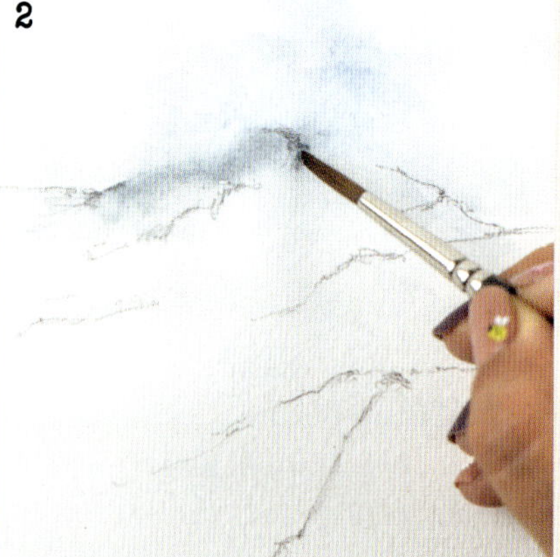

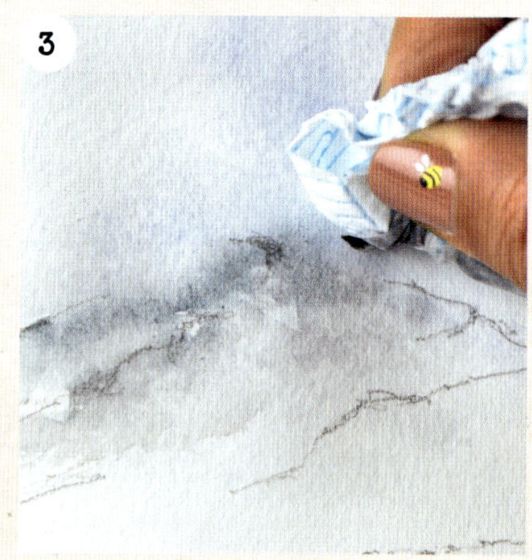

1 When painting your sky, bring the colour down over the top of the mountain ridge.

2 Wet one area of your mountain before applying the paint so that it diffuses as you work along the ridge.

3 Lift out colour with kitchen paper as required to keep the softness of the edge.

Mountain ridge: sketchbook study
This mountain in Scotland was high above me and I was concentrating on just the mountain's textures and so not including any other features to show the scale. I wanted to demonstrate that the top was disappearing into the mist, following the steps above.

Trees

Trees are one of my favourite elements of a landscape – they tell stories and stand the test of time and weather. Many trees alter through the seasons and give us the opportunity to experiment with many aspects of their design: we may wish to show the changing colours of their foliage or perhaps concentrate on the rich and varied textures afforded to us by their bark and branches.

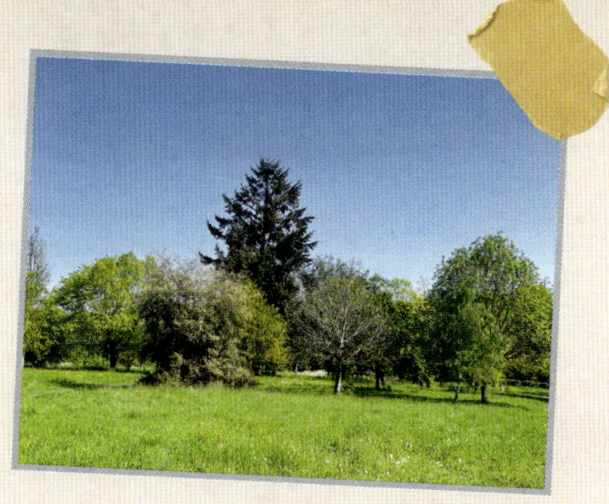

Nonsuch Park, Cheam, Surrey, UK

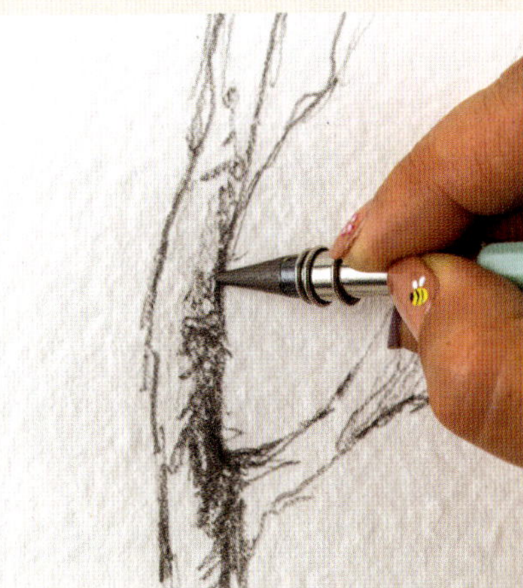

1 A graphite stick – as opposed to a traditional pencil – gives broader strokes for tree textures.

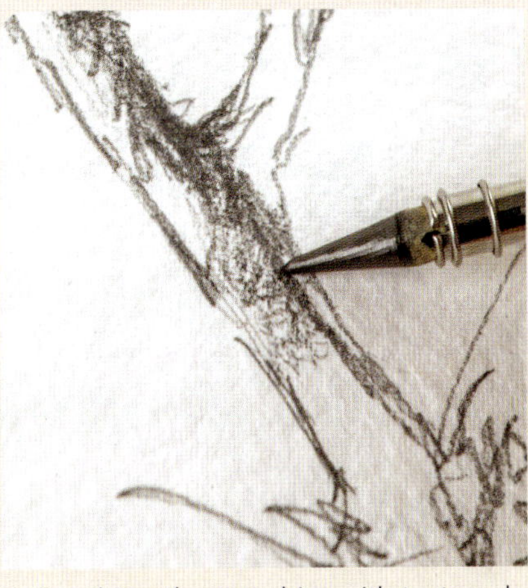

2 Combine the graphite with textured paper and experiment with how much you press down and lift off to show variation in the marks.

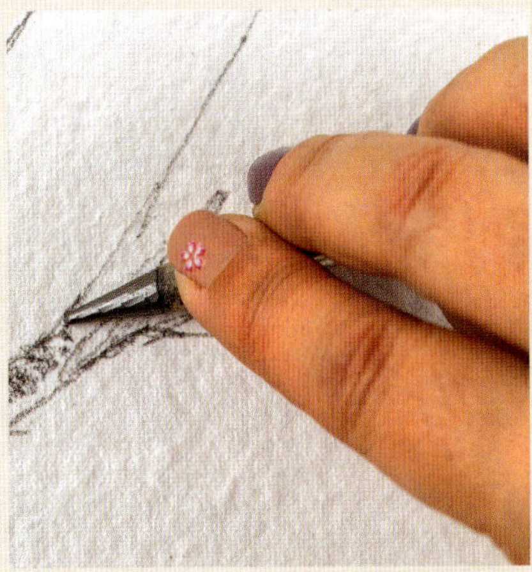

3 Hold your hand above the stick to lay down larger areas of graphite, rather than holding it in the same way as you would for writing.

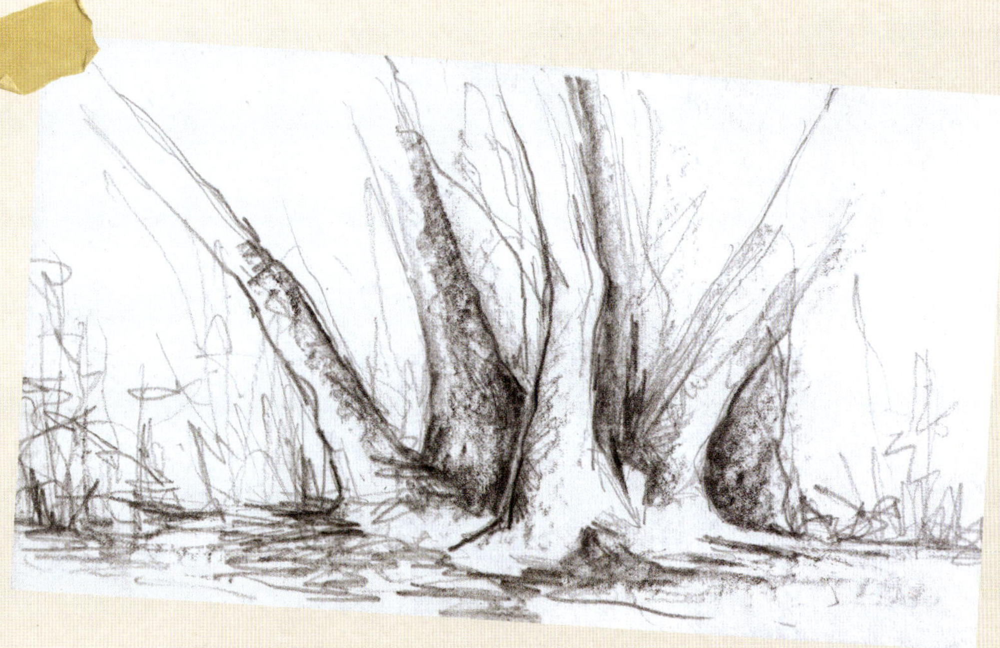

By the Lake: sketchbook study
Graphite is ideal for executing quick studies, such as this one, when I was on a walk and had only minutes to get my observations down in my sketchbook before my dogs' patience ran out.

Trees: perspective

As with hills and mountains, aerial perspective can be used to distinguish between trees in the distance and trees closer to the foreground.

Use a limited palette of colours to help depict the atmosphere and depth of a wooded area.

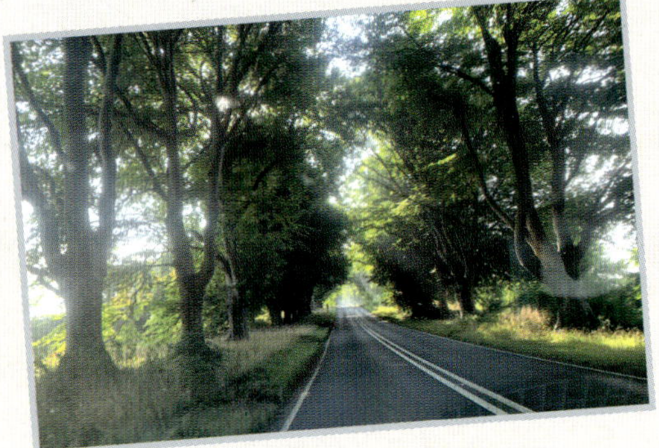

Beech avenue

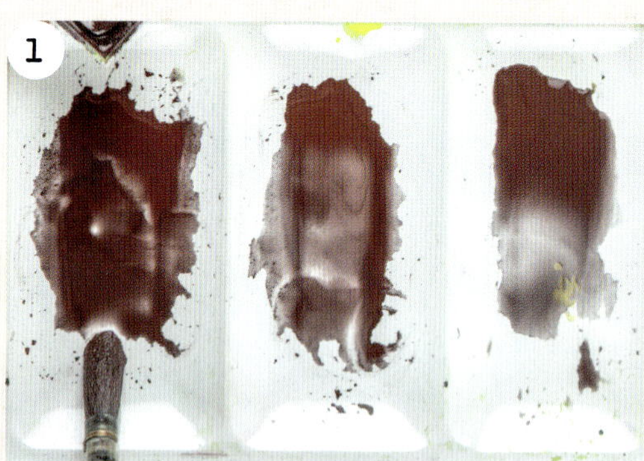

1 Choose a rich paint that is going to give you a variety of tones. Here I have used Hematite Genuine, a strong watercolour pigment.

2 Start with very diluted versions of the colour to put in distant trees.

3 Slowly build up the strength of the colour and the texture in the tree shapes that are closer to you.

The End of the Garden
This technique can take a while to get right; it's as much about understanding your paint as it is faithfully representing the distance through the tree trunks.

Trees through the seasons

Your recording of various landscape elements doesn't just have to be through sketching or painting; it can be through photography too. I have become slightly obsessed with photographing the elm tree outside my studio, which I see every single morning as I walk down the stairs. Seeing the images all together helps me to appreciate what changes occur throughout the year and at different times of day.

1 Choose a tree that you see often, perhaps where you live or on a daily walk.

2 Try to take a photo from the same position each time. You don't have to use a fancy camera – a phone or tablet will be just as good to remind you of the changes.

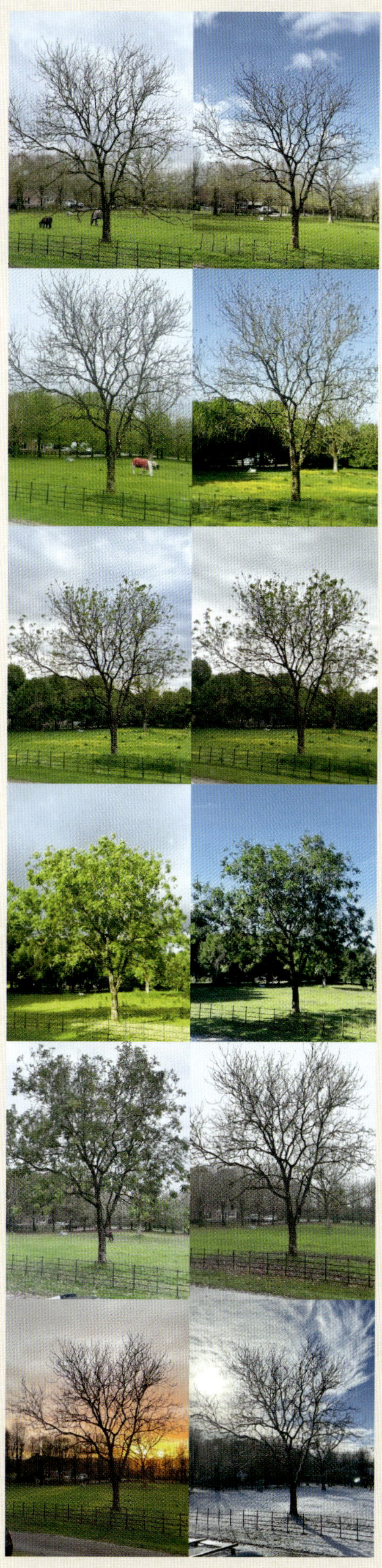

Right and below, the studio elm

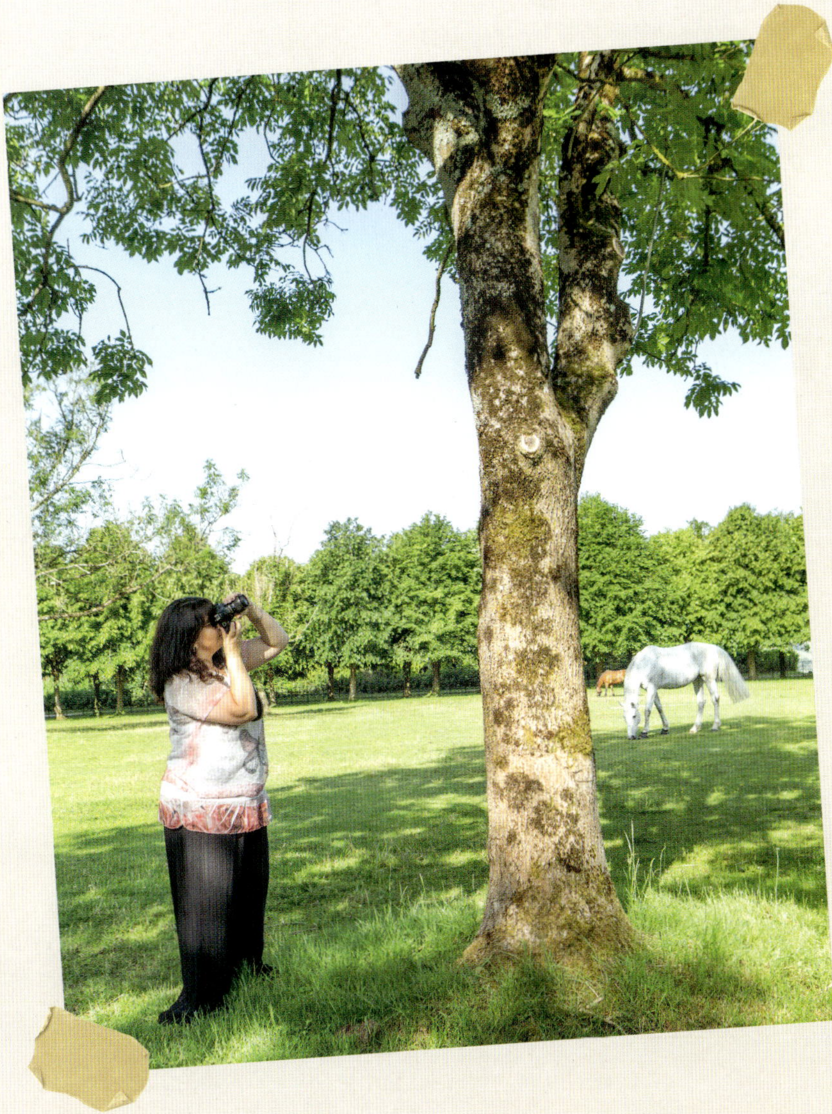

Mark making for trees

Many techniques can be used to describe the texture of bark or the foliage of a tree. If a tree forms a central part of your painting, it is worth considering how you might like to show it so that it comes forwards in your piece. I like to experiment with inks as they are unpredictable enough to be exciting, without getting wildly out of control.

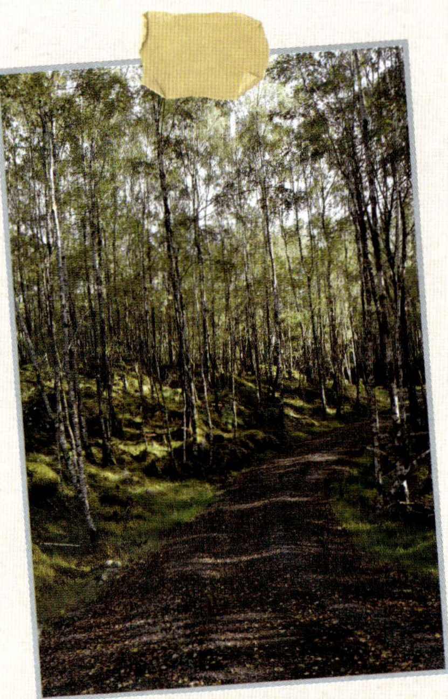

Ceannacroc, Scottish Highlands, Scotland, UK

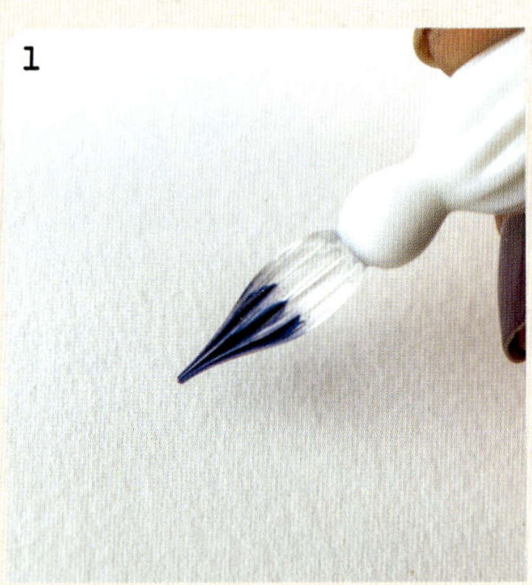

1 Use water-soluble fountain-pen ink, as it makes interesting textures when sprayed with water, and is a somewhat unusual tool with which to make marks. Here, I have used a glass dip pen, as it glides over the paper, and I can't overload it.

2 Make a variety of marks; you can choose to leave the ink wet or let it dry before rewetting it at the next stage.

3 Use a spray bottle with a fine mist, held a short distance away, to allow the water droplets to 'rain' on the paper and give you interesting results.

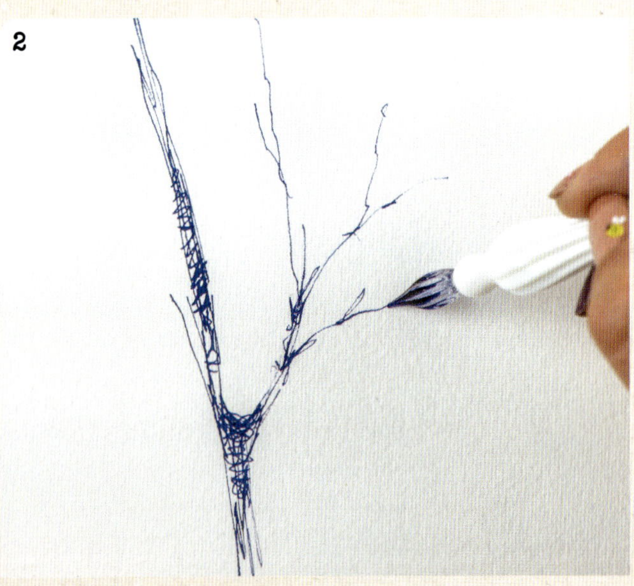

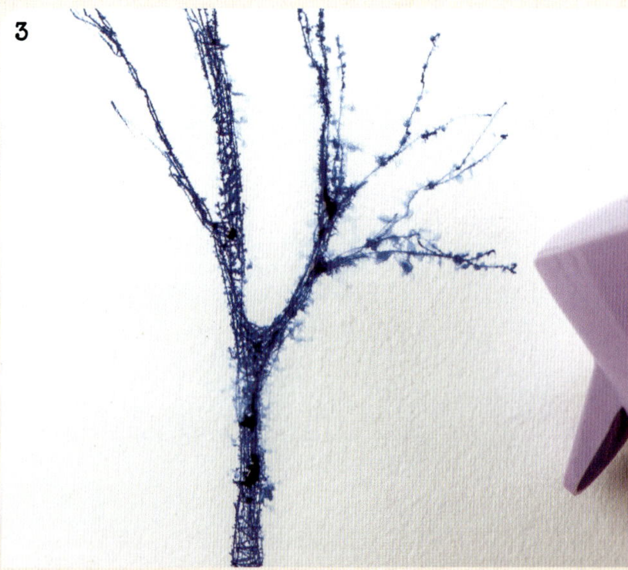

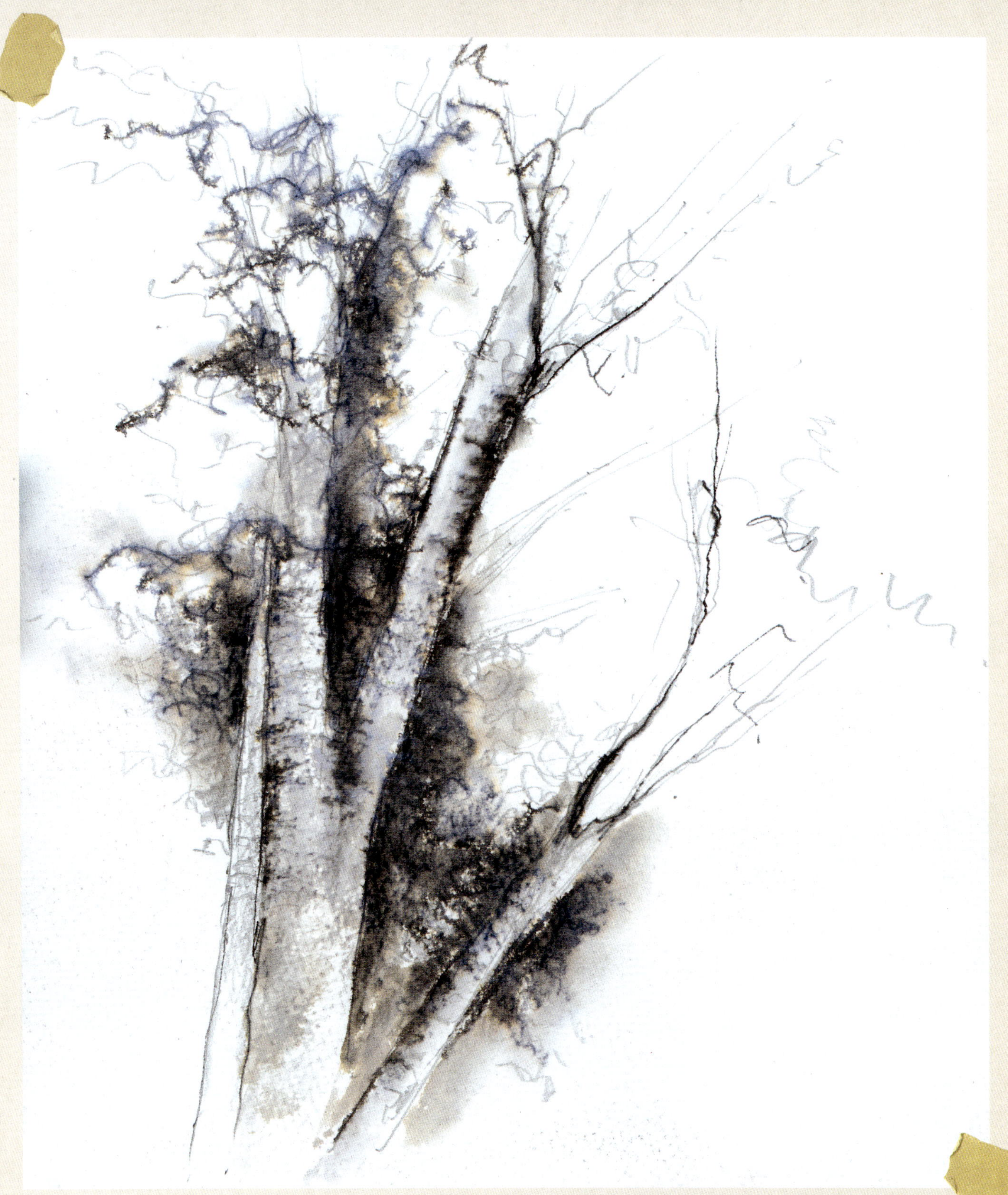

Ink tree: a study

Using the steps opposite, I created the texture in this study on both the tree and the foliage behind it. You may notice that this black ink produced a shade of brown when it was sprayed, due to it breaking down into its component pigments.

Individual trees

Trees are fascinating to paint in a group, but equally you can paint them as a simple patch of foliage or even individually if you want to replicate the species faithfully.

While it is absolutely fine to paint a generic tree, it might be that a particular landscape has a unique species associated with it or that the geography of the area is defined by the shape and contour of specific groups of trees.

1 Choose either a tree that you see every day, or your favourite species to concentrate on; in the photo below, I chose a willow tree as it is one of my favourite species.

2 Use whatever medium you feel most confident with to consider its foliage, colour and shape. In the example below, right, I've chosen watercolour as this is the medium that always performs best for me when painting trees.

3 Compare various species to see how they differ and what characteristics make them interesting to paint.

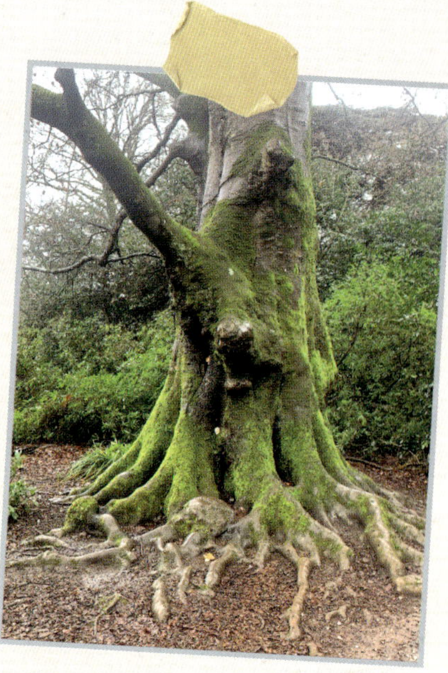

Cornish woods, UK

Different species of tree can have quite different shapes and colours. Studying these variations will help give you confidence in painting them. From top left, pine, lime, elder, holly, ash, beech, rowan, horse chestnut, sycamore, crab apple, apple and willow.

Sketching my favourite willow on location, noting the texture and shape of the trunk.

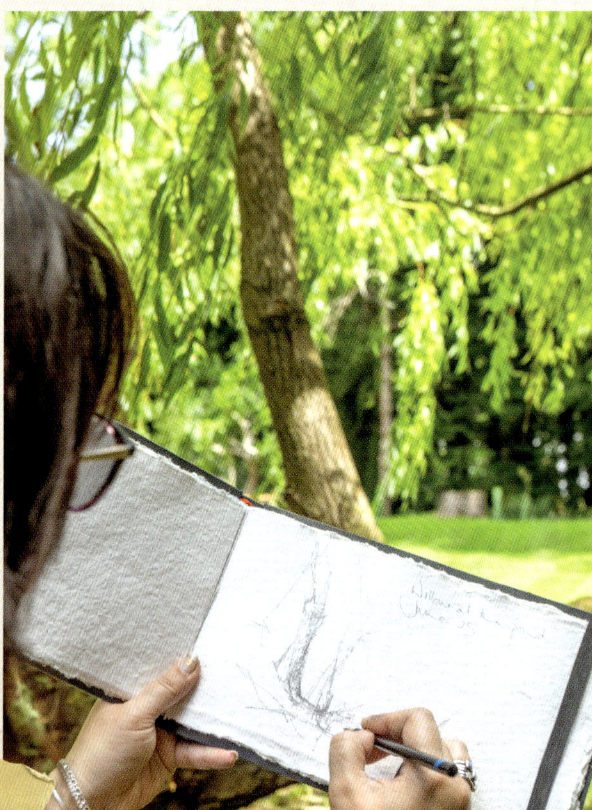

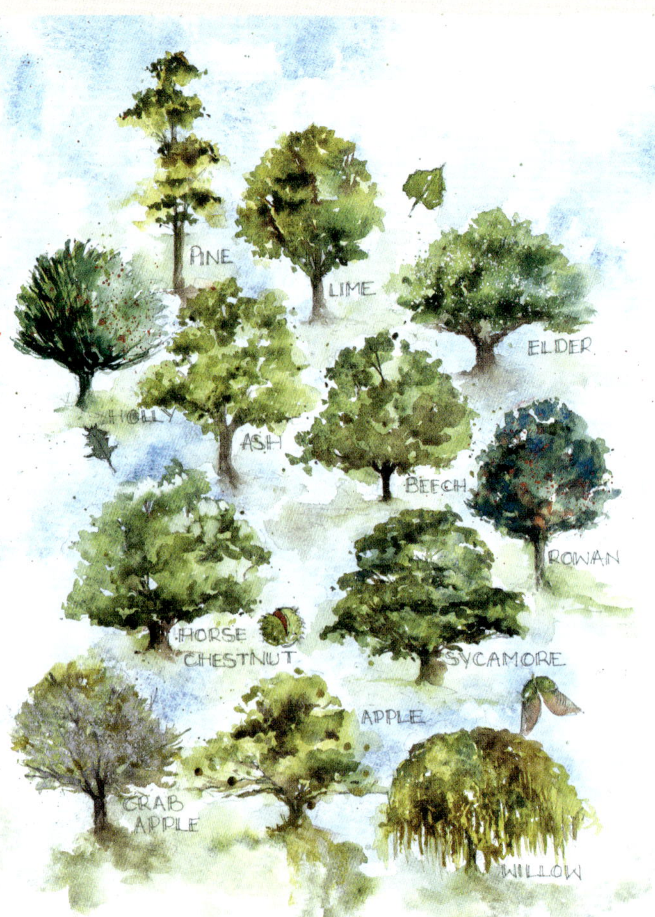

Including buildings

The addition of a building or structure in a landscape can sometimes really help tell a story; I'm a big fan of old farm buildings and stone structures as they can show age and add interesting texture to the composition. If a whole building feels too overwhelming to include, try first tackling a smaller structure, or possibly a detail of a building, to build up your confidence.

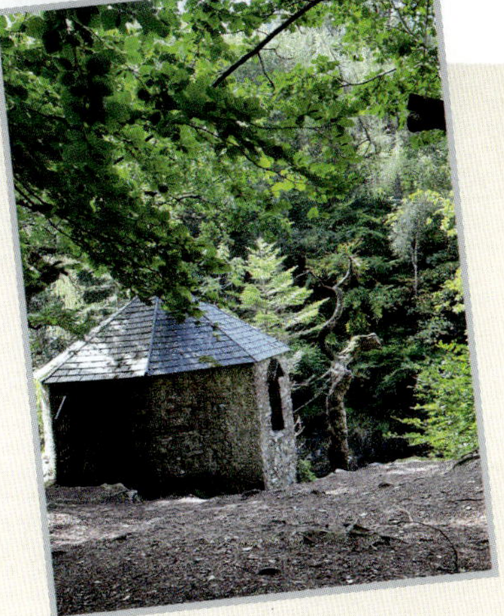
The Summer House

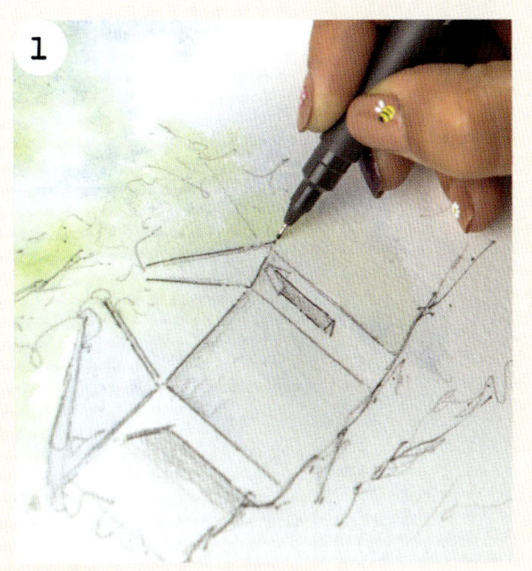
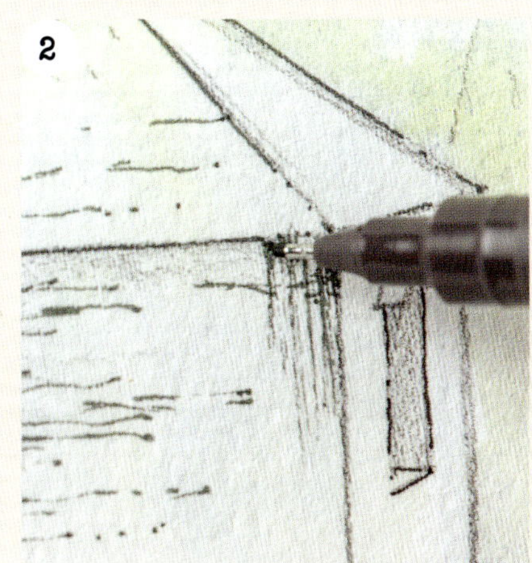
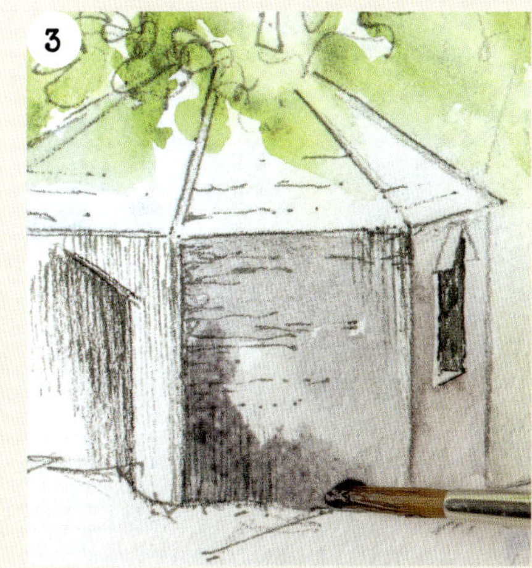

1 Use a waterproof sketching pen and paint in combination - the pen for detail and the paint for colour.

2 Employ a variety of marks to describe the surface of the structure.

3 Lay a wash of ink or watercolour over the top and add shadows as required.

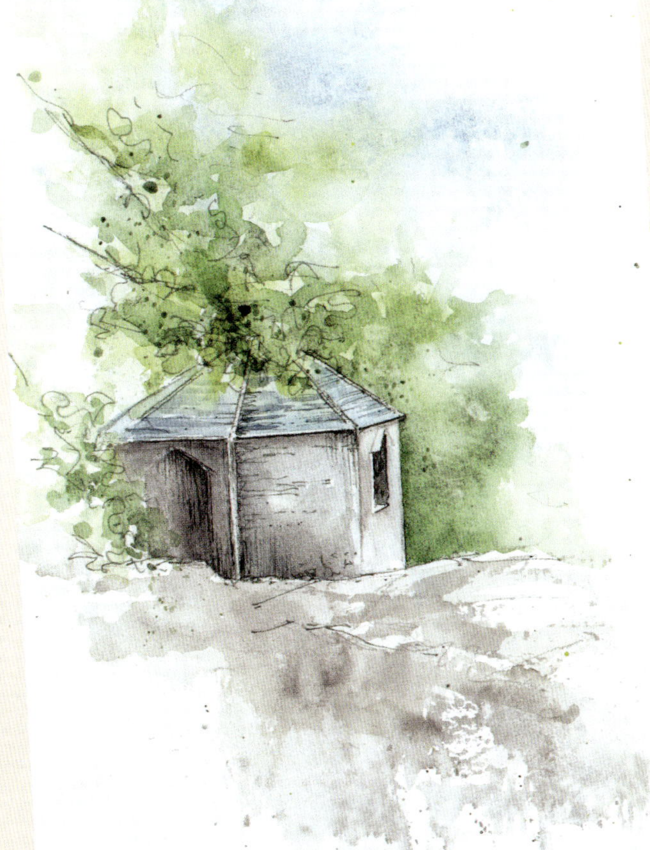
The Summer House: a study

This study allowed me to understand the structure before including it in a much more complicated painting later on (see pages 156–159) and helped me to understand how the building is formed. The jigsaw-puzzle approach in action (see page 60)!

Linear perspective

Aerial perspective uses tone and colour to show how elements of a landscape 'disappear' into the distance; however, if we are thinking of including buildings or structures in our paintings, we need also to understand linear perspective. Linear perspective is a way of realistically showing depth and distance by making objects smaller, the further away from us they are.

Both types of perspective, aerial and linear, can take a little time to accomplish results that you are pleased with, but look to specific tools and techniques to help guide you.

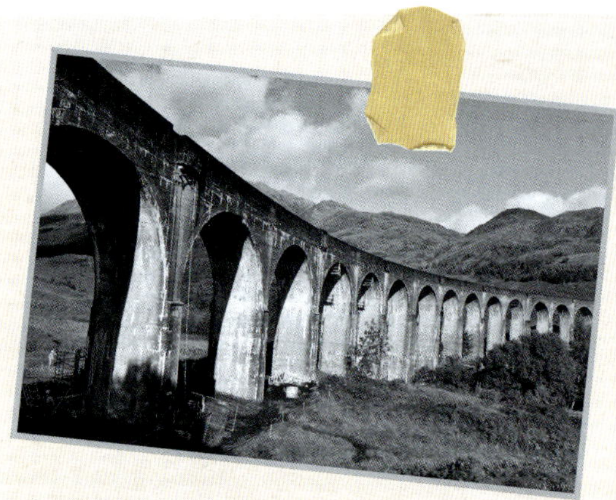

Glenfinnan Viaduct, Scottish Highlands, Scotland, UK

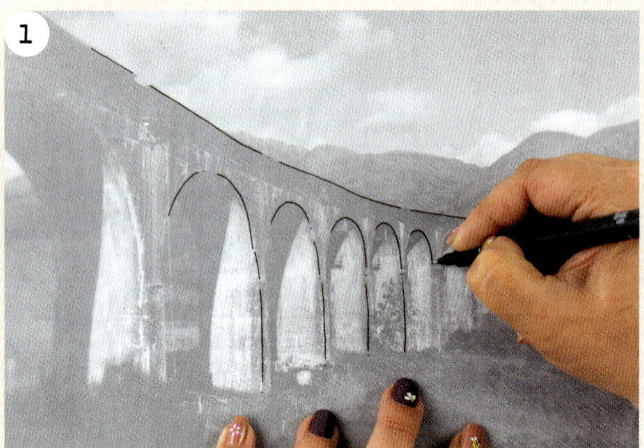

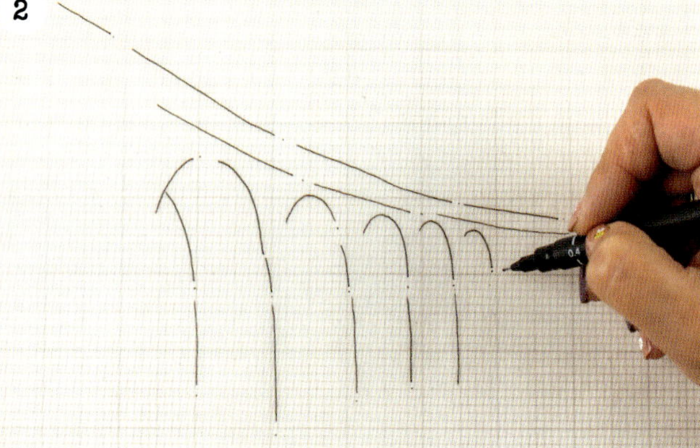

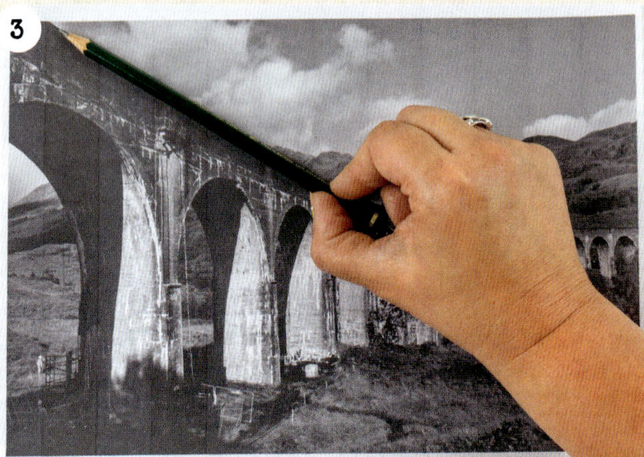

1 If you are depicting a complicated structure, take a photograph and trace it so you can see which way the lines slope. It can be helpful to work from a black-and-white photograph, which shows up the different tones better than a colour one.

2 Overlay tracing paper on top of graph paper to help you really 'see' the lines you need to follow.

3 If you prefer to draw freehand, line up a pencil along the angle that the structure forms to show you which way the building's features are sloping.

Opposite, Hurds Hill Steps

This is an example of when I wouldn't let a complicated subject get the better of me. Careful study of the angles against a freer application for the foliage helped set the mood of the painting.

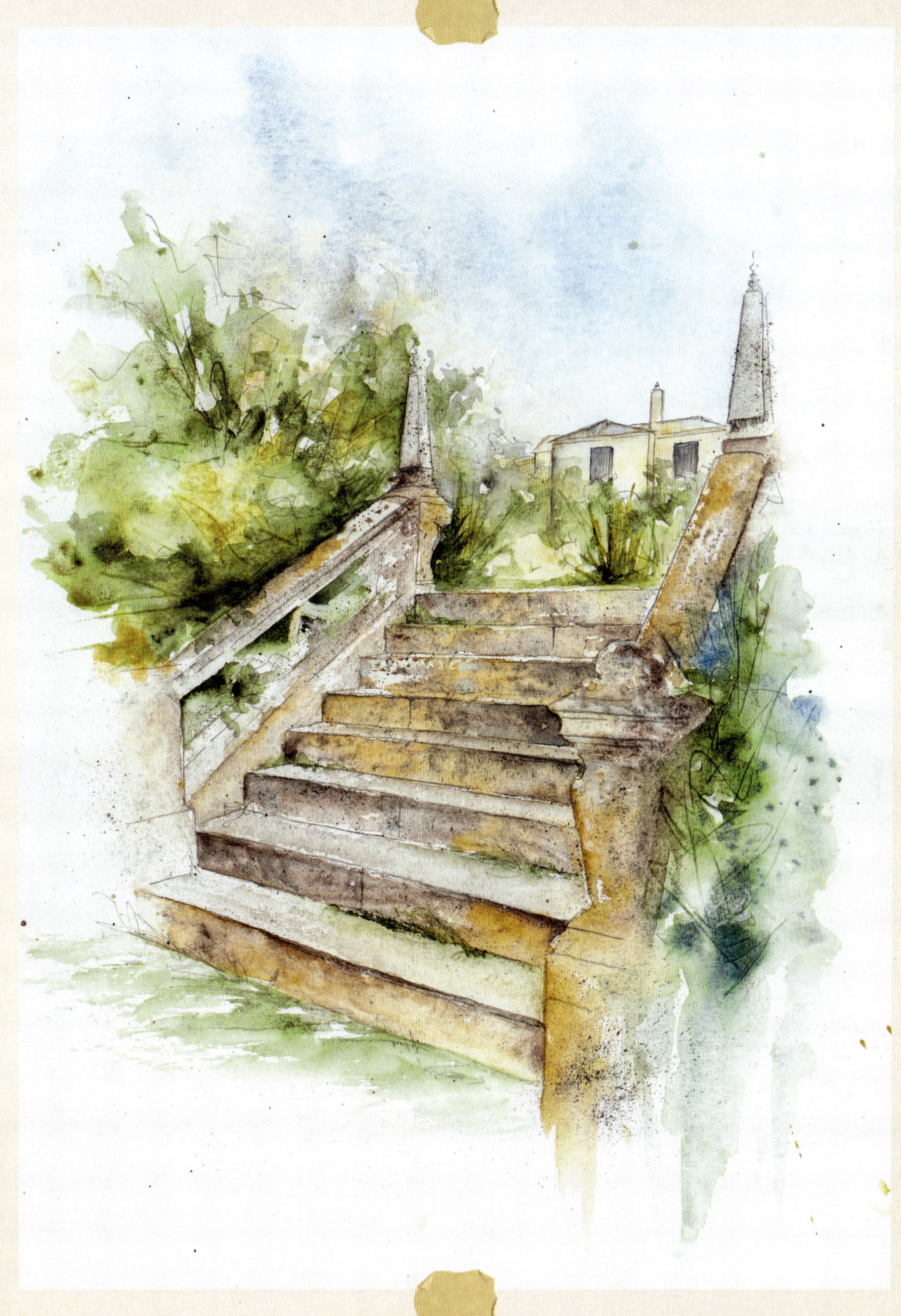

Composition for buildings and structures

It is sometimes tricky to know where to place your structure: is it a central feature or are you using it to lead the eye elsewhere? I think it's useful to get a building to hint at something else: maybe at the start of a path or perhaps dwarfed by its surroundings, showing the scale of a field. You could even use a building to evoke the memory of a walk you once took.

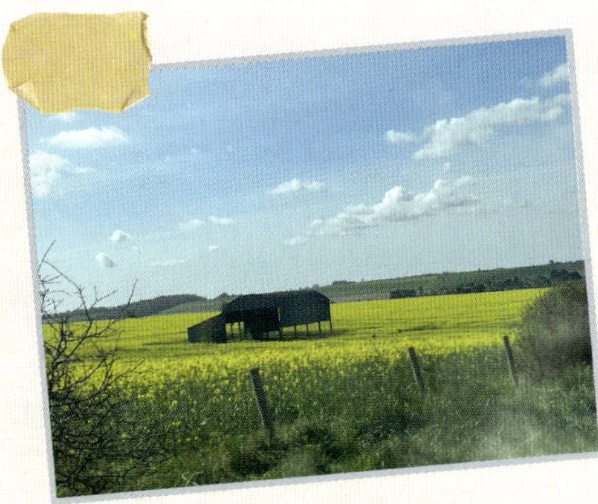

That Blue Barn, Sixpenny Handley, Dorset, UK

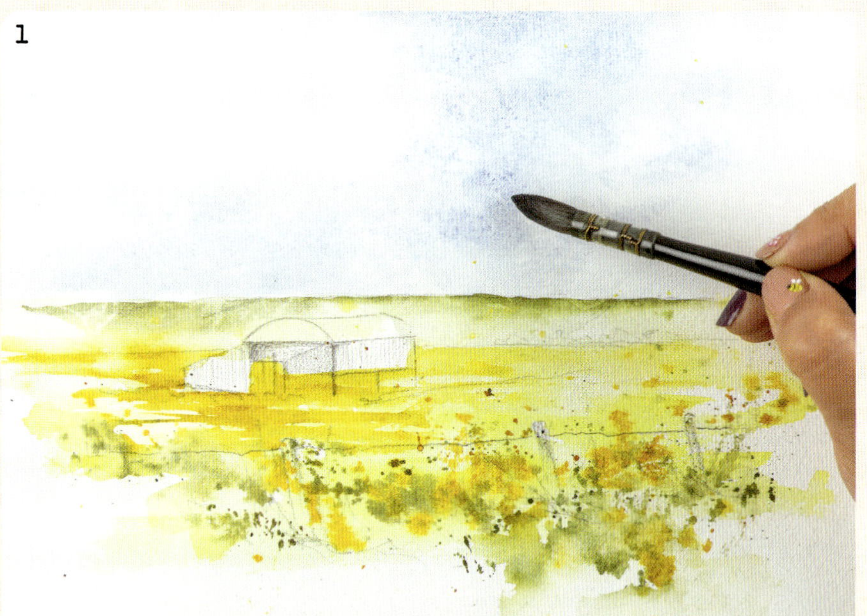

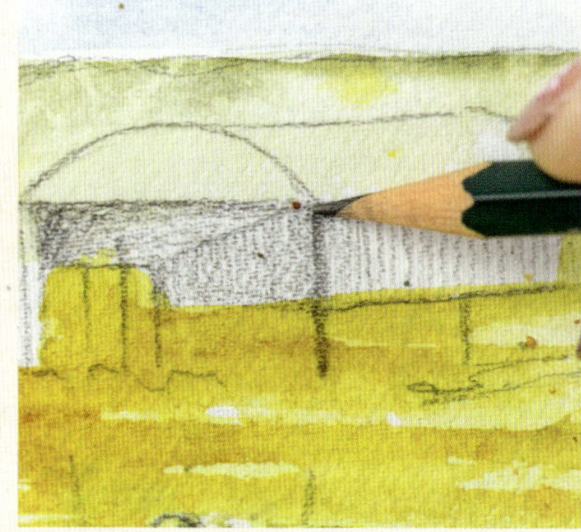

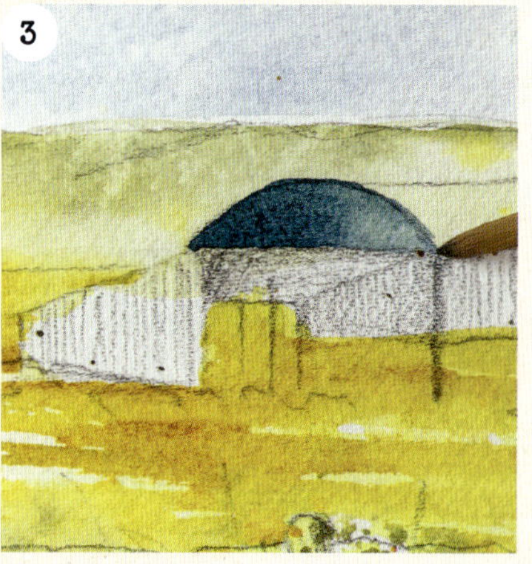

1 Use colour to show the importance of the building within its surroundings. A dark, contrasting or stronger colour can make the building a point of interest, or blend into its surroundings. Here the yellow of the crops show how moody the dark blue of the barn is by comparison.

2 A few elements of detail can often suggest much more, saving you labouring over every brick or plank. Not everything needs to be painted in, either; sometimes going back in to the structure with a pencil will make your building look more accurate than struggling with the hairs of a brush might.

3 Be brave with darks to show shadows and contours. The barn here is so dark against the surrounding fields that I need to ensure that I replicate this contrast in order to give the study a dramatic appearance.

Opposite, <u>Between the Dunes</u>
This structure is placed so as to give the impression that it leads on to another view. By dropping the sky right down on the other side it is suggested that as soon as you cross the bridge, the beach and sea will greet you, creating a sense of anticipation.

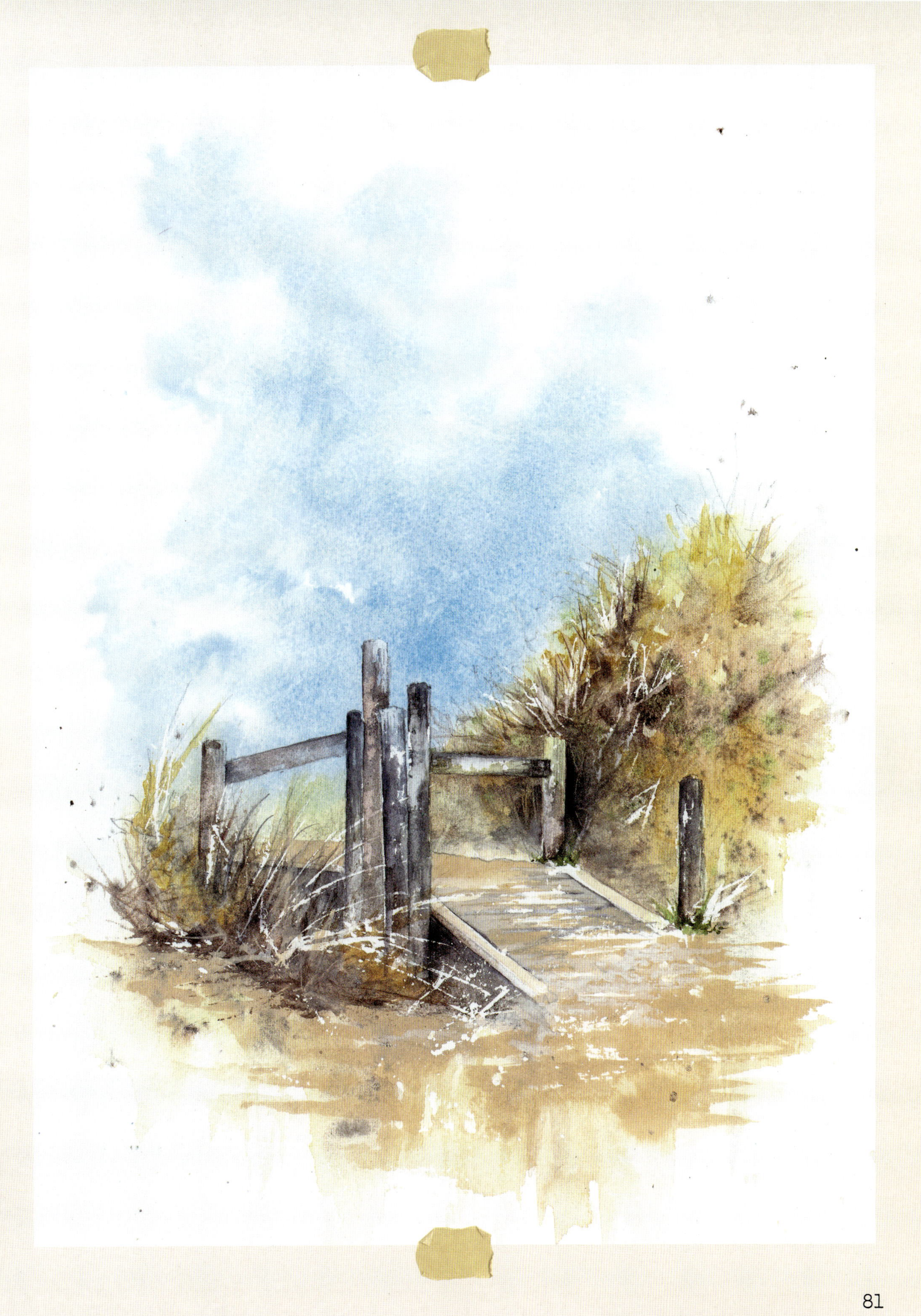

Basic water

Water can sometimes be a challenge to paint due to its many forms, colours and depths. When I first started painting, every body of water looked a lot like carpet. However, after spending many hours really looking at water, and watching how it changes, I realized that no matter the surface area, water needs both rich colour and surface tension to look realistic, and the marks that you make are an important part of the process.

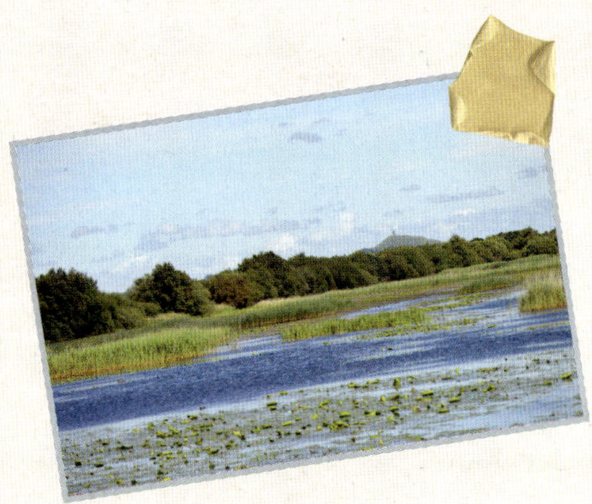

Towards Glastonbury, Somerset, UK

1 Look closely at the water you are trying to paint. Does it need texture or tension? Do you need an area of flat colour, or to skim your brush across the texture of the paper? A slightly dry brush leaves a broken trail that suggests light reflecting off the surface of the water.

2 Consider using different brush shapes to achieve the marks you are looking for – a flat brush, used on its side, is useful for depicting ripples or distant waves.

3 Do you need to vary the pressure of your brush or painting tool to adjust the weight of the mark that is required? Experiment and see what effects you can create.

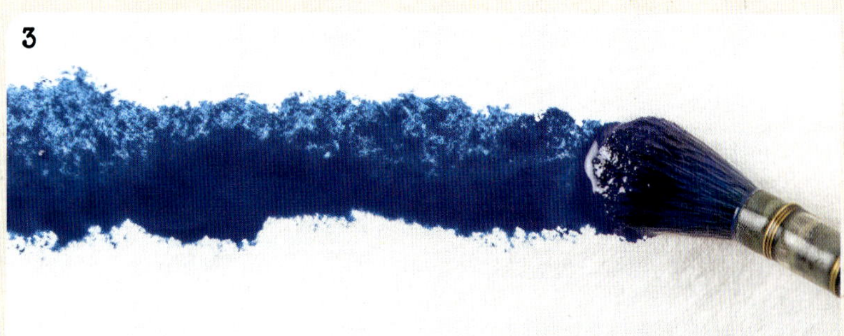

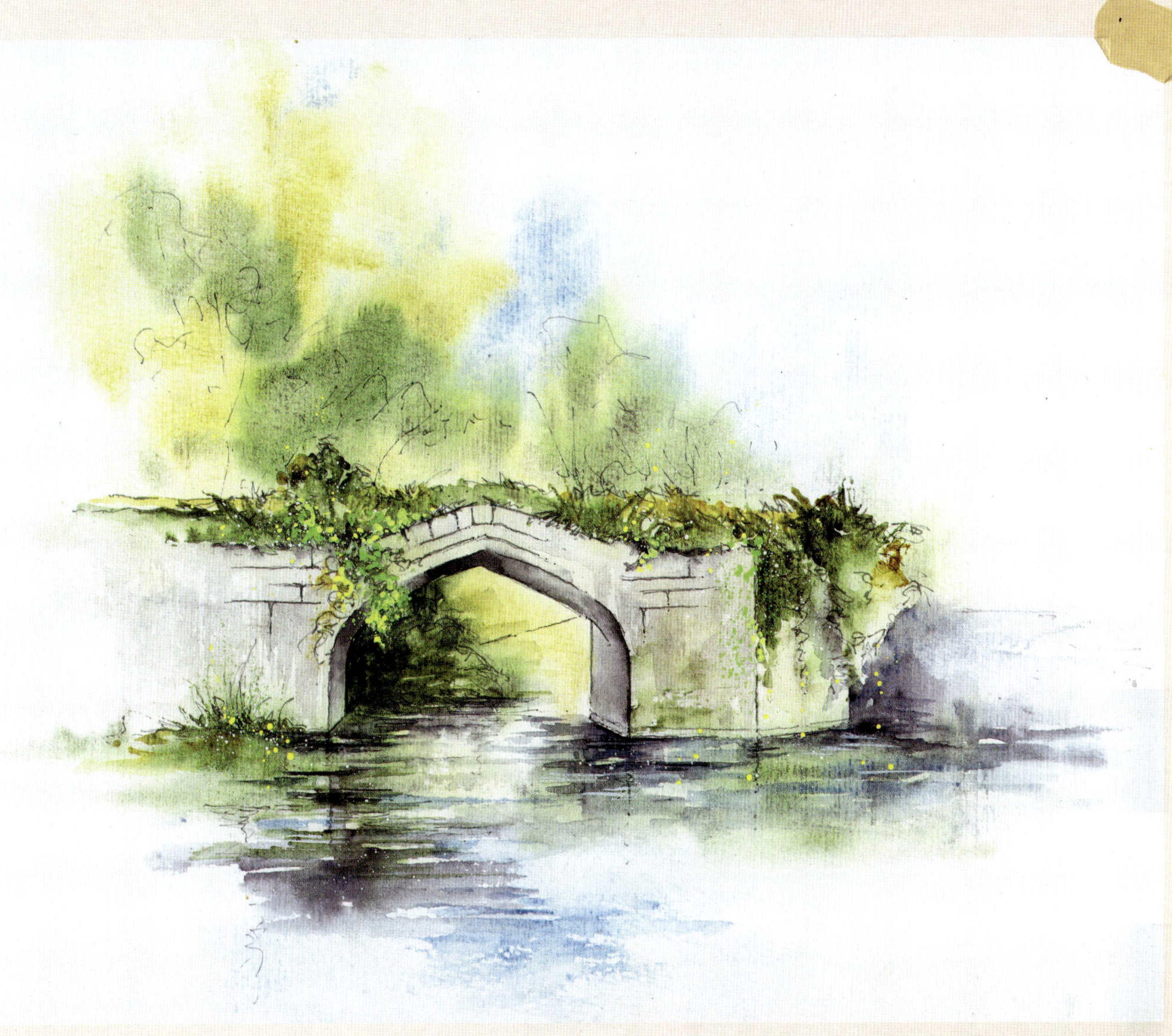

The Old Footbridge: a quick study

*This view was as much about the dark colours used as it was about how to
describe the state of the water. I used marks to show the soft foliage and the
hard structure of the bridge but also the water too – horizontal lines
where I needed the water to look flat and calm, and strong colours that
blurred together to suggest depth.*
Be as brave as you dare with those darks – your lights will thank you for it.

Landscape or seascape?

When is a landscape a seascape and vice versa? For me, a painting that incorporates both the sea and adjacent land is simply a type of landscape and is something you are probably going to come across in your exploration of painting subjects.

Painting water adjacent to rocks, and moving with force, can give great opportunities to express texture and incorporate more unusual materials to describe tone.

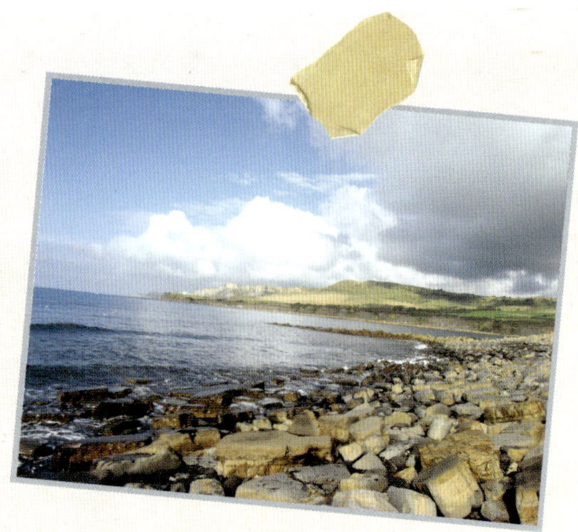
Kimmeridge, Isle of Purbeck, Dorset, UK

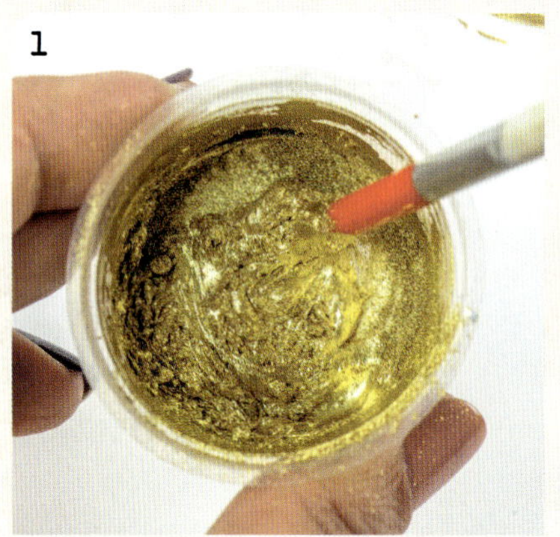

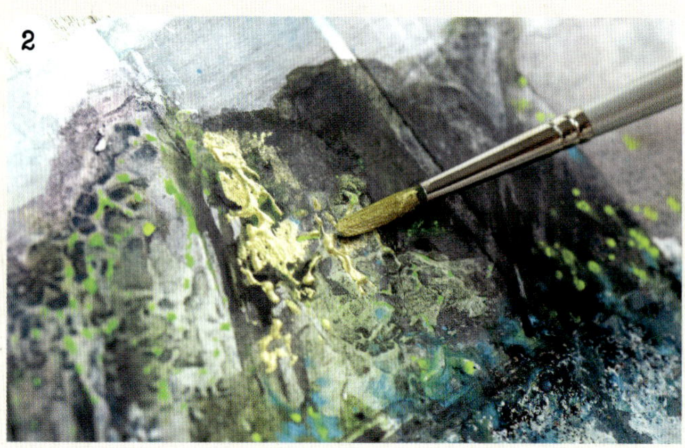

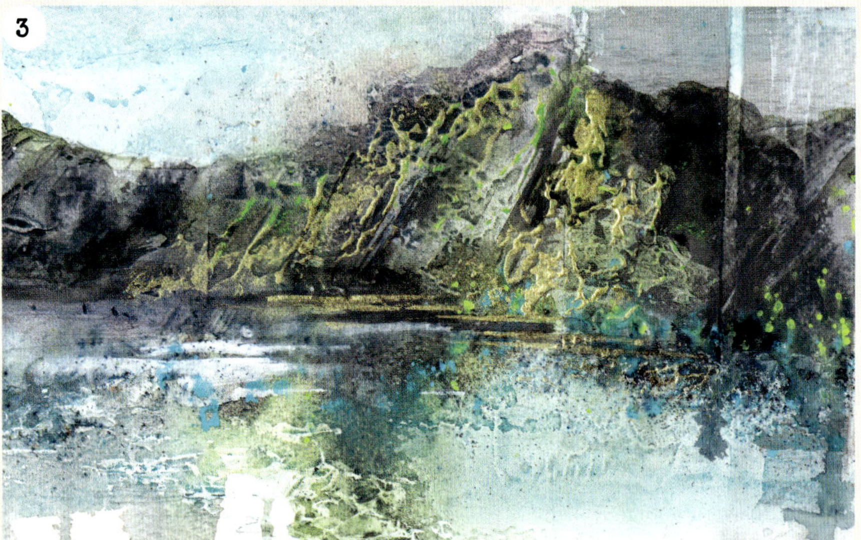

1 If you have a very heavy texture in your painting, a metallic element may help 'lift' any tones you wish to show. Try combining gouache and a metallic powder for soft marks with a strong gold or silver component.

2 Use a metallic colour for either the sand or the water, to express the glint of light on the texture.

3 Adding gouache will allow the marks to be blended or faded into the surroundings if required as it is a very forgiving medium.

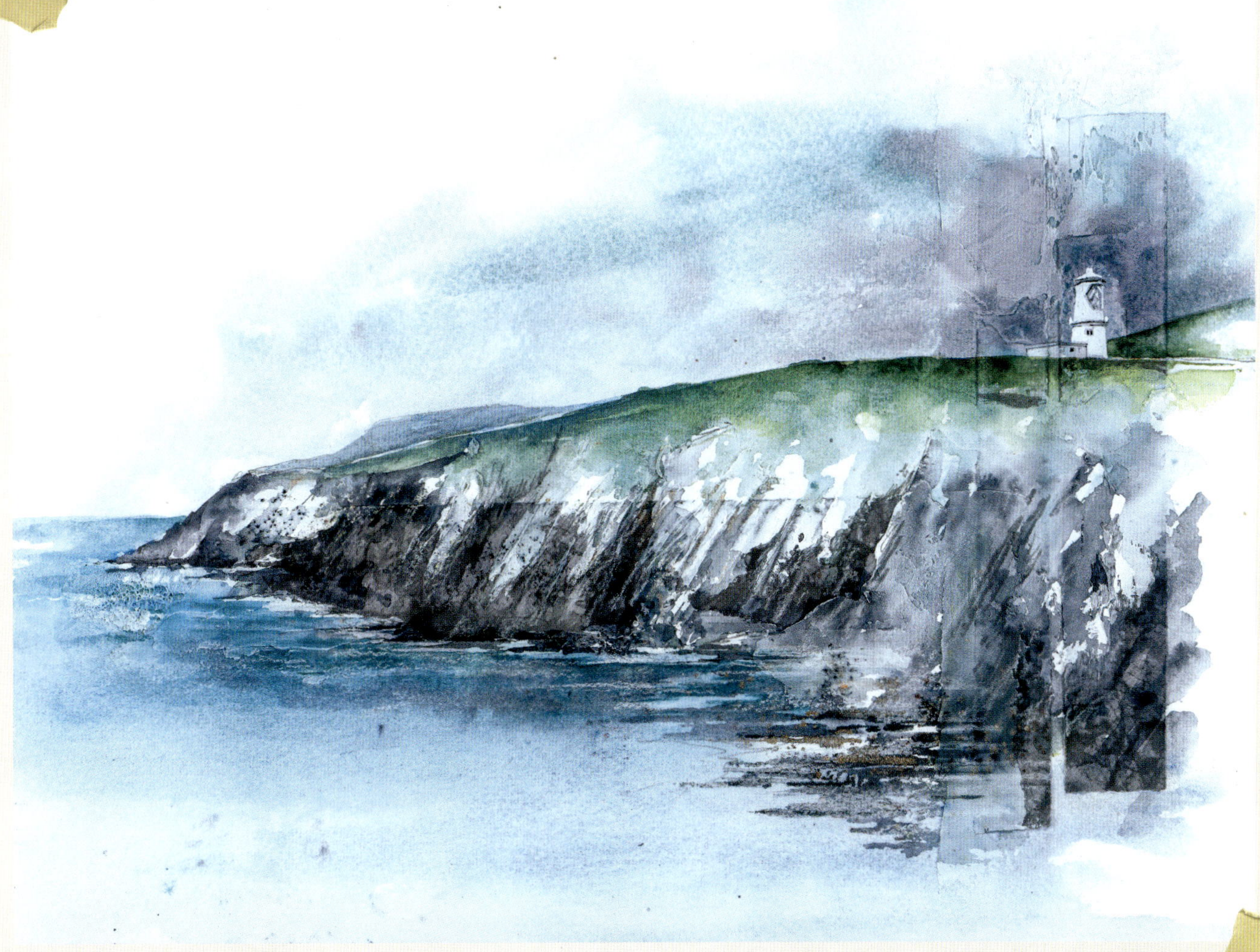

Strumble Head, Pembrokeshire, Wales, UK

Depicting a cliff that falls into an area of water is a favourite activity of mine: it gives me the opportunity to show drama and movement that can sometimes be difficult to introduce into a more conventional choice of subject.

In the foreground, at the bottom of the cliffs as they meet the water, I have used metallics to show small glints of gold and silver.

Large bodies of water

Large rivers, lochs and lakes all provide the painter with an array of textures and rich colours to be exploited in a painting. I tend to find large areas a little easier than small bodies of water (see page 88) – you can experiment with how dark you make your paint to demonstrate the weight of the water, and what can be added or taken away from the surface to show tension.

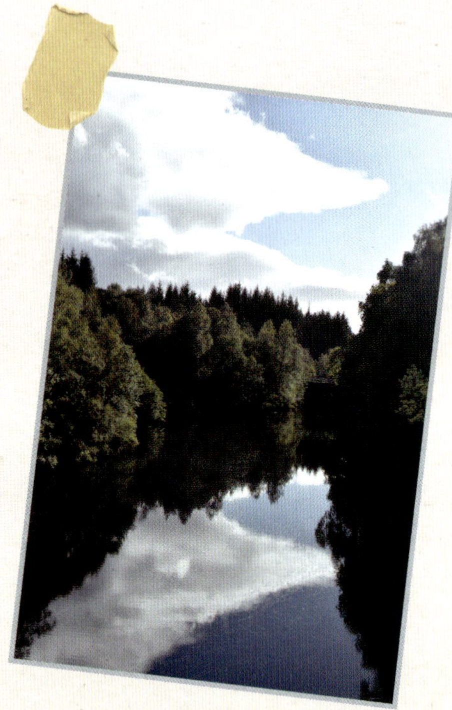

River Moriston, Inverness-shire, Scotland, UK

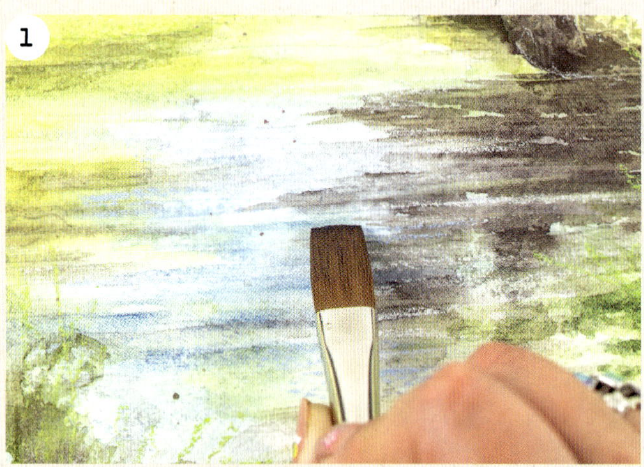

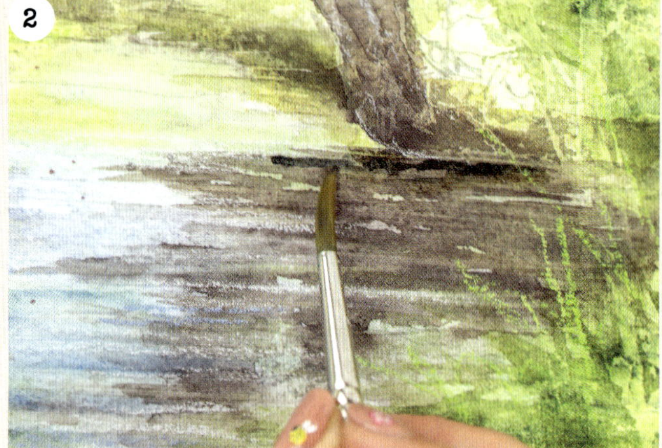

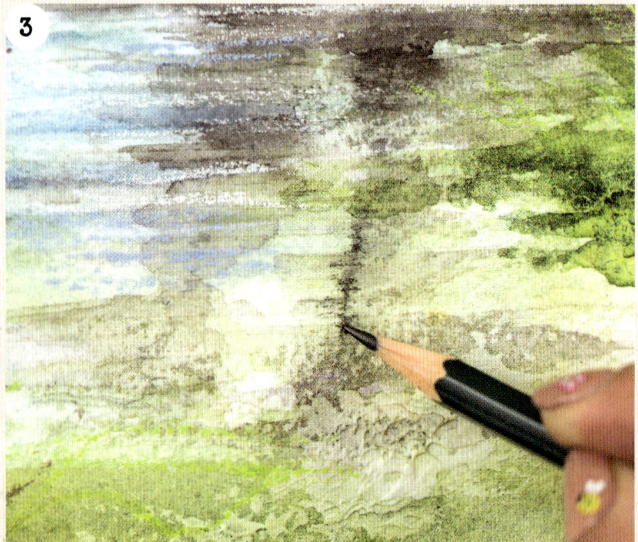

1 If your water surface needs to look flat, it's important that your brush strokes aid this – don't let them tip up or down, or the water will look as though it's flowing against gravity.

2 Mix up strong darks to show the depth of the water. Integrate some of the surrounding colour to make it relevant.

3 Play with reflections by observing what shapes are above the water and create a fuzzy version below. It may be easier to turn your painting 90° or even upside down so that you can more easily re-create the shapes.

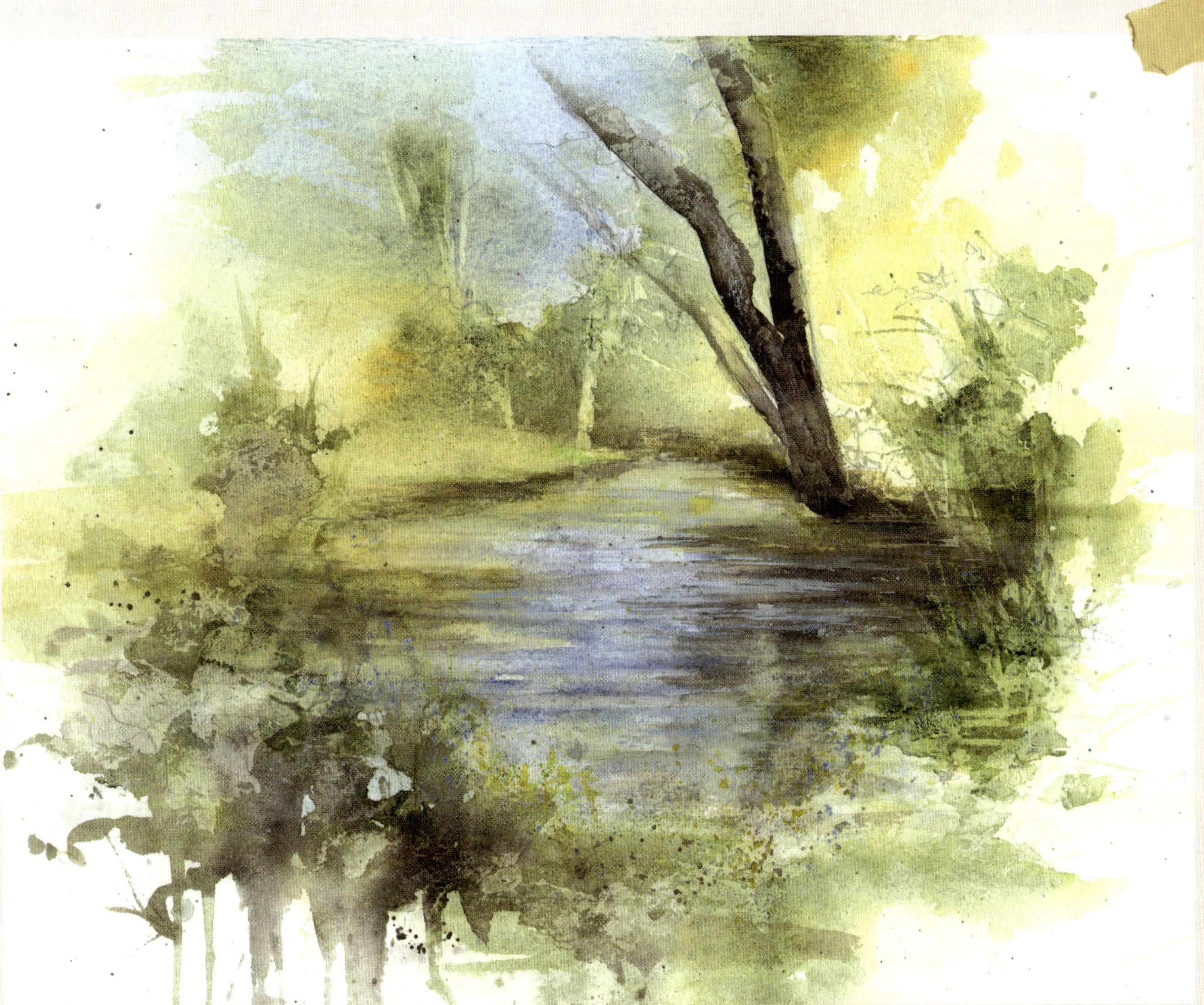

Bend in the River

I started this painting out on location and then finished it in the studio. The day was very bright, and the sun was making the white paper difficult to paint on due to glare. So I returned to the calm of the studio to work out how to depict it, adding the extra details I have described opposite to refine the composition.

Small bodies of water

Sometimes, little pockets of water such as puddles or ponds prove to be trickier to depict than large, deep expanses of water. You need to be able to capture their reflective properties and have the shape make sense in the surrounding landscape. Pay close attention to what colours you can see and how any reflected shapes show the surface tension. Make lots of sketches and experiment with different media to see which records it best.

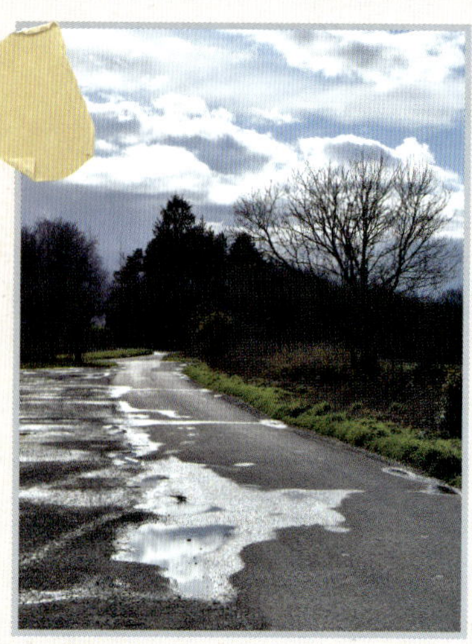

Bulbarrow, Dorset, UK

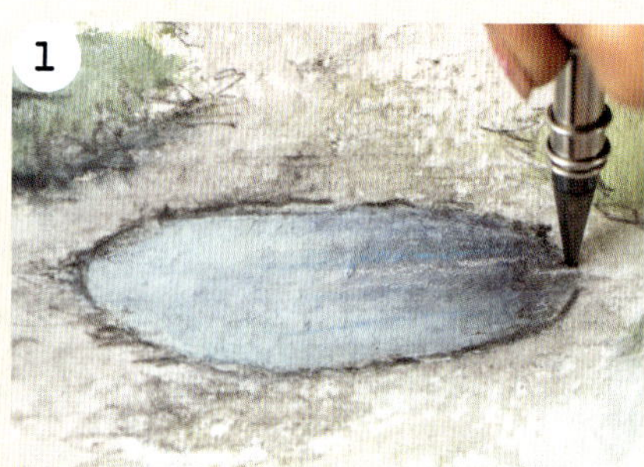

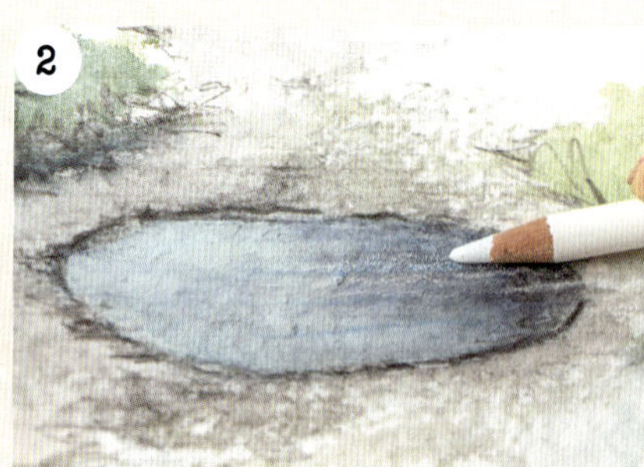

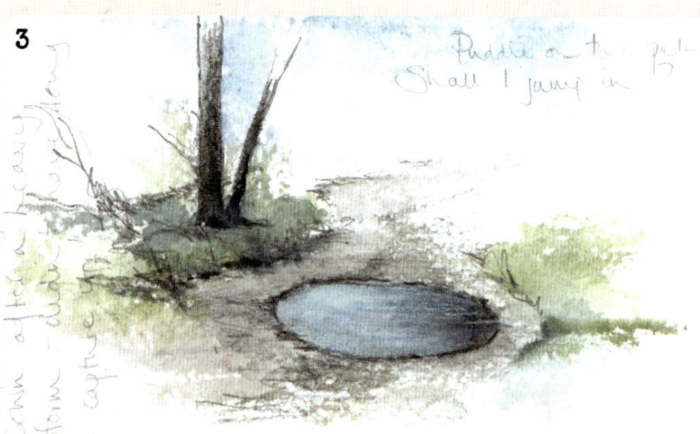

1 A great exercise if you are out on location is to spend time observing the water and how it changes with the light or weather. There are often hard, dark edges to puddles and ponds. Observe them and darken them where necessary.

2 Adding highlights to the surface with a white pastel pencil or white pen can help show the reflective quality of the water.

3 Make small sketches or notes about what you see so that if your photographs don't capture it adequately, you have more information to use.

Bulbarrow puddle study
The tarmac of the road was a real challenge to paint so here I started with a coloured paper, choosing instead to add charcoal and white pastel for the texture and water.

Moving water

Water that is moving – across a shore or over rocks, for instance – has a real draw for the landscape painter: I'm not sure if it's the drama of it or the fact that it provides the opportunity to show movement – no matter what entices you to want to paint moving water, it can certainly make a painting more exciting.

This is where my love of mixing media comes into play: rather than trying to make just one paint or tool do it all, it is much more fun to discover what textures can be made by combining them. Here, as with the experiments with mountains on page 66, I use various white media to show how the light hits the ripples in the water.

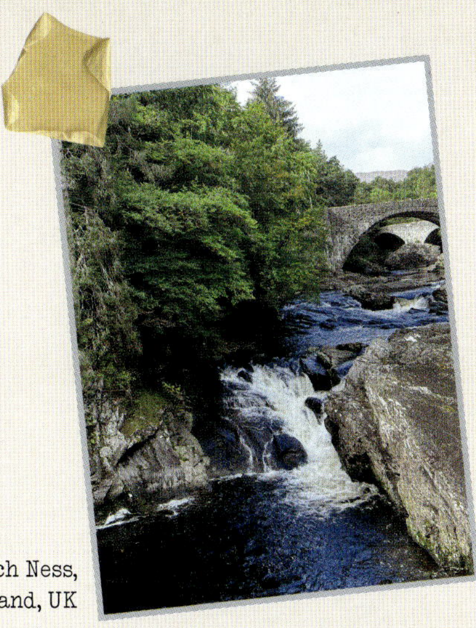

Invermoriston Falls, Loch Ness,
Scotland, UK

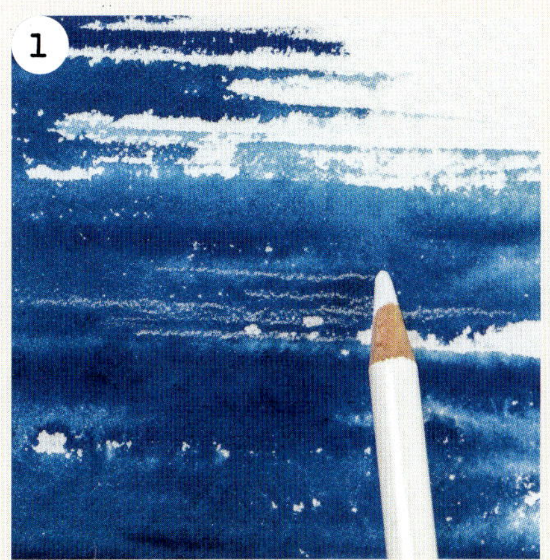

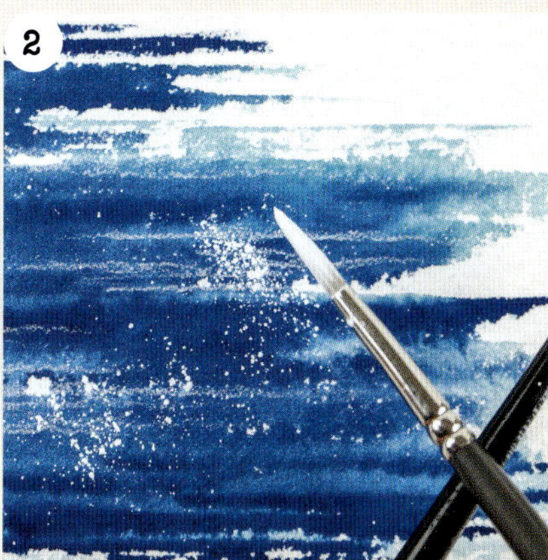

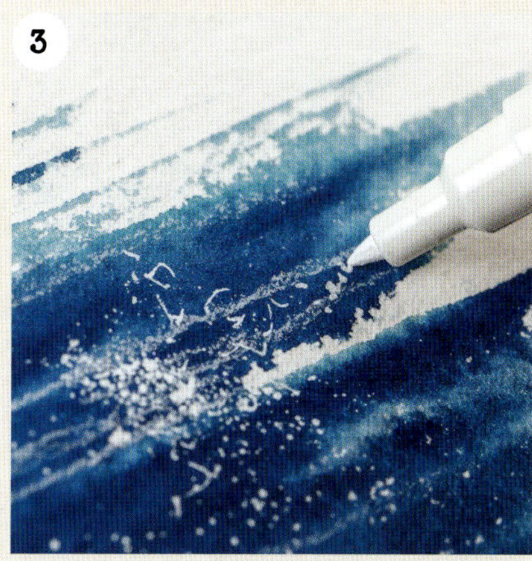

1 A white chalk pastel dragged over a dark wash can break up flat areas of colour and demonstrate the foamy quality of water.

2 Using white gouache or ink, spattered in small areas, can show where water is hitting another surface.

3 To create a swirling pattern as the water falls or pools, try applying a white paint marker over darker areas. (I favour Posca permanent acrylic paint markers.)

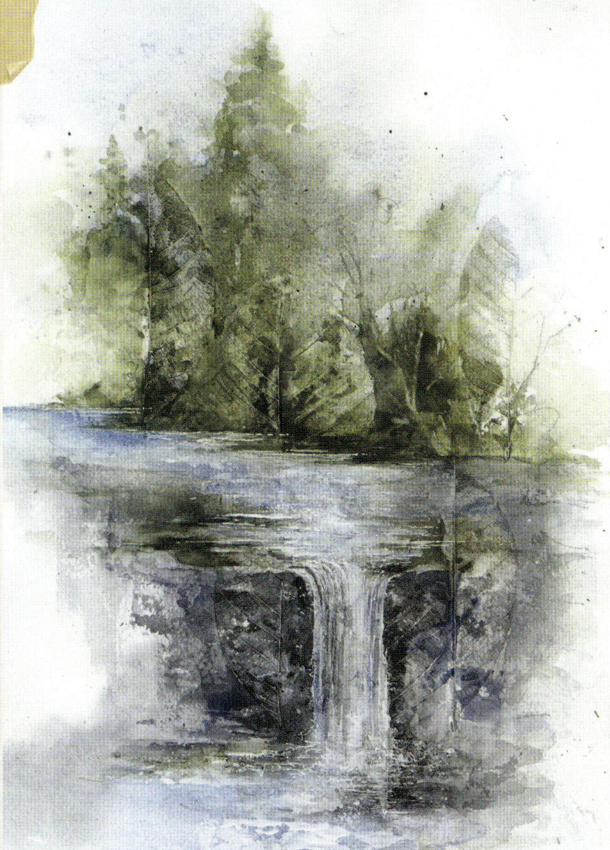

Moriston Falls

This painting, which shows a scene a little further along the River Moriston from the falls in the photograph above, combines collage in the form of dried leaves stuck to watercolour paper for the texture, and watercolour to show the clarity of the water. Not every combination of media will work but it is great fun experimenting. Here I used white gouache and paint marker to show the patterns of the water as it hit the rocks.

Weather and seasons

Capturing the weather or seasons in your painting can truly set the mood of a piece. Weather captured in your sketchbook will remind you of the time of year you were on location; similarly, capturing challenging weather such as a storm (see pages 26–27) can be a positive way of adding atmosphere. Inclement weather is exciting to express and if you prefer not to be out in it, a well-chosen window will afford you comfort while still allowing you to witness the drama.

Seasons need a carefully considered colour palette depending on your location, and different weathers themselves can require a specific set of techniques to capture the spontaneity of the event. If you compare the *Storm Bert* painting on pages 26–27 with this photograph of the Bore Hole, you can see that one is all about texture and dramatic movement whereas this is much smoother and calmer with brighter, hazier colours.

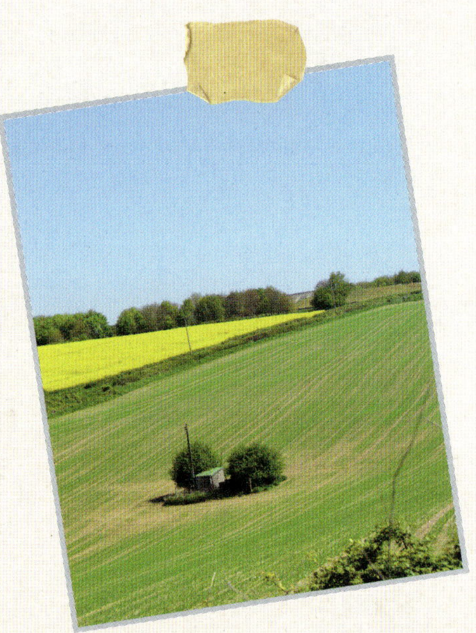

Bore Hole, Downend Farm, Dorset, UK

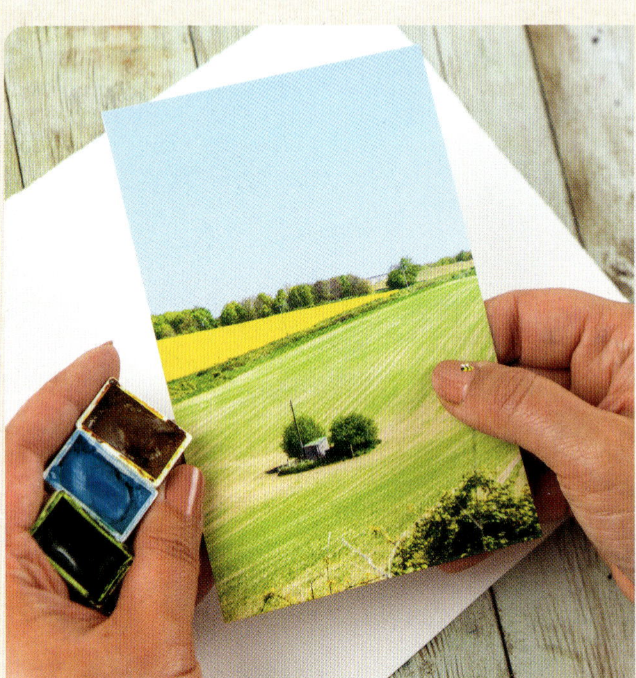

1 Besides the individual elements of your landscape (trees, water, hills and so on), observe which colours link the scene together. Can you reduce the number of colours you need so that it doesn't become too busy?

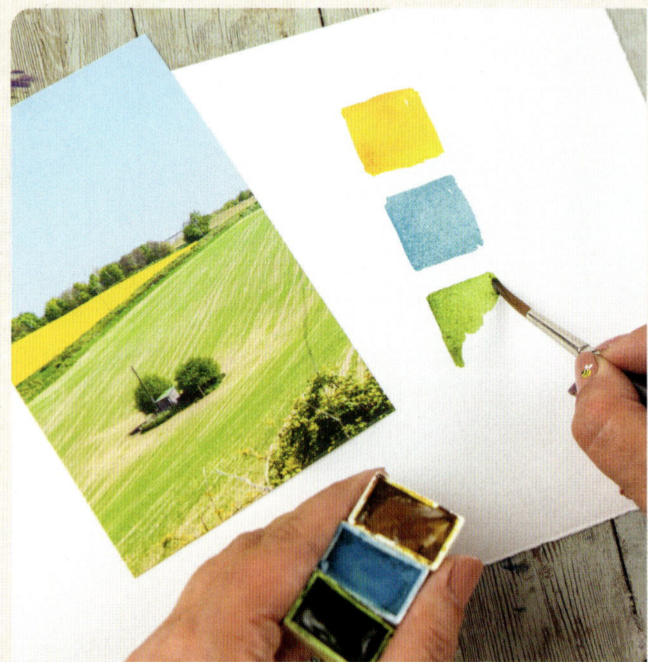

2 Test out the colours to see how they work together and what mixes can be achieved, before committing them to a painting. Memory sketches can sometimes be a great way to experiment with your colour combinations first (see pages 22–23).

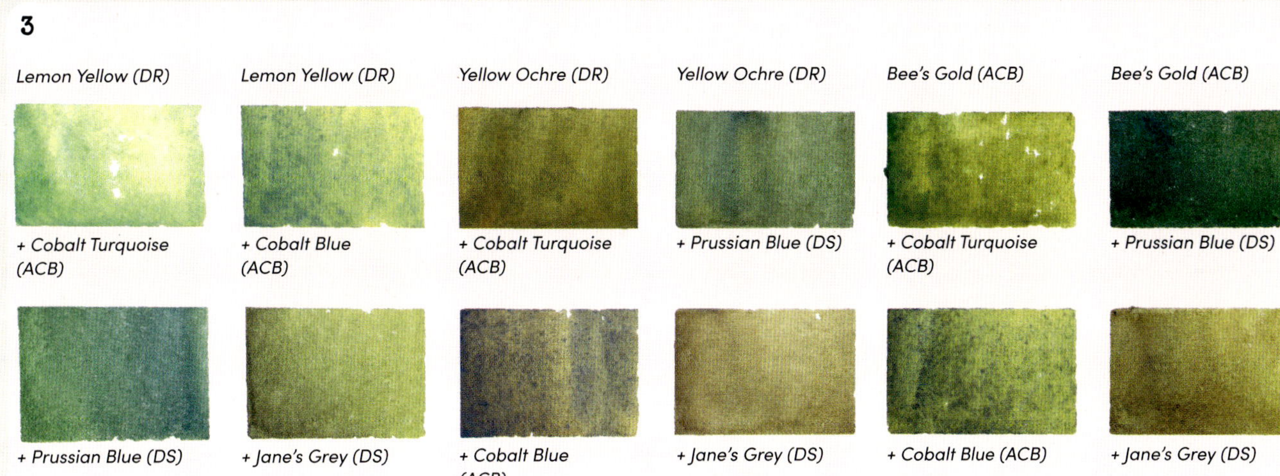

3 Keep a journal of the colours you have used so that you can refer to it next time.

Legend

DR: Daler-Rowney;
ACB: The Alison C. Board Collection;
my own brand of paint;
DS: Daniel Smith.

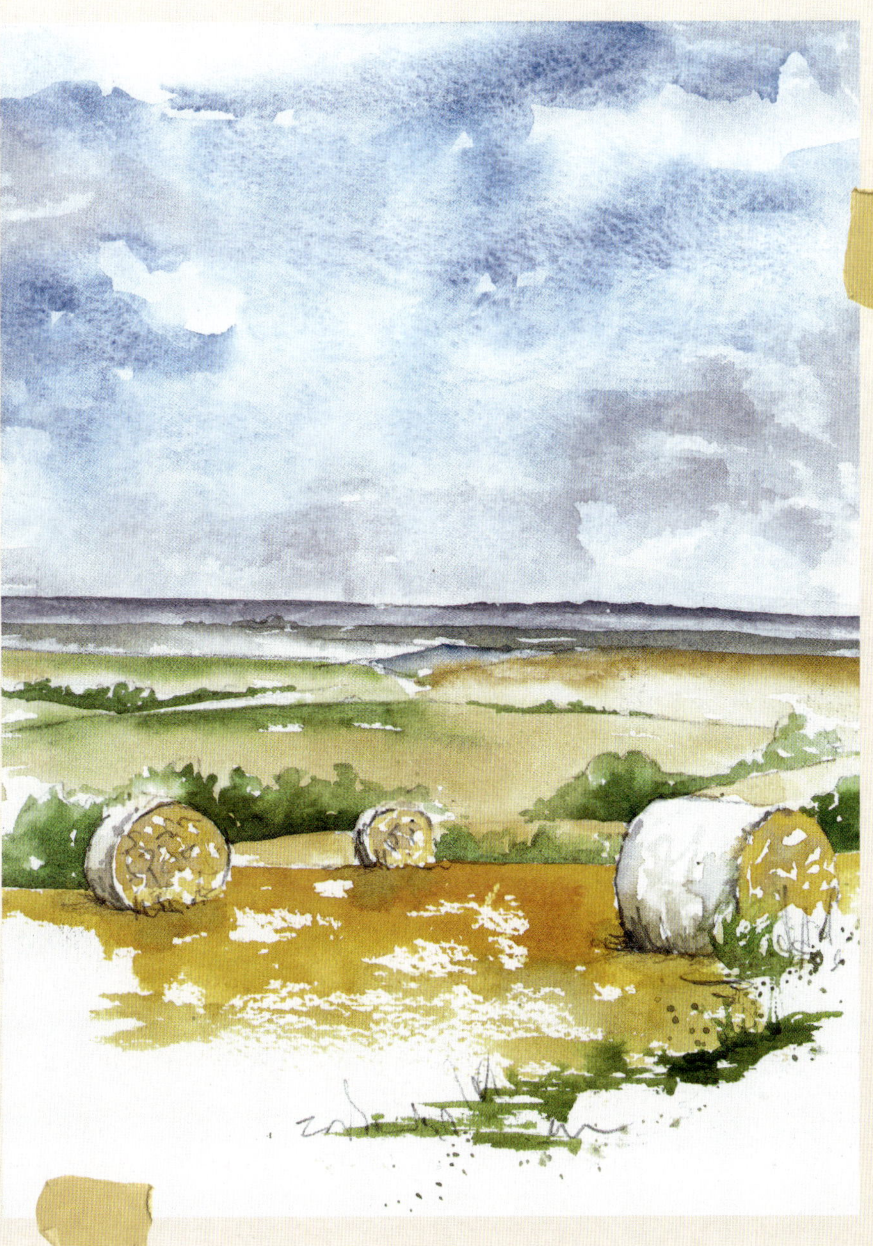

Harvest

A quick watercolour study captured the changing light and the warmth of the stubble left after the straw bales had been made.

Lost edges

When we talk about the changing seasons or weather events, in painting terms we are actually talking about the nature of light. The changing light and the properties that light bestows on objects before us are what tell us if it's hot, cold, dark, sunny – or anything in between.

On page 70, we observed that blurring the area where objects stop and start helps us to portray atmosphere; it's worth noting that doing so can also help us depict a weather event or a time of year.

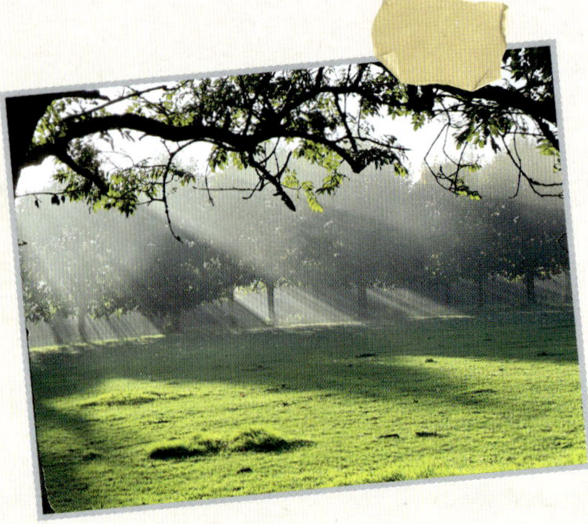

The Green, Downend Farm, Dorset, UK
As the sunlight passes in front of the trees you can see the effect it has on the shapes beyond, softening them and giving atmosphere.

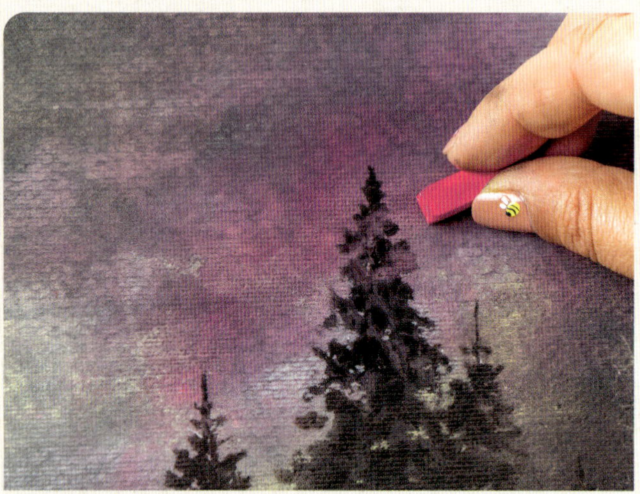

1 Soft pastels are an ideal medium for achieving blurred edges as they are highly editable. Use unusually vibrant coloured pastels – such as hot pink – to great effect in contrast with the surface colour shown in step 3.

2 Use blending tools such as sponges, cotton buds (swabs) or paper stumps to get the amount of blur you are looking for.

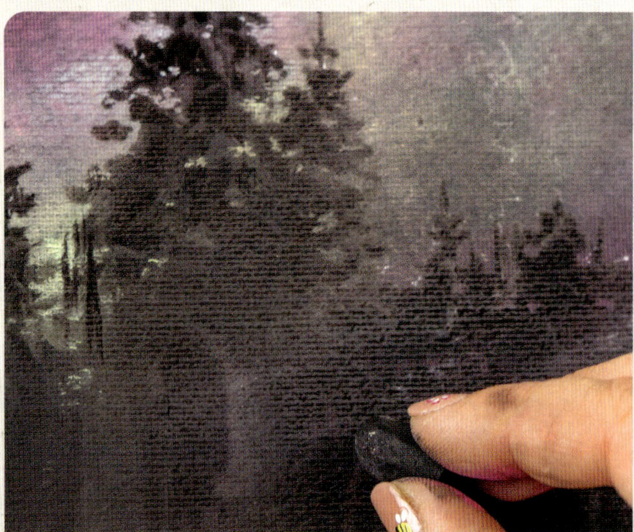

3 Consider a chalk pastel or a paint that is the same colour as the surface you are working on in order to blend shapes into the background more.

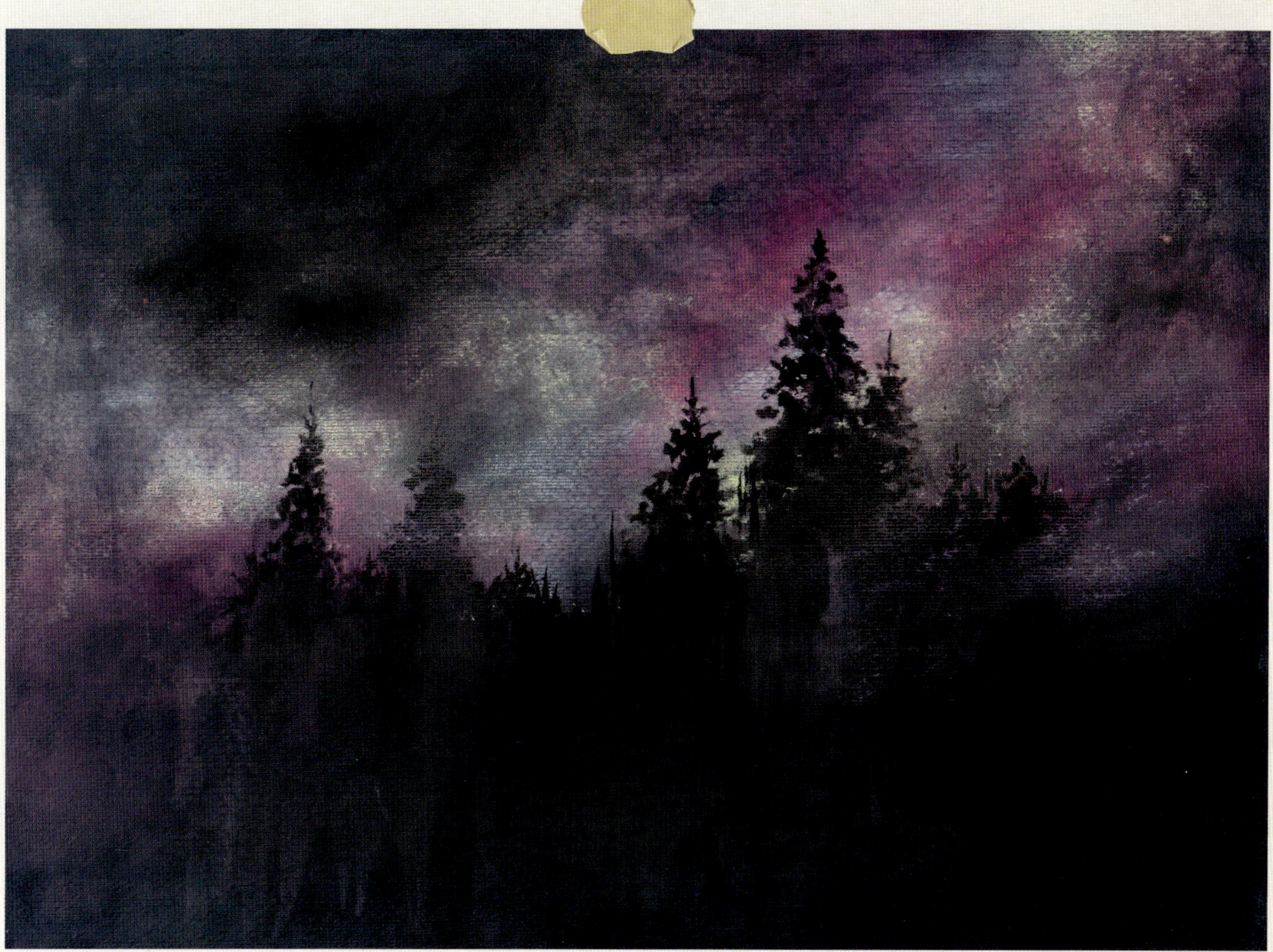

Lost Trees

This painting is a combination of two observations: one is the last, dying seconds of a sunset; the other the silhouettes of trees on a horizon.

Using lost edges can help us not only to suggest light but also to depict distance so that not all the elements appear flat and in a line.

Capturing the whole picture

By 'capturing the whole picture', I mean making sure to include the effect that the weather has on the landscape itself. It's no good coming to paint a snow scene and capturing the colours, the lost edges and the flakes falling from the sky if you don't then record how these look on the ground. Rain will form puddles; sunshine will create dry earth; and snow will settle and reflect the colours around it.

Try to tell the whole story if you are painting the whole scene – you will then fully convince your viewer of what effect the weather or season is having on the environment.

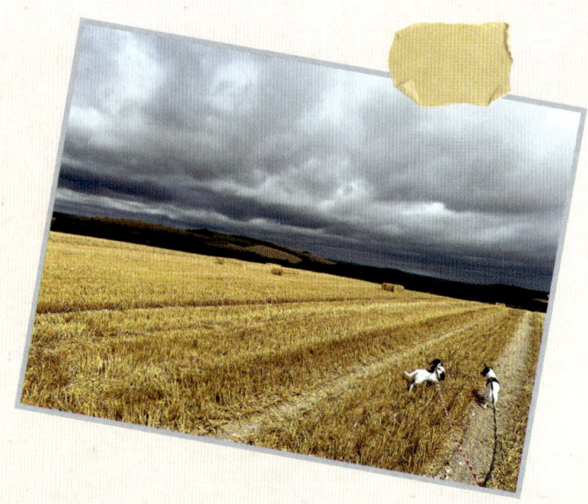
Stormy harvest, Downend Farm, Dorset, UK

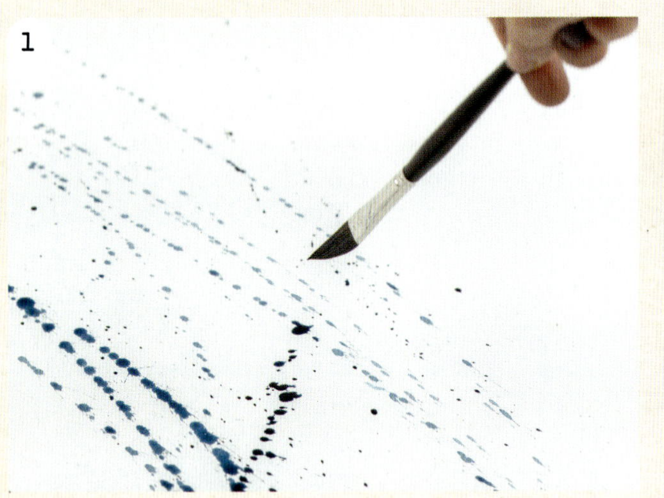

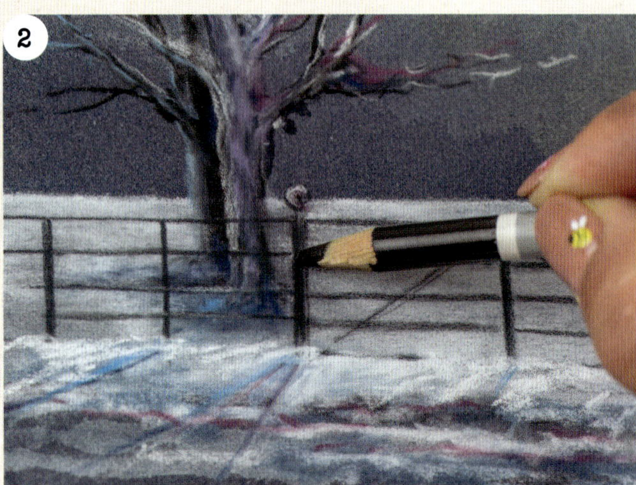

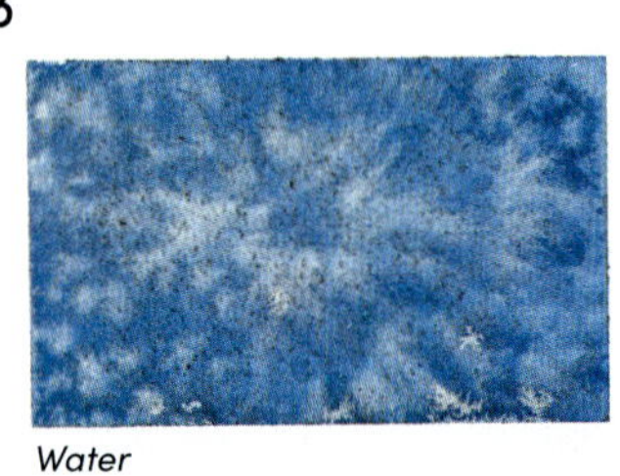
Water

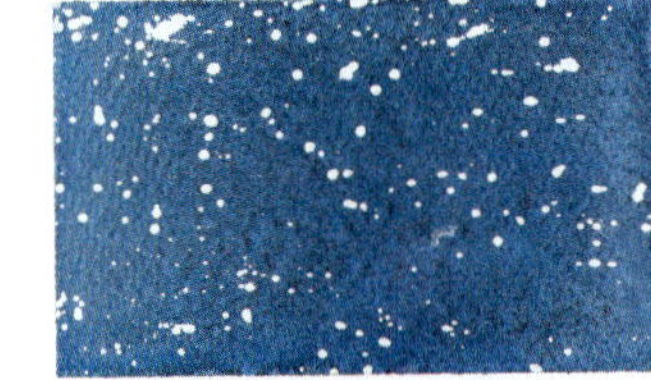
Posca (acrylic paint marker pen)

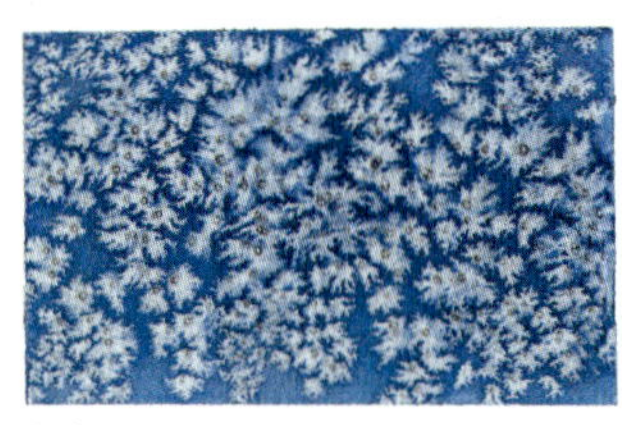
Salt

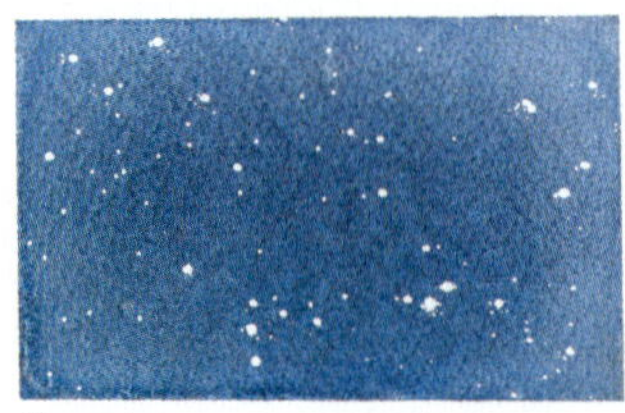
Gouache

1 Both snow and rain are fun to record – they can be shown with energetic strokes as they fall through the sky or dramatic textures when they hit the ground. My favourite technique, spattering, is helpful here.

2 Be brave with darks to show a storm on the horizon, or the white of the snow. You can use dark paint tones but here I am using a black pastel pencil.

3 Combine media to best effect: a chalk pastel ably shows off the texture of snow, while something more liquid such as paint or ink demonstrates rain falling heavily. I also love to drop water or salt into wet watercolour to create light highlights, or to spatter with a paint marker or gouache once the watercolour has dried.

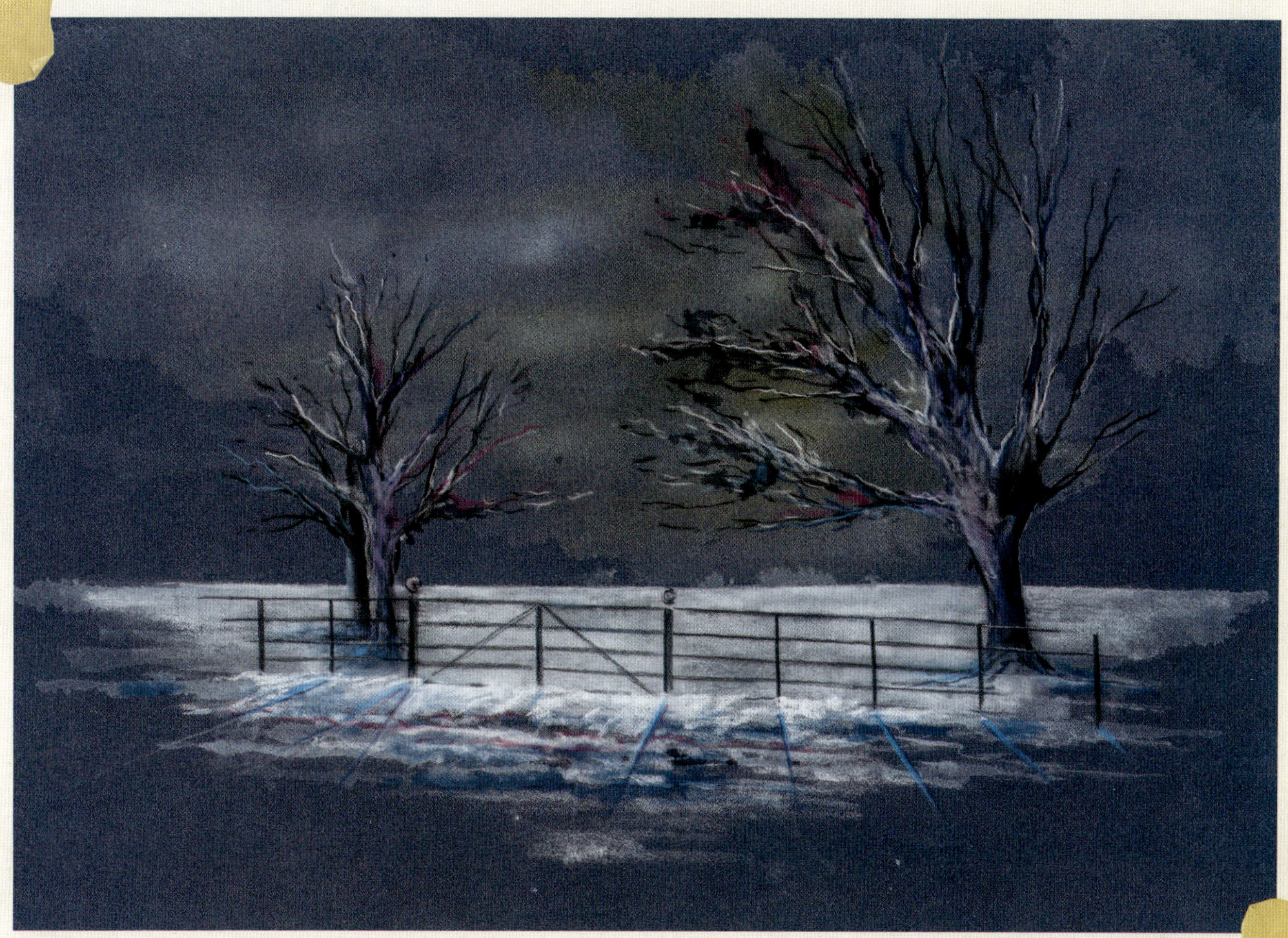

Snowy Green

This painting is a good example of how the weather emphasizes other elements in the scene. The snow shows off the structure of the fence in the same way that the storm clouds, in the photo opposite, top right, show off the warm colours of the field.

The elusive rainbow

I don't mind admitting that a rainbow is an element that I am still trying to include in my paintings. I want my rainbows to look ethereal – as if they are not quite there – but I also want them to be a key feature, so they need to stand out.

Ever the tenacious artist, I've become quite obsessed with rainbows, taking photos of them whenever and wherever I can, and experimenting with numerous mediums to see what captures them most effectively.

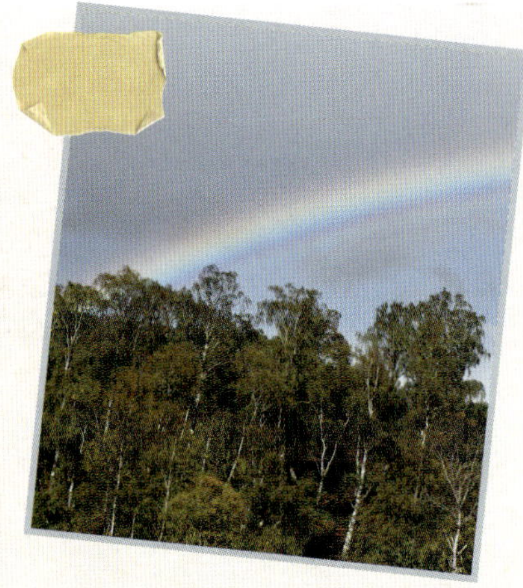

Ceannacroc, Scottish Highlands, Scotland, UK

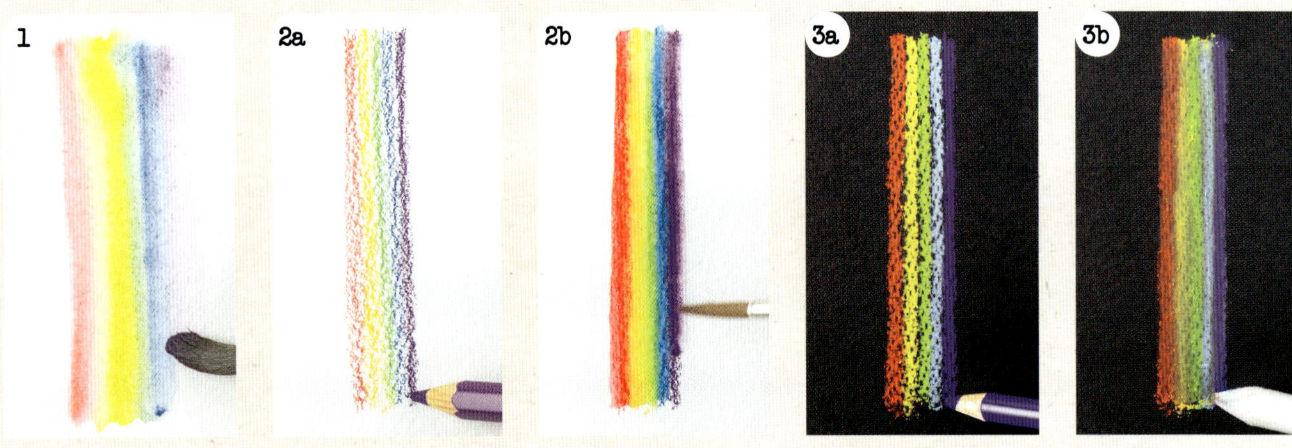

1 Wet-into-wet watercolour (adding paint to wet paper) works well to achieve blurred edges. Experiment with how long you leave the paper wet before applying any colour.

2 Watercolour pencils make adding colour easier as you have more control over a pencil than a paintbrush. The pressure with which you apply the pencil is worth experimenting with too. Then, just add water with your brush.

3 Pastels may work better than watercolour for depicting rainbows, in terms of being able to smudge them (here I'm smudging with a paper blending stump) and also being able to control where the colour sits.

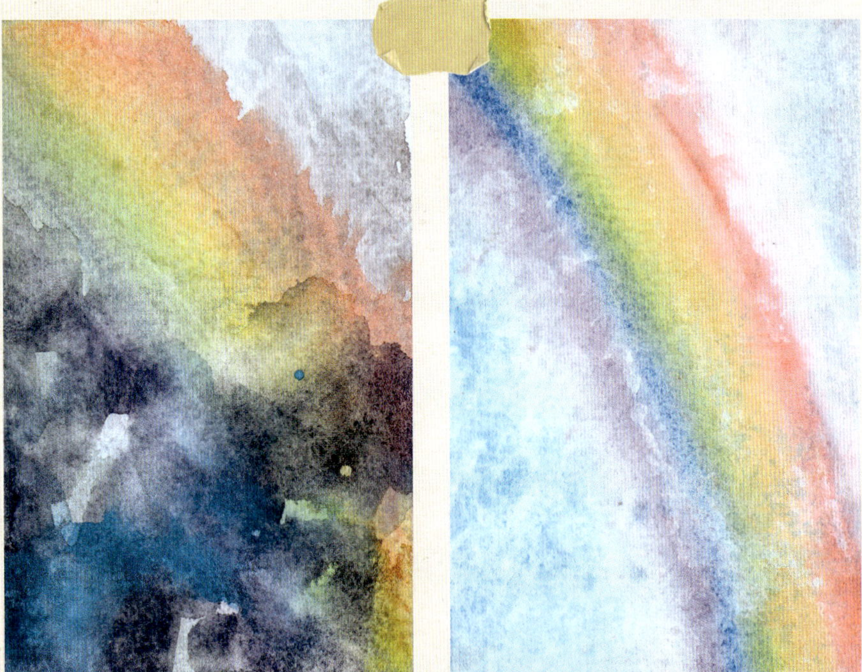

Rainbow memory sketches
Not bound by the formality of a final painting, I have enjoyed featuring rainbows in my memory sketches to experiment with how to apply them in my future work.

CONCLUSION

There is a never-ending array of pieces to the jigsaw puzzle of a painting; and there are several ways of approaching each one; this chapter has covered only a few. Some methods covered are favourites of mine; some are common to all landscape painters, and others have been included as I am currently battling with them myself.

My advice is to practise each element in isolation and then slowly introduce it to more complicated compositions, experimenting with different mediums as you go. This is not the only way of tackling these landscape elements, however – we will move on to some imaginative ways of interpreting them in the next chapter.

5 Creative thinking

It can be very easy to feel overwhelmed when contemplating a painting project, and we often revert to our default settings, trusting what we know in order to be able to tackle it. These defaults can help us to develop <u>some</u> skills but can also hinder us in discovering something new. We might default to using materials that we haven't necessarily thought through, settling for painting the first view we come across, or losing confidence in the process, all of which serves to put us off from putting brush to paper.

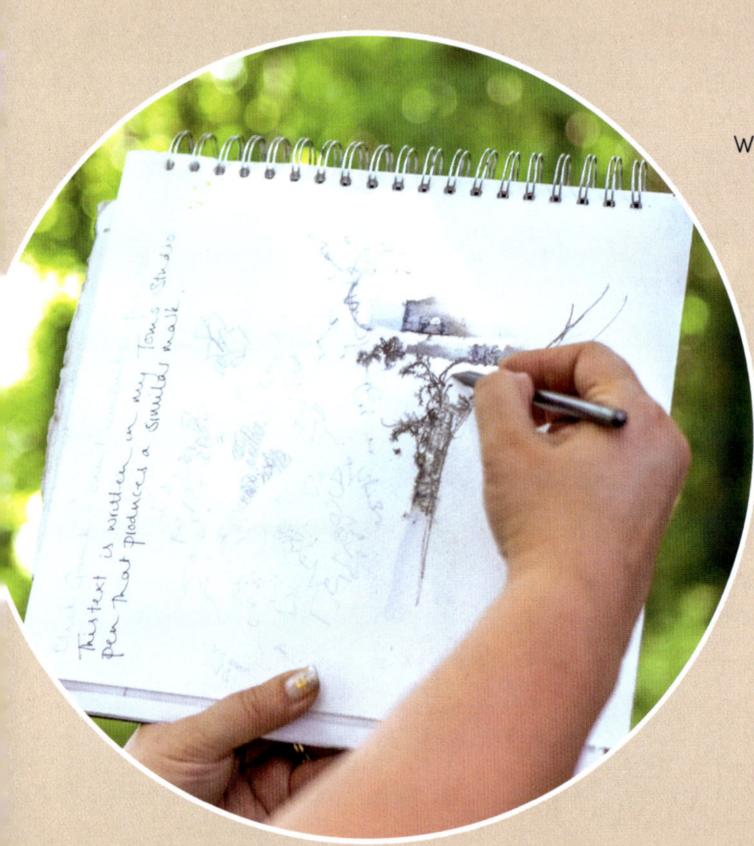

What I try to do, every time I put my creative hat on, is ask myself what it is that I want from what I'm about to do. Then I prod myself a little harder and think about how I can make it happen in an exciting way that means I'm truly expressing myself and starting to think creatively.

Creative thinking isn't necessarily about making everything new and unique – it's about exploring your individuality. It's a way of discovering ideas original to you, and making connections between them. For me, this usually happens in the form of a technique or a way of including an unusual element in a painting. These novel techniques help me to communicate something extra – a way of showing the viewer the story of the location, or its importance to me in the hope that it will trigger understanding or familiarity in others.

Combining traditional and unusual techniques is what I always strive for in my work; that way, the result is unique to me and therefore very fulfilling to achieve.

Opposite, <u>Cornwall Birches</u>

530 × 730mm (20⅞ × 28¾in)
A painting created with collage techniques. The collage has the words 'Silver Birch' printed on it in a medieval language. (See page 108 for more information on my collage techniques.)

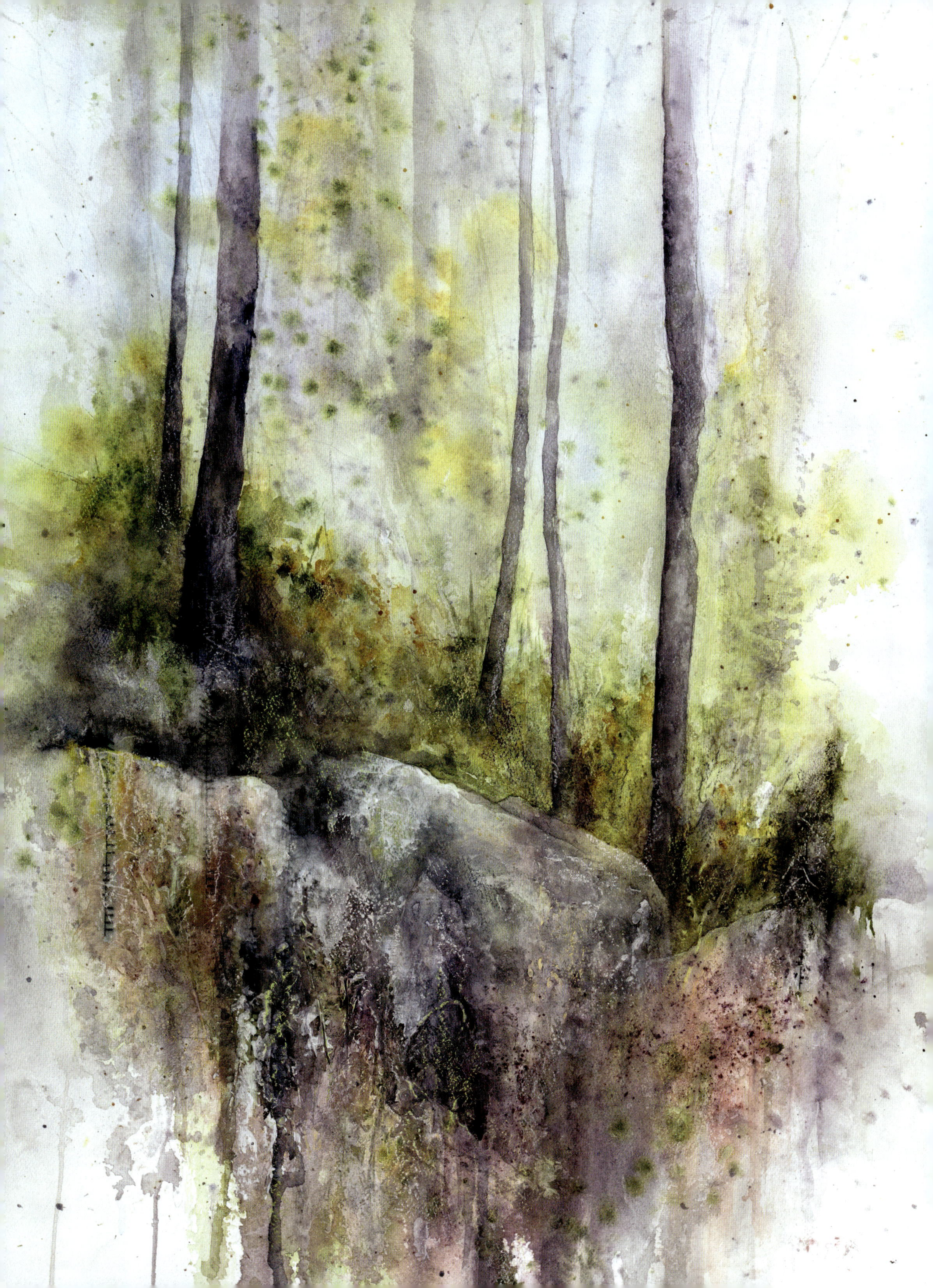

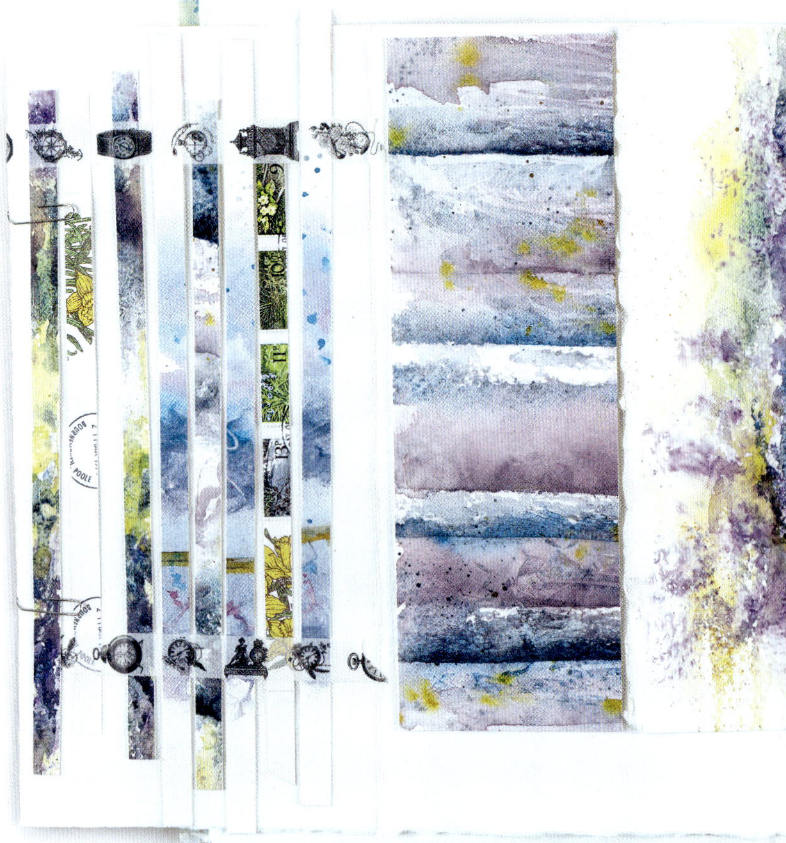

CONSIDERING CREATIVE THINKING

It's important to note here that, when I use the word 'thinking', I don't mean that you should spend your whole time hypothesizing about what you are about to paint. Creative thinking can be done on the page through experimentation, annotation, using new materials or tools or mark making, to name just a few examples.

For me, another advantage of creative thinking – aside from artistic output – is that it has an incredible effect on my wellbeing, leading to positivity which, in turn, helps me to think more creatively.

At the risk of getting cerebral, and not wanting to dive too deeply into the perils of artistic angst, there will inevitably come a point when you want to find connections between you and your subject. When I first started painting, I'd paint anything and everything – whatever felt most achievable. It was only when my skills grew that I started to be more selective with what I chose to paint and why.

As we touched upon in chapter 1, landscapes are a brilliant artistic gateway into asking yourself why you want to paint a subject, and what it means to you, as we all have personal connections to a location.

When you have identified your connection to your subject, the next step is to find creative ways of expressing that in your painting. Your instant reaction to what I am suggesting throughout this chapter may be, 'I've never been able to do this' or 'I don't know how to go about this' so I'm pleased to tell you that it is something you can learn.

By sharing the way I approach my personal projects, you may be inspired to try out some of the techniques, find those that work for you and expand on them with confidence.

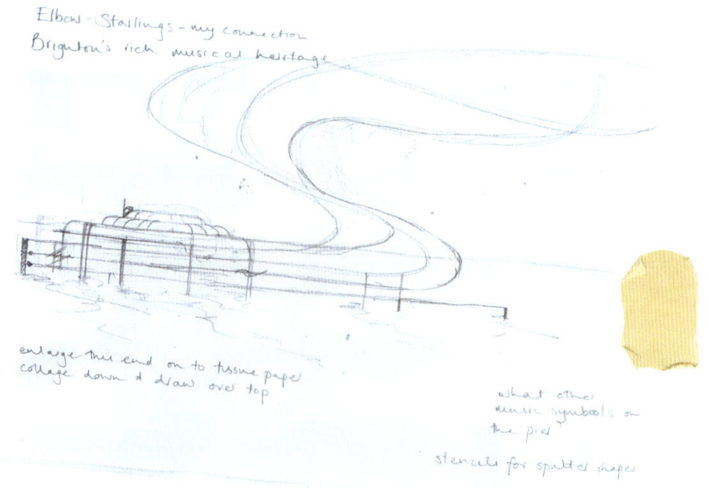

Top-left, memory sketches (see pages 22–23) of a walk in the countryside with my dogs, through fields where I grew up; top-right, using unsuccessful paintings woven together to find new colour and texture combinations; bottom-right, sketched ideas from a trip to Brighton that informed the project on pages 104–105.

CREATIVE LANGUAGE

In chapter 3, we explored how painting fundamentals such as colour, composition and tone can be used to make your landscapes represent what you see – but what if the very thing you are trying to portray can't be pinned down so easily?

I have found that not all traditional painting techniques can describe what I want to communicate, so I regularly look to other disciplines, and appropriate methods from other branches of the creative arts to help me express myself better. I call this 'using creative language'. These might not necessarily be the creative techniques that inspire you personally but they can certainly be a good place to start.

CRAFTS

Assemblage, weaving, paper sculpting, collage – I enjoy exploring techniques that are more three-dimensional alongside the two dimensions of my painting.

PRINTMAKING

Stamping, etching, relief and *chine-collé* (the addition of tissue paper) are some of my favourite printmaking techniques.

THE WRITTEN WORD

Poetry, prose, creative and descriptive writing can be powerful to include. I find the words of other writers inspiring, and even on occasion take the time to write something myself.

THE PROJECTS IN THIS CHAPTER

The four projects I share over the next few pages illustrate the practicalities of adding alternative techniques to my repertoire. Each of these projects has a particular significance to me, and uses methods of connecting ideas that you might not have previously considered.

Ahead of creating each of these four projects, I worked through my ideas in my sketchbook and through photographs I had taken or discovered, and undertook a little online research to fill any holes in my knowledge:

- *Brighton Pier* (pages 104–105) explores storytelling through punched text, using the words of poet and polymath Oliver Wendell Holmes Sr;
- *Frosty Sunrise* (pages 106–107) uses maps of a specific geographic location to add a layer of collage to the painting;
- *Abereiddy* (pages 108–109): a rubbing of a wall provides the textures and colours of a location, and is collaged on to the surface before painting;
- *Letters from the Rock* (pages 110–111) incorporates text, including my own creative writing, to 'tie' me to the location and the meaning behind the painting.

The last things I did before embarking on any of these projects were to create a set of memory sketches (see left) and to use the flow chart on page 13 so that I could test out my thoughts before committing to a final piece.

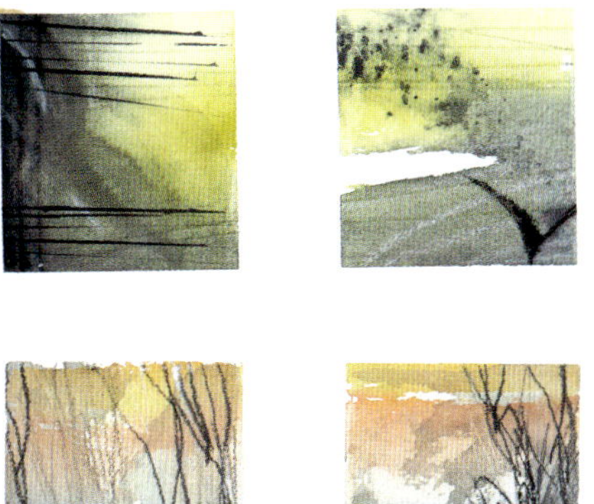

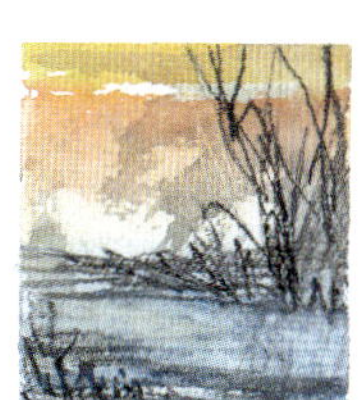
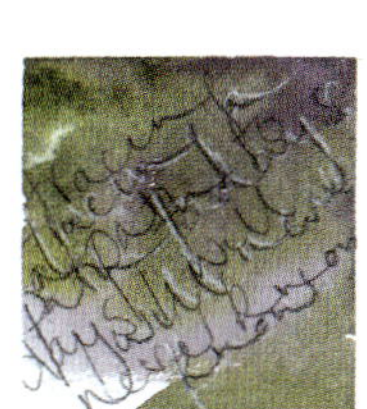
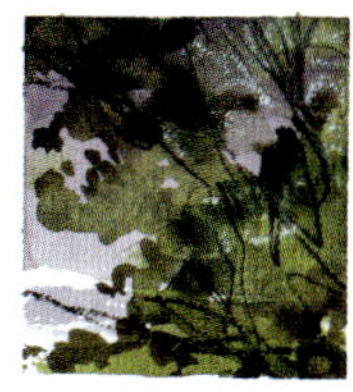
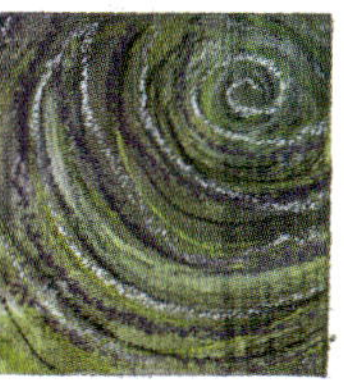

Memory sketches
Brighton Pier, Frosty Sunrise *and* Letters from the Rock.

CREATIVE LANGUAGE MATERIALS

In order to express interesting ideas and techniques, you need materials that can turn them into 'language' – that is, the way you express or communicate those ideas.

I have already touched on a few of these ideas – the addition of chalk pastels and inks being one example – but there are myriad other materials, some of which you may find you already have or can acquire at low cost.

GLUES AND TEXTURES

If you are thinking of including collage, you will need a good adhesive to anchor it to your surface. My favourites are those that are waterproof when dry so that you can't disturb your collage when painting or drawing back over the top.

I also enjoy adding gesso or watercolour ground, often over the top of collage to disguise or emphasize it, while interfering with my colour in some way.

TEXTURE-MAKING TOOLS

From a humble piece of Lego, through sponges and sticks to more complex texture stencils, anything that has the potential to make marks can be interesting for your paintings. On pages 52–55 I explain how these are integral to my work; you may wish to push the techniques further by using these tools to remove colour, or use them alongside textures to create interesting patterns.

PRINTMAKING

Any tool or object that transfers colour to (or removes it from) your surface can be classed as a printmaking tool. Even the most basic print from a leaf or a potato can often break up large areas of a composition and give them greater significance. Alternatively, you can include alphabet stamps and punches to convey the written word.

UNUSUAL COLOUR CHOICES

There is no reason at all why you have to stick to conventional colour schemes if they don't inspire you. The addition of metallics (as described on page 84) or even fluorescents (see page 34, and pages 140–145) can provide a 'pop' of colour where it is most needed.

Some of my favourite tools and materials

1 Bindex – an acrylic medium that acts as an adhesive
2 Gesso – an acrylic medium for texture
3 Watercolour ground – a medium applied to a surface to make it suitable for painting in watercolours
4 Lego
5 Charcoal pencils
6 Pastel pencils
7 Acrylic paint markers
8 Pastels – these are soft pastels, but oil pastels can be investigated too
9 Inks – acrylic, fountain pen
10 Crystalline (powder) watercolour
11 Metallic powder
12 Gouache
13 Acrylic paint
14 Pastelmat® paper
15 Texture stencils
16 Dip pen
17 Watercolour pencils
18 Tissue paper
19 Sponge
20 Bamboo skewers for mark making
21 Spoon for burnishing paper or collage materials
22 Hammer for letter punches
23 Graphite stick in holder
24 Blending tools
25 Letter punches (lower case).

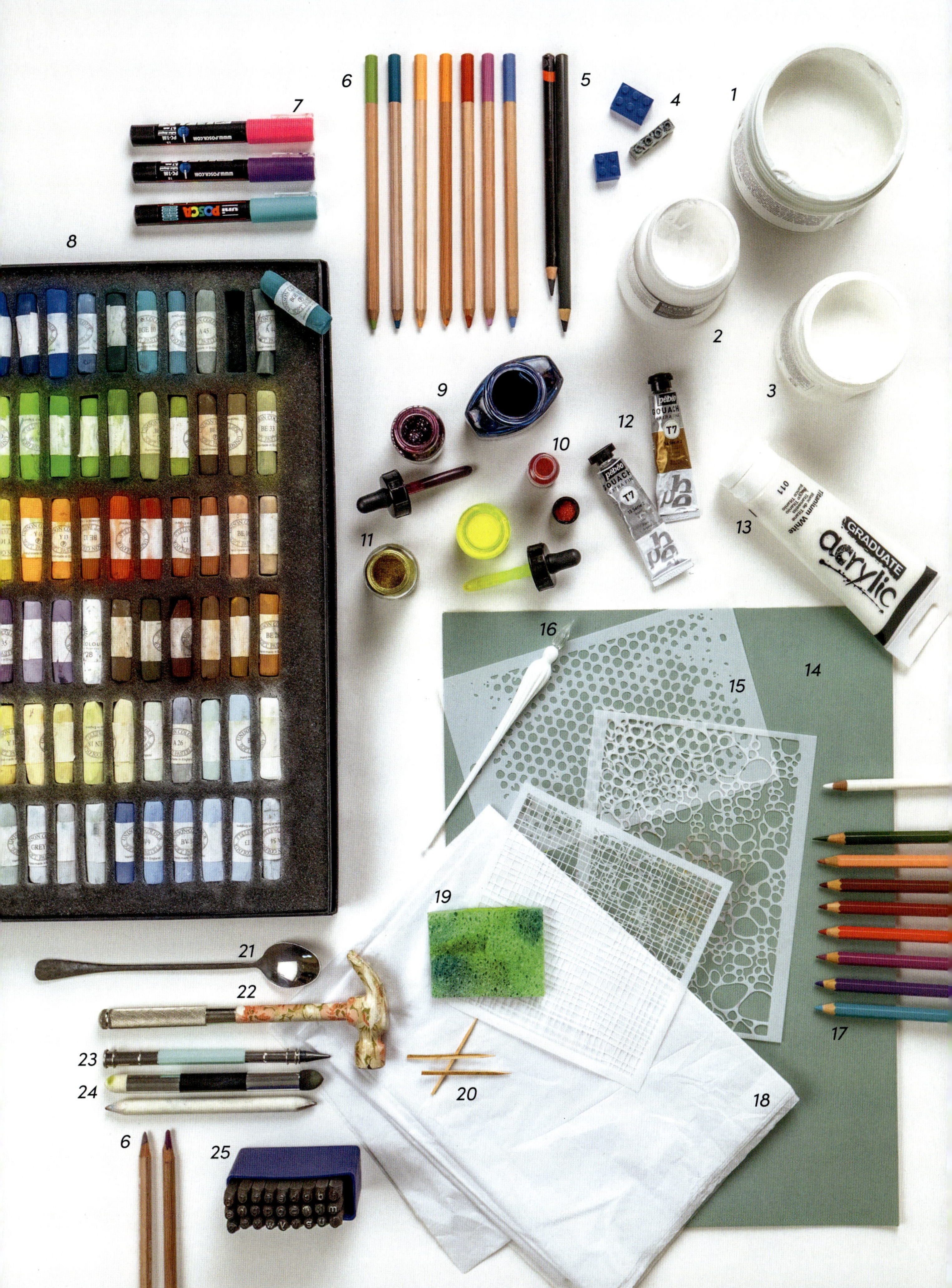

1
2
3
4
5
6
7
8
9
10
11
12
13
14
15
16
17
18
19
20
21
22
23
24
25
6

BRIGHTON PIER

STORYTELLING

Storytelling is your opportunity to share something with the viewer of your painting that goes deeper than just a conventional view of your subject.

I have suggested several things you might consider (*Storm Bert*, pages 26–27; *Ancient Trees*, page 35; and *Between the Dunes*, page 81), one of which is using your imagination to tell more than you see. This was the case with this painting, *Brighton Pier*.

In this piece I wanted not only to convey the significance of Brighton using an element as recognizable as its West Pier, but also to try to portray that, while the structure has long since perished in a fire, the music that is so synonymous with the city lives on.

After a little research, I discovered a poem by Oliver Wendell Holmes Sr. (1809–1894) about Boston Pier; one verse resonated with me, which describes the history of the structure, and the community associated with it:

**For the Centennial Dinner of the Proprietors of Boston Pier,
Or the Long Wharf (April 16, 1873)**

They are gone, friend and foe,—anchored fast at the pier,
Whence no vessel brings back its pale passengers here;
But our wharf, like a lily, still floats on the flood,
Its breast in the sunshine, its roots in the mud.

Using punched text, I was able to include a short phrase that leads along the lines of a musical stave. The text, intertwined with the pier's structure, uses texture and colour to describe it not only as a place but also a feeling.

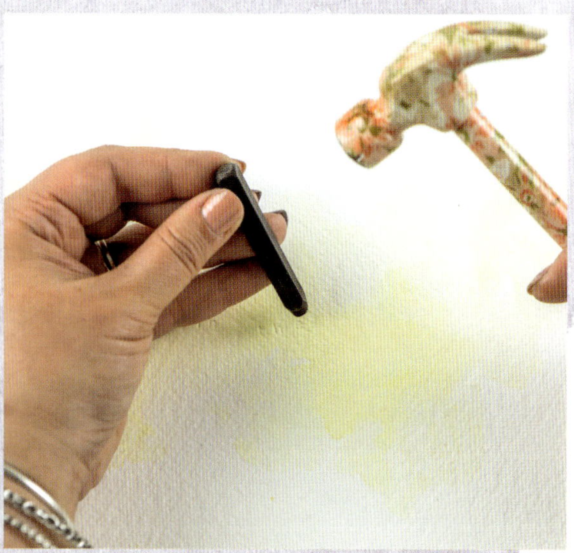

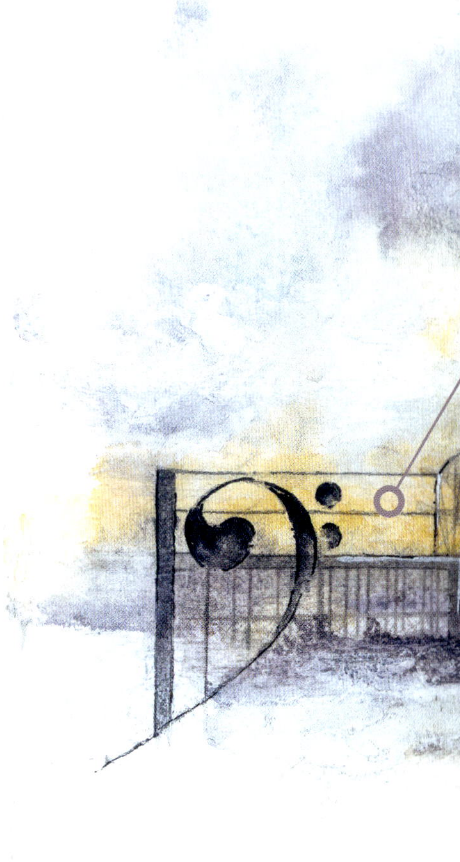

Punches designed for leather and jewellery-making indent the watercolour paper so that the paint settles there.

1 Using the pier structure as a stave;
2 Turning the stave into a murmuration of starlings, a sight famous in Brighton;
3 Textures applied to the water using gesso and a palette knife to repel watercolour;
4 Punched letters spelling out a phrase from the Oliver Wendell Holmes poem.

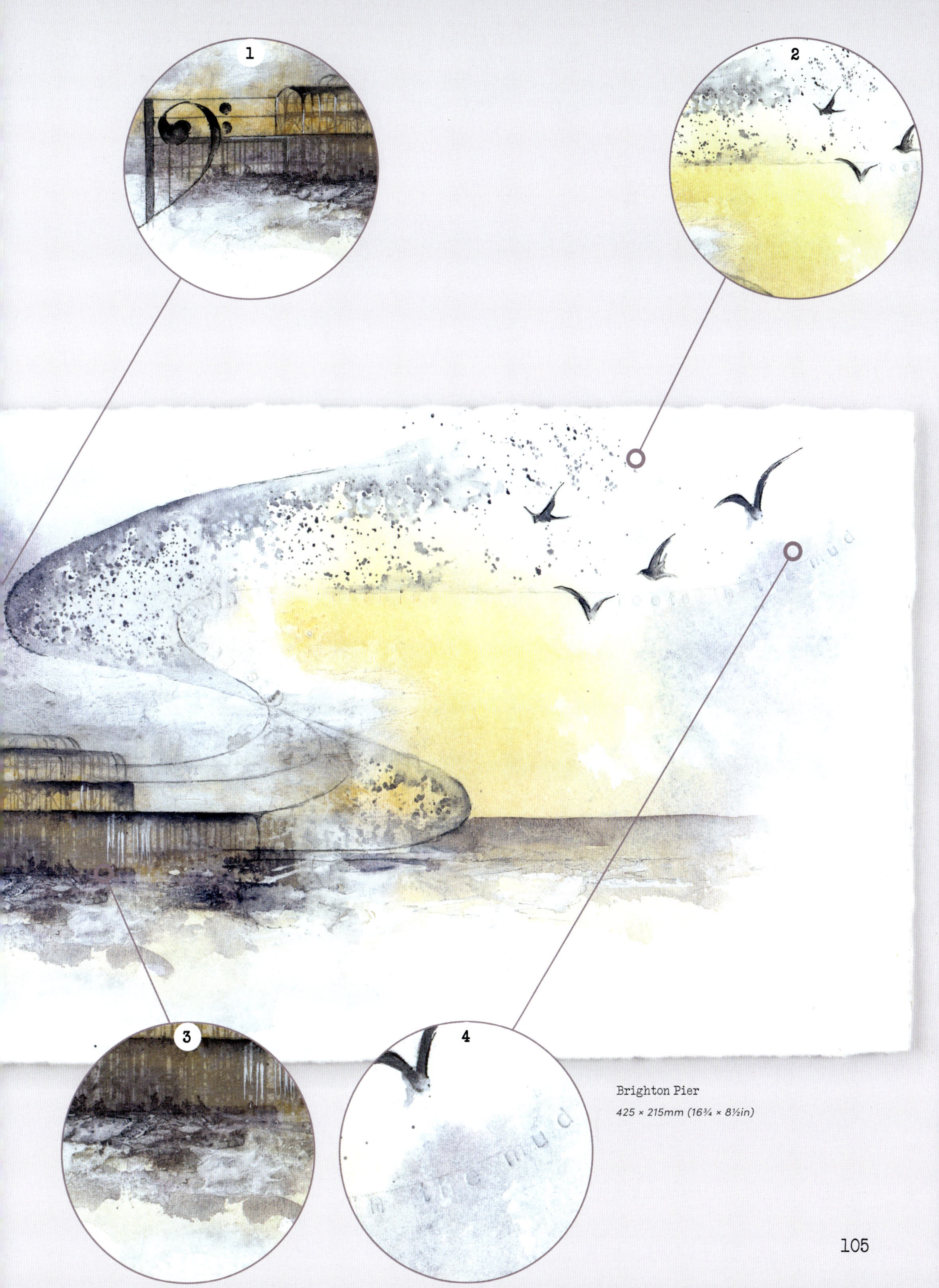

Brighton Pier
425 × 215mm (16¾ × 8½in)

FROSTY SUNRISE

MAPPING

Mapping is a long-used art technique that not only incorporates the use of maps but can also use images or symbols of specific geographic locations to record or tell a story. Authors have often included maps at the start of novels to explain the location of areas so that the reader can envisage where the plot takes place. It's no different for an artist who wishes to ground where they are painting as I have done in *Frosty Sunrise*. I used a very old map of where I live and painted how it looks now, in the cold light of winter, over the top of it.

A WORD ABOUT COPYRIGHT

You can't incorporate any map you find into your work if you intend to sell it; you will need to research what is in the public domain and thus available for you to use without infringement of copyright.

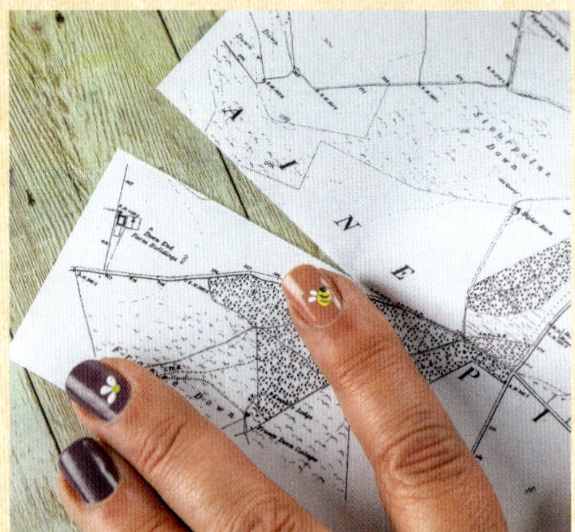

I tore sections of the map that I'd found to exactly match the area of the geography; I tend to prefer torn edges to cut ones as they are softer in appearance. Some I placed off centre to fit the composition and some were in the exact right spot.

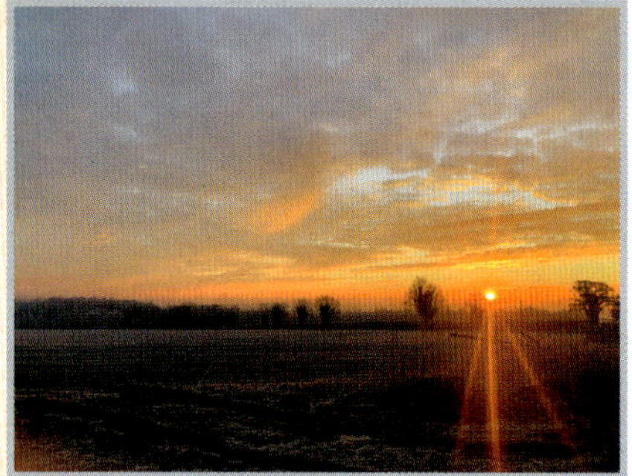

The reference photograph.

DETAILS

1 Sections of map adhered to watercolour paper;

2 Using tissue paper to create further texture on top of the map;

3 Map showing the location and using it for the texture of the distant trees;

4 Using sympathetic colours to complement both the map and the scene.

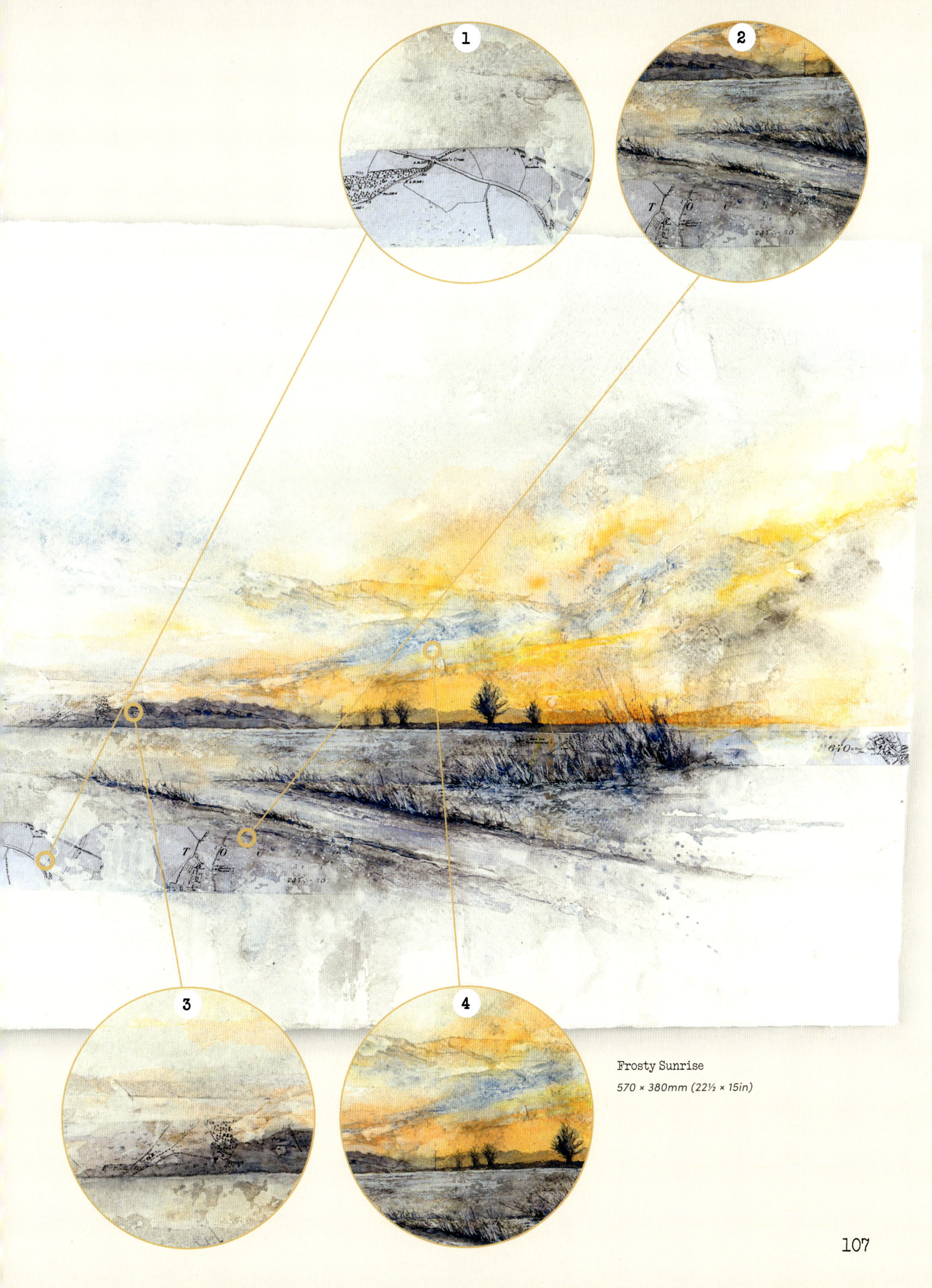

Frosty Sunrise
570 × 380mm (22½ × 15in)

ABEREIDDY

COLLAGE

Collage is a staple technique for me; an element of creativity that I have loved since I was small. I love it because it is so tactile, and it excites me that on occasion I have no control over it, which makes the outcome a surprise.

My painting of Abereiddy, in Pembrokeshire, Wales, incorporates both collage and mapping. While I was on location, I didn't have time to stop and sketch, only to take a photo and to take a rubbing of the wall using tissue paper, which is another technique for mapping a location. When I returned to my studio, I had not only the photograph but also the actual textures that I had collected from the wall, that I could then collage back into the painting.

For these sections of collage, you can apply a glue that will dry clear underneath the texture you are adding. Experiment with the combination of media you have chosen to achieve the most successful results.

Even if you aren't able to visit the exact location of your landscape and take a rubbing, you don't need to deny yourself the opportunity to use this technique. There are numerous surfaces that you can use to take a similar texture sample: a house brick can also make a superb surface for a rubbing.

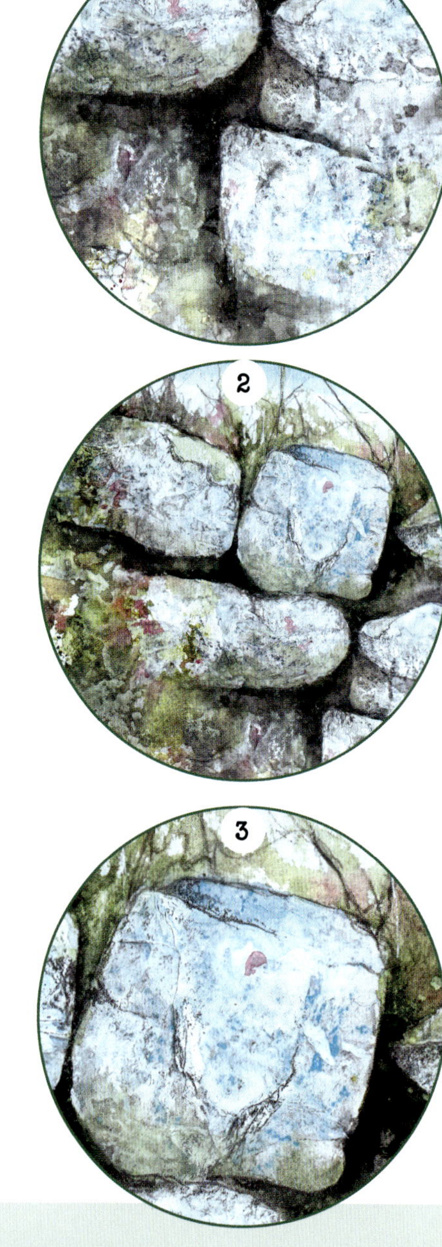

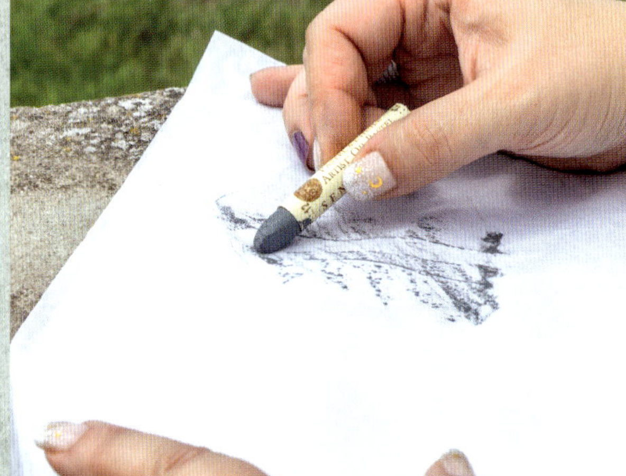

Taking a rubbing using oil pastel on tissue paper.

DETAILS
1 Sections of collage on the rocks;
2 Using dark tones between the rock areas so that the texture of the collage is prominent;
3 Adding graphite back over the top for detail.

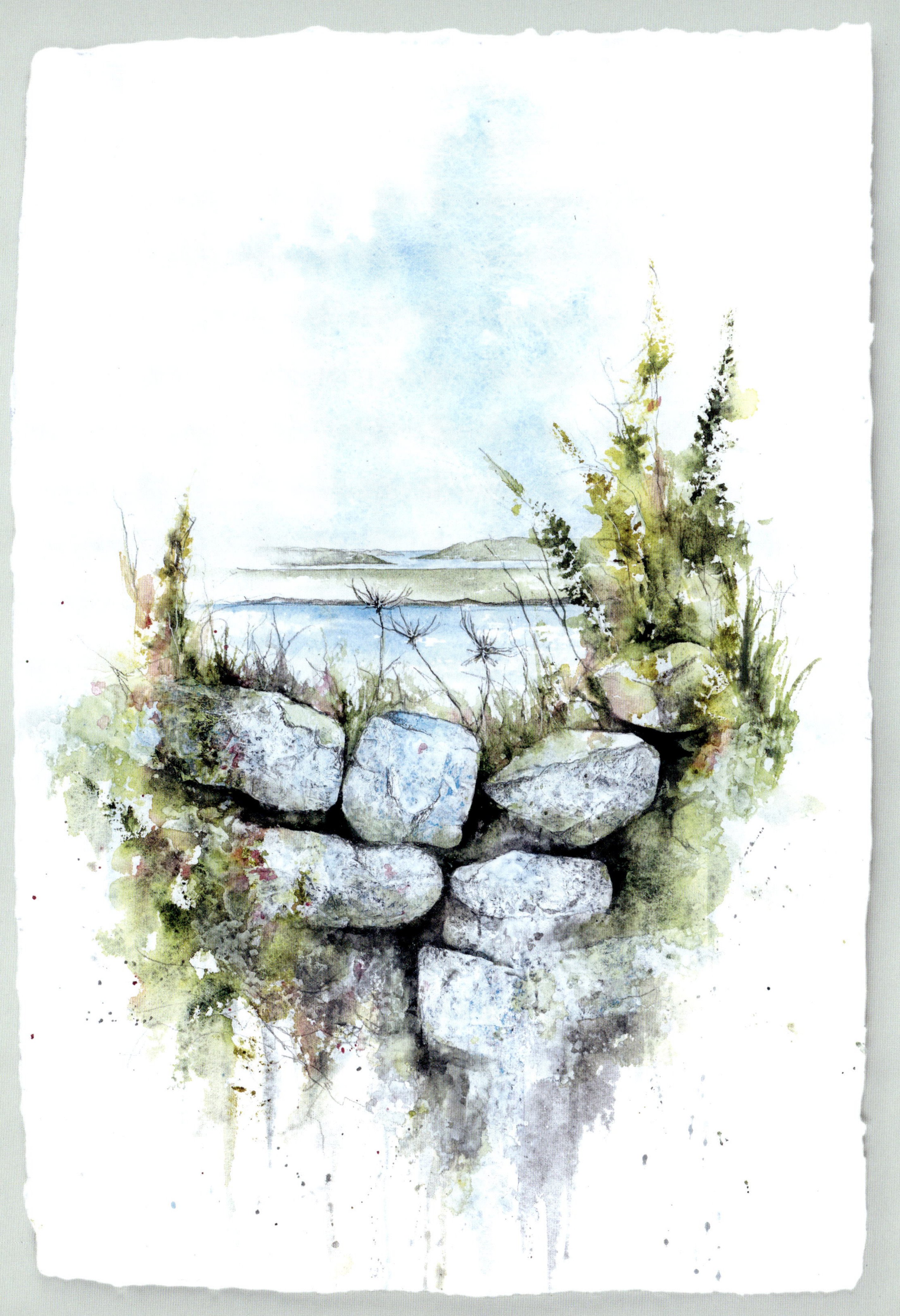

LETTERS FROM THE ROCK

INCORPORATING TEXT

This is probably my favourite technique and one that has become a huge part of my work, giving me the ability to tell stories and make meaningful connections.

Letters from the Rock is a depiction of a place that I haven't visited yet – Gibraltar. It has special significance to me as a female ancestor wrote letters from her home there in 1805 that are of cultural importance, and I have used her as inspiration many times. Due to copyright constraints, I was not able to use any of the text from her letters, but I have read them many times and for this piece, chose to write a short sentence myself in the style of her writing to include in the painting.

Alongside collaging, stamping and punching text, it is also possible to write directly onto your work – many artists do this to record an observation or a sentiment.

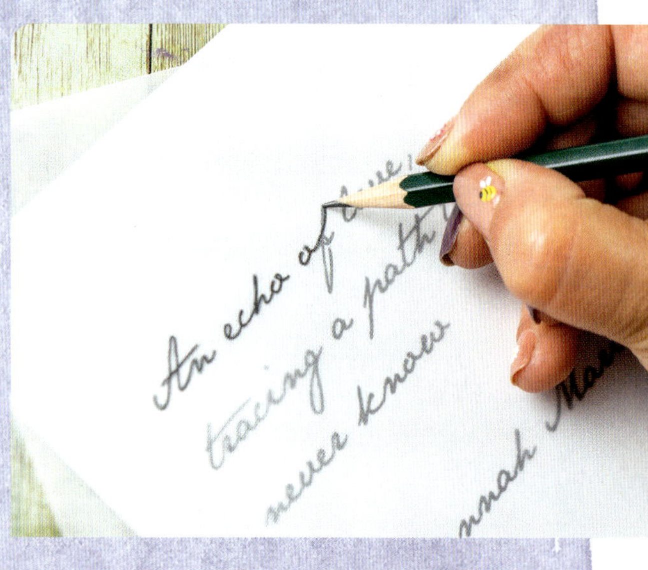

CONCLUSION

I hope the projects I have shared here have given you some inspiration for your own work and as starting points for considering unique and creative ways of interpretation. Test out the techniques and try not to overthink them; allow them to develop and, if they don't quite work, we will do a little problem-solving in the next chapter.

DETAILS

1 Culmination of techniques using maps and postage stamps (be mindful of copyright here too);

2 Using a simple graphite pencil to write directly on to the painting (see also bottom left); or you could trace your text onto tissue paper and then use it for collage;

3 Using a vintage-inspired colour palette to suggest the time span between my ancestor and myself.

Right, <u>Letters from the Rock</u>
510 × 380mm (20 × 15in)

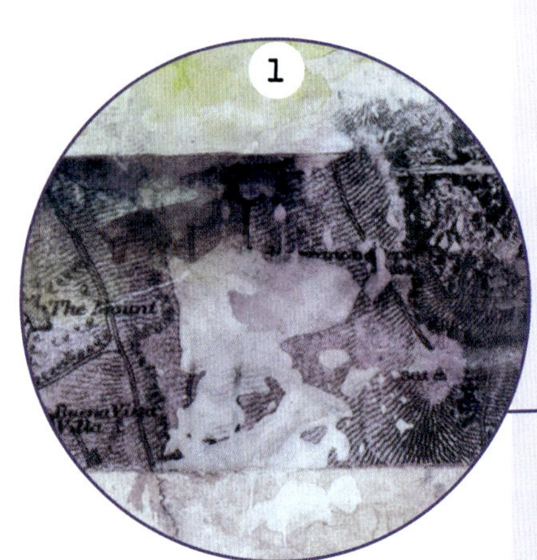

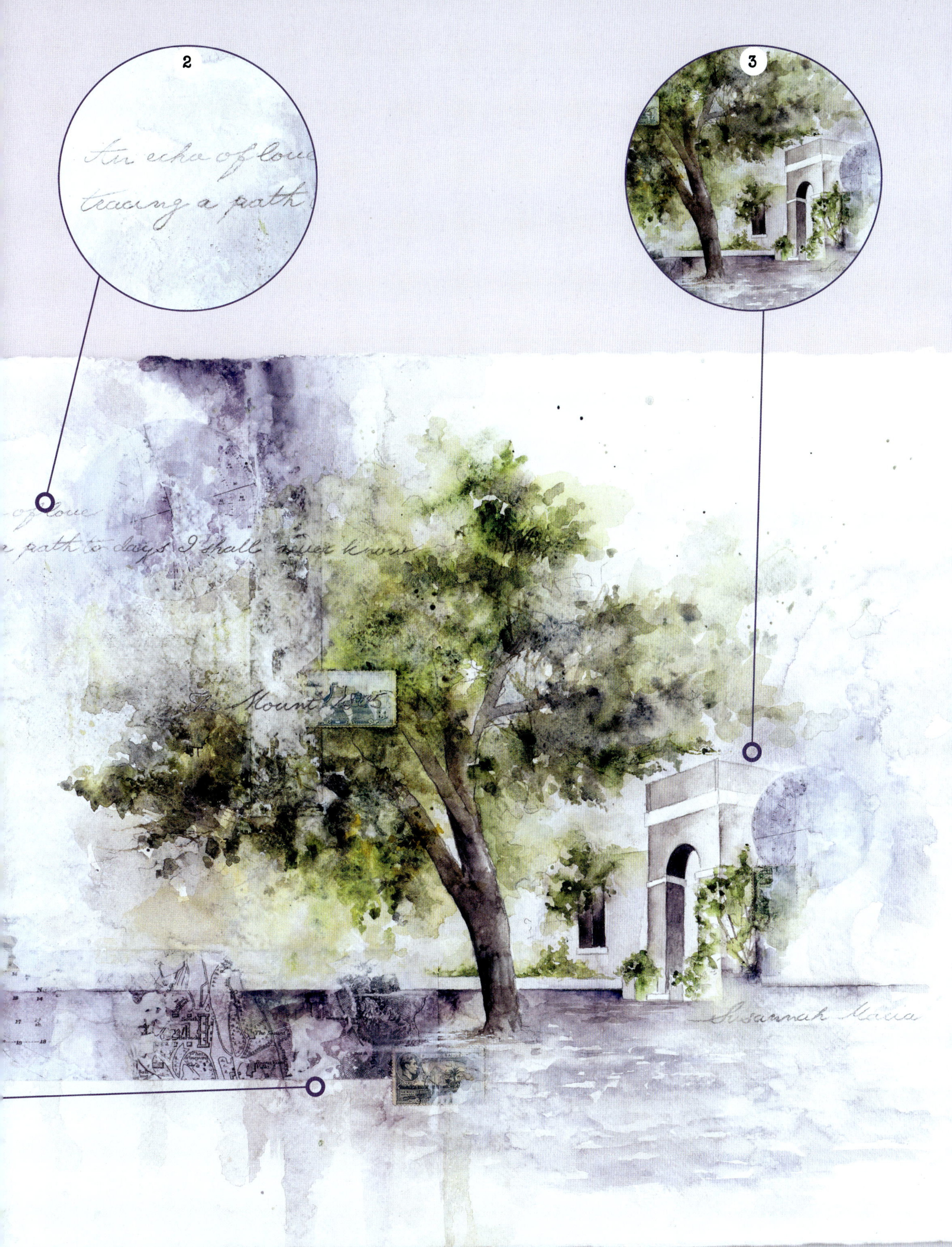

An echo of love
tracing a path
of love
a path to days I shall never know
The Mount
Susannah Maria

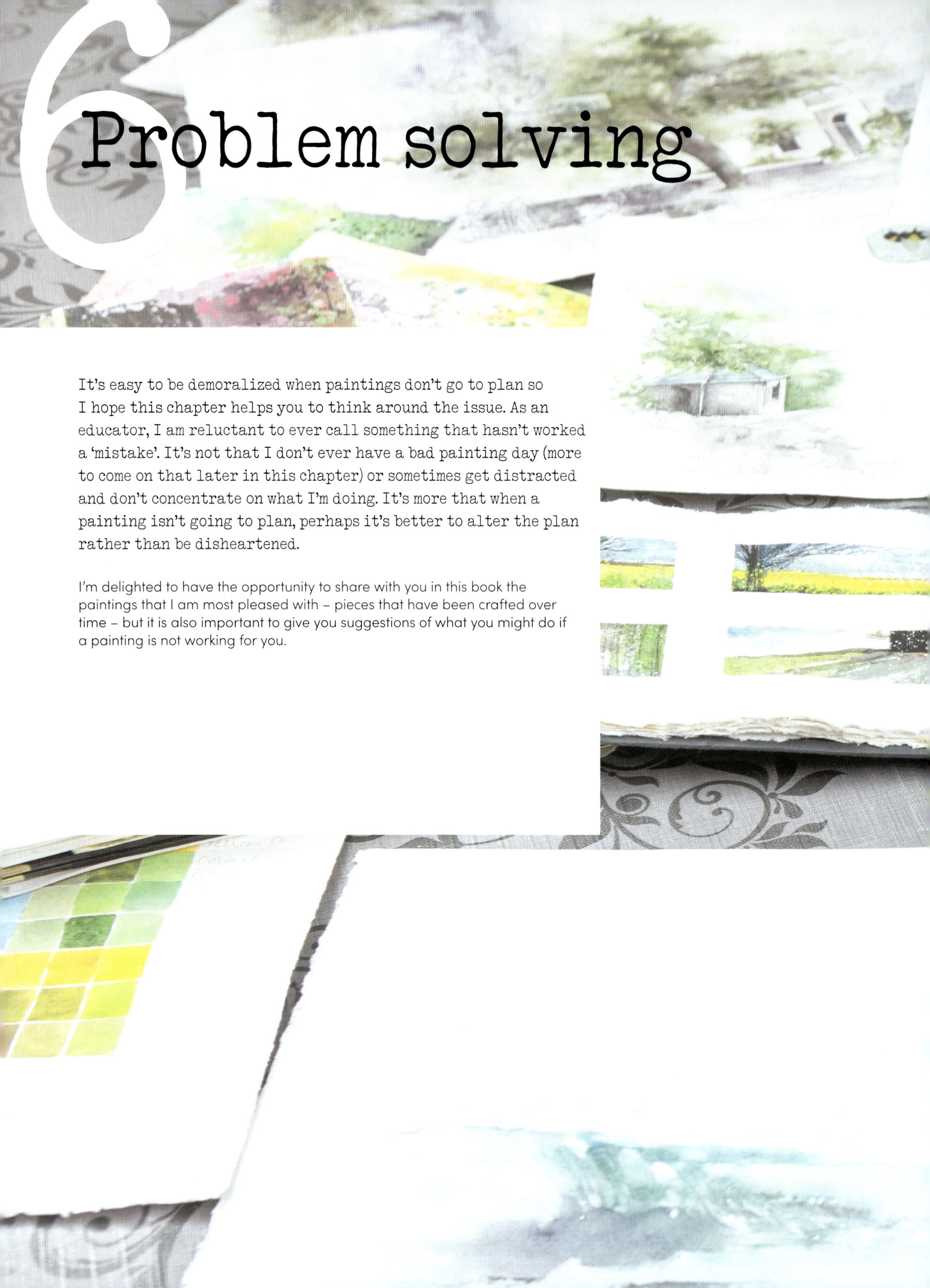

Problem solving

It's easy to be demoralized when paintings don't go to plan so I hope this chapter helps you to think around the issue. As an educator, I am reluctant to ever call something that hasn't worked a 'mistake'. It's not that I don't ever have a bad painting day (more to come on that later in this chapter) or sometimes get distracted and don't concentrate on what I'm doing. It's more that when a painting isn't going to plan, perhaps it's better to alter the plan rather than be disheartened.

I'm delighted to have the opportunity to share with you in this book the paintings that I am most pleased with – pieces that have been crafted over time – but it is also important to give you suggestions of what you might do if a painting is not working for you.

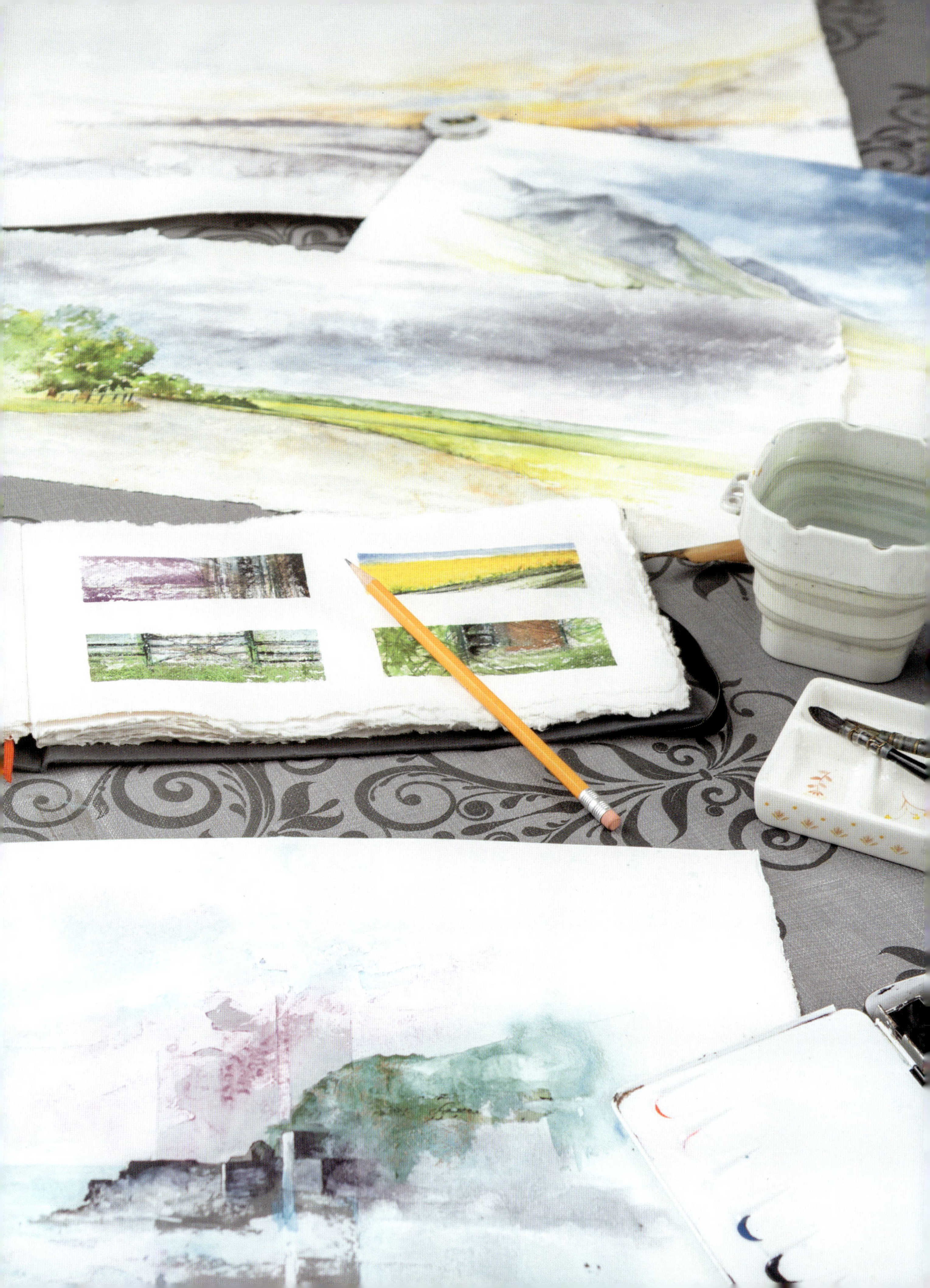

When you are being creative, your underlying personality traits will inevitably bubble to the surface. Creativity is deeply personal, and no matter how laid-back you are on any given day, this is *your* expression and has the potential to be profoundly fulfilling.

The act of creating is also a way of developing problem-solving skills so, while you may want to pitch your painting across a room when it's not going to plan (just me?), problem solving can also guide us towards lateral thinking – a way to think sideways about whatever is eluding you.

Therefore, in this chapter, I want to identify some of the problems that you may encounter, based on my own experiences, and suggest solutions that might help you to resolve them. The issues are not exclusively related to landscape painting, so the solutions will hopefully help you with many other creative subjects too. I have shared my own work to demonstrate where something hasn't quite hit the mark, so that you can understand the backstory to many of the finished paintings in this book.

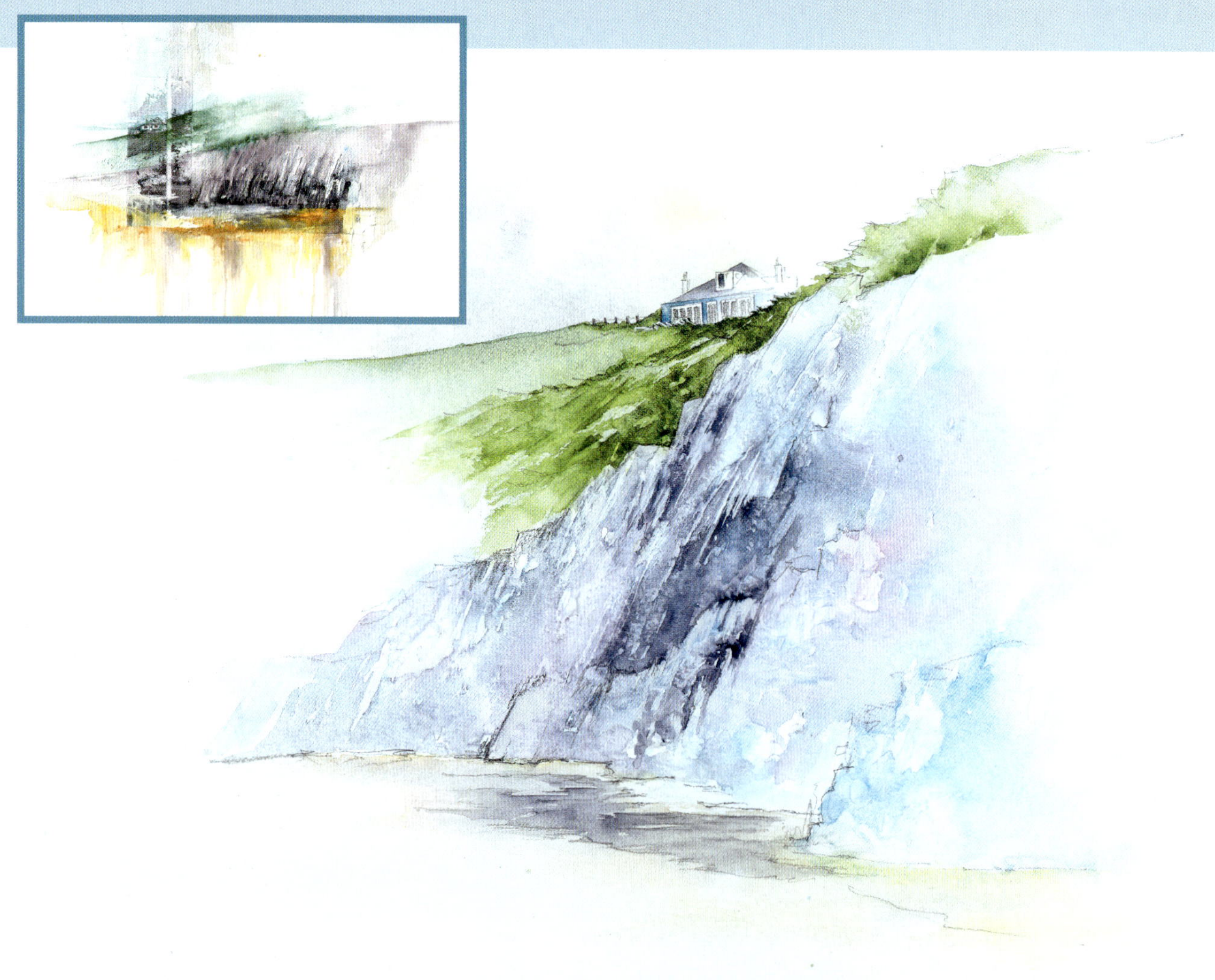

Test piece for Craig Yr Awel

This piece was intended as a finished painting, but it never got that far – I felt it was too safe, it was taking too long and didn't contain any of my signature, unexpected marks. This is an example of how, when a piece doesn't sit quite right, it needs a rethink or a new approach with techniques to better reflect your intentions.

A completed version of the painting can be seen inset, left, and on page 7.

PROBLEM #1:
BATTLING YOUR MATERIALS

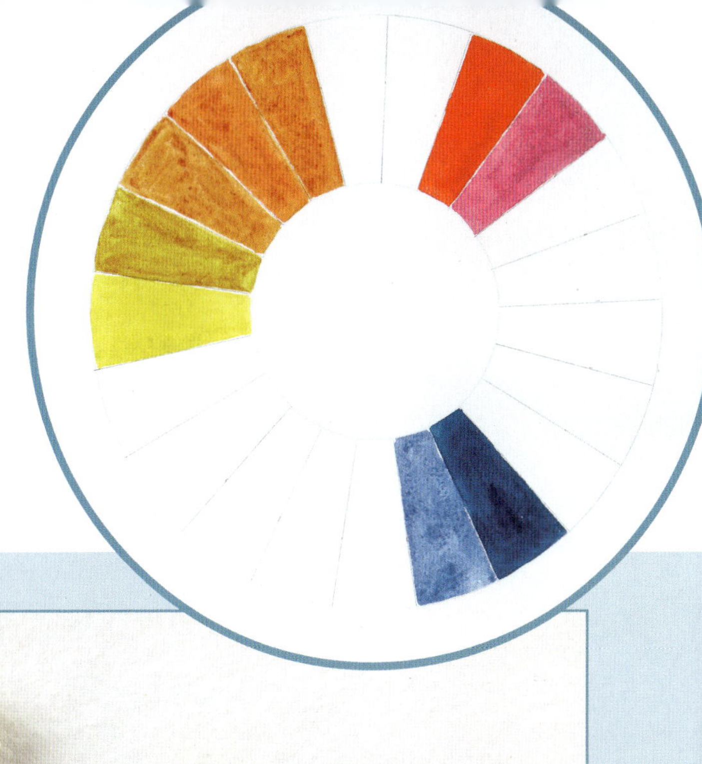

Occasionally, you may find yourself working through a project and while you are applying your medium in the way you usually would, the effects are not materializing as you anticipated, or you are fighting to get the results you want.

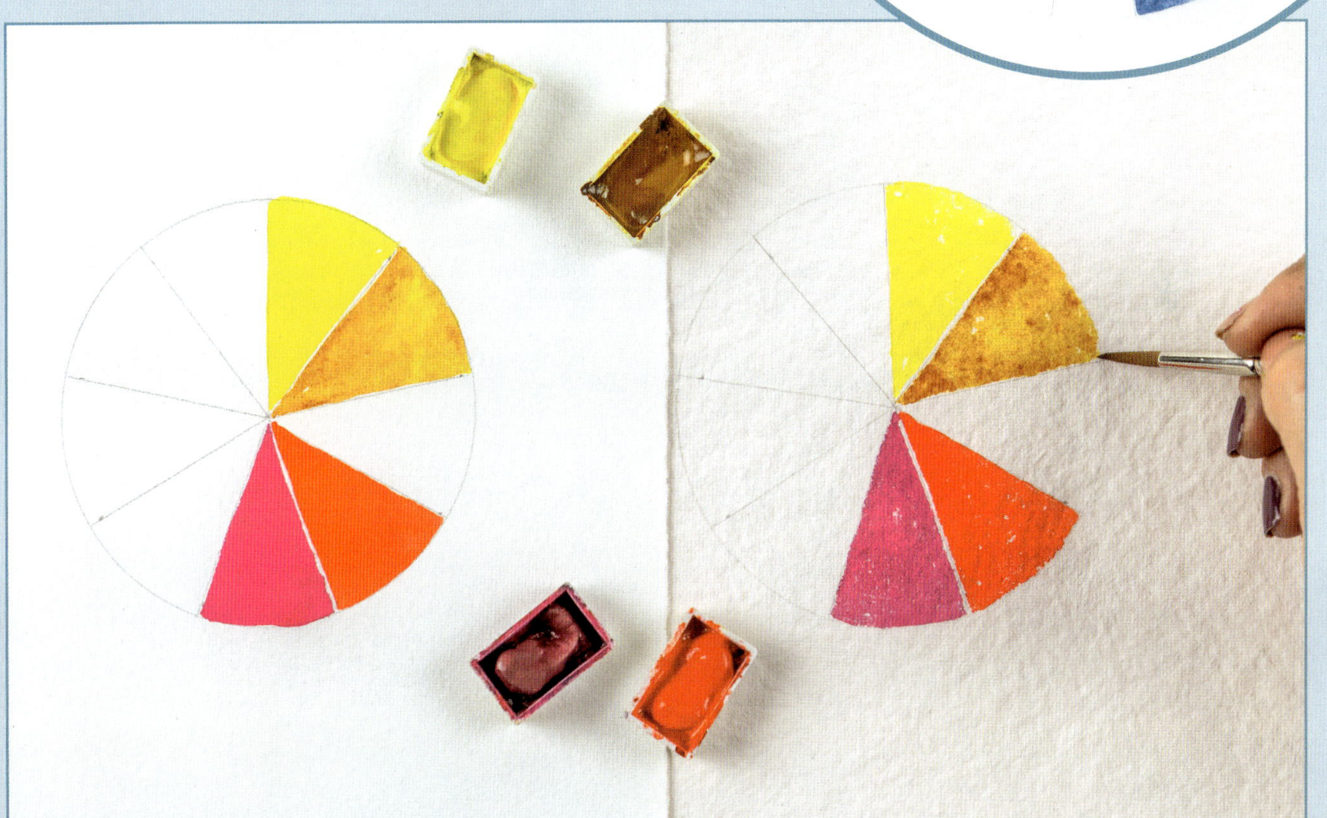

EXAMPLE

Problems with getting your paint to behave how you want it to often happen when you are using a watercolour paper that doesn't suit the technique you are using, or the material you are applying. If you want time to float your colour on the surface, you need a paper that will allow the paint to sit while you soften or move it into position.

Here (top right), you can see that some peculiar patterns appeared in my paint when I was constructing my colour wheel (on page 40). As I brushed the paint on, it felt greasy and I was struggling to apply it evenly.

SOLUTION

Try a different paper, perhaps one that contains a higher amount of cotton as these tend to allow the paint to settle on the surface more evenly and therefore provide you with a more satisfactory result.

The examples above show the same paint colours applied to two different paper surfaces. Your preference will depend upon the look you are trying to achieve.

PROBLEM #2:
A COMPLICATED VIEW
OR REFERENCE

Whether you are working from a photograph or painting out on location, sometimes the number of different elements or all the details can be overwhelming. As a result, you feel you are going to struggle to simplify it in your interpretation.

EXAMPLE

When you are on location you can be easily overwhelmed when you see all 360 degrees of your surroundings but the same can be said if you are working from a photograph. The photograph on the right is very busy and full of green textures so has the potential to look flat or repetitive as a painting.

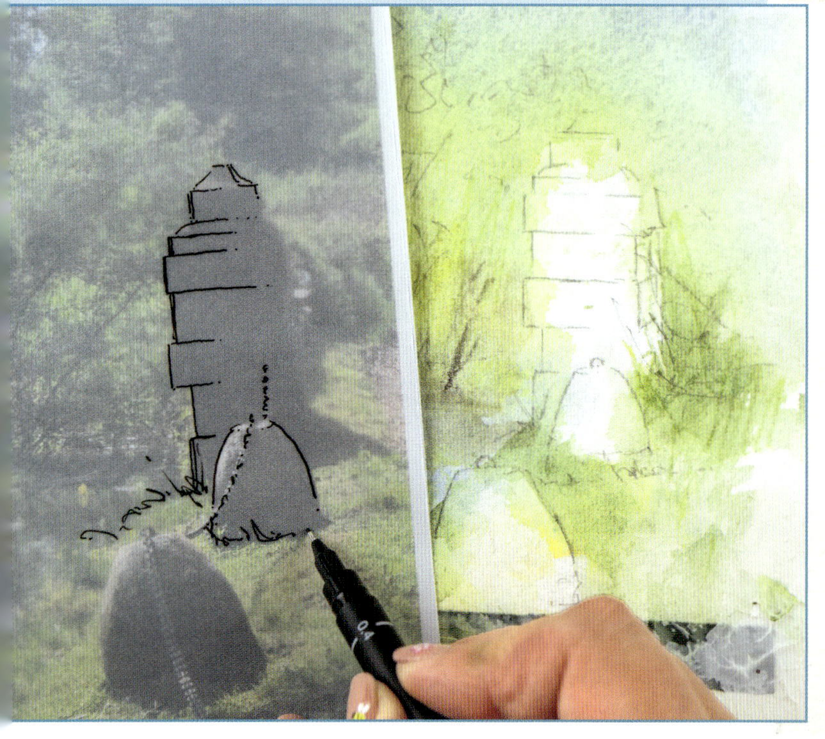

SOLUTION

Use a piece of tracing paper to break down the view into more manageable parts. Drawing the outlines of certain elements can often help you to isolate those features that are more important and reduce the subject to the items that interest you. You can find the completed painting on page 45, where you can see how I simplified this complex scene.

PROBLEM #3: OVERWORKING

Often, particularly when we are getting near the end of a painting, we think that adding more to it will somehow improve it or get it to the finish line. I often say that if the question is 'Shall I just...', then the answer is probably 'No'.

Overworking can happen for all sorts of reasons. It's common for artists to look back at a painting and wish they had stopped a few brush marks ago. I call the process of overworking 'faffing' as I think it sums up my mindset as I am doing it; deep down I know I'm overworking, but I can't seem to stop.

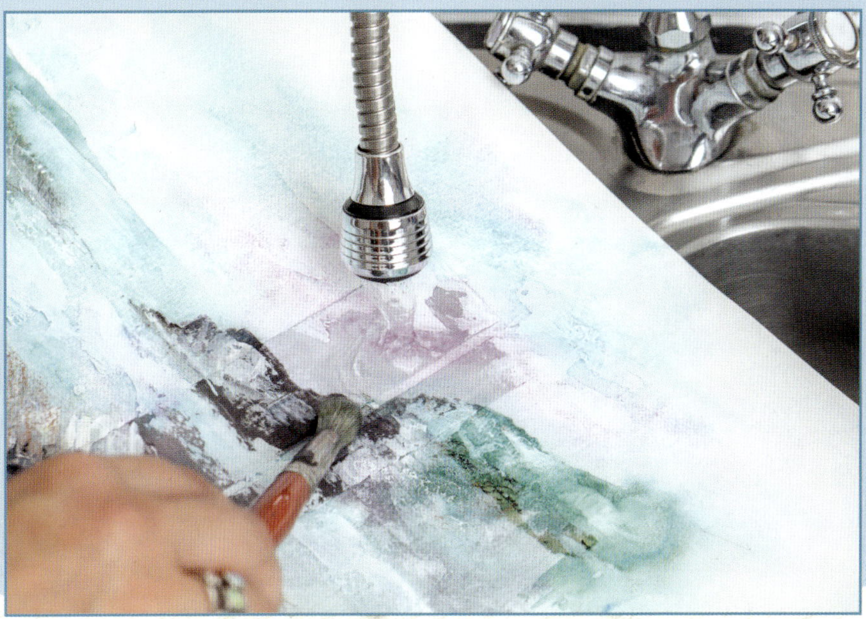

EXAMPLE

Overworking doesn't always affect a whole painting; sometimes just a small section, as you can see here in a painting of Abereiddy that I had been working on. I got far too excited about including textures and then made *everything* textured, which had the adverse effect of flattening everything out so I was no longer sure what was distant and what was in the foreground.

SOLUTION

Occasionally, a drastic move is the best one, particularly if you don't like the painting and therefore can't make it any worse. Washing away a section of colour either under running water or with a sponge can get you back to a point where you can reset and think again.

PROBLEM #4: UNEXPECTED MARKS

Sometimes, no matter how hard you try, something will appear on
your surface, and you will wonder how it got there. You may have lost
concentration, have faulty equipment or, in the case of this example, spilt
something and not realized. Rather than start the painting again, which
is demoralizing if you have already spent a long time on it, you need to find
a way to deal with what's in front of you.

EXAMPLE

My *Glencoe* painting on page 135 incurred two such incidents. The first (**1**) I'm
going to blame on my dogs, who barked at the postman and distracted me,
leaving a pale bloom in the sky that I didn't really want. The second (**2**) is my
fault for not cleaning up properly so I ended up with red powdered pigment –
used in a separate painting – in the foreground.

Stepping away. I was cross with myself and so left the painting to one side so
that I didn't make changes that I would regret and overwork it.

SOLUTION

Sometimes, living with a tiny error –
or two – is better than tying yourself
in knots trying to fix it. Ask yourself
the question, are you unhappy with
the result on the paper or it is more
that you have got frustrated that
the process didn't go to plan and
that actually, in the grand scheme
of the whole painting, you can live
with whatever has occurred and look
past it?

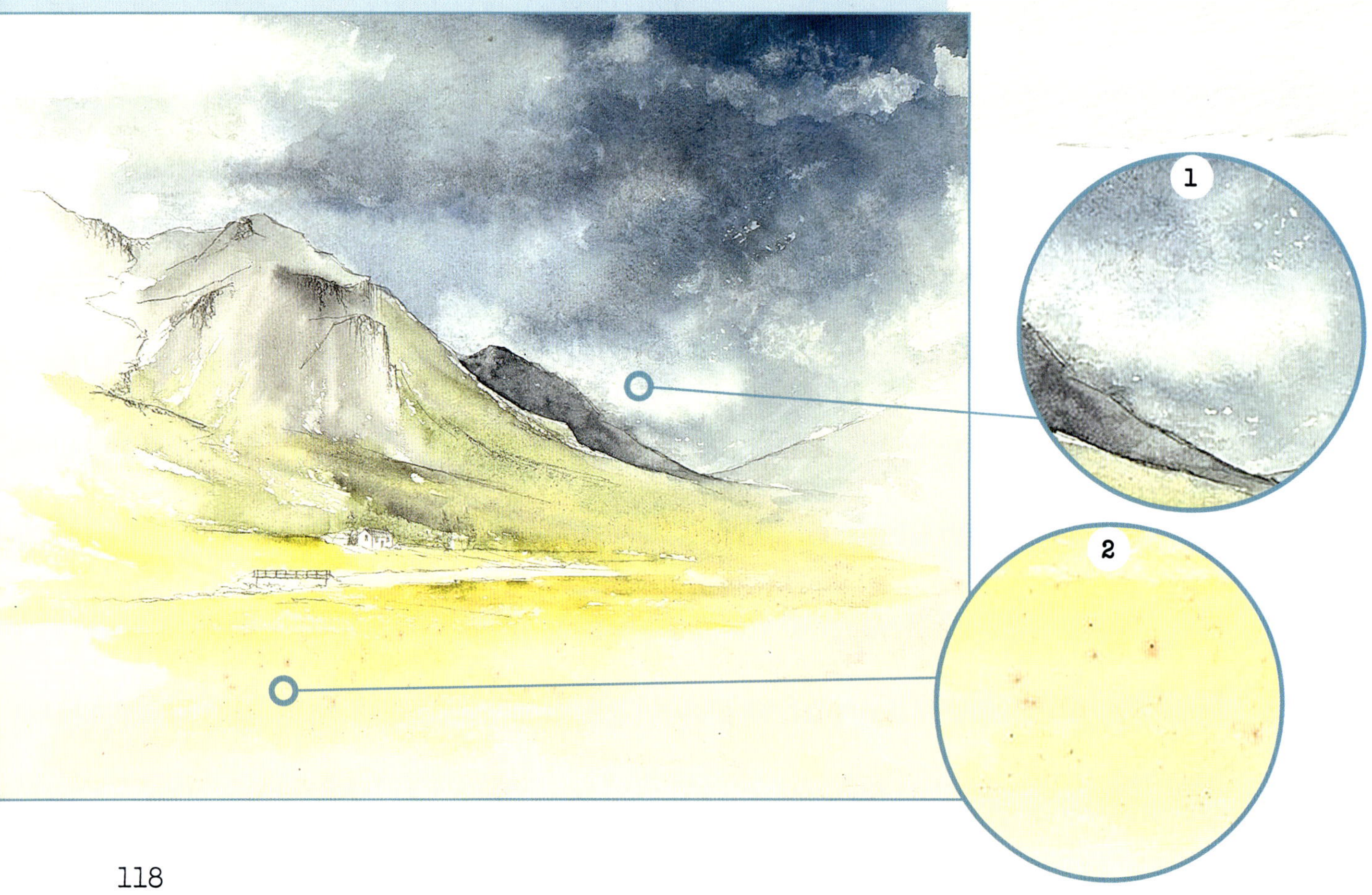

PROBLEM #5:
WHEN YOUR BRUSH MARKS DON'T WORK

Sometimes, you can choose the right materials and the right colours, and have your tones spot-on but the way that you have applied the paint to the paper looks too forced, as if it were done by a machine, rather than a creative human being.

It shows up most in landscape painting when you are trying to describe an organic element but your marks have become repetitive or ordered that they don't give the sense of a natural form. Perhaps your trees are all the same height, perhaps the texture on each of them is identical or maybe the marks (or lack of them) look bland and uninteresting. As humans, we find comfort in making things repetitiously that somehow the act of repeating the same thing over and over again is the 'correct' way of doing it, but we must override this mindset if we wish to have more spontaneity in our work.

Very often though, it's too late, we have made the mark and now we think we are stuck with it, but that's not true – there are ways we can go back to it and find a method of creatively improving it.

EXAMPLE

I have spent many years working on my mark-making skills and on pages 52–55 I introduced you to a few of the techniques that I enjoy. Repetition where I don't want it, or the making of marks that could be improved upon, still happens to me and so I have a selection of techniques that I use to get me past the problem.

The example below illustrates one of my favourite solutions. The foliage that I was attempting to paint came out looking flat and monotonous, the marks were a bit too even and the colours all very similar.

SOLUTION

Using stencils to add or take away colour can often help to break up a flat area. Use a damp (not wet) sponge to lift colour through the pattern with a very gentle rub. Be careful, because if your surface is very soft (as some watercolour papers can be), you may need to apply the lightest of touches to avoid damaging it.

Below, top-right, applied greens that all look very similar; bottom-right, using a sponge and a craft stencil to scrub out some colour; left, the result.

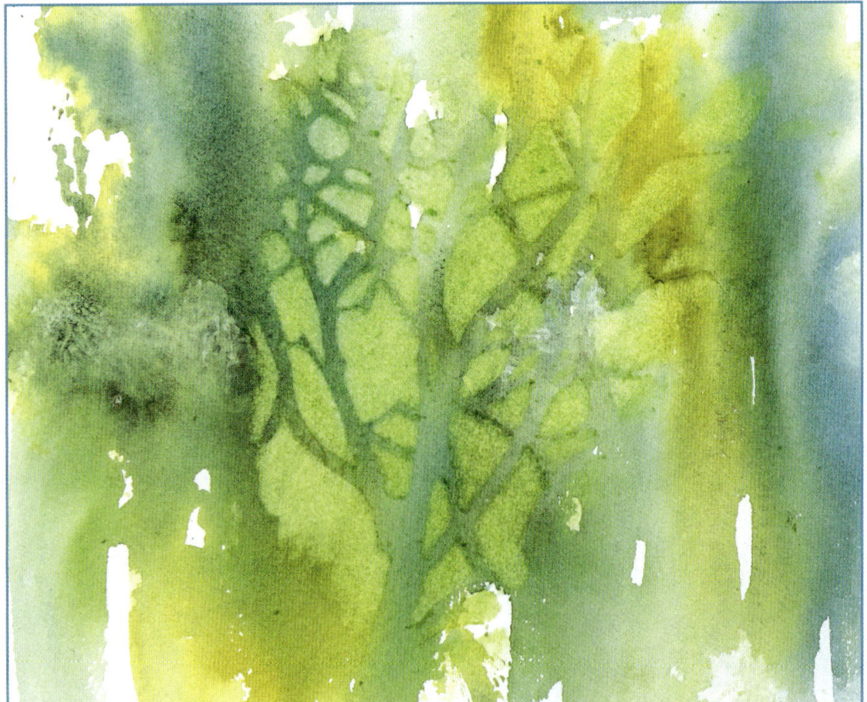

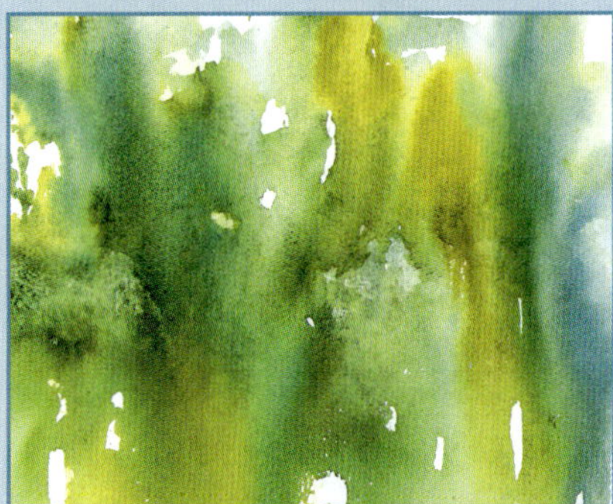

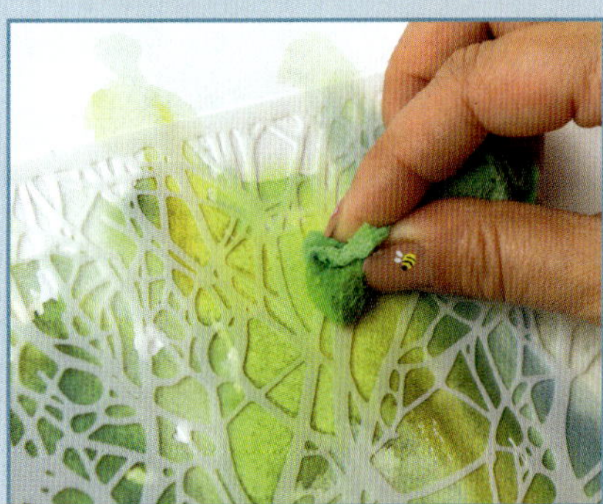

PROBLEM #6:
NO DRAMA OR RANGE OF VALUES – ONLY MID-TONES

Adding rich darks, particularly in watercolour, can be scary: it seems very final to make such a bold application of colour that you might not be able to retract if you aren't then happy with it. So you risk being left with a bland painting; there's nothing essentially wrong with it – it simply lacks punch.

EXAMPLE

Green is an exceptionally difficult colour with which to create a range of tones, as it can be hard to deepen without too much black and hard to lighten without it appearing wishy-washy.

There's nothing 'wrong' with the study above-right but you could argue the composition isn't as daring as it might be, and it definitely lacks 'oomph'.

One of the issues was that the post divided the foreground green from the fields beyond and so I needed to lighten the fields, which I did by lightly scrubbing the surface with a damp toothbrush. Then I added more detail to the post, darkened the green just behind it and added a few thoughtful highlights in white pen to the wire in the foreground.

SOLUTION

Occasionally, you think a painting is complete and then when you look at it with fresh eyes later you realize that your darks tones were not as brave as you had thought. With watercolours it can be that you walked away from the painting before it had time to dry fully – watercolour always dries lighter than when you apply it – and so you need to reassess and probably add further darks to the piece to make it work. Going back in and adding more when you think you have finished is not a negative process; you are simply pushing your painting further than your first assessment.

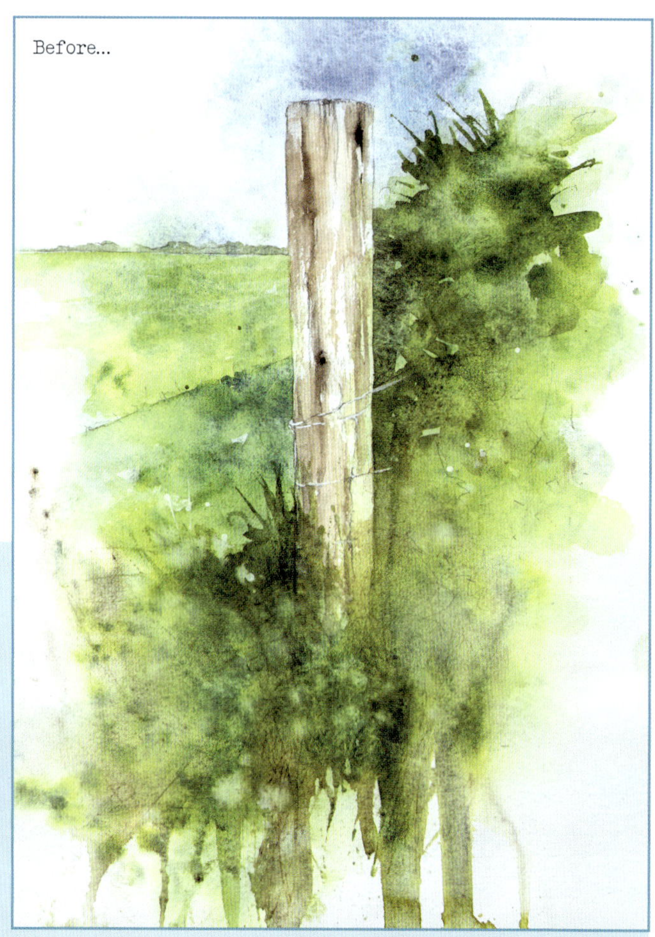

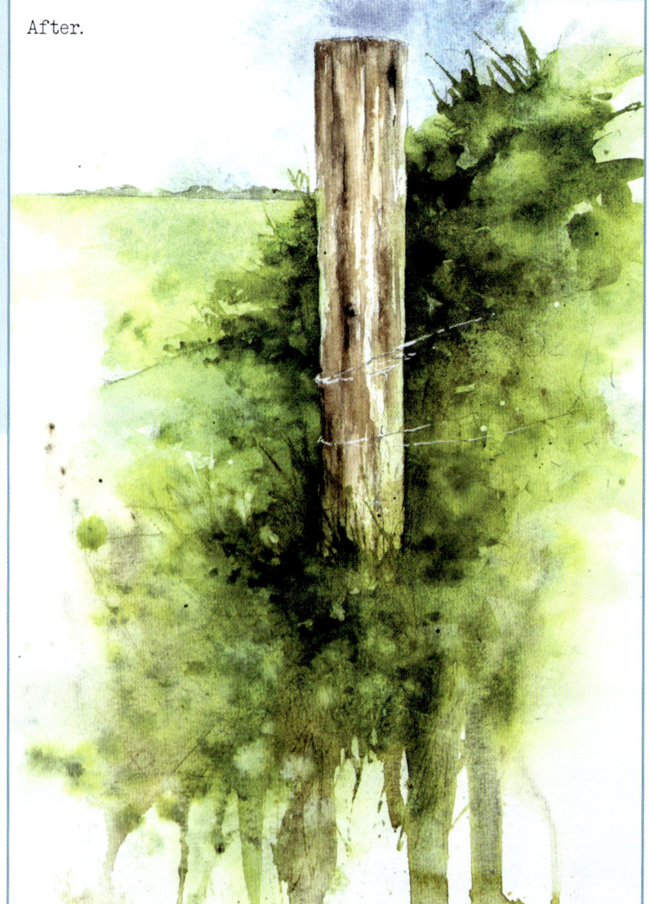

PROBLEM #7: LACK OF CHARACTER/ STORYTELLING/ATMOSPHERE

Not every painting has to have a deep, significant meaning; it doesn't have to draw you in and make you ask what inspired the artist. Every so often I paint a picture to test my skills or to teach a class, so it has a different function from my other paintings.

This can be dangerous, though – if I don't feel a connection to the subject, then it shows – the painting lacks atmosphere because there is no passion driving it.

EXAMPLE

The painting below definitely falls into that category – and it actually makes me wince to share it here – but it's good to try to get to the bottom of what isn't working and add it to our experiences so that, hopefully, we don't repeat them.

The sky appears to be divided into formal bands; the soft edges around it are too rectangular, the buildings don't look very three-dimensional and the colour palette isn't exactly adventurous.

SOLUTION

It's easy to say and not so easy to do but try to chalk this one up to experience. Keep the painting so that it reminds you of where you have come from and where you are going; it will prompt you to remember that not everything you create is going to be your very best work.

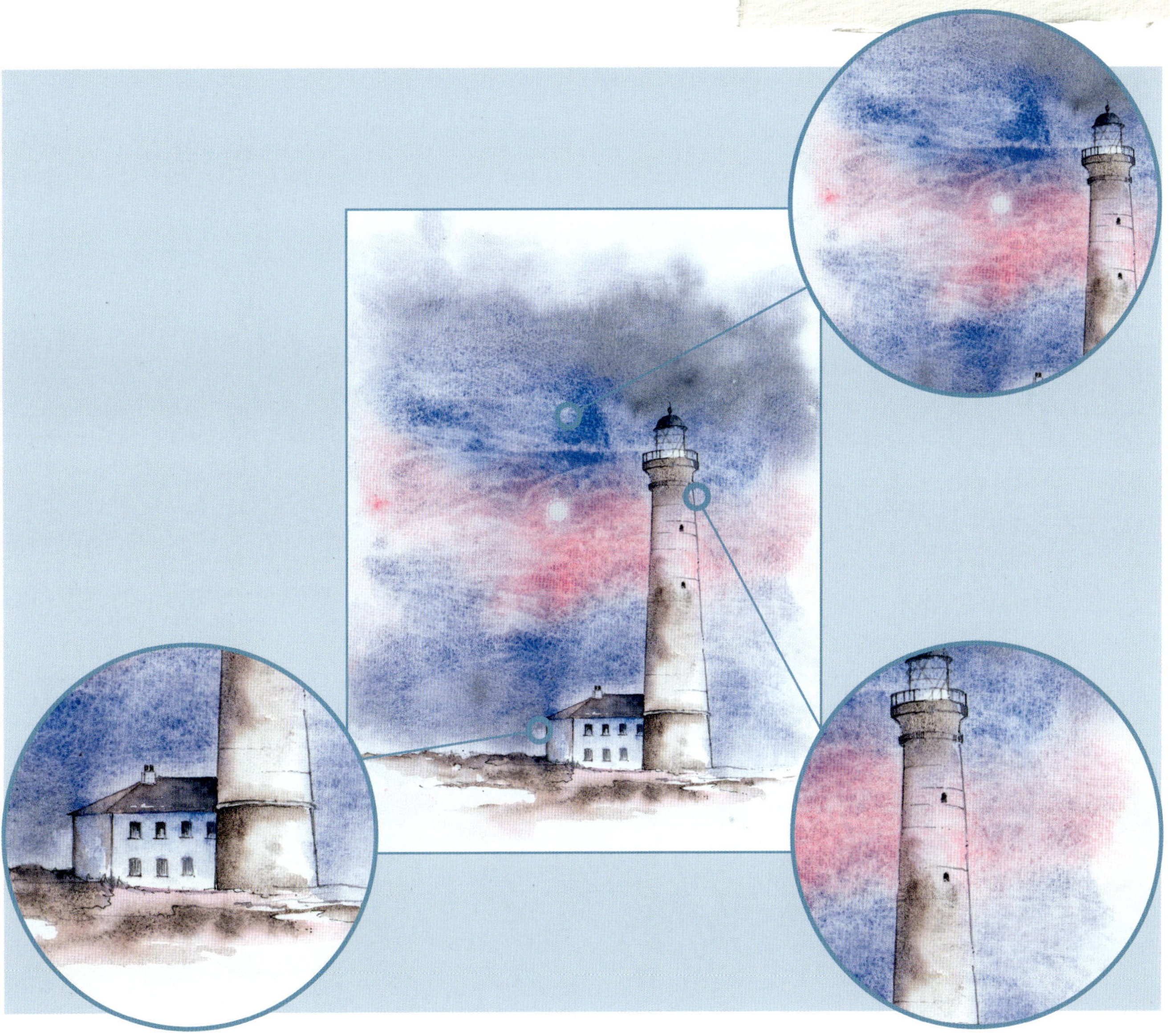

PROBLEM #8:
UNBALANCED COMPOSITION

Despite considering all the elements discussed on pages 46–47, your chosen composition isn't working and the painting looks forced or contrived. Composition is one of the fundamentals that is much discussed between artists; the rules are debated, often broken intentionally for effect and individual preferences become partof the signature of each artist.

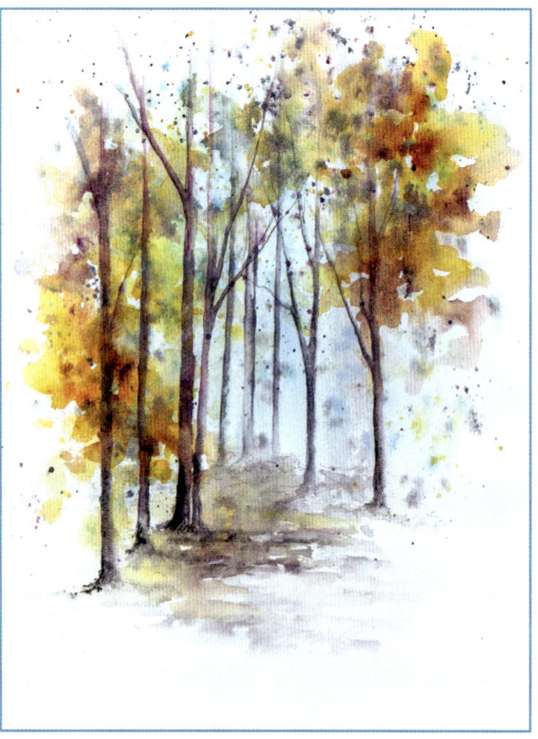

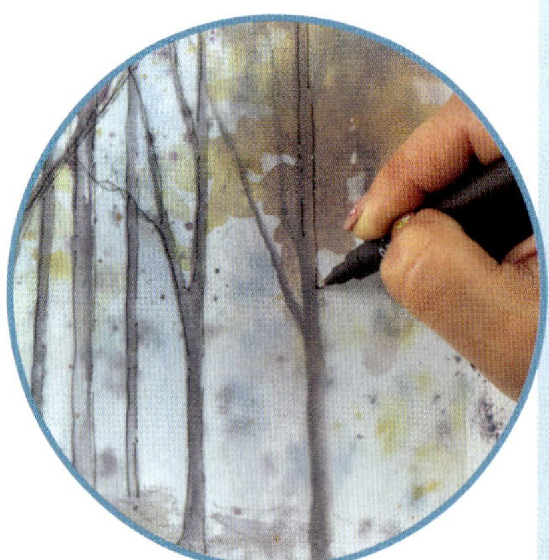

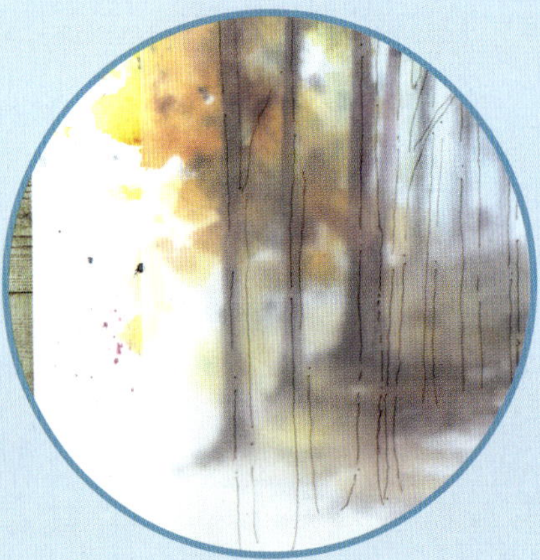

By tracing over what I have painted and then moving the tracing paper around, I can see more clearly where things should have been. I use a black pen to do this so I can see the lines clearly and it reinforces my suspicions that the subjects are too far up the paper. You can see a more developed version of this painting, with an improved composition, on page 43.

EXAMPLE

Above is a painting I did quite a few years ago now. At first glance it doesn't look too badly composed: the trees are asymmetrically placed, there are both warm and cool colours, textures, suggestions of distance… OK, the tree canopy was painted in a rush and so lacks detail, but it was a very fast painting.

It was a real turning point for me when I realized what wasn't working: I had painted the foliage to the edge of the paper. I had squashed in my elements because I didn't want them to go off the page and started the whole scene too far up the paper, thereby making it cramped and awkward.

SOLUTION

To see what could have worked better, trace over the main components and move the tracing paper to where they might work better – just for your own understanding.

This study is a reminder of my epiphany of what wasn't working; I vowed to always leave plenty of space around my paintings for them to grow and develop, and not be restrained by the arbitrary size of the paper I was working on.

Good composition now forms a huge part of my work so I am grateful for one unsuccessful piece to show me the way.

PROBLEM #9: SOMETHING IS NOT QUITE RIGHT

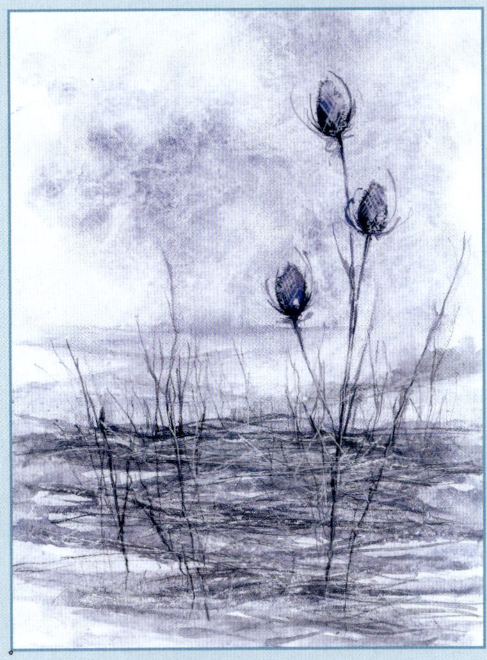

Above

The final piece.

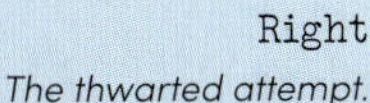

Right

The thwarted attempt.

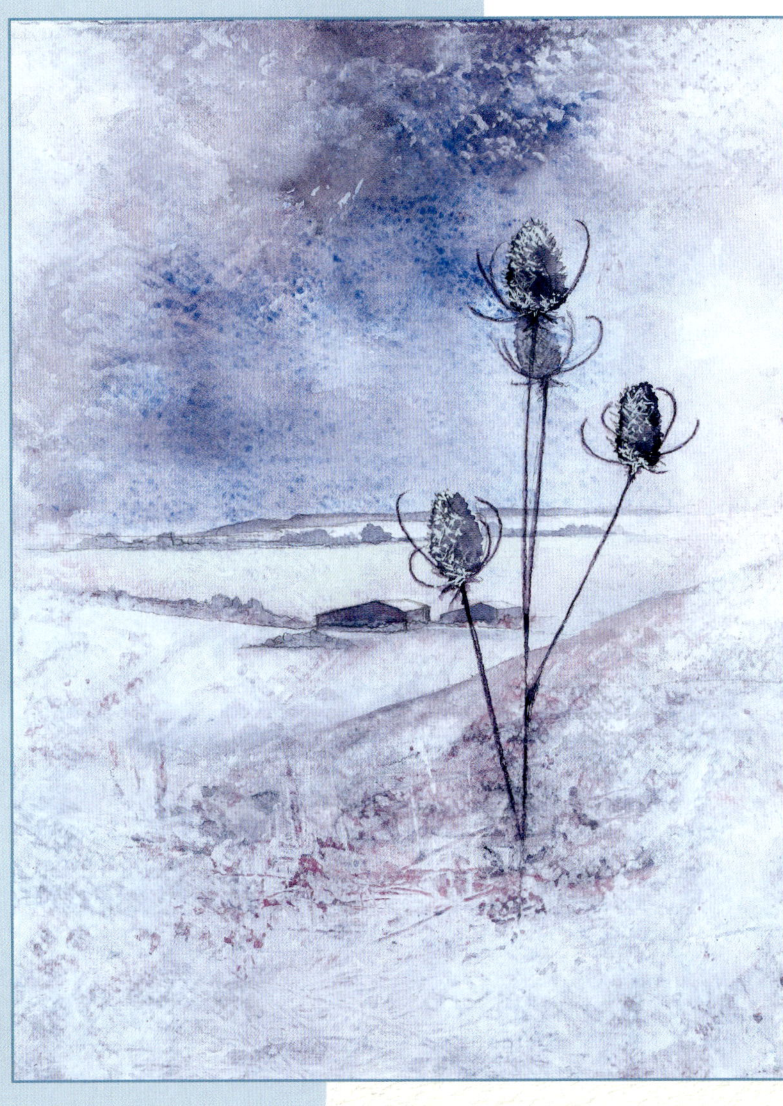

Some paintings just don't work. You can't always define what isn't happening, and no matter how many outside observers tell you all the good points, something in the painting feels 'off' and you know it in your bones. Take other people's encouragement with grace: they are trying to get you to see the positives, and try not to let the fact that the painting didn't work concern you, because sometimes the pieces just don't fit.

EXAMPLE

The version of my *Downend Snow* painting shown above right didn't make the cut. I had tried out a couple of techniques that hadn't worked so I used watercolour ground over the top to block out what I didn't like. When that had dried, I realized that this painting had run out of steam, and I needed to simply start again.

In the final version (shown above left and in process on pages 146–149) the two elements of thistles and landscape are now fully integrated and the thistles are more thoroughly grounded.

SOLUTION

Knowing when to stop and regroup is as important as knowing when to be tenacious and push on through the problem. Make peace with the fact that not all paintings will reach a conclusion. It's no reflection on you or your skills; it just happens sometimes.

PROBLEM #10:
A BAD PAINTING DAY

As artists, we all have them. Sometimes they don't happen for a while and we think they're never to return; but often they come in a flurry, and it seems we can't see a way out. Bad painting days are rubbish, and I wouldn't wish them on any of you as they undermine your confidence and make you feel like you're not getting anywhere. They can come in the form of tiredness, of being overwhelmed by the wider world, a lack of inspiration or a feeling that you are going around in circles.

It's because painting is so personal and reflects who we are that we find bad painting days difficult to navigate, as if those days are somehow making a statement about us, but the good news is that you can find your way out with a bit of help.

SOLUTION

Bad painting days are sometimes a glitch. I often have one if I haven't painted for a while, and I have learnt that if I say to myself, 'this might not work' then I often surprise myself as I let go and the painting turns out successfully.

If a bad painting day turns into more than one and you are scared that you have hit a rut, change what you do to break the cycle. Gardening, walking, photography, reading, baking, crochet, music, watching a film are all creative pursuits and still 'feed' you, so try very hard not to beat yourself up if something isn't working.

My other best piece of advice for a bad painting day? Gravitate to people who empathize and who will lift you up when you are creatively stuck. Maybe it's another artist, a creative friend, a mentor or perhaps just a family member who sees how hard you work.

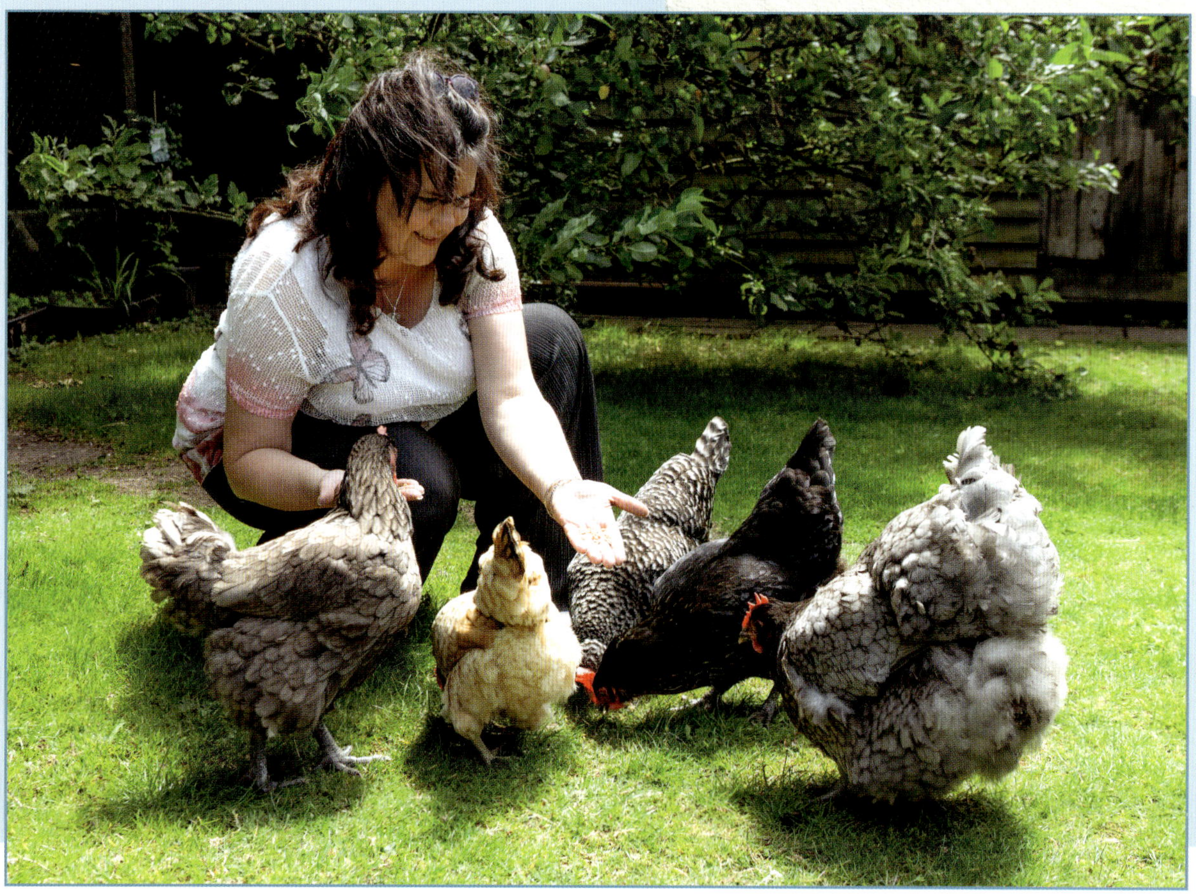

I often discuss creative block with my hens; they may not have the solution but they definitely keep me sane and help me to step away.

CONCLUSION

As I said at the beginning of this book, painting is not a linear process: it has to be considered from all angles, and there will be bumps in the road. We are, after all, human; we cannot be robotic in our approach to creativity, always being the very best versions of ourselves.

Learning to solve our creative problems is as much a skill as knowing how to paint a sky, create depth in a body of water or where to place a building in the landscape – useful to have up our sleeves for when our painting doesn't go as we might like.

Reflecting on everything we have talked about so far, we now find ourselves nearing the exciting bit: when we learn how to put it all together and build further confidence in our ability to interpret what we want to express.

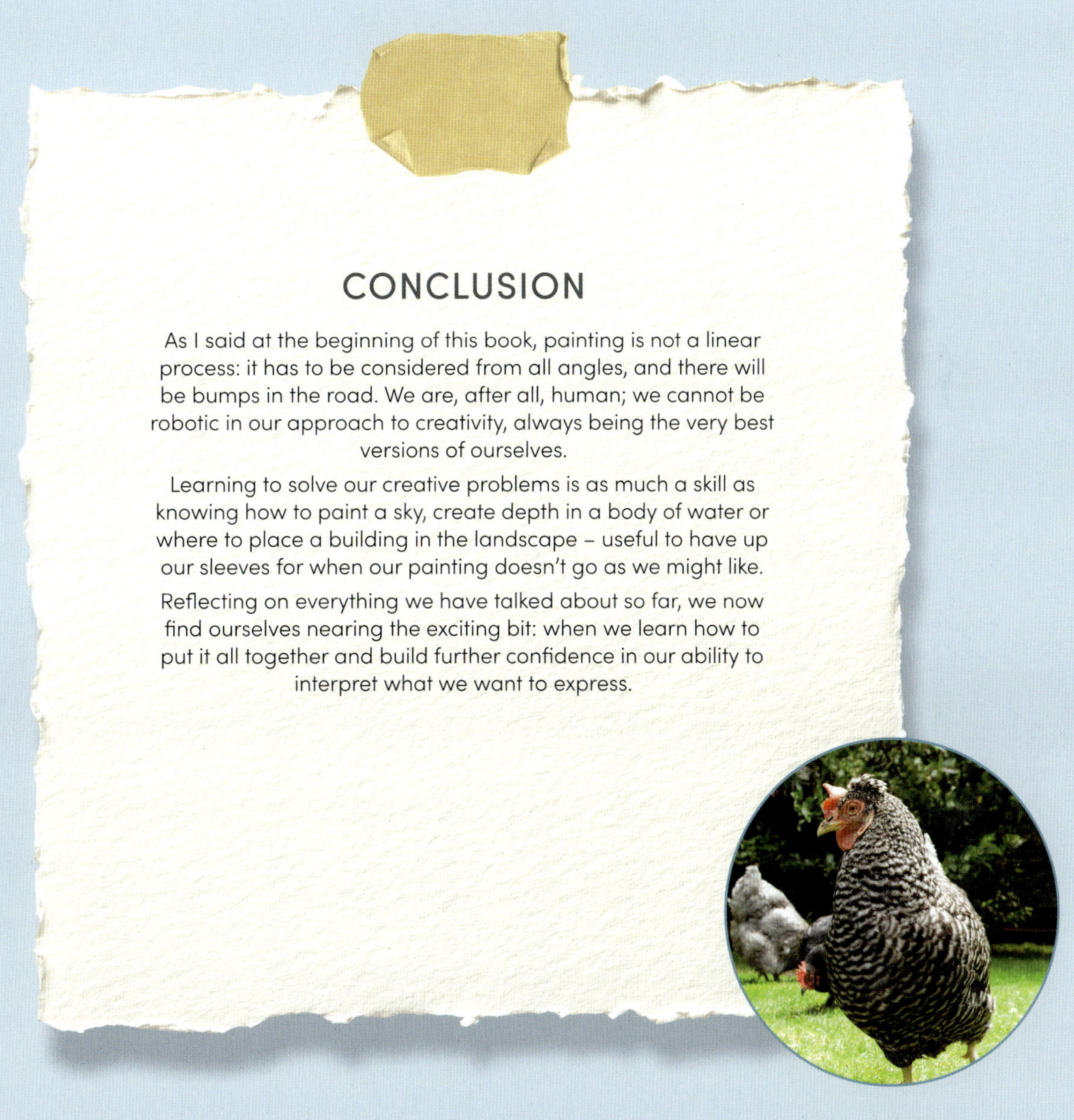

Pick-and-mix projects

If I could wish anything for your landscape painting adventures, it would be that this book gives you the confidence to assemble your own interpretations of what you experience. With that in mind, I would like to share the process that I encourage in all of the classes that I teach – the concept of 'pick and mix'.

'Pick and mix' is my way of encouraging you to use different materials, to put elements in or leave them out, appropriate them from elsewhere and generally have a lovely, creative time.

There isn't ever only one way of creating something, and you will respond to your subject in different ways on different days, piecing together the jigsaw of the landscape as your artistic intuition guides you.

This chapter aims to demonstrate different ways in which I have tackled a painting from the same starting point. They vary in style and media to show the myriad potential outcomes for how your landscapes could be presented, creating a unique interpretation every time.

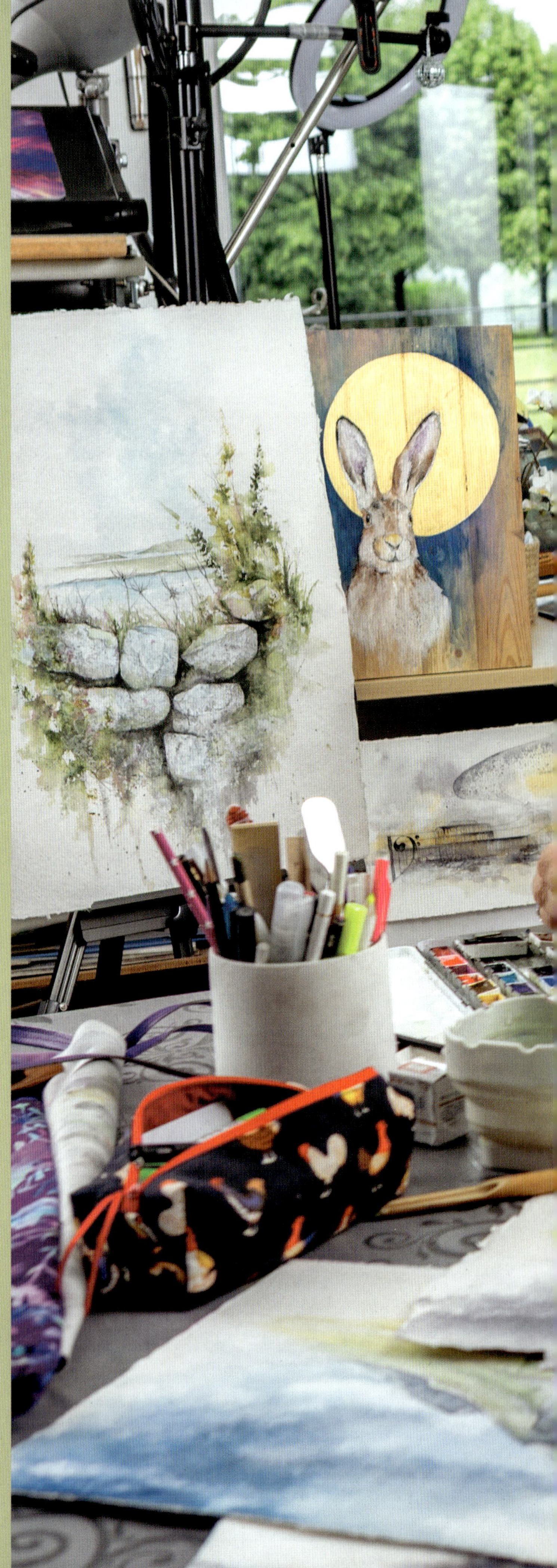

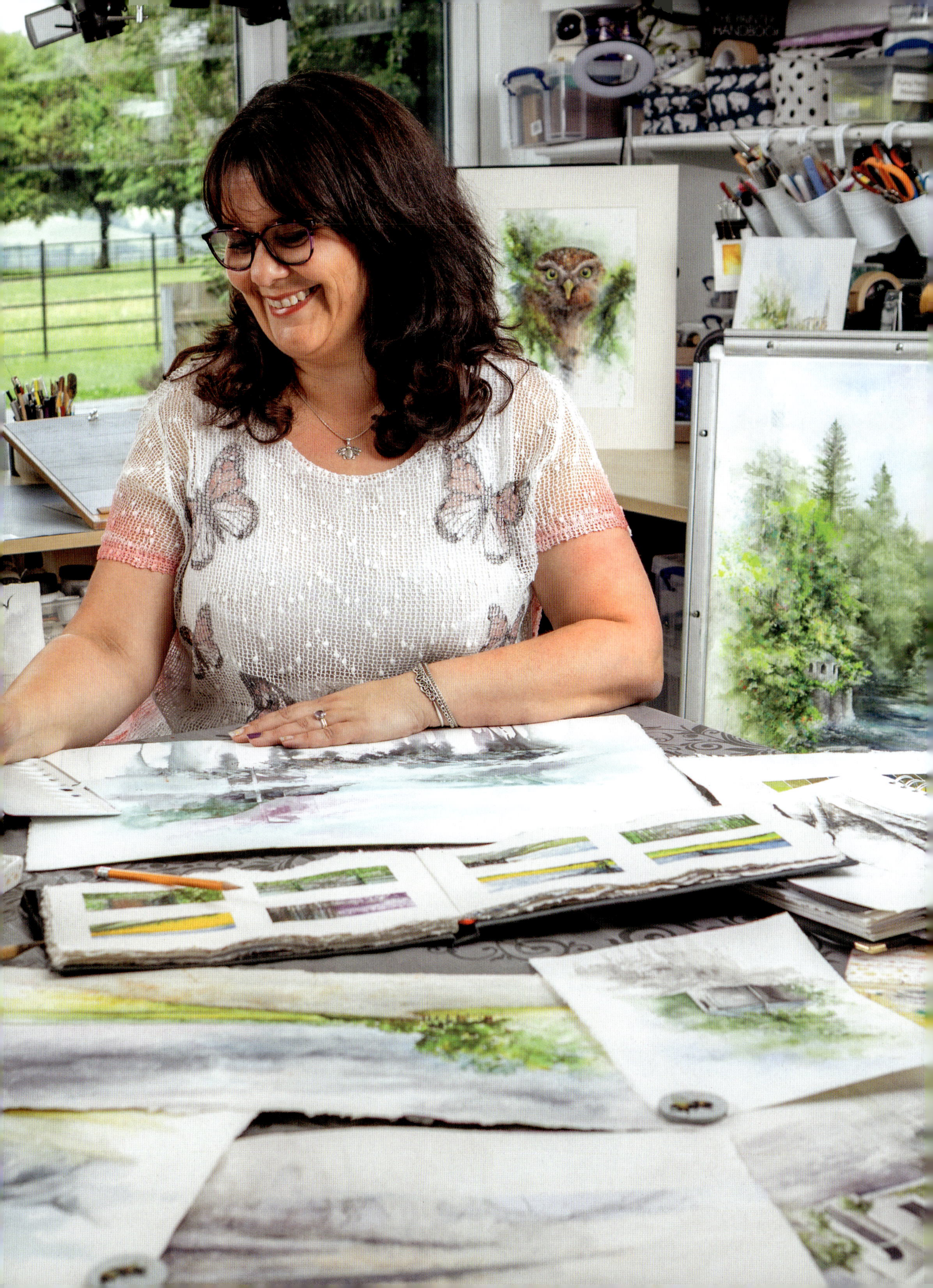

HOW THESE PROJECTS WORK

In this chapter I have chosen five different landscapes, all visited by me; some fleetingly with a camera and others more deeply investigated, through sketches and observations.

Each view has two outcomes that explore different media, techniques or variations in composition, sharing ideas for how you might like to experiment with your own landscapes.

Badbury Poppies

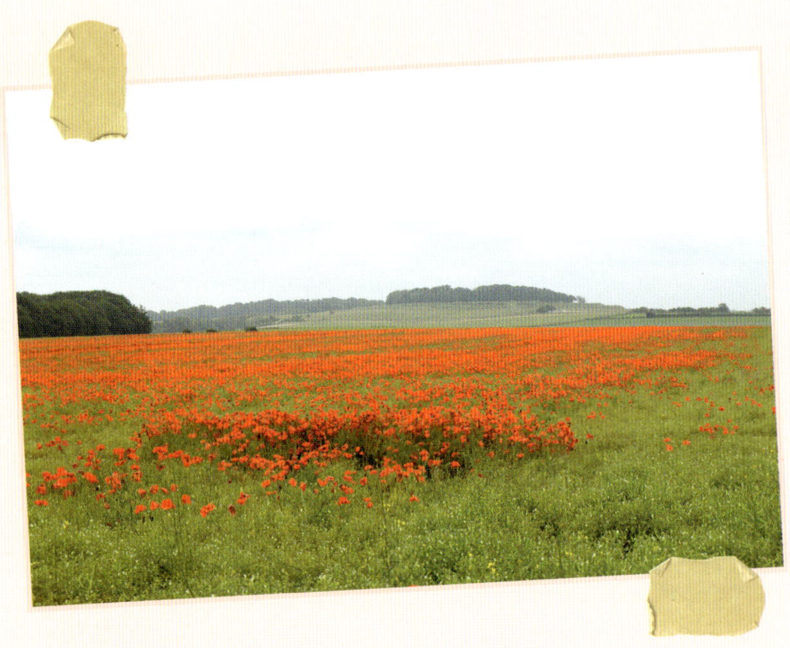

INSPIRATION

This is Badbury Rings, a Roman hill fort not far from my studio in Dorset, UK. The photograph was taken on a dull day as I passed by this incredible sea of red in my car. It doesn't provide me with much information apart from how broken up the flowers are, but I grew up here, so I have memories of how I felt about the place as a child.

You will need...

VERSION 1 (PAGES 128–131)

SURFACE: Fabriano Artistico, 300gsm (140lb), Extra White, Cold-Pressed, 350 × 270mm (13¾ × 10⅝in) – approximately quarter-imperial

MATERIALS AND TOOLS: watercolour paints in Cobalt Blue, Foliage Green, Green Gold and Scarlet Lake

VERSION 2 (PAGES 132–133)

SURFACE: Artway INDIGO, 250gsm (no imperial equivalent), Mid Texture, 297 × 420mm (11¾ ×16½in)

MATERIALS AND TOOLS: watercolour paints in Cobalt Blue, Dusky Violet and Foliage Green; Crystalline (powder) watercolour in Poppy Red

BEFORE I START PAINTING

This location is linked to my childhood and is recalled with fondness, so I have quite a romantic notion that I want to capture the way my memory gives a soft quality to the scene. I don't want to make the painting too busy as I think the flowers will give plentiful texture, so I need to keep it simple.

I want to keep my materials to a minimum, but I also need to experiment with the combination of media and techniques to see what transpires.

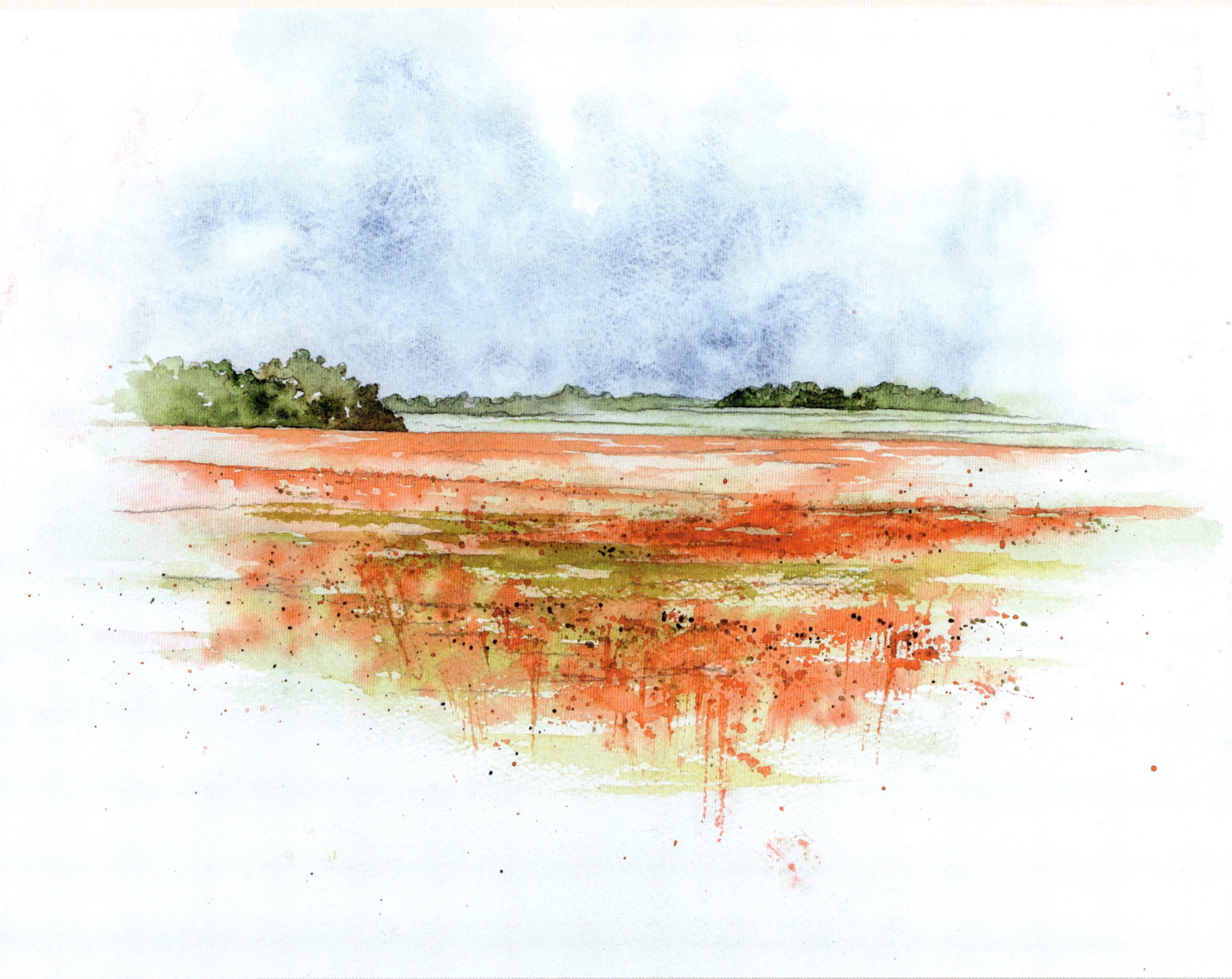

Badbury Poppies: version 1
350 × 270mm (13¾ × 10⅝in)

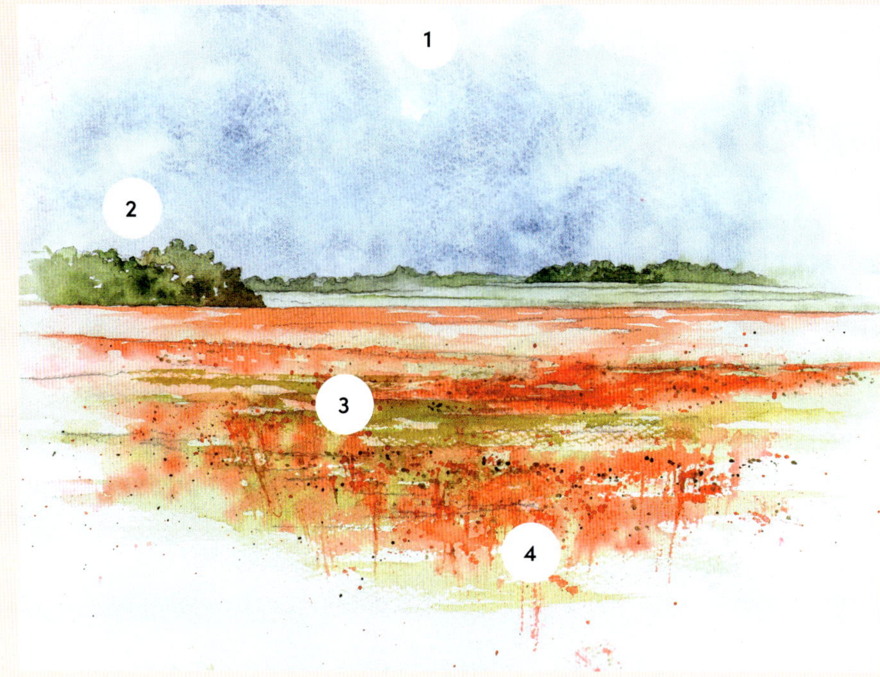

Techniques featured in <u>Badbury Poppies</u>: version 1

TECHNIQUES

VIGNETTE

Begin with a soft vignette, using lots of water to create lost edges in the sky (see page 61). Here, I have kept the sky very simple so that it doesn't detract from the red flowers and reflects my memory of summers spent at the location. This softness gives the whole painting a nostalgic, dream-like quality with atmosphere.

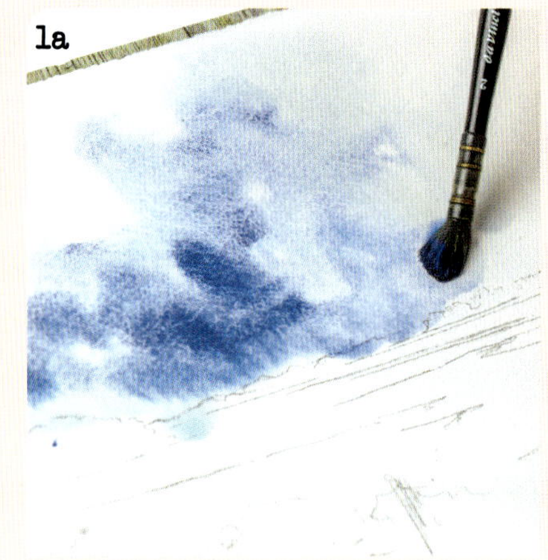

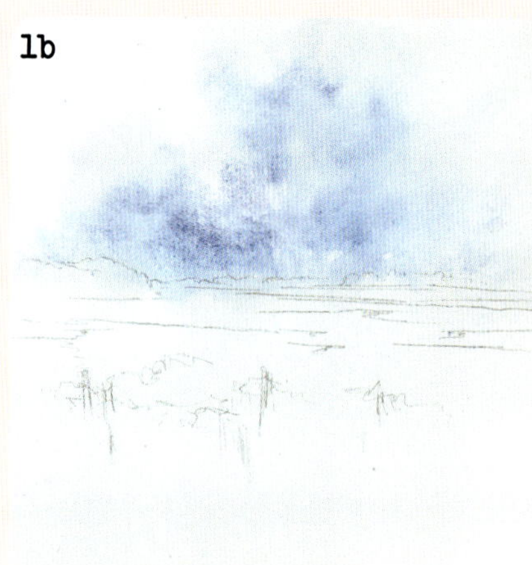

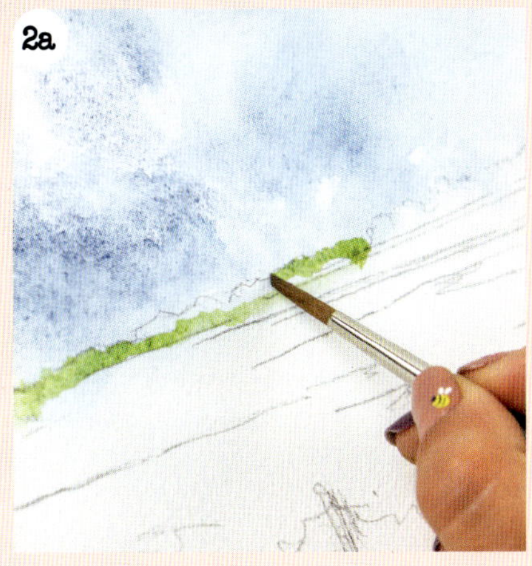

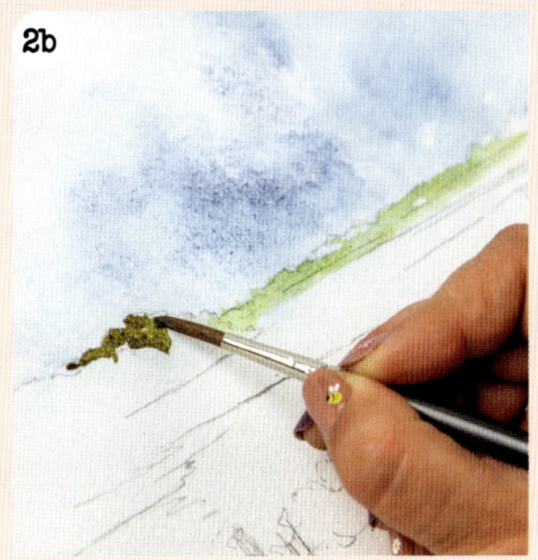

BALANCING TONES

Balance the tones and colours of the foliage to give distance to the trees: you can add the blue from the sky to make the trees colder, and then, as they become darker and closer to you, perhaps mix in a touch of red for a warmer feel.

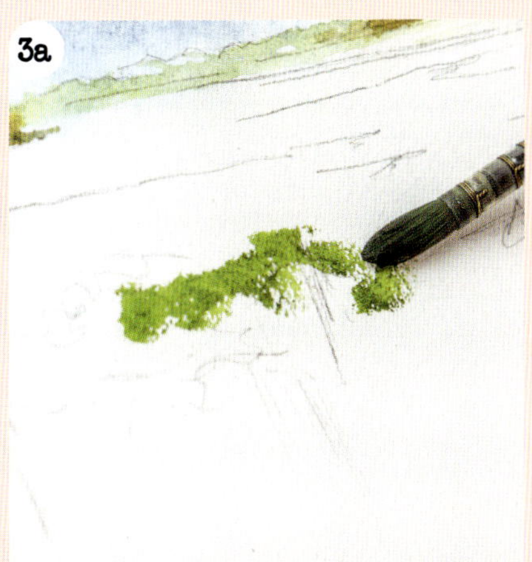

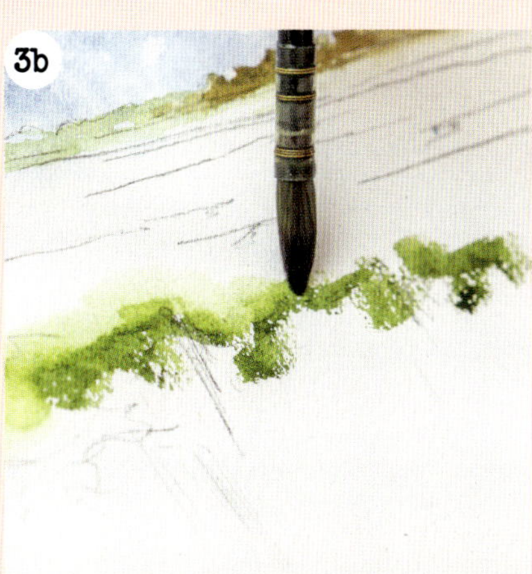

DRYBRUSH

To describe the grass and stems in the foreground, use a sticky consistency of paint, dragged across the surface of the paper so that it hits and misses. Use different parts of the brush to provide an assortment of marks.

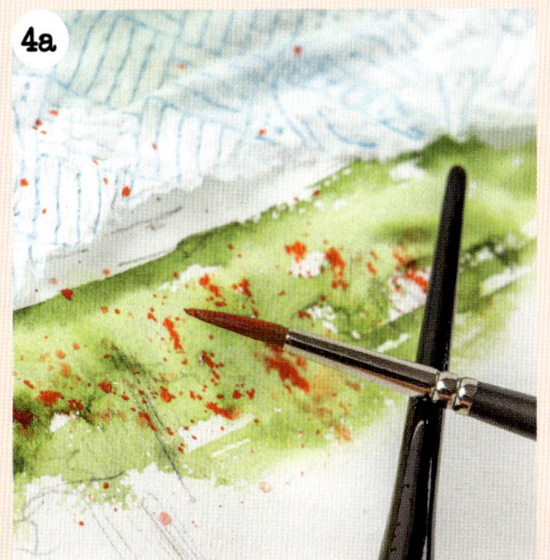

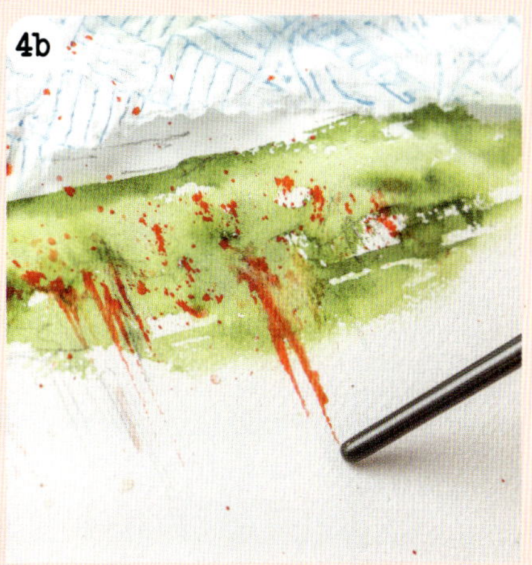

SPATTER

Add spatter for additional texture in the foreground by loading up the brush with colour and tapping it over the top of another brush handle or pencil to create small splashes. Then, use the handle of the brush to pull the colour into a suggestion of stem shapes.

(Make sure you cover any areas of your painting that you don't want to affect with spatter!)

Spatter isn't the only texture you could consider here; consider the mark-making tools and techniques we discussed on pages 54–55.

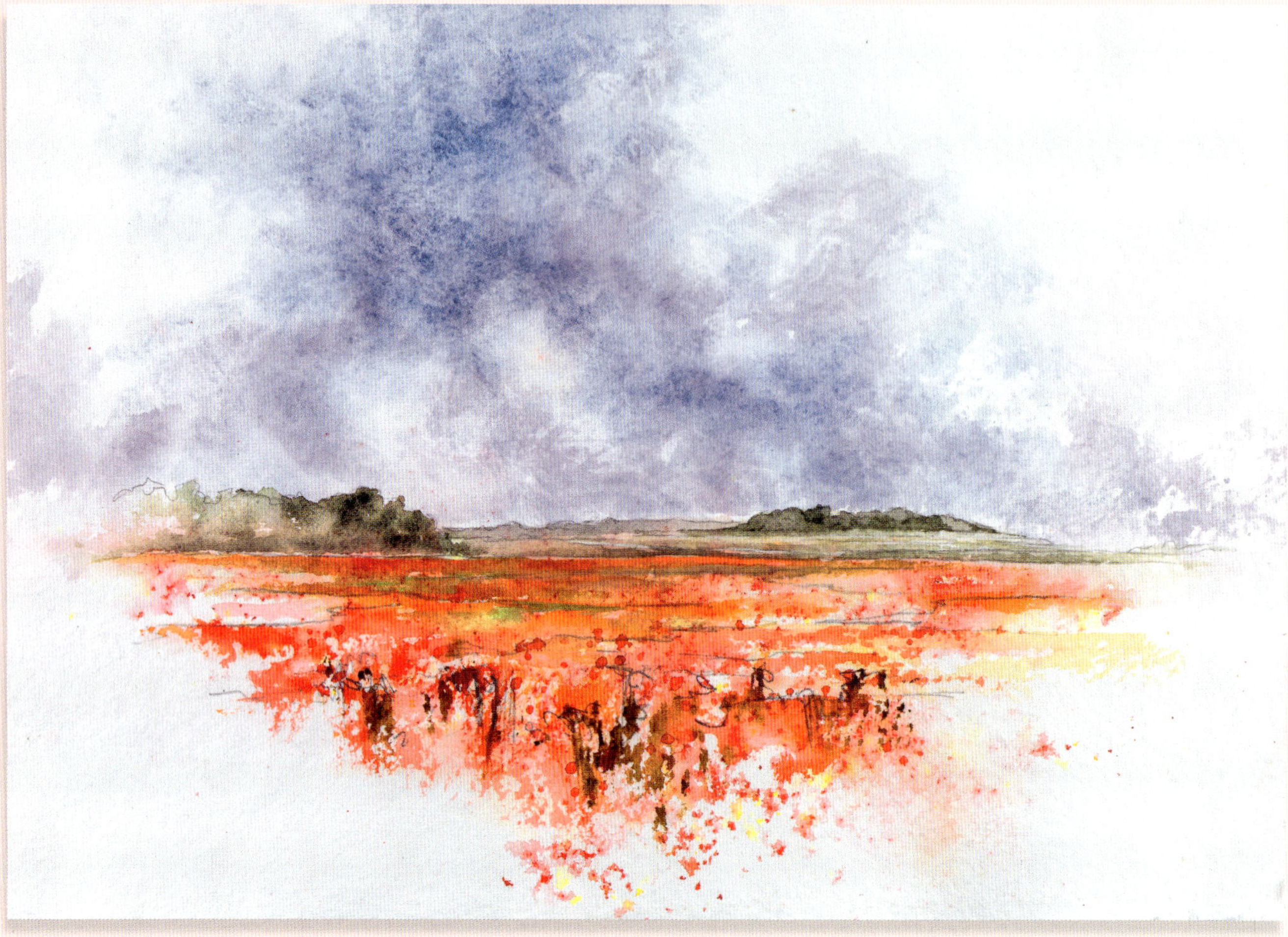

The first version worked well but in developing it further, I felt that more emphasis could have been placed on the foreground texture, giving the painting greater depth and distance.

Badbury Poppies: version 2
420 × 297mm (16½ × 11¾in)

TECHNIQUES

'DOUBLE' SKY

Put two layers into the sky area to provide more drama and depth.

Allow a basic sky (see page 61) to dry and then add more texture within a second layer; just make sure that the first layer is completely dry, and use a very light touch for the second.

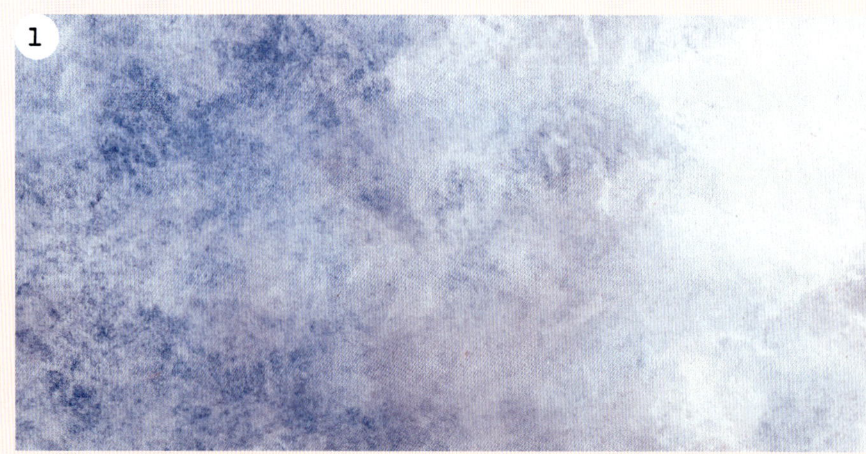

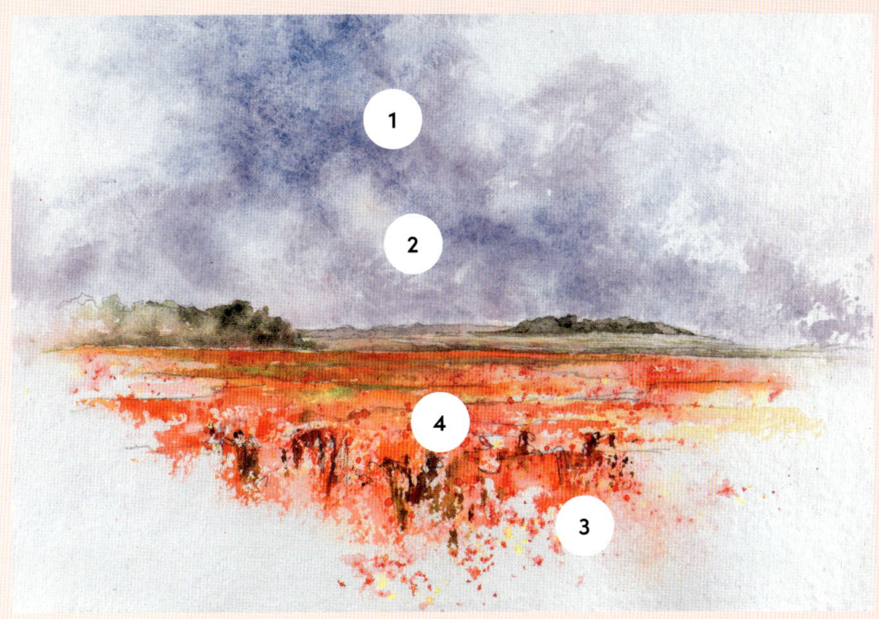

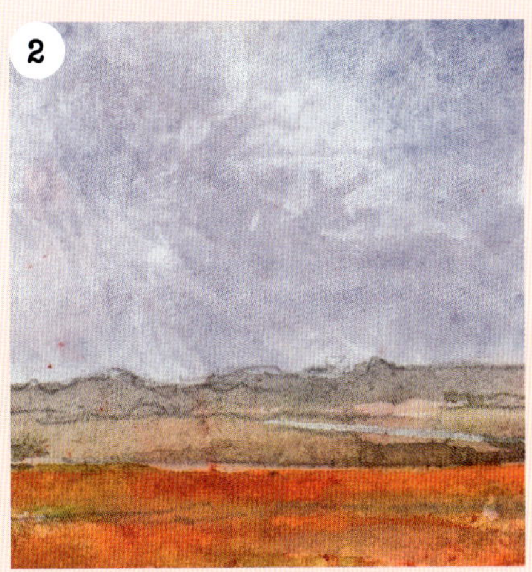

USING THE TEXTURE OF THE PAPER

The uneven texture of the paper helps to split the pigments in the watercolour, giving the illusion of more detail. This effect is sometimes referred to as 'granulation', but a heavily textured paper can lead to interesting marks when using even the most solid of colours.

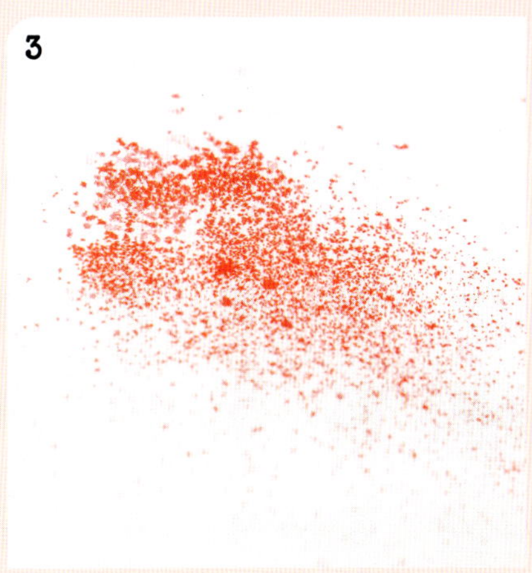

CRYSTALLINE (POWDER) WATERCOLOUR

Use Crystalline watercolour (by Jackman's) or a similar powdered pigment such as Brusho Crystal Colour to add both texture and unpredictability in the foreground. Any powdered pigments that bloom when they come into contact with water are fun to use but (as I mention on page 118) be sure to clear up your workspace after use!

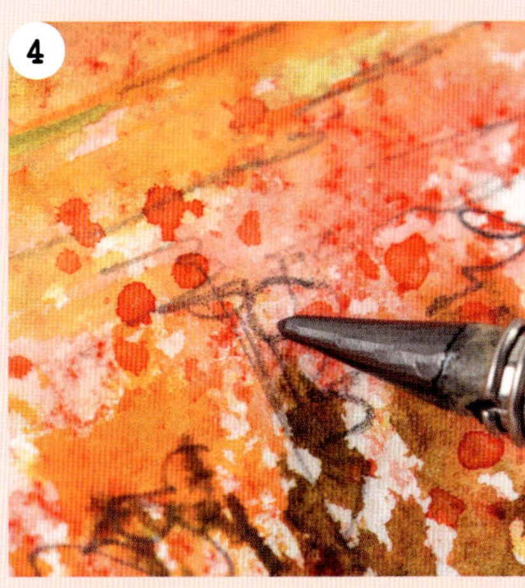

STRATEGIC MARK MAKING

Add detail and further marks through spatter, extra water and marks with a graphite stick when the previous layer has dried. With these types of finishing touches it can be tricky to know when to stop and so they are sometimes best done when you have stepped away from the painting for a little while.

Glencoe

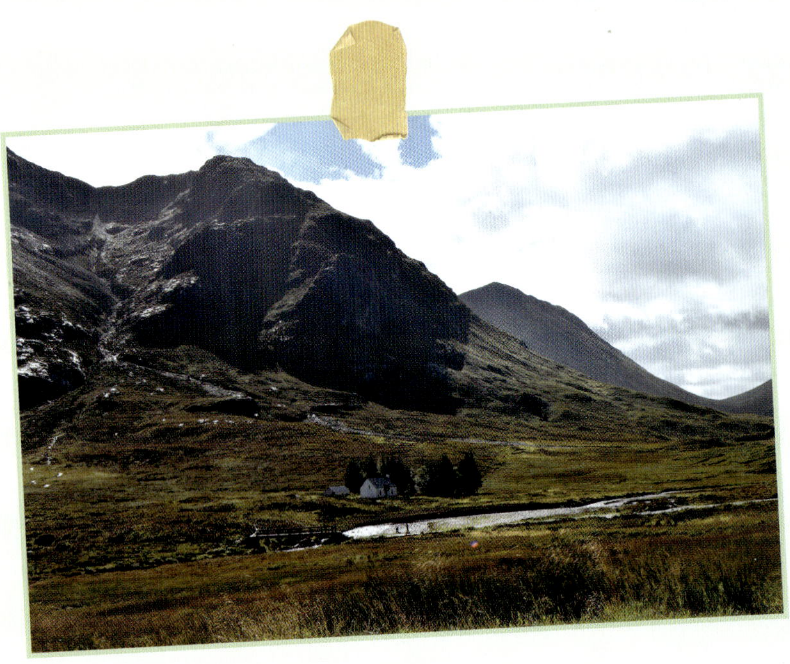

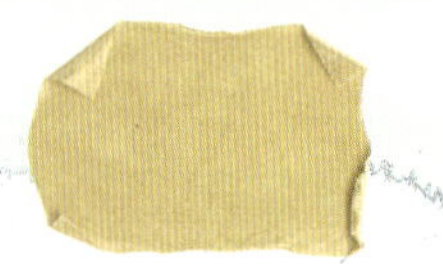

VERSION 1 (PAGES 134–137)

SURFACE: Fabriano Artistico, 640gsm (300lb), Extra White, Cold-Pressed, 380 × 280mm (15 × 11in)

MATERIALS AND TOOLS: watercolour paints in Prussian Blue, Green Gold, Grey, and Foliage Green

VERSION 2 (PAGES 138–139)

SURFACE: Pastelmat® in Light Blue, 360gsm (170lb), 300 × 400mm (11¾ × 15¾in)

MATERIALS AND TOOLS: Unison pastel sticks in assorted heather, green, blues and greys; Stabilo® CarbOthello pastel pencils in green, tan, black and white

INSPIRATION

I have adored the Highlands of Scotland for many years. Even if the weather isn't great, you can still find drama and history around every corner. This photograph was actually taken from a moving car as the exact spot I wanted to capture was too dangerous to stop at. So I made my husband drive backwards and forwards a couple of times before I managed to capture the scene I was looking for.

BEFORE I START PAINTING

The potential for using different media here is enormous. I often don't see just one way that I want to capture a view on paper and therefore experimenting with different media to capture the essence of geography is very important to me.

There is quite a challenge here in balancing the height of the mountain against the small detail of the cottage, so it will be interesting to see how the balance appears on the paper.

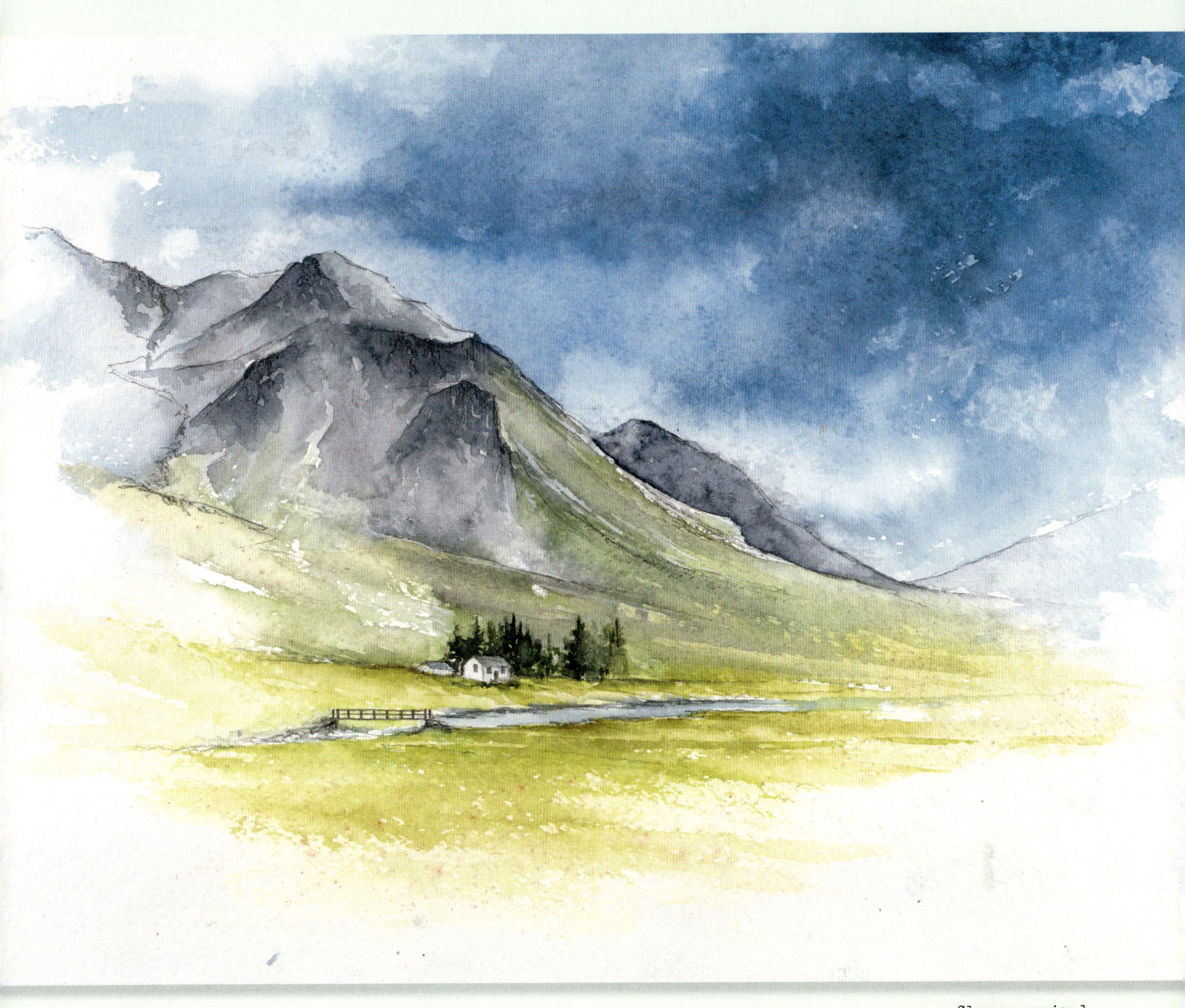

Glencoe: version 1
380 × 280mm (15 × 11in)

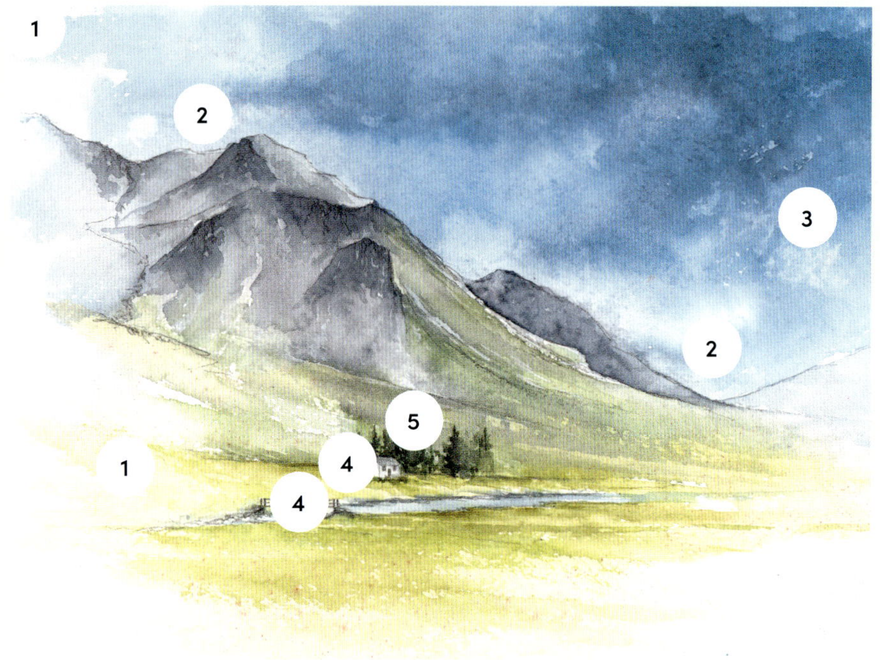

Techniques featured in <u>Glencoe</u>: version 1

TECHNIQUES

VIGNETTE WITH A STRONG COLOUR

Giving soft edges to the painting suggests both atmosphere and distance, which can be difficult when you want to use a colour that is bold. If you are using watercolour, make sure you give the paint plenty of clean water to escape into and diffuse.

1a

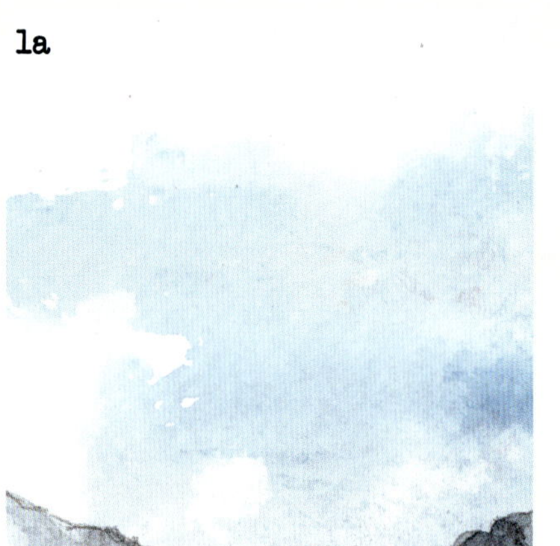

1b

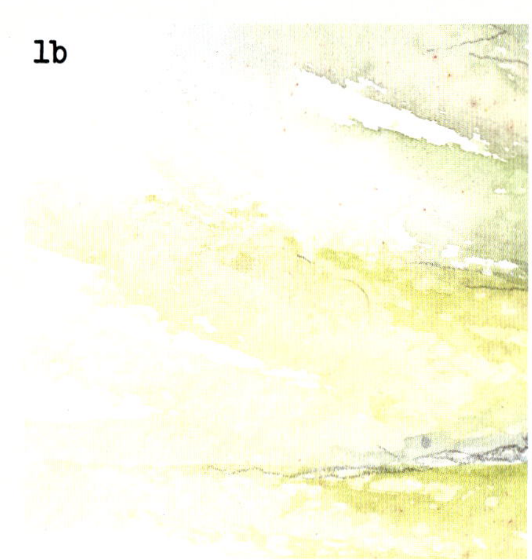

EXPERIMENTING WITH COLOUR PALETTE

Use cooler colours for the mountains in comparison with the foreground to show distance without holding back the dark tones for drama. Experiment with sharp and lost edges as this will also help with showing how far away objects are (see pages 68, 92 and 93).

2

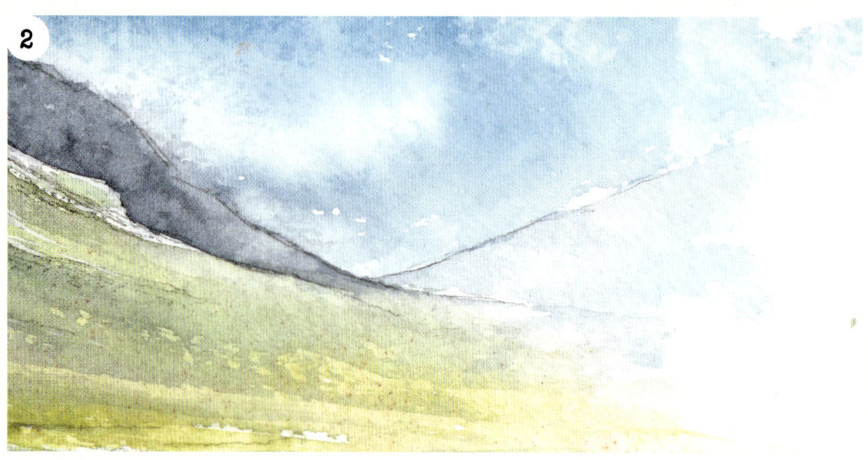

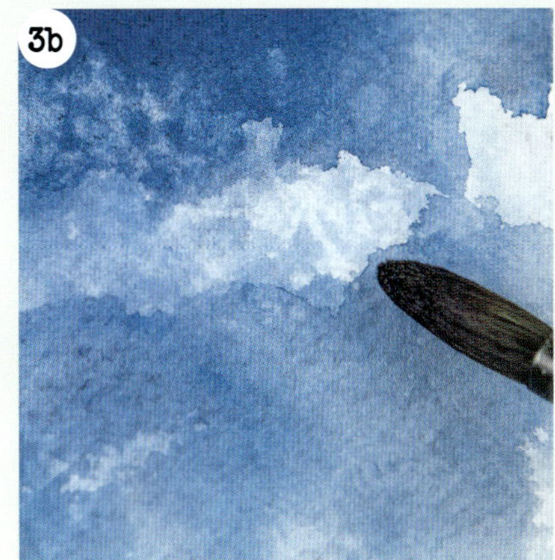

DOUBLE SKY

Create a 'double' sky with two layers of paint so that a sense of distance can be achieved. You can see how I used this effect in the second *Badbury Poppies* painting on page 132.

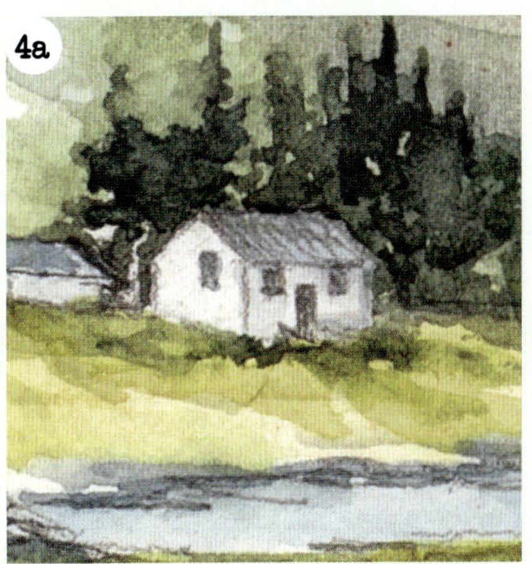

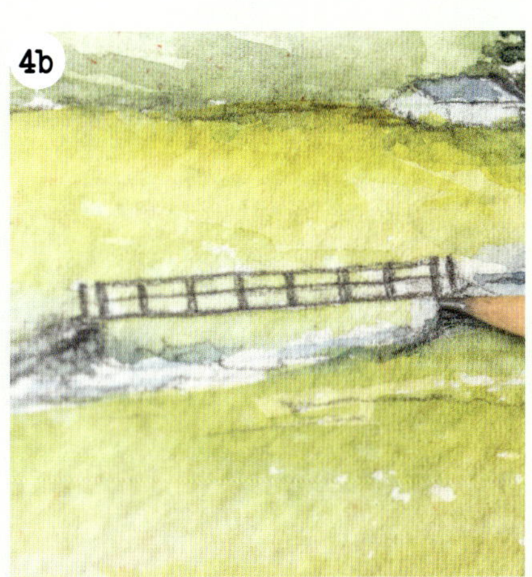

DETAILS WITH GRAPHITE

Apply small details for the buildings and the bridge to give scale to the mountains. You may wish to experiment with the most accurate tool for this job; here I am using a pencil so that I have full control over the small marks – I would struggle with a brush, and a pen would perhaps give too bold a mark.

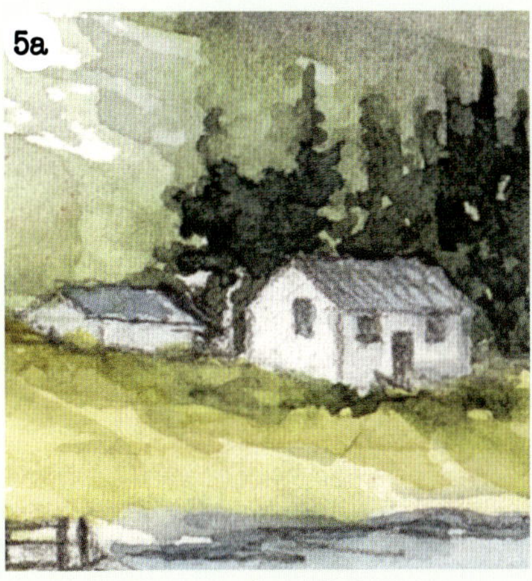

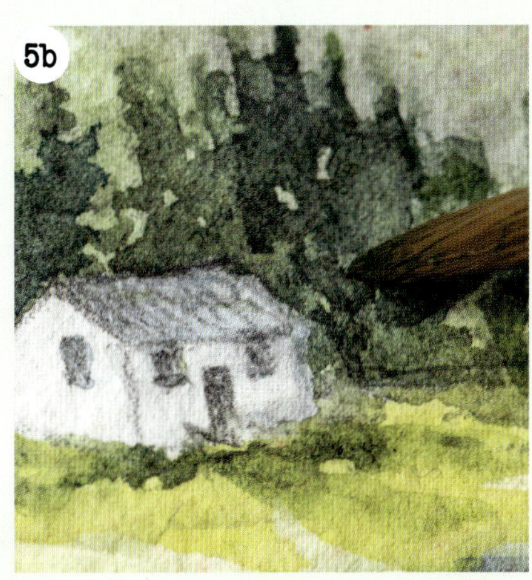

NEGATIVE-SPACE DARKS

Place rich darks into the trees, to throw the brightness of the buildings forwards. It is sometimes better to work on the marks around a subject rather than on the positive image itself.

GLENCOE: VERSION 2

After assessing how much drama and atmosphere was being created with watercolour, I wondered if there was an opportunity to test a totally different medium. So, I am experimenting with chalk–pastel techniques here. I have also included a coloured paper so my choice of colour palette is influenced by what would work well with this grey tone.

Glencoe: version 2
297 × 420mm (11¾ ×16½in)

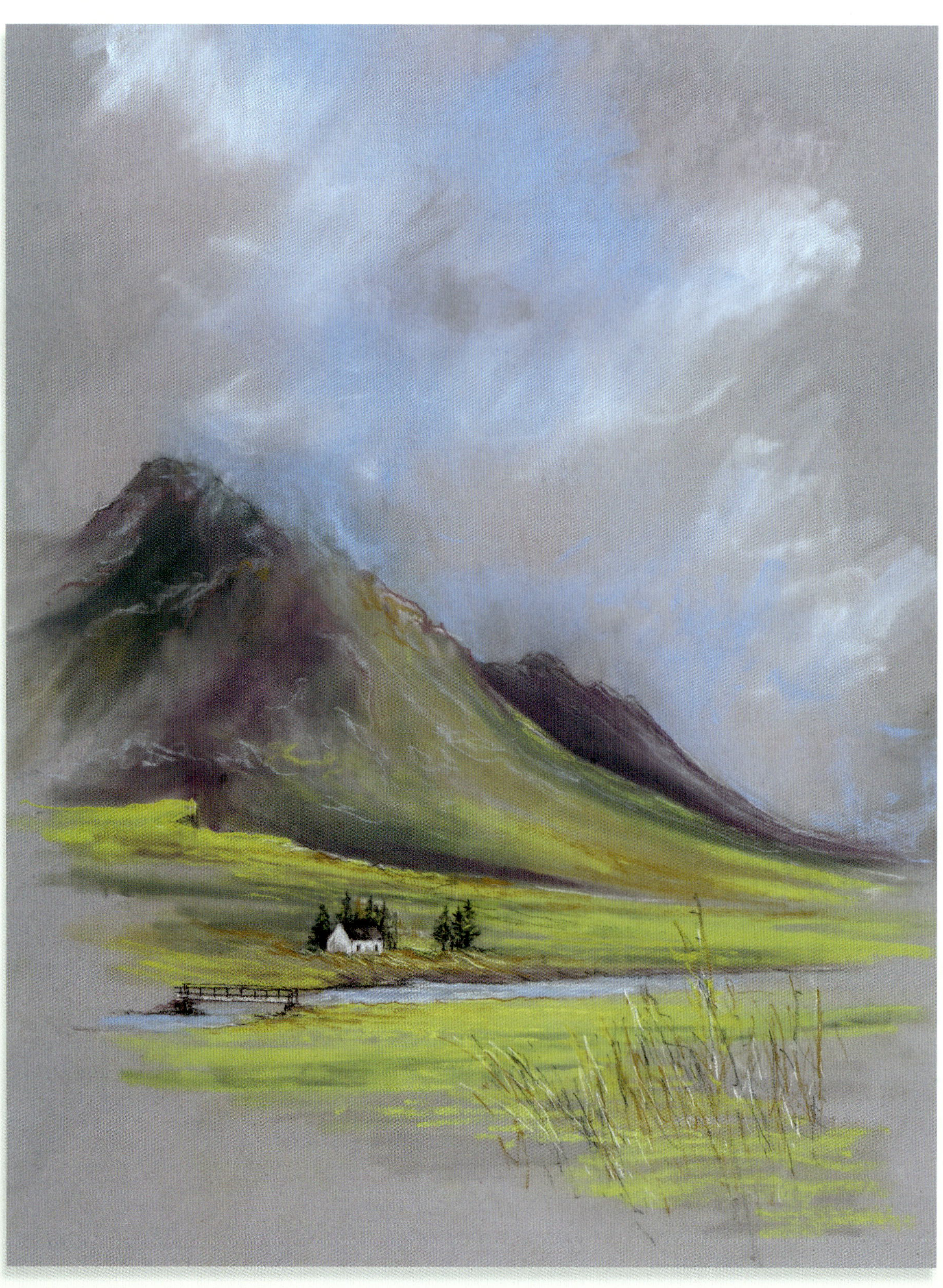

TECHNIQUES

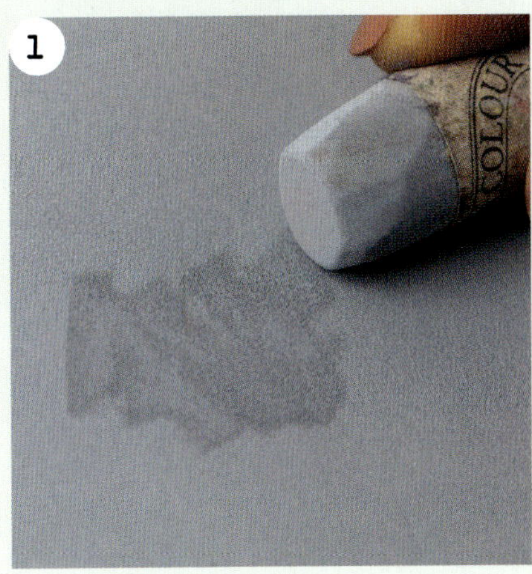

BLENDING EDGES

Find a pastel very close in colour to the surface colour, so that edges can be blended out. This has the same effect as using water to fade out the colour in a watercolour technique. Page 92 has more information on blending pastel.

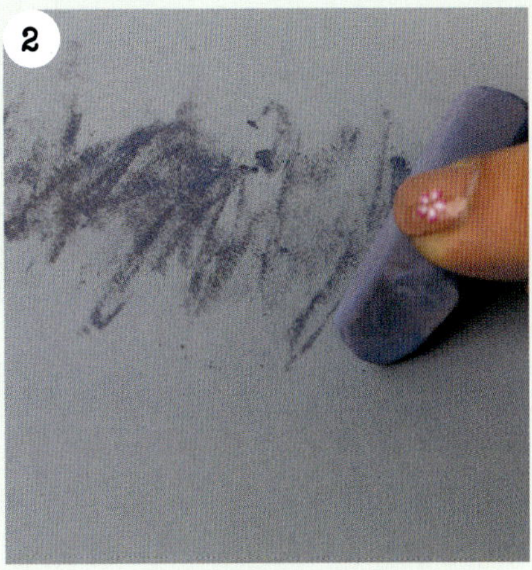

ROLLING A PASTEL STICK TO CREATE TEXTURE

Don't be afraid to leave marks on the paper to depict texture: in this example I have laid the entire pastel stick on the surface and rolled it like a log.

It can be tempting with chalk pastel to blend everything, but you need some texture and definition somewhere in your painting to achieve the balance between the lost edges and the sharp focus.

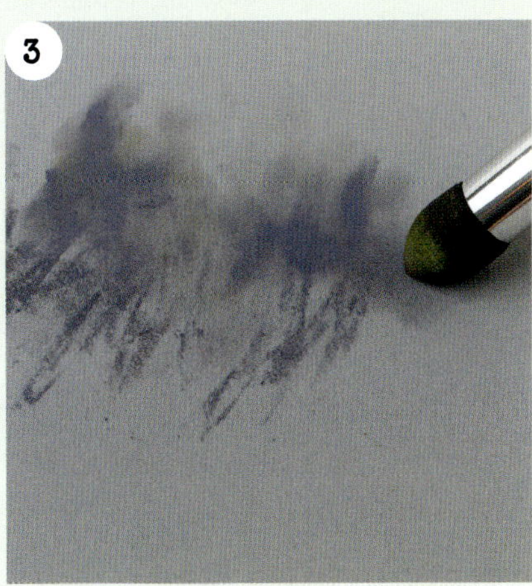

DIFFERENT BLENDING TOOLS

Use different types of blenders with pastel so that you can vary the appearance of your marks. This tool is a pastel blender that has a sponge end for soft marks in small spaces.

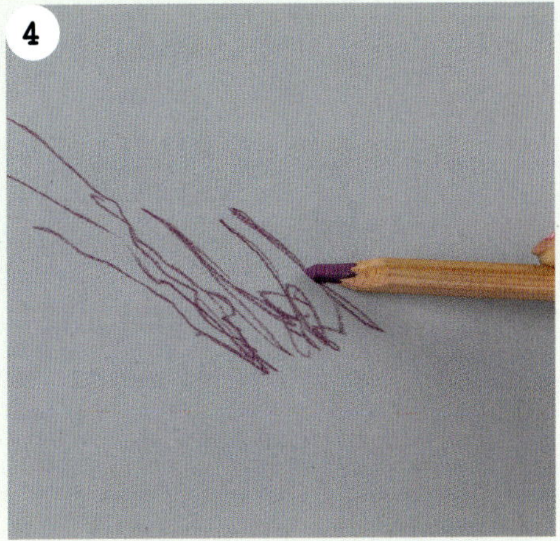

PUSHING A PASTEL PENCIL

Push, instead of pull, a pastel pencil for more natural foreground marks. You will be surprised by the textures that can be created just by this small change in application. I have used this technique for the grasses in the foreground.

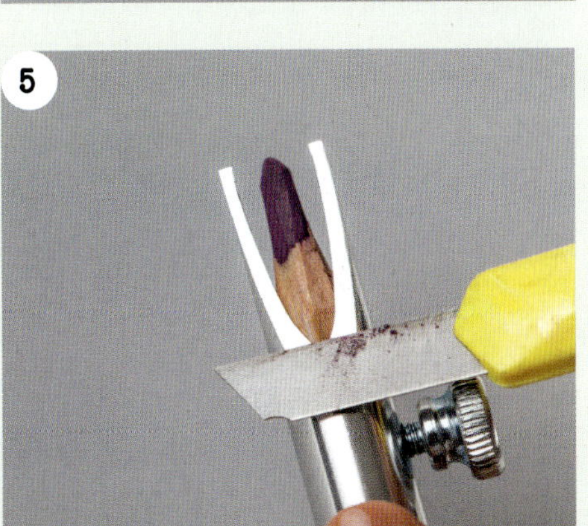

SHARPENING A PASTEL PENCIL

Make sure your pastel pencil is super-sharp and will hold its point for the tiniest of details. If you struggle with using a knife, a sharpening guide like this one may help; a fine grade sandpaper works well too.

Melin Tregwynt

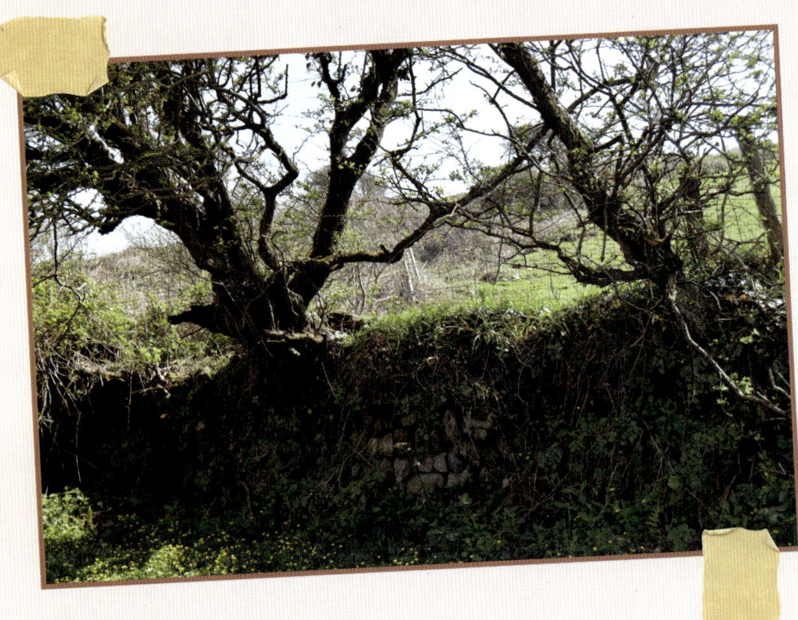

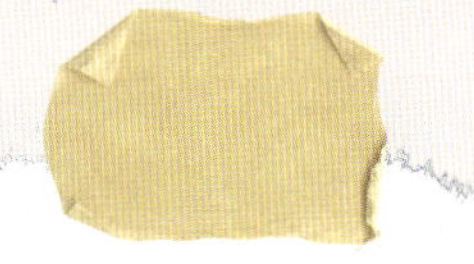

You will need...

VERSION 1 (PAGES 140–143)

SURFACE: Fabriano Artistico, 300gsm (140lb), Extra White, Cold-Pressed, 380 × 280mm (15 × 11in)

MATERIALS AND TOOLS: acrylic inks in fluorescent yellow, phthalo green, muted violet and black; Posca (acrylic paint marker pens) in black, yellow, green and white

VERSION 2 (PAGES 144–145)

SURFACE: Pastelmat® in Anthracite, 360gsm (170lb), 380 × 280mm (15 × 11in)

MATERIALS AND TOOLS: gouache paints in Leaf Green, Olive Green and Cool Grey; Caran d'Ache pastel pencils in greys, tans, violet-greys and greens; charcoal pencil

INSPIRATION

My family and I have often taken this walk down to the sea in Pembrokeshire, Wales; it's full of old walls and shows where nature has found a way through the various structures, creating a canopy of shade as you walk along. It doesn't matter what time of year you walk this path, you are always sheltered from the elements and surrounded by nature.

BEFORE I START PAINTING

It isn't the wall that draws me to this scene, it's the patterns of the branches, grasses and the wire of the fence that you can just about see in the photograph.

I have several photos of exactly the same spot at various times of the year and so I am eager to create two experiments, one that is all about the colours and the other, all about the mark making. Two paintings of this scene will probably never be enough as I have many more ideas beyond my first experiments.

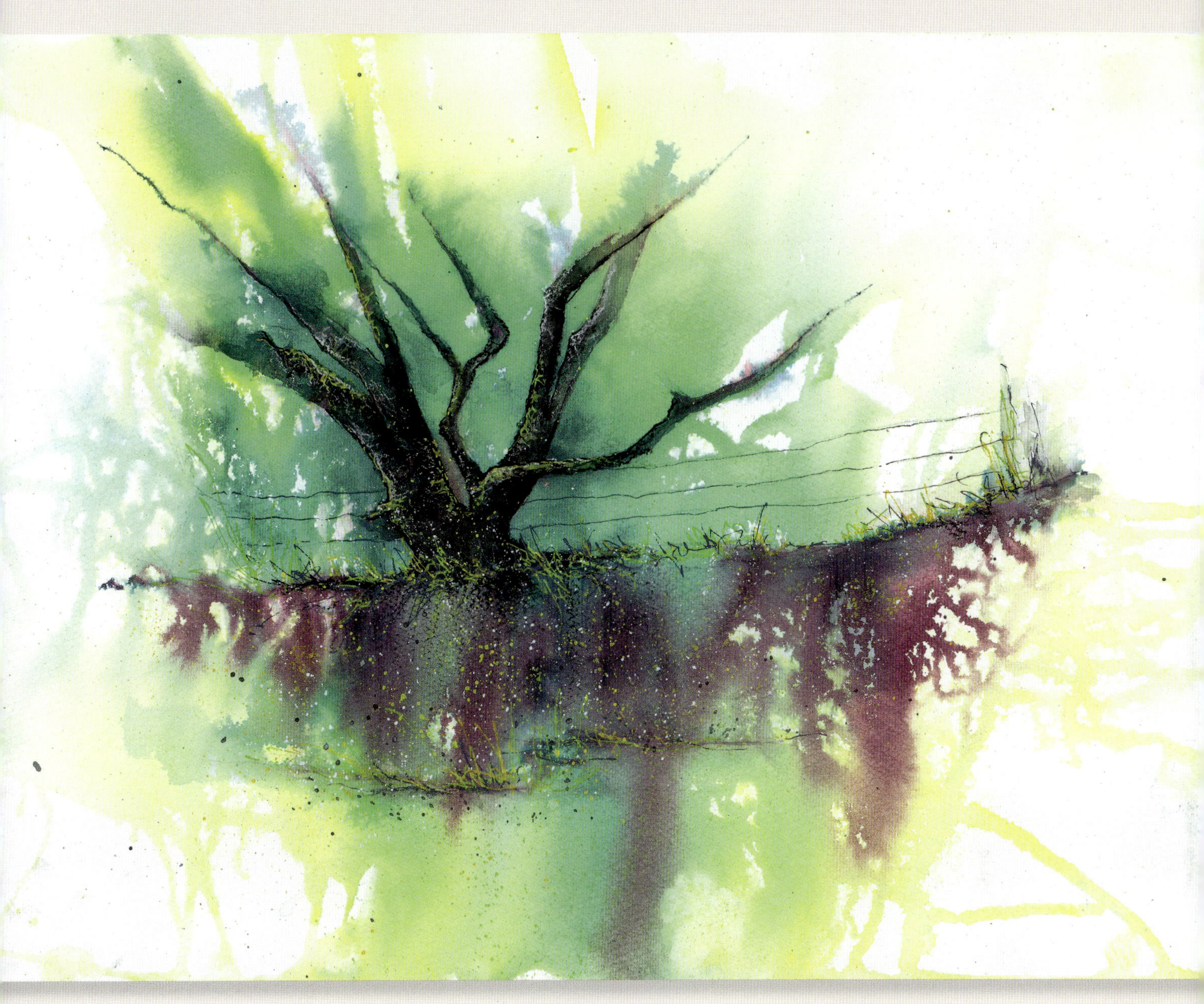

Melin Tregwynt: version 1
380 × 280mm (15 × 11in)

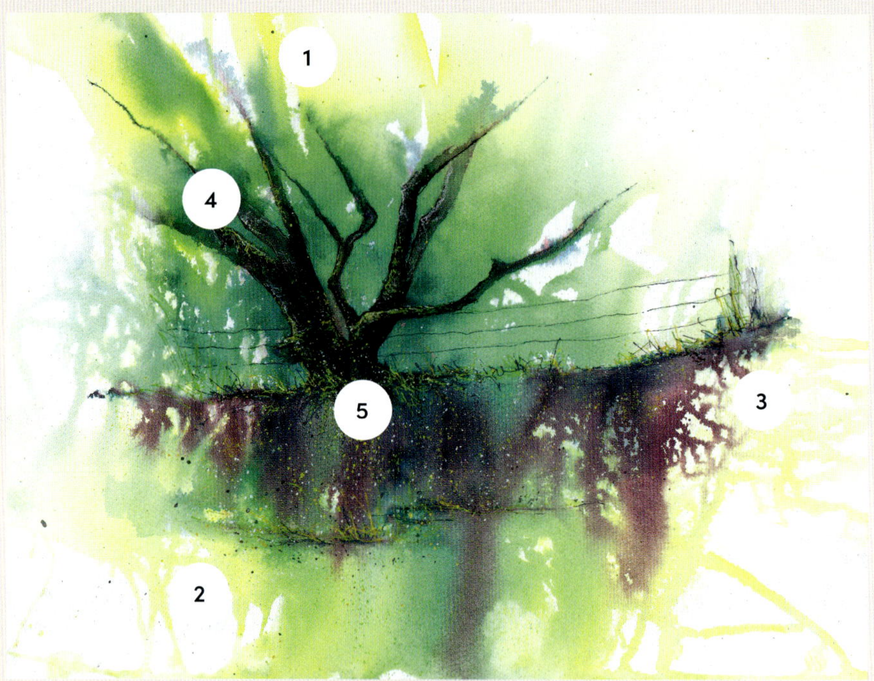

Techniques featured in Melin Tregwynt: version 1

TECHNIQUES

CHOOSING BRIGHT COLOURS

I enjoy choosing to paint a subject in non-natural colours and so I invite you to be daring with your choice to suggest the sunlight beyond the dense structure.

In my recent experiments, fluorescent pigments – such as these inks – have started to feature, as they provide a delicious 'pop' of colour and can bring an added dimension to a painting.

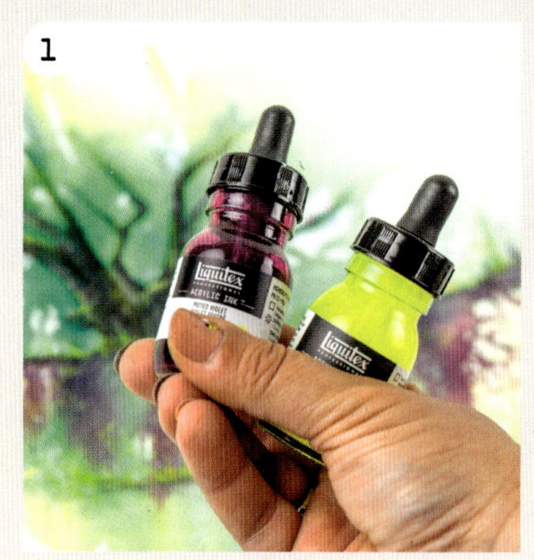

DRIPPING AND TURNING

Allow the liquid colours of acrylic inks to drip and flow by turning the paper several times during application. It may feel as if they are out of control but you will be able to manipulate them by trying different angles or simply letting the colours run off the surface.

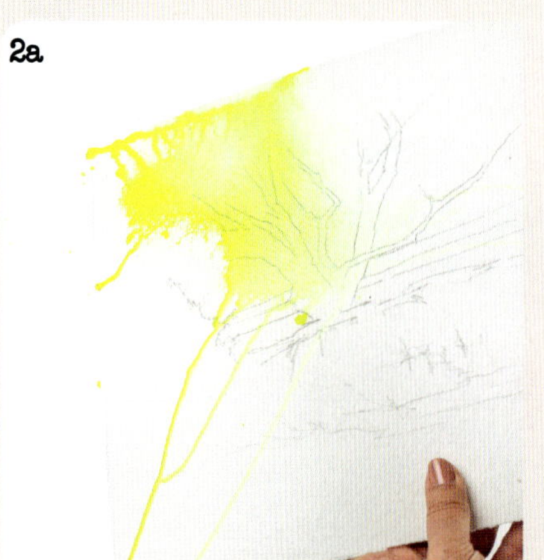
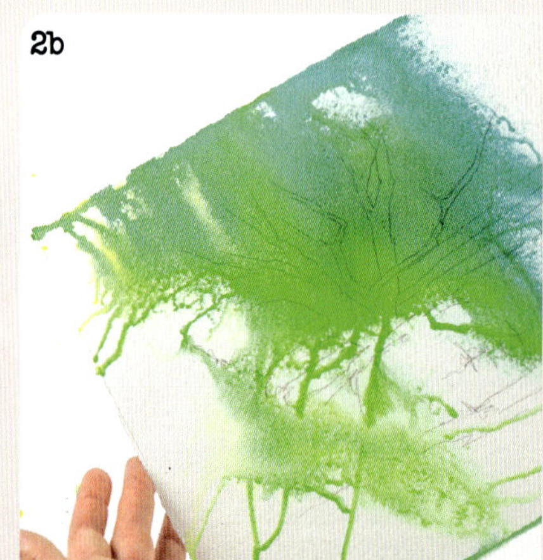

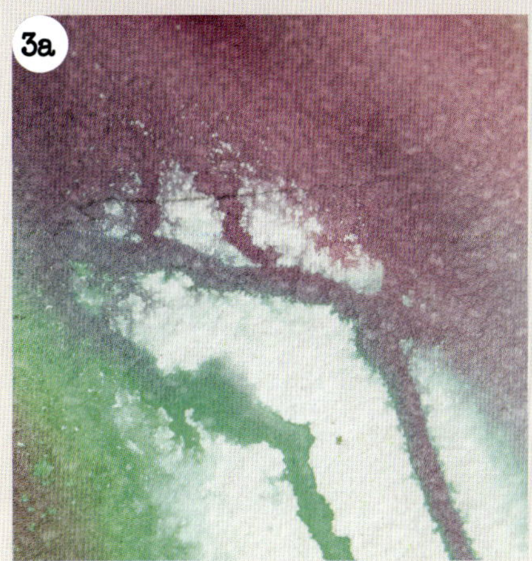

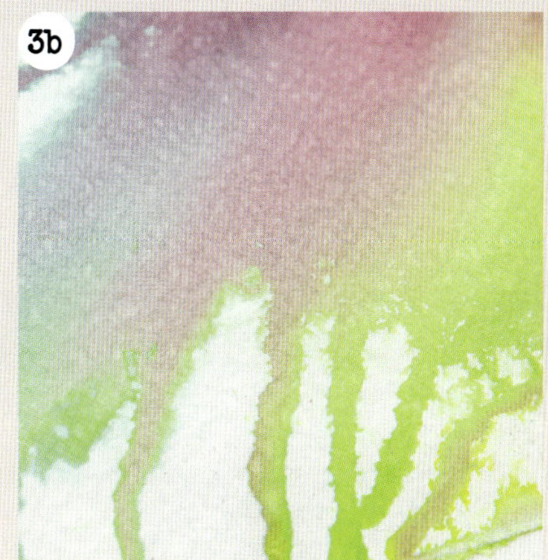

EMBRACING UNUSUAL MARKS

Keep some marks that have happened through serendipity to suggest the textures you are trying to capture. They may feel scary, but embrace them as they can often provide an interesting textural element.

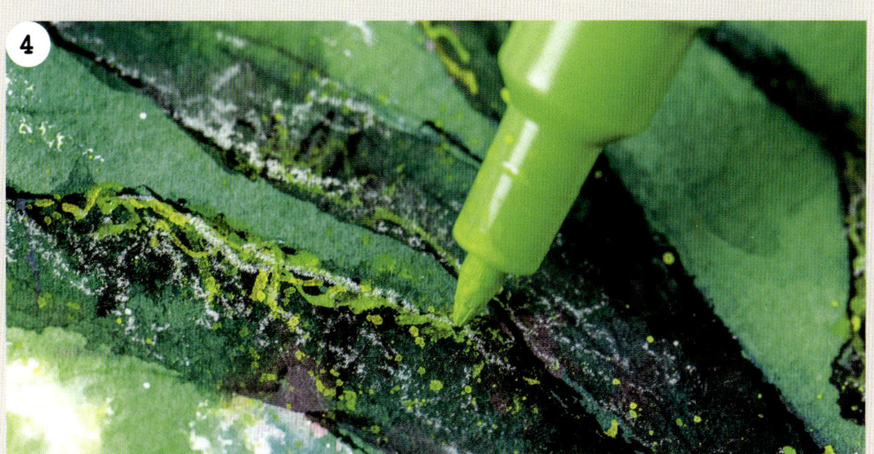

REFINING WITH DETAIL

Pull the piece together by embracing the chaotic and adding detail to refine it.

Alongside acrylic inks, I enjoy using Posca pens (acrylic paint markers) as their bright colours and painterly look bind the liquid areas with the structure.

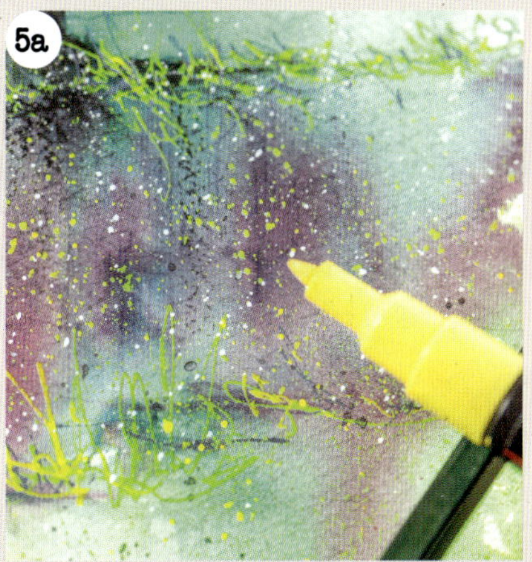

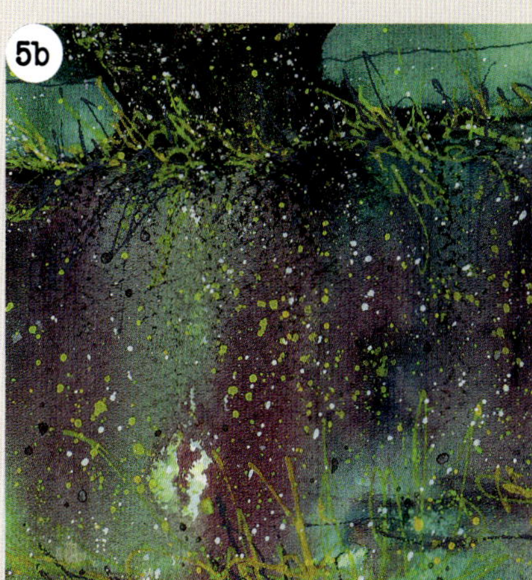

SPATTER

Spatter with acrylic paint markers for very fine texture.

Spatter with a paint marker pen is just as achievable as with a brush (see page 131) but you may need a much stronger tap across your pencil or brush handle for the ink to leave the nib.

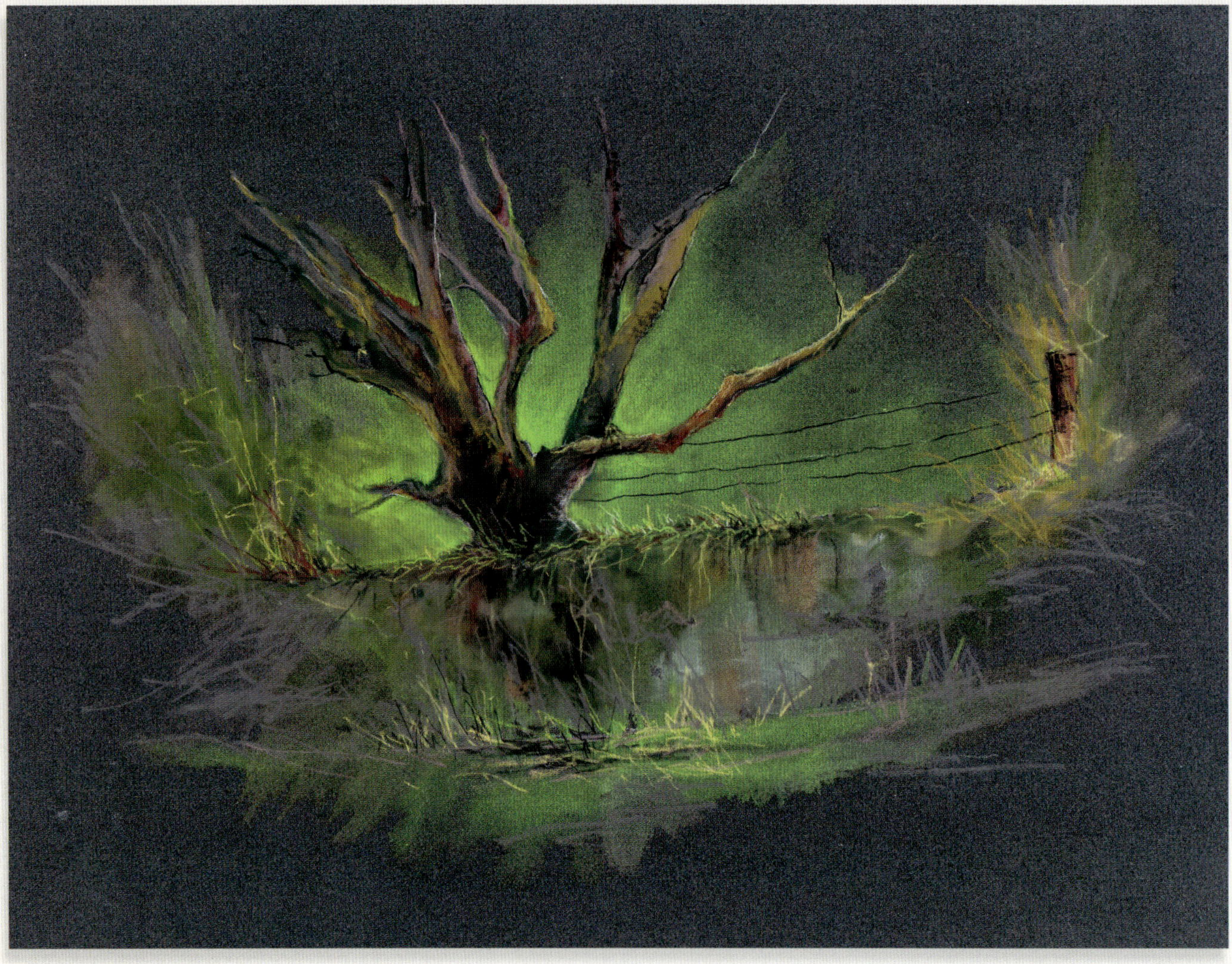

Melin Tregwynt: version 2

380 × 280mm (15 × 11in)

To marry liquid and drawn areas together (see page 143, step 4), you could consider a combination of paint and chalk pastel, even a coloured paper as used on page 139 for the second version of *Glencoe*.

To allow the paint to show up on a near-black paper, I have chosen to use gouache, a more opaque and robust medium similar to watercolour, so my painting skills can be used in combination with drawing in pastel pencils.

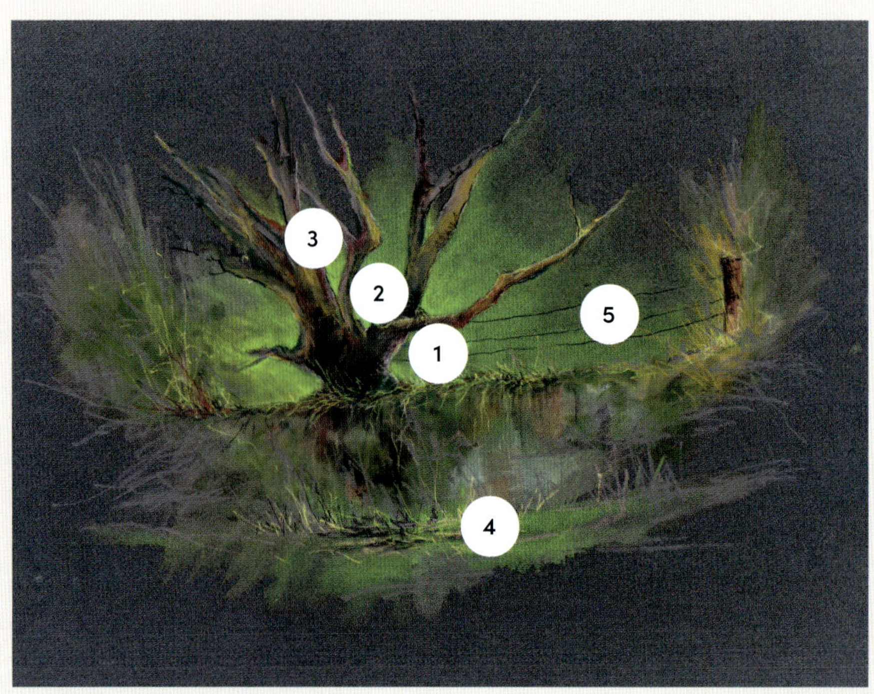

TECHNIQUES

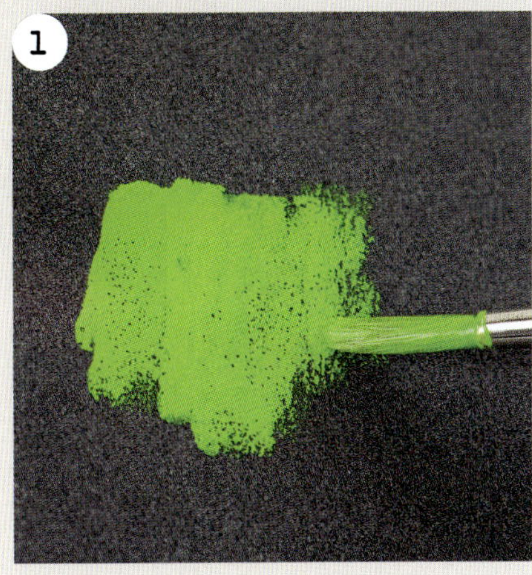

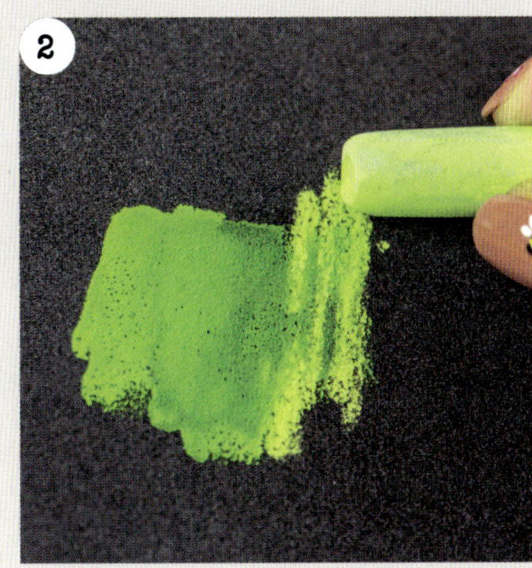

GOUACHE ON PASTELMAT

It may surprise you to learn that even though a pastel surface is meant for chalk and other dry media, many take paint very well. Gouache in particular is one to consider due to its opaque properties – I often describe it as 'liquid pastel' for this reason.

PASTEL STICKS ON GOUACHE

The combination of gouache and chalk pastel is fairly seamless, so you can use them together to make bold colour statements.

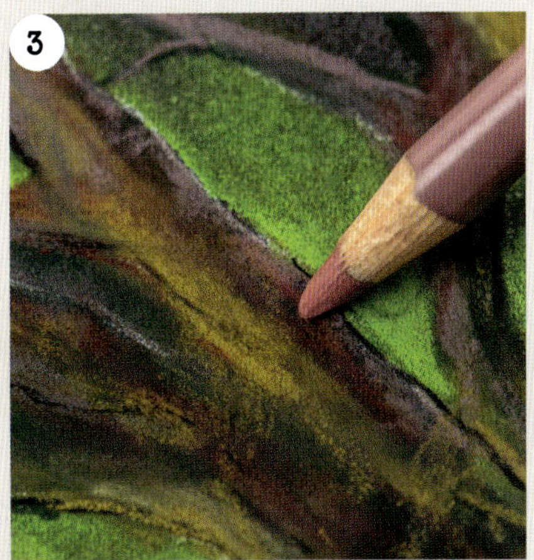

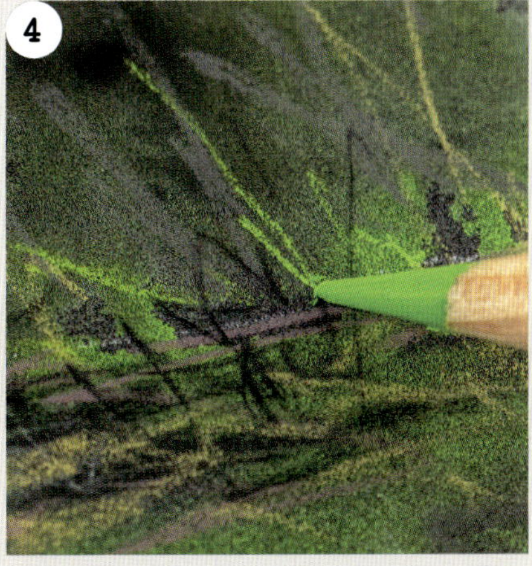

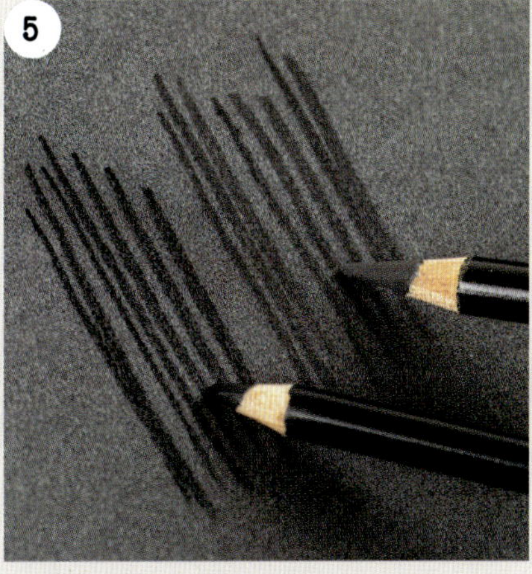

BUILDING LAYERS OF PASTEL PENCIL

Use pastel pencils to give detail that sticks of pastel cannot. A pastel surface, depending on the brand, will allow you to build up layers of elements such as grasses or branches to give depth.

MARK MAKING WITH PASTEL PENCIL

Natural forms such as grass need a variation of marks applied to make them look realistic, so avoid making them too uniform in width and length. Change the angle of your strokes and try pushing the pencil away from you (see page 139).

PASTEL PENCIL VERSUS CHARCOAL PENCIL

Continuing to think about the quality of marks that you can make, you can achieve even greater subtlety by using a charcoal pencil instead of a black pastel pencil to give a softer dark line. You can see a comparison here; the pastel pencil is on the left and the charcoal pencil on the right.

Downend Snow

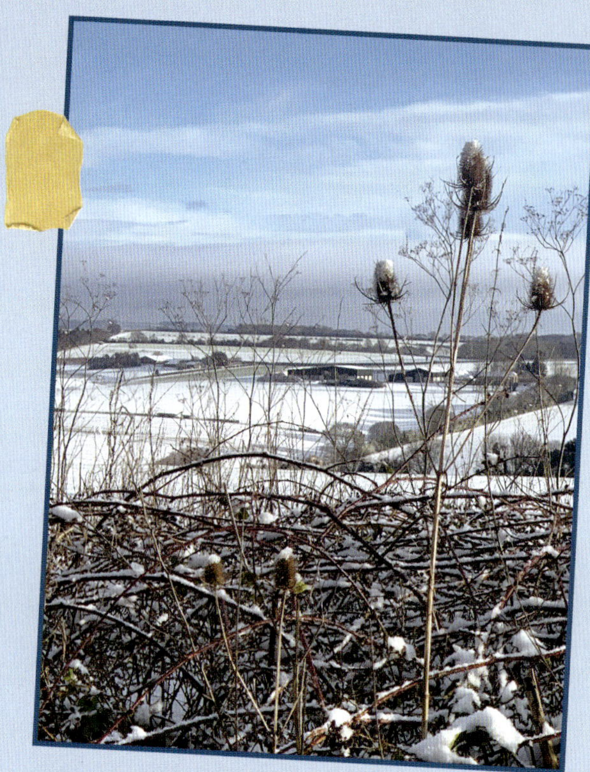

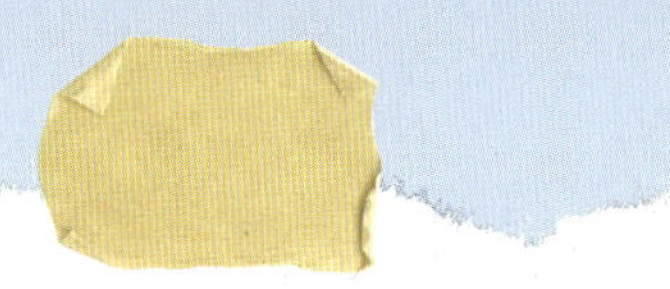

VERSION 1 (PAGES 146–149)

SURFACE: Hahnemühle Andalucia, 500gsm (230lb), 300 × 400mm (11¾ × 15¾in) – quarter-imperial

MATERIALS AND TOOLS: watercolours in Cobalt Blue, Ultramarine Violet, Prussian Blue and Hematite Genuine; charcoal pencil, pastel pencil and tissue paper

VERSION 2 (PAGES 150–151)

SURFACE: Pastelmat® in Dark Blue, 360gsm (170lb), 300 × 400mm (11¾ × 15¾in)

MATERIALS AND TOOLS: Unison pastel sticks in blues, greys, whites and maroons; Caran d'Ache pastel pencils in greys, white, blues and violet-greys

INSPIRATION

Behind my studio are some of the most breathtaking views in all of Dorset. They are not accessible to most and so are teeming with wildlife and fields that seem to go on for miles. Being so high up, you can often get battered by the elements in the colder months of the year.

This photograph sums up all of those things to me, featuring distant farm buildings, an expanse of sky and the tight knit of the brambles at my feet.

BEFORE I START PAINTING

I know this view was going to be a challenge, particularly in achieving the criss-cross pattern of the brambles, so I am looking forward to seeing how I can make meaningful marks but still keep it simple. I have already made one attempt at this composition as you can see on page 123 and have learnt a great deal about what to put in and what to leave out. One of the key lessons is going to be keeping my colour palette cold and being brave with my darks.

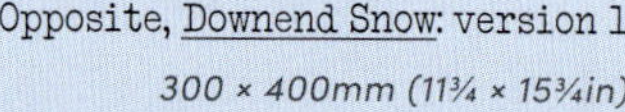

Opposite, <u>Downend Snow</u>: version 1
300 × 400mm (11¾ × 15¾in)

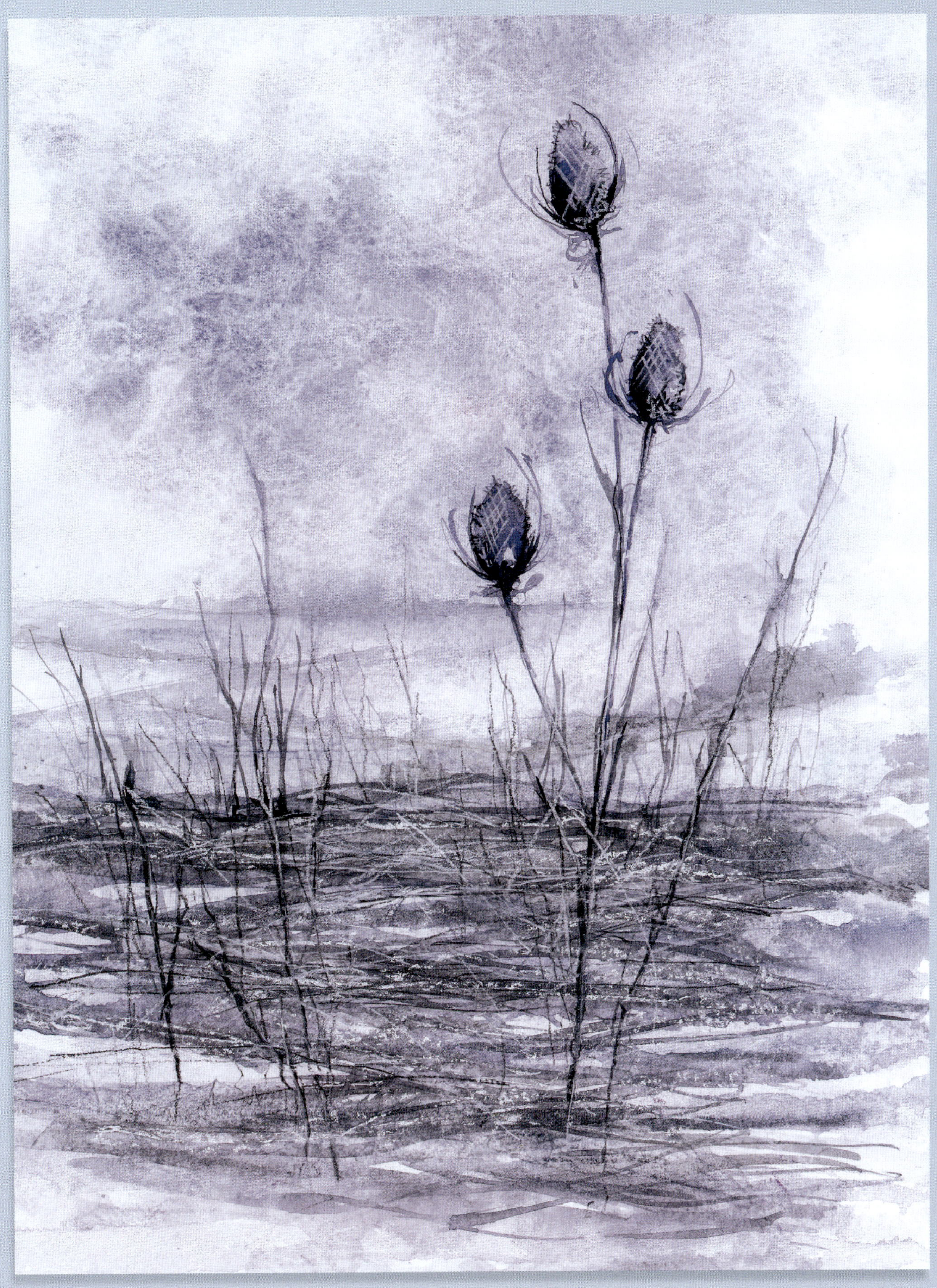

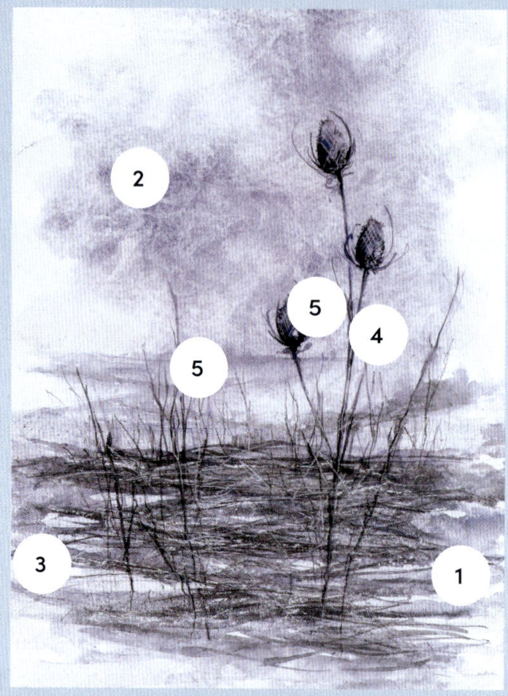

Techniques featured in <u>Downend Snow</u>: version 1

TECHNIQUES

ADDING TISSUE PAPER

Glue folded or scrunched tissue paper to the surface with an adhesive that isn't going to repel your colour. My favourite is to use an acrylic medium that I have watered down or washed away from the top layer and this will give interesting textures when you add liquid colour.

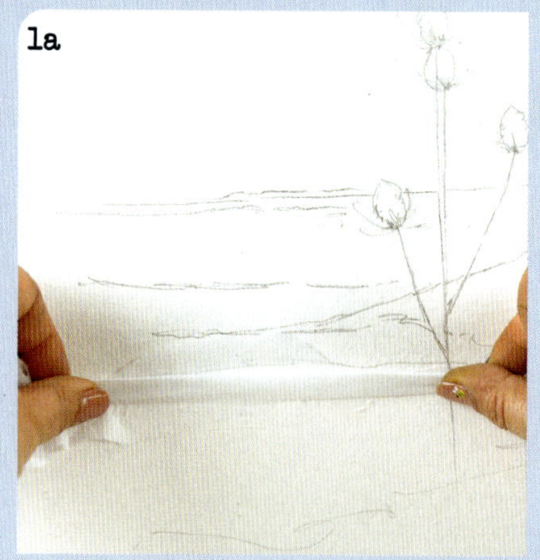

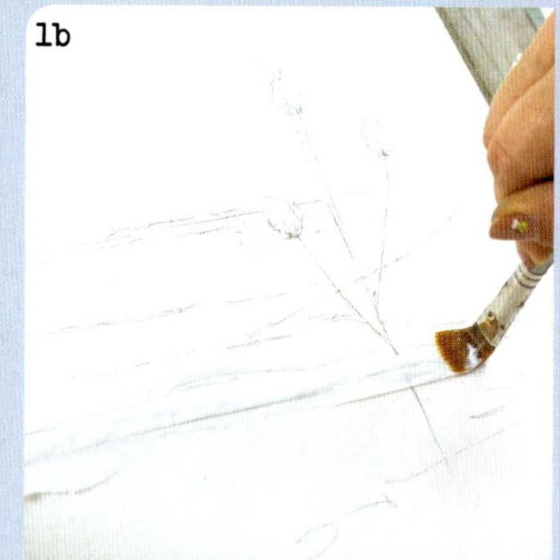

SOFT WET-INTO-WET SKY

Add soft edges to the sky to counterbalance the intended hard textures in the foreground. Here I have added a watered-down pink to balance the cold and dark colours I have chosen for other parts of the painting.

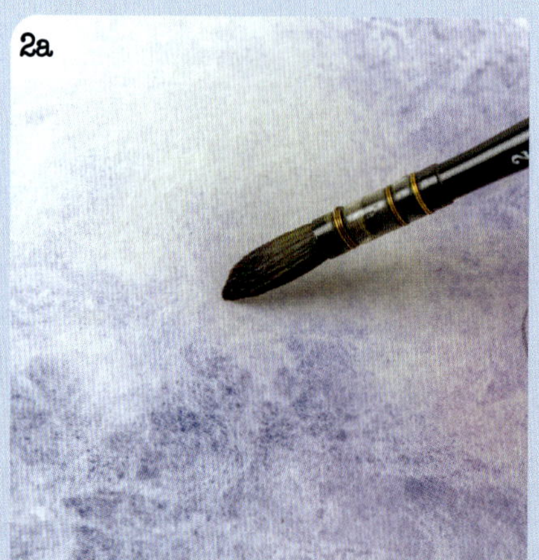

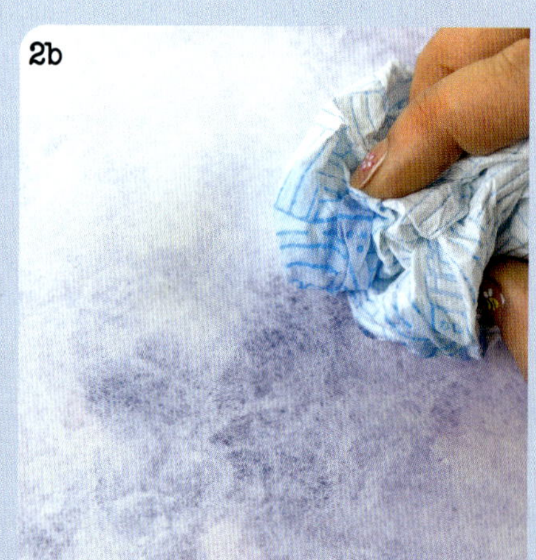

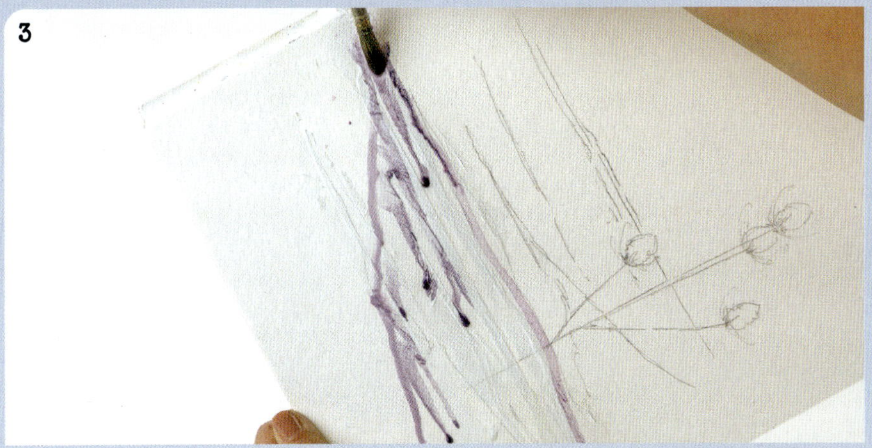

ADDING PAINT TO TISSUE

Be brave and allow liquid colour to drip; tip up your surface to allow gravity to help you. The textured tissue added earlier will guide the liquid along avenues that you cannot predict, providing marks that look more natural.

CHANGING BRUSH TYPES

You may find a change of brush shape helpful to make the stems of the brambles and seedheads – here I'm using a dagger/sword brush, which is excellent for painting long lines: I often use a brush that holds a decent quantity of colour while providing a soft and structured shape.

Experiment with the brushes you have and how you can manipulate them to make the mark of your choosing.

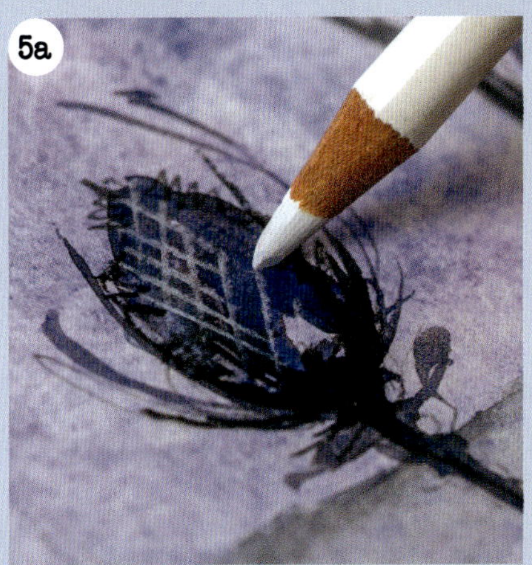

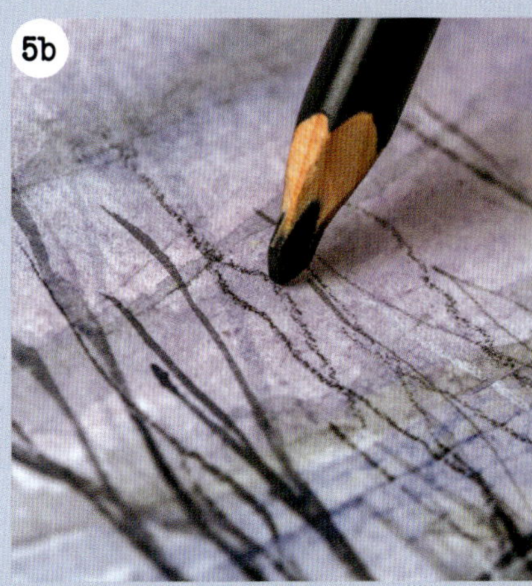

ADDING CHARCOAL AND PASTEL PENCIL FOR DETAIL

Pastel and charcoal don't just have to be used on pastel-specific surfaces. Use them in layers on watercolour paper; they are often good alternatives to graphite and ink when you want to add fine lines or details.

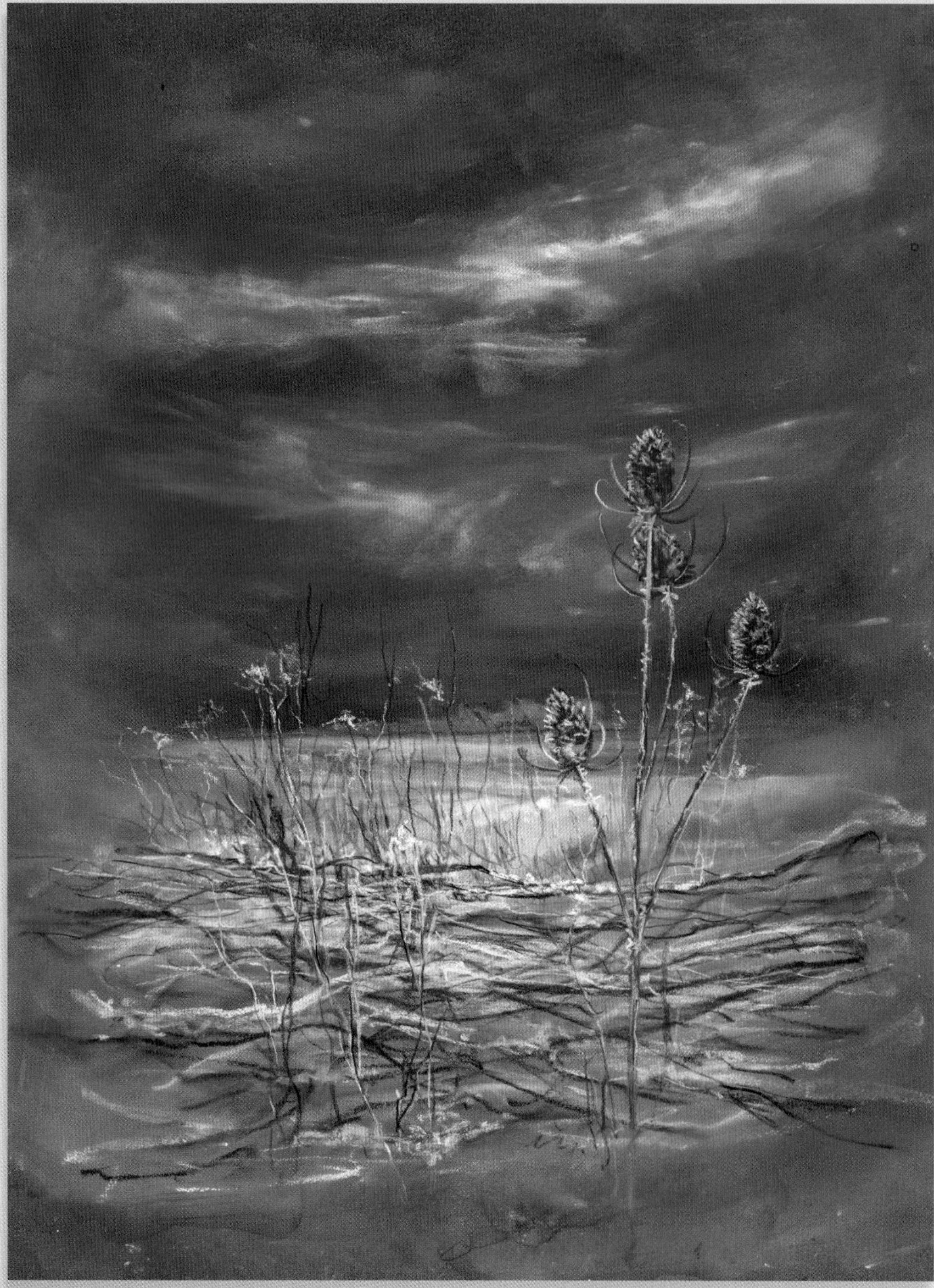

Downend Snow: version 2
300 × 400mm (11¾ × 15¾in)

This view provides me with so many ways to interpret it and after the success of my experiments with *Melin Tregwynt* on pages 140–145, I have fallen in love with the idea of presenting it with an entirely different atmosphere.

I will try a dark base colour for the surface and then use highlights and warm tones to bring out the textures and distance across the fields.

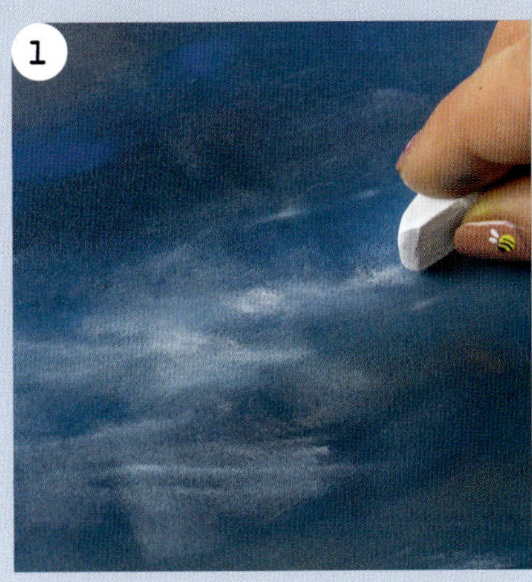

CLOUDS IN PASTEL

We have discussed using more than one layer of colour in a watercolour sky (see page 132); this effect can also be achieved with pastel, as you can count the dark colour of the surface as the primary layer. Add highlights and cloud shapes to help your composition.

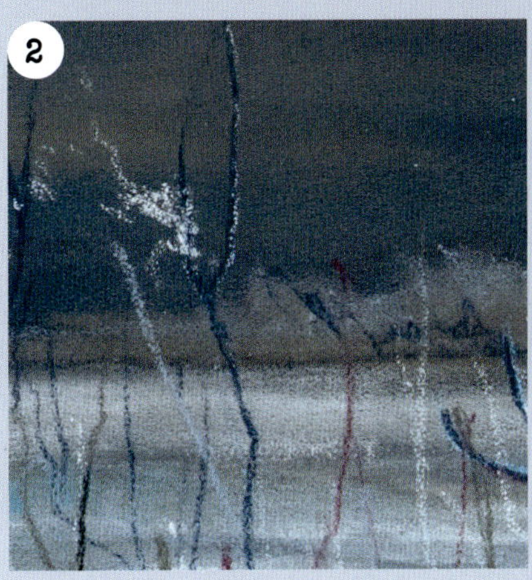

SIMPLE MARKS FOR SNOWY HILLS

Simplify the landscape beyond to make it seem further away, leaving out the buildings to concentrate on other textures.

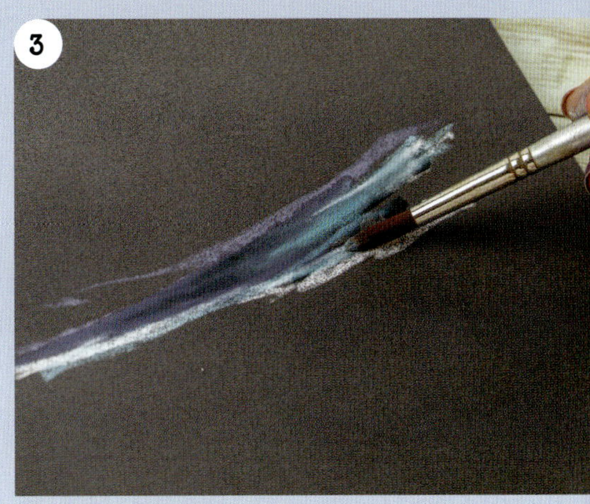

ADDING WATER TO CHALK PASTEL

You can blend soft pastel with water to create soft edges. If this is a technique that you enjoy, try it with a liquid that evaporates more quickly, such as alcohol. I have used both high-proof vodka and isopropanol (rubbing alcohol) with great success.

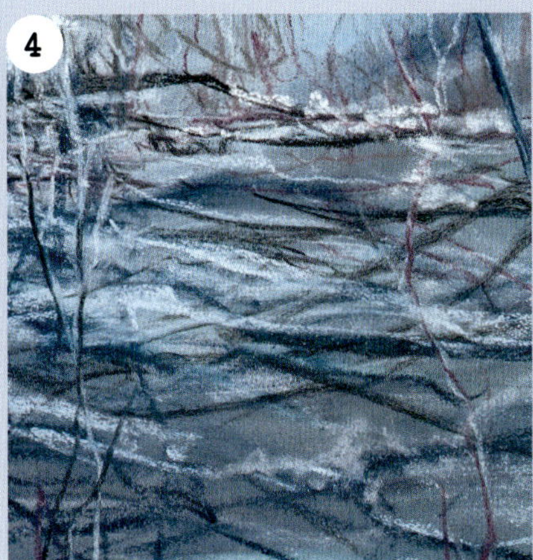

PASTEL-STICK ROLLING TECHNIQUE

As the texture of the brambles requires lines that cannot appear too contrived, try rolling a pastel stick across the area rather than dragging it. This will deliver more spontaneous marks.

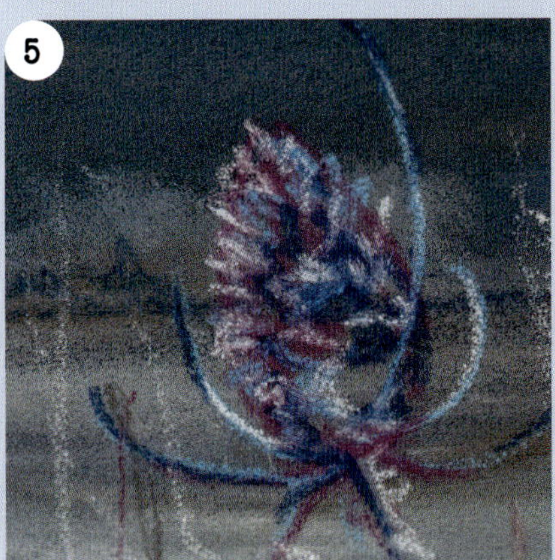

COMBINING COLD AND WARM COLOURS

Experiment with combinations of cold and warm colours, layered over each other for any foreground details, as this will show variegation in the vegetation and the high contrast will also help to bring these elements forwards.

The Summer House

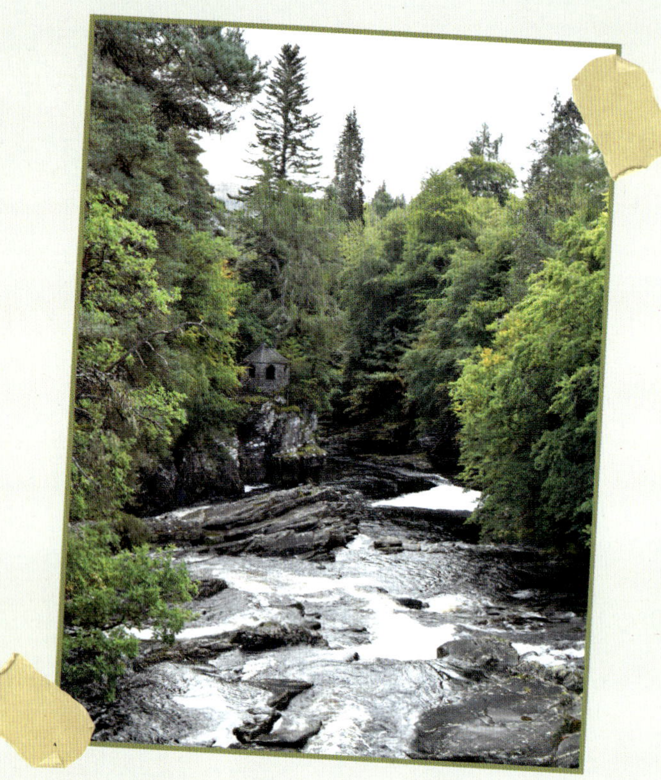

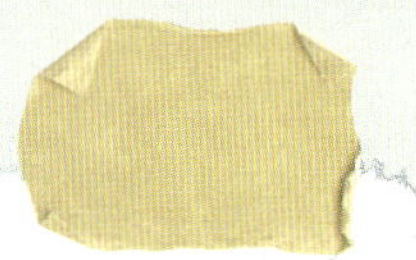

VERSION 1 (PAGES 152–155)

SURFACE: Artway INDIGO, 250gsm (no imperial equivalent), Mid Texture, 300 × 420mm (11¾ × 16½in)

MATERIALS AND TOOLS: watercolours in Cobalt Turquoise, Foliage Green and Hematite; dark grey sketching pen; gouache in Titanium White, Leaf Green and Cobalt Turquoise Light

VERSION 2 (PAGES 156–158)

SURFACE: Fabriano Artistico, 300gsm (140lb), Extra White, Cold-Pressed, 560 × 762mm (22 × 30in) – full imperial

MATERIALS AND TOOLS: collage materials: vintage map and printed poem; watercolour ground and gesso, both in Titanium White; watercolours in Cobalt Blue, Grey and Foliage Green; gouache in Titanium White; chalk pastels and charcoal pencils

INSPIRATION

This area of Scotland (Glenmoriston) is not well known, but I have been drawn to it for many years and have taken endless photographs of this particular view.

The photo was taken on a very dull day in early September and, while it doesn't show the colours as well as it might, what it does offer is the opportunity to interpret all of those incredible tree species.

BEFORE I START PAINTING

Very often, I set myself the ultimate challenge to paint a subject that I know I struggle with, in the hope that if I am tenacious, it will mean that it is no longer an issue and I can get past it with confidence.

My first thoughts when I see these trees are: how will I show all of the greens, make the different marks for the different species and also retain the atmosphere of the area?

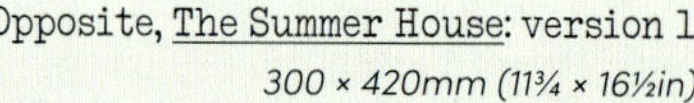

Opposite, The Summer House: version 1
300 × 420mm (11¾ × 16½in)

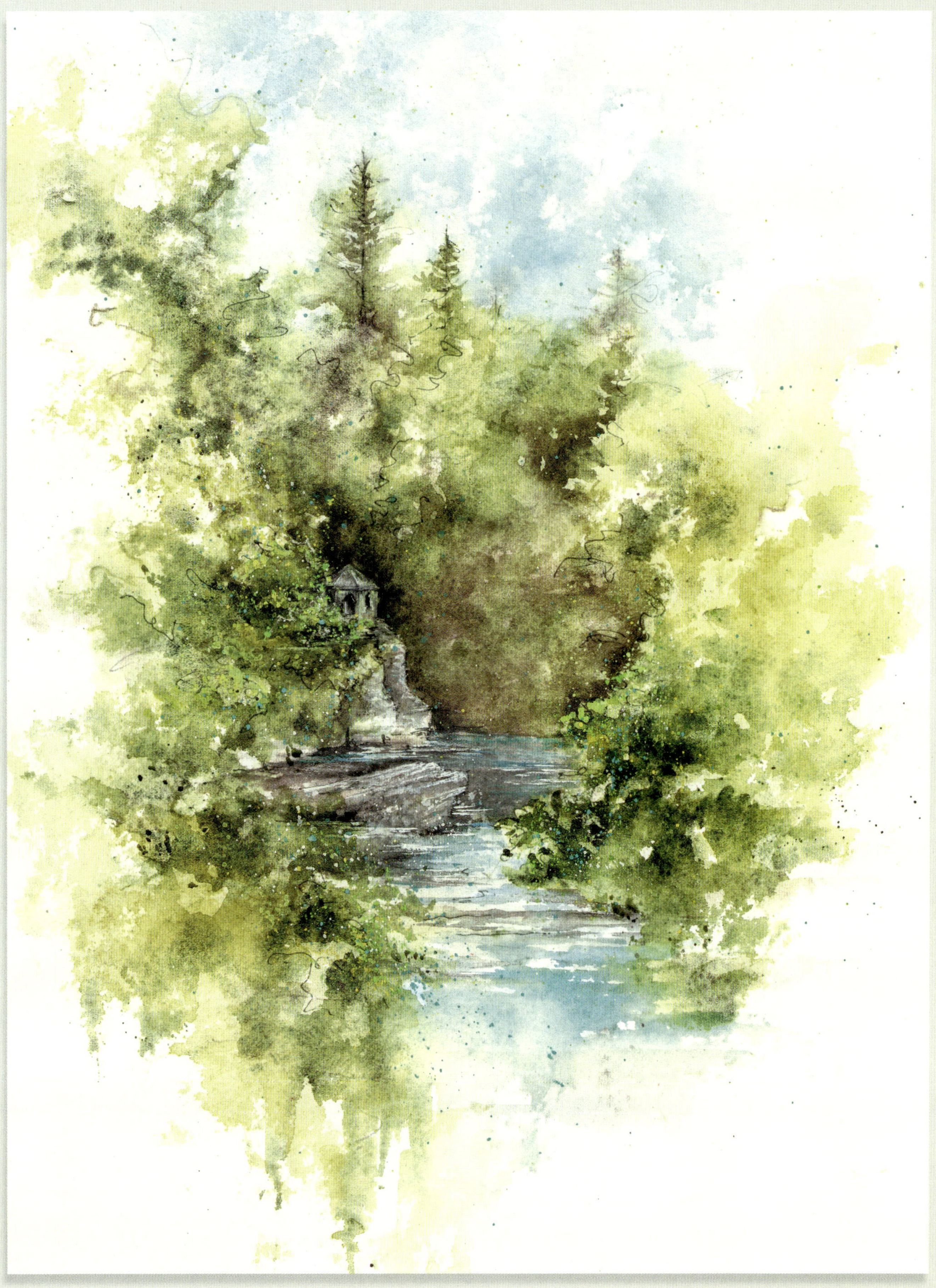

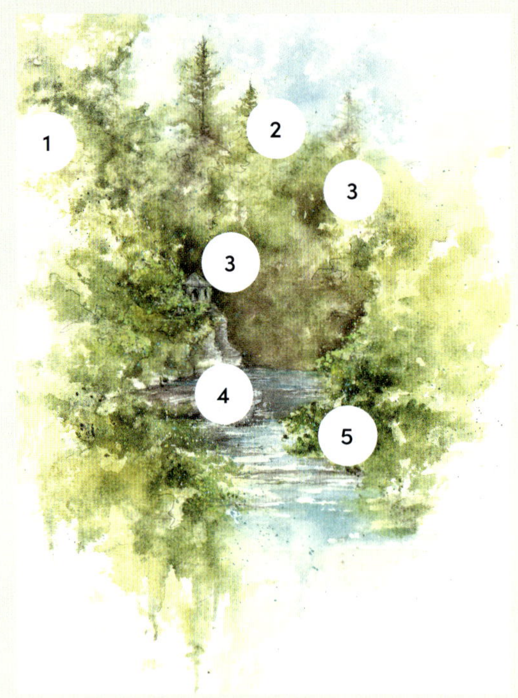

Techniques featured in <u>The Summer House</u>: version 1

TECHNIQUES

CONSIDERING AND TESTING A VARIETY OF PAPERS

Make your paper choice work for you. Will it give you soft edges? Will it provide texture for foliage? Will it allow you to layer up your colours so that they have depth and atmosphere? All these elements can be ably assisted by a good choice of surface.

USING A NATURAL GREEN RICH IN TONE

As this scene is predominantly green, and I want to use a realistic palette, I need to make sure that the greens I choose will create both pale and deep versions without becoming muddy or flat (see pages 44 and 49).

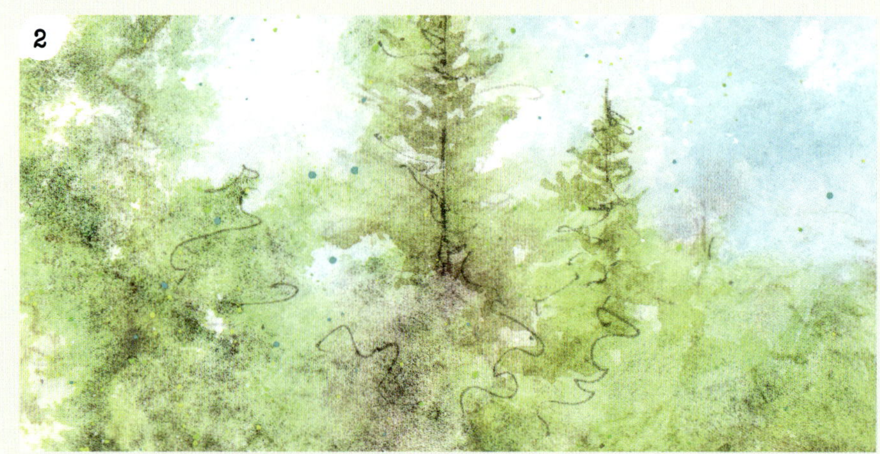

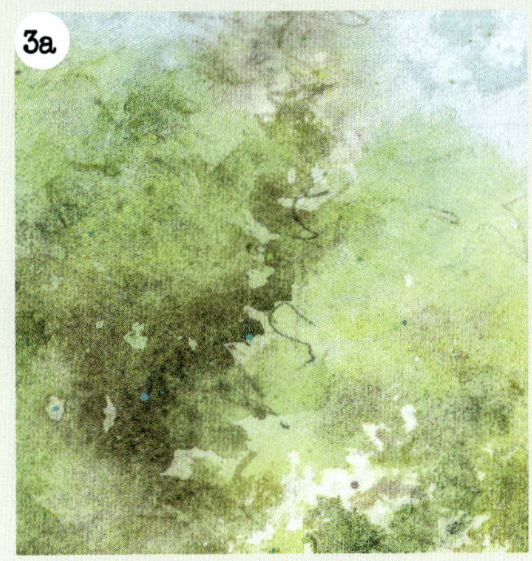

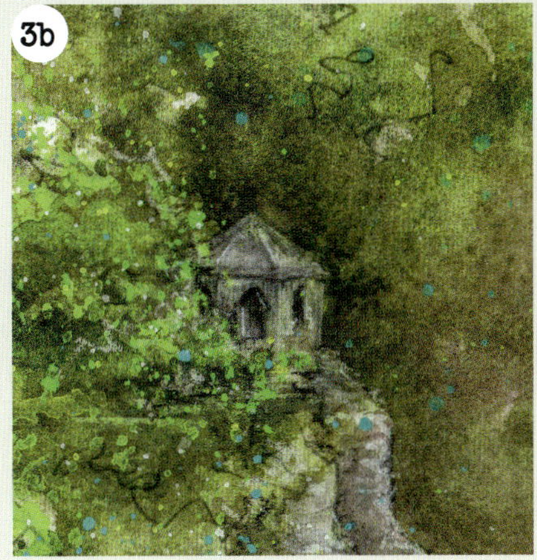

MIXING DARKS AND CREATING NEGATIVE SHAPES

Pay close attention to the dark areas behind shapes that you want to pop forward. This is the same technique employed in the first version of *Glencoe* (page 137, stage 5) where we concentrate more on the space around an object than the object itself.

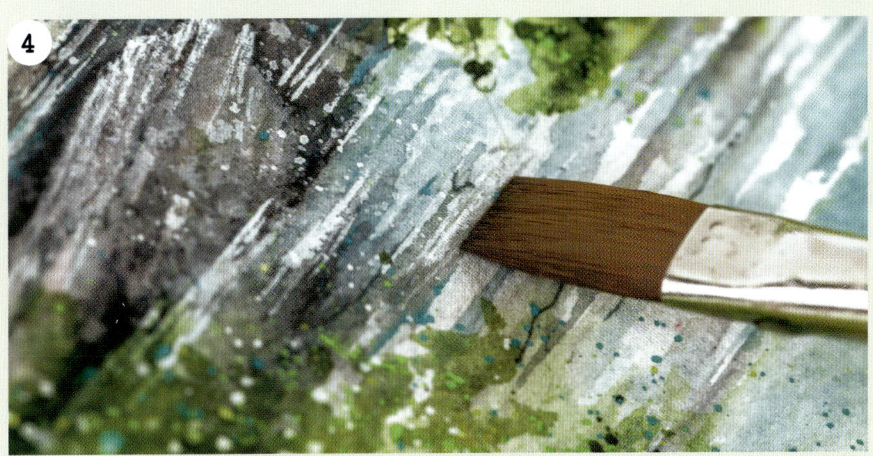

USING FLAT OR FINE BRUSHES FOR SURFACE TENSION

This view also has the challenge of featuring water that is moving, but at a slow pace, so, darks are required but so is the impression of surface tension. Use flat or fine brushes to create small, horizontal marks (see page 86).

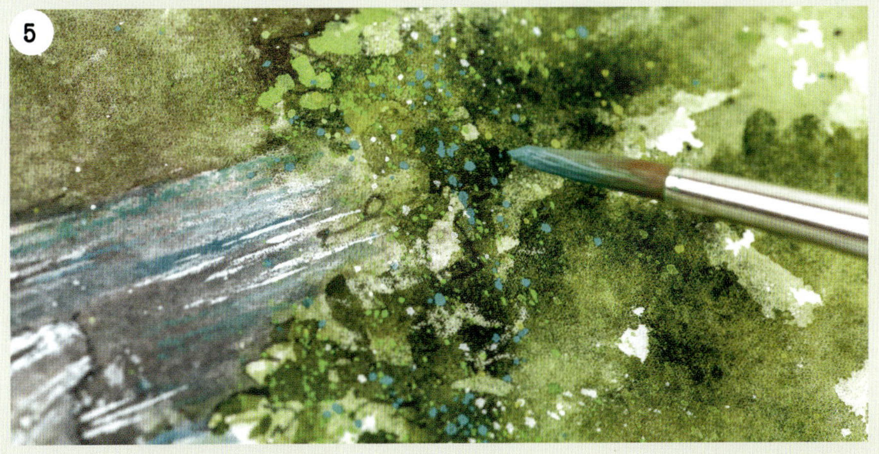

SPATTERING GOUACHE IN CONTRASTING COLOURS

For a final textural flourish, try a spatter technique with gouache so that its opaque properties cover well in the foreground. I enjoy using highly contrasting colours: here I have used a turquoise to mirror the colours in the sky and the river.

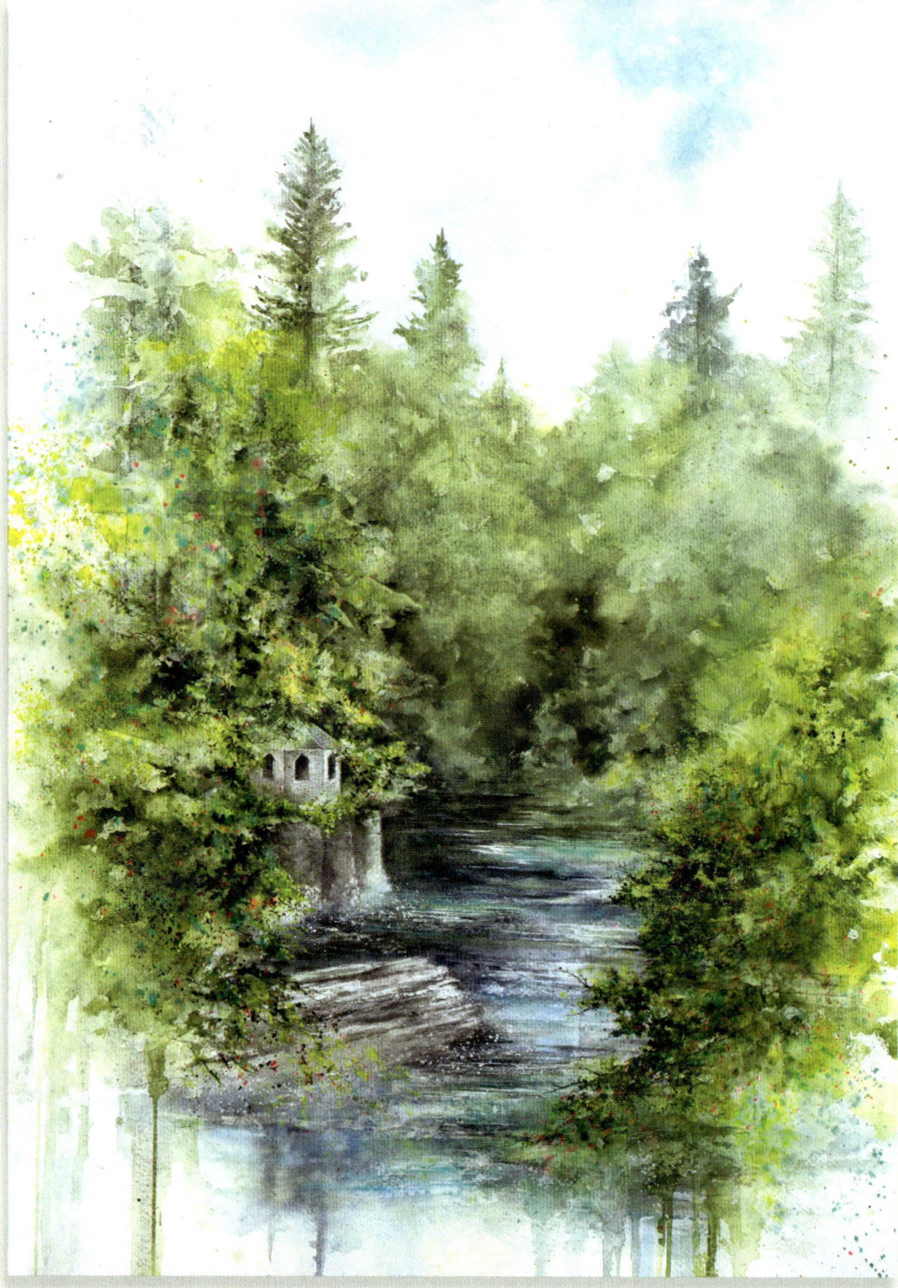

The Summer House: version 2
560 × 762mm (22 × 30in)

Taking everything into consideration from the first version of this painting, and the desire to combine some of the techniques discussed in chapter 5, I want this piece to be a culmination of ideas and influences.

This can make things creatively dangerous as I don't wish to make the piece too busy, so one of the first things I will do is scale up the size of the piece.

In version 1 I concentrated more on the water and foliage; this time, I want to give more attention to the building, in the hope that the viewer will discover something new each time they see the painting.

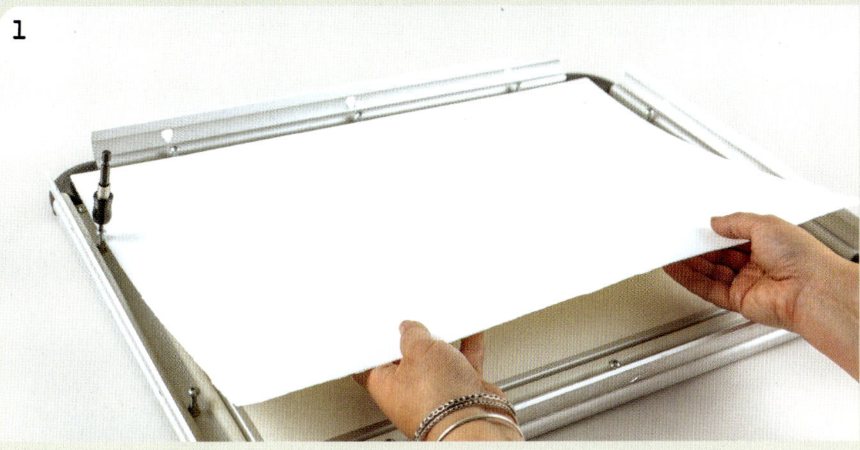

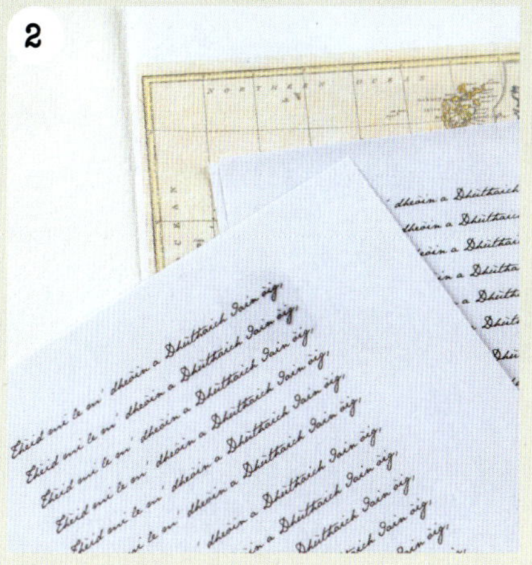

STRETCHING LARGE PAPERS TO PREVENT WARPING

Stretching paper is a traditional technique that stops it buckling when it gets wet, but it's not something I often bother with as I tend to use paper that returns to being almost flat after painting. When using a sheet of this size however, stretching is a safety precaution so that warping is not something I have to battle along with everything else.

Stretching can be done in a simple way on a drawing board using gummed tape to hold down the edges; or paper stretchers such as this one can be purchased to make the process faster, as the sheet is clamped between aluminium rails instead of using tape.

SELECTING AND APPLYING COLLAGE

In the same way as for *Letters from the Rock* on pages 110–111, I chose to feature text, this time printed onto thin – 80gsm (54lb) – paper with the phrase 'I will go gladly into Glenmoriston' in Gaelic. I also found a vintage map of the area, which I will add in places to create texture and interest.

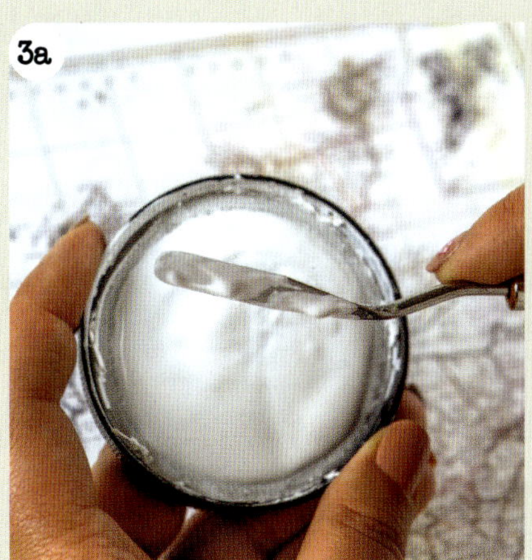

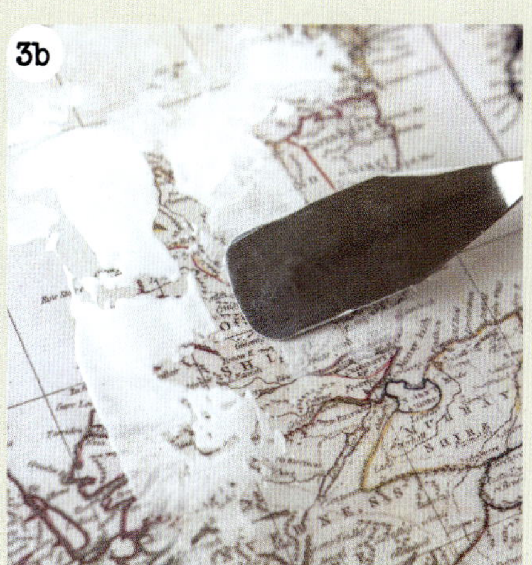

ADDING MEDIUMS OVER THE TOP

Adding textures over the top of the collage gives me even more opportunity to play with texture. I have used a combination of gesso, which will slightly repel my watercolour in the rock and water areas, and watercolour ground, which will be more accepting of colour but provide interesting textures in the foliage (see stage 4 overleaf). I use small quantities, applied with a palette knife, sometimes using the lid of the pot that the texture comes in, as a way of dispensing the ground.

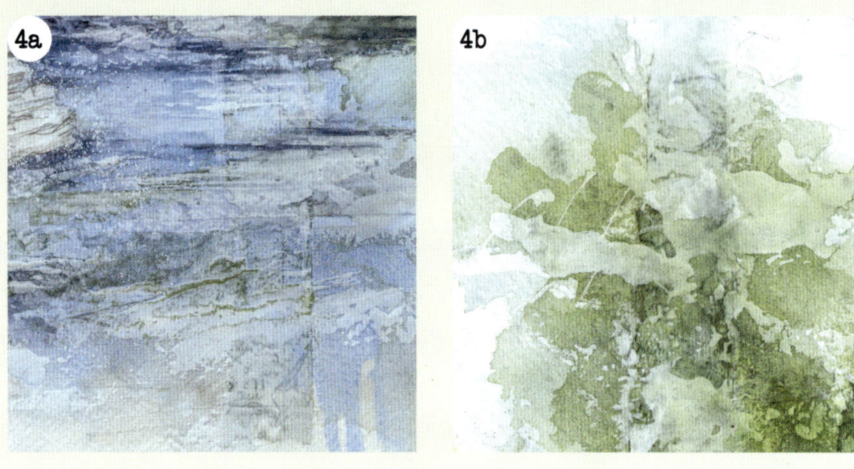

EMBRACING THE UNPREDICTABILITY OF WATERCOLOUR OVER TEXTURES

These two images show, in greater detail, what watercolour can look like when it comes into contact with gesso and watercolour ground. Some effects are exactly what I am looking for, some are a serendipitous surprise, and others are not what I need, and will require extra work either through other media being added, or by washing them off to get them to how I want them (see page 117).

CREATING DETAIL ON A LARGE-SCALE PAINTING

One of the biggest challenges on a painting of this size is balancing the amount of detail so that my painting is texturally interesting, tells a story, is tonally balanced and works both close up and far away. Keep stepping back to view your piece or place it in a room where you can walk past it, asking yourself if it requires anything else or if you should call it complete.

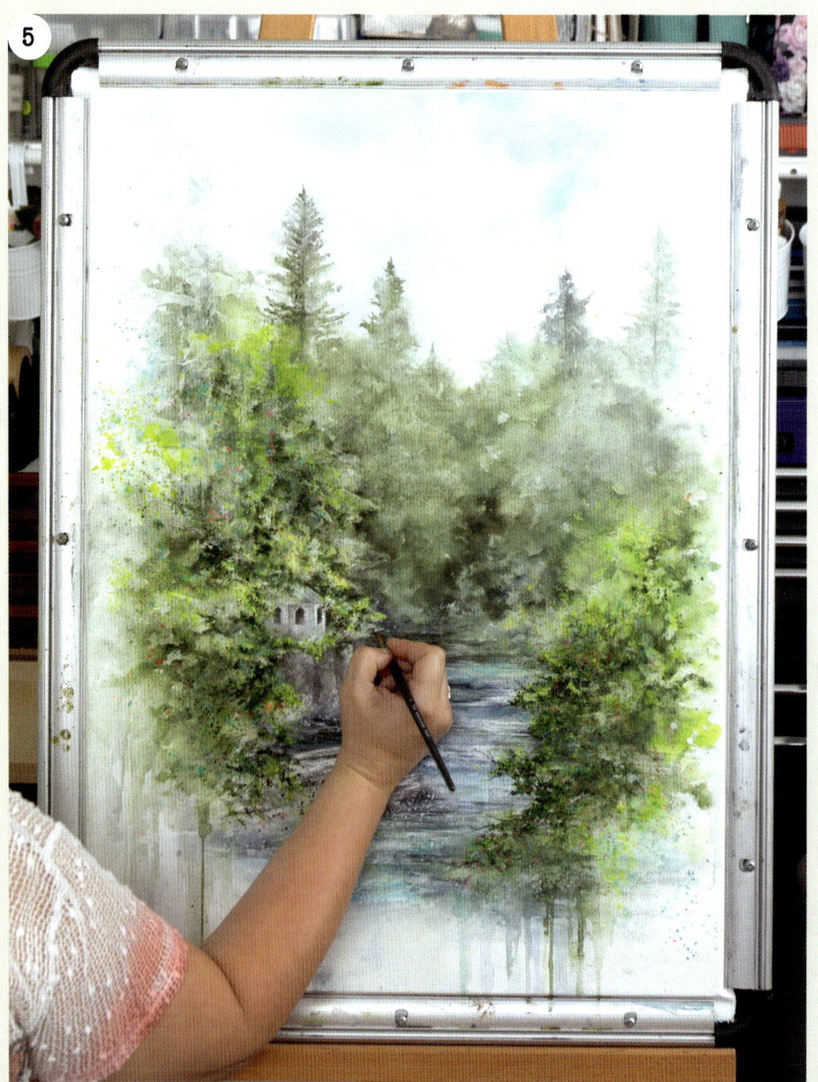

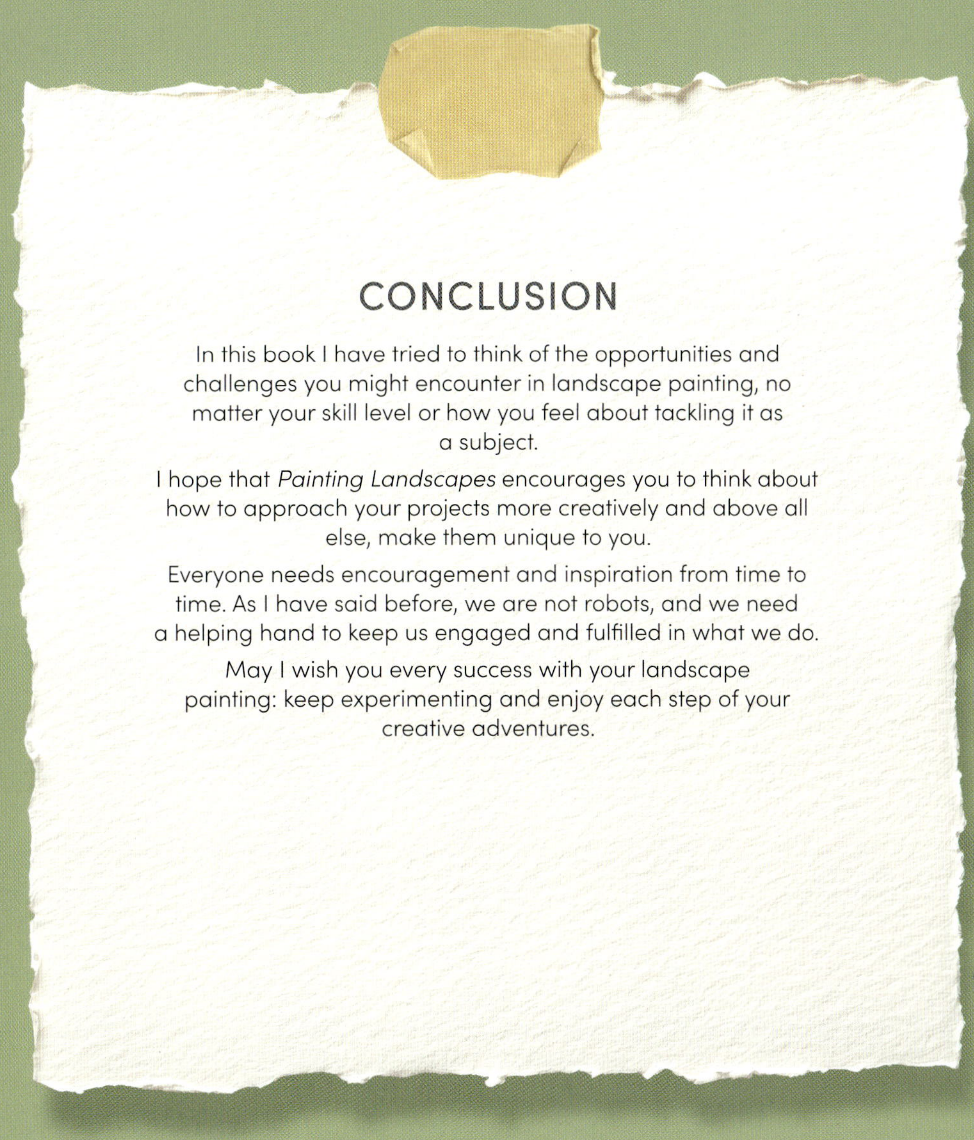

CONCLUSION

In this book I have tried to think of the opportunities and challenges you might encounter in landscape painting, no matter your skill level or how you feel about tackling it as a subject.

I hope that *Painting Landscapes* encourages you to think about how to approach your projects more creatively and above all else, make them unique to you.

Everyone needs encouragement and inspiration from time to time. As I have said before, we are not robots, and we need a helping hand to keep us engaged and fulfilled in what we do.

May I wish you every success with your landscape painting: keep experimenting and enjoy each step of your creative adventures.

INDEX